Women's Suffrage Memorabilia

Women's Suffrage Memorabilia

An Illustrated Historical Study

KENNETH FLOREY

McFarland & Company, Inc., Publishers
Jefferson, North Carolina, and London

LIBRARY OF CONGRESS CATALOGUING-IN-PUBLICATION DATA

Florey, Kenneth.
Women's suffrage memorabilia : an illustrated
historical study / Kenneth Florey.
p.   cm.
Includes bibliographical references and index.

ISBN 978-0-7864-7293-2
softcover : acid free paper ∞

1. Women — Suffrage — Collectibles.
2. Women — Suffrage — United States.
3. Women — Suffrage — Great Britain.   I. Title.
JF851.F56 2013   324.6'23074—dc23   2013019610

BRITISH LIBRARY CATALOGUING DATA ARE AVAILABLE

On the cover: *clockwise from top left* Belva Lockwood official campaign card;
Carrie Chapman Catton, a New York State Woman's Suffrage Association button;
card from Suffragette series, Dunston Weiler Lithograph Co., 1909; button advertising
the 1908 Rochester, N.Y., march; 1915 Tin Bird Eastern campaign advertisement;
1848 Suffragette hat pin; "Votes for Women" American suffrage button; Connecticut
Woman Suffrage Association's Mrs. Toscan Bennett, pictured here with her children;
Advertising Booklet for the Brown Shoe Co. (all objects from author's collection photographed
by Paul D. Sprague); background floral wallpaper (Ingram Publishing/Thinkstock)

Manufactured in the United States of America

*McFarland & Company, Inc., Publishers
Box 611, Jefferson, North Carolina 28640
www.mcfarlandpub.com*

For Emmy, Katherine, Genevieve, Sean, and Miranda,
who of all the wonderful people in my life are my favorites

Contents

Contents

Preface and Acknowledgments

The purpose of this study is to provide the historian not only with a detailed survey of the various types of memorabilia and artifacts that were produced during the suffrage period, but also with a discussion of the context and history of those types, including their significance and meaning to the suffragist movement. I have examined suffrage pamphlets and journals, period newspapers, magazines and books, and assorted library clippings, along with various period sales lists for accounts both of the production and distribution of memorabilia and for the various reactions of suffragists, their supporters, and the public at the time to these various artifacts of history. Additionally, I have had access in preparing this manuscript not only to my own collection of suffrage material, which is extensive, but also to those of valued friends, whose holdings of women's rights memorabilia are among the largest currently in private hands in America.

Suffrage scholars have long been aware of the importance of suffrage "novelties" to the movement, and have alluded to them in their studies, but often have had little personal experience in dealing with the objects close at hand; thus, their analyses of suffrage artifacts have necessarily been limited. Part of the difficulty is that such objects generally are scattered widely about, and comprehensive collections of suffrage artifacts can be quite difficult to access, even though some museums in both America and England do have impressive holdings in limited areas. Another problem is that most scholars do not have ready knowledge of the general nature and history of the type of objects (postcards, badges, advertising cards, valentines, etc.) that suffragists both ordered and sold to advance the cause. To a degree, one must know something about the developing traditions of celluloid buttons, postcards, sheet music, collector's spoons, various types of souvenir photography, campaign pennants, Cinderella stamps, and other forms of memorabilia to appreciate the ways in which suffragists utilized and manipulated the potential of these forms to help achieve their ultimate goals.

This study attempts in part to address both problems by providing numerous photographs of suffrage memorabilia in concert with discussion about that memorabilia. Whenever possible, I also have included information about which organization produced what material, production numbers, and the original purchase price for items in single quantities and sometimes also in bulk. Production numbers have much to say about the relative importance of different and sometimes competing items to suffrage supporters. Specific objects, too, often have a fascinating history, a fact reflected in the abundant stories about campaign memorabilia that appeared not only in suffrage publications but also in period commercial venues such as newspapers and magazines. The pages of the major suffrage papers and journals such as the *Woman's Journal, The Suffragist, Votes for Women,* and, to a degree, *Woodhull and Claflin's Weekly* as well as Susan B. Anthony's *The Revolution* were filled with stories and pictures of new memorabilia and the excitement that a recent button, postcard, photograph or ribbon had generated among supporters.

1

The focus of this book is on American objects, but I have included significant material from the British campaign as well. Suffrage in a larger context was an international movement, and American suffragists were in constant contact with activists abroad. American women borrowed much from their English counterparts, in terms not only of merchandising and marketing but also of iconography, slogans, and an understanding of the importance of the propagandistic and emotive value that "official" colors held for any organization. It worked the other way too. American and English publications shared information, urging their readers to subscribe to journals from the other country, and activists on both sides of the Atlantic were quite aware of both innovative and provocative designs and of new novelties that had been created and manufactured by their counterparts across the ocean.

This study also examines to a degree the anti-suffrage material that was manufactured in abundance by both commercial sources and organizations of determined men hostile to the franchise, groups that were, at times, fronted by reactionary women. Often the struggle between those who supported and those who opposed suffrage was reflected in a symbolic battle between the collectible ephemera that both sides produced. A pro-suffrage button, for example, would mimic an anti-suffrage effort. An anti-suffrage leader would complain about the sentiments expressed on a movement postcard that satirized their positions. Suffragists wearing sashes in their official yellow color would dress up a dummy with apparel in the corresponding anti-suffrage red or pink and then rescue it from drowning, mocking the iconography of the opposition in the process.

Ultimately, what I hope emerges here is a portrait of the movement from a popular culture perspective. Literature published by suffragists tells us about the movement's ideologies and strategies, but may reveal too little to us about its human side. Memorabilia, on the other hand, whether sent through the mails, preserved at home, displayed at conventions, or worn at marches and demonstrations, tells

us something about the basic character of the suffragists themselves and of the organizations that manufactured and distributed these objects. The eagerness to buy, display, and collect specific memorabilia indicates that many suffrage sympathizers wanted, in part at least, to ingest the movement, to have it become part of them in a tangible way that was not otherwise possible through campaign literature and speeches alone.

I have arranged this study into sixty-nine different sections, each dealing with a specific subject, such as advertising cards, buttons and badges. I chose this approach because, I think, by isolating types of memorabilia into their own separate discussions, it provides easier access for the reader, thereby creating a structure for clearer definition and analysis. The term "memorabilia" is applied here to any object that was produced with any sort of keepsake value, however minimal, in addition to its suffrage message. The concept of "keepsake value" varies from individual to individual, and the inclusion of certain categories and the exclusion of others here is, obviously, arbitrary. In general, I have avoided discussing pamphlets, leaflets, autographs, and books, even though one legitimately could regard such printed material as memorabilia also, although not quite in the same way that buttons, ribbons, sashes, and postcards are generally perceived. I also have included categories that are not specific types of memorabilia in and of themselves, but are nevertheless related to the topic. There were, for example, a variety of objects produced that were associated with the presidential campaigns of Belva Lockwood and Victoria Woodhull, each of which is discussed in a separate listing. The casting of a liberty bell by Pennsylvania women for their 1915 state campaign resulted in the appearance of several types of innovative memorabilia, and that event, along with its aftermath, is featured in a section all its own. Finally, any formal examination of suffrage artifacts would be remiss if it were not to include a discussion of official suffrage colors and of suffrage stores, where much of the memorabila was dispensed, so those categories appear here also.

A work of this sort is never the product of one person, and I would like to thank those who have helped me along the way, some of whom have read the manuscript in parts or as a whole and have provided valuable suggestions, others with whom I have shared my interest in suffrage memorabilia over the years, and whose valued friendship and thoughtful ideas I have certainly cherished. Robert Cooney, author of *Winning the Vote,* was especially gracious in reviewing my manuscript and providing me with research materials that I otherwise would have had difficulty obtaining. I would like to thank Frank Corbeil, Gil Gleason, Rose Gschwendtner, Chris Hearn, Ronnie Lapinsky Sax, and Chase Livingston for allowing me access to their wonderful collections; to Coline Jenkins, direct descendant of Elizabeth Cady Stanton, for passing along fascinating stories about her ancestor and for giving me private viewings of the suffrage materials preserved in the Elizabeth Cady Stanton Trust archives; to Jill Norgren, one of the most helpful scholars that I have ever met; to Elizabeth Crawford, who was always willing to assist when I had a question about the English movement; to June Purvis, editor of the *Women's History Review,* for both her encouragement and assistance in passing along otherwise difficult-to-attain research materials; to Robert Bradbury for his help relating to Cinderella stamps; to Dr. Danny O. Crew, the guru of political sheet music, for his careful review of the suffrage sheet music section; to the staff at Sterling Library at Yale University for their very kind help and for allowing me access to buried-away materials; and to Paul Sprague, my photographer, for his skills in capturing these images so well. Finally, I would like to give especial thanks to Emmy, my helpmate in life, for not only encouraging me in this project but also listening to my constant and at times, I fear, tedious accounts of my problems and progress, and, in general, for being herself. I could ask for nothing more.

litical Union (WSPU) established The Woman's Press in 1907, a division devoted to the sale of suffrage literature as well as memorabilia. Between 1907 and 1914, there were at least nineteen shops in London and throughout the rest of the country that sold WSPU suffrage products. By 1910, the press averaged sales of a thousand pounds a month for various items, including a significant variety of postcards, tea sets, brooches, card games, ribbons, and buttons. In addition, *Votes for Women,* the WSPU official organ, carried numerous advertisements for the WSPU product line, particularly around Christmastime. Much of this material was printed or stamped in the official WSPU colors of purple, green and white. The WSPU, attempting to show the large public support for suffrage, urged women to "wear the colors," and its memorabilia was designed in part to help with that effort. The WSPU suffrage shops were usually more than shops where one could only buy things. They served also as lecture and study rooms and as places where women, surrounded by movement literature and memorabilia, could congregate and discuss various political and cultural issues without fear of interruption from a male voice.

Suffragists in America did not develop as extensive a system of stores and merchandising as did their English counterparts. Still, their efforts were quite respectable. The headquarters of most major organizations had at least a small sales area, if not a room, that could serve as a shop in some capacity. They issued catalogs and advertised in suffrage papers, which were always eager to print news of a clever postcard or button. Certainly, most of the products that suffragists sold were intended primarily to advance the cause in some way. That activists also understood that there was a collector's market, however, can be illustrated by the fact that several "shops," including that incorporated by NAWSA as part of its headquarters in New York, sold English posters and postcards, even though the images portrayed often alluded to specific events in that country unrelated to happenings in the United States. These creations by their English sisters, nevertheless, resonated positively with many American suffragists who had interest in collecting cause memorabilia.

A study of suffrage memorabilia, then, is another pathway to a larger understanding of the movement itself, with all of its diversities and complexities. Memorabilia reflects the personalities and concerns of its designers. But it also makes a statement about those women who enthusiastically wore suffrage buttons, ribbons, and sashes, carried suffrage pennants, played songs from suffrage sheet music on their pianos, mailed suffrage postcards embellished with suffrage stamps on them to their friends, and saw in even minor collectibles something to treasure and keep as souvenirs of the social and political struggles with which they were currently engaged. The emerging evolution of women into consumers obviously also played a role. As women were encouraged to buy "things," they began to accumulate and even collect "things," and for suffragist activists, those "things" often had a suffrage connection.

THE MEMORABILIA

Advertising Trade Cards

Various phases of the suffrage movement in America often coincided with the creation of new types of collectible memorabilia, the development of modern consumerism, and the advancement in advertising techniques. The period from 1869 to the mid 1890s, for example, which saw the split among activists, the resultant establishment of the American and National Woman Suffrage Associations, their merge in the final decade of the century, and two women presidential candidates, included also an American fascination for the creation of scrapbook collections of a recently metamorphosed form of an earlier type of advertising, the trade card. Suffragists had not as yet fully mastered the art of producing and merchandising products for the cause the way they would a decade or so later, and, thus, for the most part, saw little need for printing cards themselves. The topic of "equal rights for women," nevertheless, had a substantial visual presence on trade or advertising cards. In general, that "presence," however, was not created by those women who promoted social change and who were the topic of the cards, but by manufacturers, merchants, and card illustrators who stood on the sidelines as bemused observers and commentators. Thus, suffragists unintentionally ceded to others by default, primarily to shopkeepers and manufacturers, the ability to define the movement to the public through what was a very popular and collectible form of advertising for two and a half decades.

The advertising trade card was a small piece of thin cardboard upon which a merchant or manufacturer advertised his services or his product, generally through the use of a highly colorful graphic illustration. It had its antecedents in the early 19th century, with some examples known from the late 18th century as well. It was not until the late 1860s and early 1870s, however,

when a variety of factors, including an increase in the number of printers in the country and the development of new printing techniques, coalesced to enable the trade card, in a revised and advanced form, to become a major mode of advertising and one that became highly collectible. Their introduction by a number of Philadelphia printing firms at the Centennial Exposition of 1876 also helped to spread their popularity.[1]

Chief among these printing advances was the ability to use vibrant forms of color through the process of chromolithography as opposed to what Kit Barry terms "the formal, austere black-on-white" printing that characterized cards of the pre–1870s.[2] Thousands of designs were created, some in a generic stock format on which a merchant or manufacturer could affix his imprint to a predesigned picture, others on a card that had been designed for a particular manufacturer, where a specific product was incorporated into the image itself.[3] Many designs, particularly on stock cards, consisted of little more than pictures of cherubs, children, animals and birds, especially frogs and owls, flowers, and pre–Gibson Girl "pretty women." Other designs, particularly those that were created with a specific product in mind, were far more elaborate and extremely colorful. In addition to incorporating illustrations of products into designs, manufacturers' cards often reflected cultural and political attitudes of the period, portraying happy families, hardworking farmers, and beautifully arrayed housewives but also many containing satires of errant husbands, domineering housewives, shady politicians, blacks, Jews, immigrants, Oscar Wilde and the aesthetic movement, as well as suffragists, sometimes seen as harridans, sometimes treated with a modicum of respect.

In size, these cards could range up to ten inches or more, but the typical specimen was about the dimensions of an index card. Merchants distributed them in stores, by either setting them on the counter or handing them to customers; others were wrapped in packages or mailed out by salesmen or by the manufacturers themselves.[4] They were widely collected and pasted in scrapbooks. Some cards even contained the message "for your album" or instructed the customer to send in money to complete a set "to put in your album."[5] But the heyday of the trade card was to last about only twenty-five years, to the mid 1890s when the collectible gave way to other forms of advertising, particularly to the colorful advertisements that appeared in popular magazines, and, to a certain extent, to both the advertising postcard and the poster stamp that evolved a decade or two later.

Because suffragists during this period generally lacked products to sell apart from pamphlets and broadsides, there was little commercial reason for them to exploit this newly popular form of advertising.[6] However, they did on rare occasions employ the medium for ideological purposes, and several cards are known in which the issue itself, as opposed to a suffrage product, was the *raison d'être*.

One such card has on its front a generic portrait of a smiling little girl in a bonnet. On the back are printed "Eminent Opinions on Woman Suffrage" from Bishop Hurst, William Lloyd Garrison, Frances Willard, and others. The theme of "Eminent Opinions" was popular in suffrage literature, which suggests that this card may have been an official issue of sorts, handed out at fairs and bazaars and not in stores. The Iowa Woman Suffrage Association distributed a large card in the form of an artist's palette (a shape common to many stock cards) that also contained a number of quotations in support of suffrage, along with the organization's name. The product, then, that the suffragists were selling on these cards was not a physical item such as malt bitters, celluloid cuffs, sewing machines, soap, or thread, but rather a concept, that of suffrage as a fundamental right, and they were using a contemporary form of advertising to do it.

But if suffragists did not advertise tangible suffrage products on trade cards, at least one company, the Phoenix Manufacturing Company, did, with an item that they called "Woman's Suffrage Stove Polish," a product whose concept appears somewhat paradoxical today. The company imprinted six different stock cards with the name of its product, all featuring in their design elaborately dressed children set against a background of gold, a typical color, used originally in French cards, for many such generic pieces. The back of these cards listed in bullet fashion twelve reasons why women should buy the polish, imitating the template that suffrage literature had established in outlining various and sundry reasons why women should support suffrage. There is no known connection between the polish and the suffrage movement, so the naming of the product may have been a sales gimmick to appeal to the developing ability of women to be consumers and to respond to commercial messages. In any event, the cards themselves are fairly common even today, but cans of the polish are virtually nonexistent.

One type of image common to many sets of commercial stock cards was that of a simple black-and-white portrait of a contemporary or historical personage such as an actor, politician, writer, or religious leader. Suffragists so pictured included Elizabeth Cady Stanton, Belva Lockwood, Anna Dickinson, Victoria Woodhull, and Tennie C. Claflin, but not, curiously enough, Susan B. Anthony.

More elaborate caricatures of some suffragists do exist. Anna Dickinson, who was an actress as well as an orator and suffrage supporter, is caricatured as "Anna D..." and dressed as Hamlet on an 1882 card lithographed by the firm of Hunter of Philadelphia, this one in full color.

Another card, also in color and advertising Kerr's Spool Cotton, portrays Tennie C. Claflin, dressed as Shakespeare's Portia from *The Merchant of Venice*, on the floor of the New York Stock Exchange. The image is an allusion to the fact that the sisters Victoria Woodhull and Tennie C. Claflin had taken up with the recently widowed Cornelius Vanderbilt after their arrival in New York in 1868, and he set them up as stockbrokers in a business called Woodhull, Claflin, and Company. Claflin is not specifically identified by name on the card, the manufacturer apparently assuming that her notoriety would allow her image to be easily identified. One of the investors pictured in the background has a hooked nose, characteristic of the anti–Semitic representations on many cards of the period.

Suffragist Anna Dickinson was also an orator and a Shakespearean actor.

Card mocking Dr. Mary Walker's gender identity by questioning her habit of wearing men's clothing.

This card portrays Tennie C. Claflin, who was at one time a stockbroker, as Shakespeare's Portia.

Dr. Mary Walker, who had earned a medical degree in 1855 and was a lecturer on such issues as health care, temperance, dress reform, and women's rights, was caricatured as a "Man Baby" on a set of ten cards that poked fun at politicians and famous personalities of the day, including Ulysses Grant, Benjamin Butler, Charles Darwin, and Mark Twain. Walker's satirical portrait derives from the fact that she wore men's clothing. Her sexuality

MORTON. SCHURZ. THURMAN. CLEVELAND. GRANT. HANCOCK. HARRISON. FISK. BELVA LOCKWOOD.

Satiric image of Lockwood, a known teetotaler, serving beer to other presidential candidates.

was also questioned on a card in a set with the generic title "Ye Great Men of Ye Day." The card shows Walker from the back and asks, "Ye What is it?" George Francis Train is satirized in the same set as "Ye Philosopher."

Belva Lockwood appears on at least two cards depicting political figures, including such presidential aspirants as Grover Cleveland and Benjamin Harrison. Finally, an especially long-necked Elizabeth Cady Stanton is depicted on a card in still another series as a medieval knight with shield and spear.

In general, the theme of suffrage when it arose was presented as simply an aspect of a contemporary scene that had little or nothing to do with the product advertised. There were definitely negative portrayals of suffrage advocates on these cards, but advertisers had to be careful lest they offended potential buyers of their products. Even women whose views were not necessarily pro-suffrage could conceivably take offense at a negative image of a woman that was drawn by a man. Some negative cards were produced nevertheless, and they include an illustration of a Wagnerian woman with a scowl on her face pulling the "stop" cord of a trolley under the cap-

tion "An Advocate of Woman's Rights"; another of a Susan B. Anthony–type figure slamming her umbrella on top of a lectern proclaiming, "I will assert my rights and buy my T where I can get the best, at Lester's"; and a third, much gentler satire, of a girl, dressed as Santa Claus, standing on a chair as a mouse runs across the floor. She has just hung up a wreath emblazoned with the phrase "Votes for Women," and the card's caption reads "Santa Claus Up to Date." It is not known what effect these cards had on potential women consumers, but one might assume that it was not positive. Obviously not all advertisers had fully mastered the psychological intricacies of modern consumerism and the proper appeal to the audience to whom they were attempting to sell their products.

One set of four stock cards may resonate differently today than it did in the nineteenth century. Two of the cards picture boys with the caption "He May Yet Become President." The corresponding two cards depicting girls contain the counterpoint response of "She May Yet Wed a President."

Fleischmann's Yeast and the New Harvest Cooking Stove issued other cards with a neutral or even positive view of suffrage, although perhaps in somewhat reductive domestic terms. In the Fleischmann's ad, three women are casting their ballot into a ballot box surrounded by the caption "The Candidate who always receives the Ladies Vote — Fleischmann's Yeast."

A New Harvest Stove card portrays a woman speaking to a meeting of what presumably are suffrage supporters. The back of the card begins with the headline of "Victims of Man's Tyranny" and reductively satirizes suffrage arguments by ascribing man's injustice to women throughout the ages to be a neglect in providing the proper cooking range to wives and not as one involving a denial of the ballot.

A card for a rival stove, "The New Uncle Sam Portable Range," pictures Uncle Sam and his wife, Columbia, expressing delight over their new acquisition, not "Votes for Women," but a kitchen range. Their three children, wearing hats or sashes indicating different parts of the country, take part in the general merriment. New England is represented by a little girl holding a

The only known card on which Stanton is portrayed.

The card pictures a typical ballot "box" of the 1880s.

book inscribed "Woman's Rights and Other Issues," reflecting the perceived popularity of the subject in that region of the country.

Suffragist activist and author Charlotte Perkins Gilman attempted to support herself for a while in the early 1880s, when, with her cousin Robert Brown, she designed trade cards for several soap companies, including Curtis Davis and Company and the Kendall Manufacturing Company, producers of Soapine. Her original sketches are preserved among her papers, and close to fifty different cards including variations have been attributed to her. Not specifically suffrage related, her designs on occasion depict women working hard at their domestic chores. Others show a female archer, a young boy lassoing a star, a sailor amid the rigging of a ship, and a magician touching the fingertips of a woman. One set of six cards shows girls and women, including a nun, with their heads inside of various flowers, the type of which may have had period iconographic implications.[7]

The popularity of the advertising card led to the development of other forms of small cardboard or paper giveaways. One was the "Prize Puzzle," or rebus card, which contained a riddle composed of words or syllables depicted through pictures that supposedly suggested the sounds of the words and syllables that they represented. One of the pictures found on a generic card distributed by a variety of merchants shows a young girl turned away from a polling booth by a rather stern election official and a policeman wielding a threatening club. What specific sound this scene may have represented is difficult to determine. Victorian rebus cards were so difficult to solve that merchants often gave away prizes to those who could successfully interpret them.

Sapolio, a brand of soap so noted for its advertising that even Bret Harte wrote some of its jingles, distributed a set of small stand-up paper figures, one of which was a woman holding up a "Votes for Sapolio" sign. The back of the figure had the following poem: "A suffragette is Mrs. Brown/Who's cleaned up in Sapolio Town./ When she discovers wrongs to write,/The mails assist her in her fight./De-voted readers high and low/Are voting for/SAPOLIO."

Other such novelties include a fold-up puzzle from the 1888 campaign distributed by the manufacturers of Oliver Chilled Plow. When a 5½-inch-square piece of paper that contained what was seemingly a discordant grouping of random images was folded in the proper way, it revealed a series of candidates for the current election, including Belva Lockwood. The same firm distributed another paper piece, this one in color, which displayed a series of figures representing some of the major political issues of the 1888 election, such as prohibition, free trade, and protection for American industries. The topic of "Woman's Rights" is represented by a woman with a broomstick threatening her cowed husband, who is holding their baby.

Small, colorful advertising booklets also supplemented trade cards as a way of reaching the public. Perhaps the strongest pro-feminist statement of the period came from the Brown Shoe Company of St. Louis for their product line of women's shoes called "White House." The cover of this extremely colorful booklet shows a young woman resting against a tree, with the image of the White House in the clouds, and the accompa-

Often Gilman's trade cards featured whimsical scenes such as this.

nying phrase, "Her Ambition." The inside pages, in addition to picturing the product line, discuss a number of various possible "ambitions" or occupations for women, including that of violinist, painter, golfer, actress, and doctor. This booklet is one of the few advertising pieces of the period that actually envisioned social change for women positively.

English trade cards with suffrage themes are almost unknown. Collis and Company, "The Peoples' Clothiers," of Castle Street in Bristol, did distribute a "puzzle card" sometime in the early part of the 20th century depicting a woman going off to a suffrage rally and leaving her perturbed husband to cook dinner. When the card is held in a certain way, the image of Mrs. Pankhurst can be seen.

There are a number of other advertising cards from the period of 1870–1895 that in one way or another mirror both positive and negative images of the suffrage movement. They make an excellent study into just how suffrage was seen in terms of popular culture and what an impact it was beginning to obtain, despite the lack of solid legislative victories. Because women were responsible for buying many of the products advertised on these cards, the negative images of women that they contained were generally but not always muted, but they were present, nevertheless. Basically, advertising cards portray a world in transition, one that was not always happy about the emerging political and economic power of women, but one that also had to respond to and respect that emergence.

Baked Goods and Other Foodstuffs

In October 1909, the Home Restaurant of Friday Street in London advertised in the English publication *Votes for Women* "Home-Made Cakes iced in the colours of the WSPU."[1] Undoubtedly other restaurants and bakeries sold baked goods with suffrage themes. What is interesting here is that the restaurant believed that there would be enough response to the ad from women engaged in the movement to justify its expense. Moreover, the Women's Social and Political Union's color scheme of purple, white, and

green apparently had become so firmly embedded in the public's mind at this time that there was no reason to add words to the cakes to indicate their connection to the suffrage cause. At Christmas in the same year, the WSPU offered a variety of Christmas goods for sale, including "Christmas Crackers." However, these special crackers, which ordinarily would have contained prizes for children such as paper caps and toys, were stuffed with articles of "prison dress, miniature handcuffs, etc."[2] The WSPU also sold more conventional foodstuffs, including "Official Suffragette" crackers that were made by the firm of C.T. Brock and Company at one shilling and six pence (1/6), two shillings and six pence (2/6), and three shillings and six pence (3/6) per box of 12.[3] In America, a firm that was noted for its "health crackers" named one variety "The Suffragette."[4] Because of the perishable nature of such products, it is difficult to imagine any being preserved in a contemporary suffrage collection.

IVELCON, a bouillon cube consisting of beef and vegetables for consommé, was not packaged specifically to indicate a suffrage tie-in, but its English manufacturer, St. Ivel Con-sommé, did advertise extensively in the WSPU's *Votes for Women*. However, one of its more graphic advertisements seems inappropriately satirical and reductive to the spirit of the movement. It pictures a suffragist, who is identified as "Miss Tinkabel Spankhurts," ringing a bell. Addressing her "suffering sister Suffragettes," this comic depiction of suffrage activist Christabel Pankhurst notes that "we have had to tread the Holloway—pardon me, I mean narrow way." She goes on to outline her plan "for the subjection of that tyrant—man." Her strategy is to "lure him on by feeding him with Ivelcon ... and thus make him so pleased and satisfied that he will grant us anything—especially votes."[5] Plays on the name of "Pankhurst" occur also in anti-suffrage cartoons of the period, such as on a postcard that features a beleaguered speaker named "Miss Ortobee Spankdfirst." However, such derisive satire of a movement leader along with the trivialization of the Holloway Prison experience in an official suffrage publication is highly unusual. In any event, this particular ad ran only once in the WSPU journal.

In America, a "Suffragette Biscuit," made and distributed by the Johnson Educator Food Company of Boston, Massachusetts, made its first appearance at the Boston Suffrage Bazaar held at the Copley Plaza in 1913. It later was available nationally, and was extensively advertised in the *Woman's Journal*. The Educator Food Company had been founded by Dr. William L. Johnson, a strong believer in equality for women. Upon his death, it was taken over by his daughter, who originated the "Suffragette Biscuit." The new biscuit received a highly favorable review in the *Woman's Journal*, in part because of Johnson's enlightened views, which he had expressed publicly forty years previously, but probably also in appreciation for the firm's extensive advertising in the paper for another of its products, the "Educator Cracker."[6]

Balloons

One of the more popular forms of suffrage novelties that made its way into fairs, bazaars, demonstrations, and movement shops throughout the country was that of the printed balloon. Unfortunately, the survival rate of this new type of memorabilia was minimal. Blown-up balloons were difficult to untie and deflate. Unused balloons were subject to the variables of the weather, cracking in the winter and melting in the summer. Accordingly, despite suffrage interest, very few, if any, of the many thousands of balloons that were manufactured for the cause likely survive today.

Still, Harriet Taylor Upton, president of the Ohio Woman's Suffrage Association. commenting on the distribution of a multitude of suffrage balloons in the 1912 Ohio campaign, noted, "The yellow balloon seems to be the last novelty in the campaign. At the Mississippi Conference a friend donated 10,000 such balloons for the State work."[1] The Kansas Equal Suffrage Association held a "Balloon Day" on Saturday, June 29, of the same year to "keep up the interesting campaign for equal suffrage." The idea for the event came from Mrs. C. Charles Clark of Rosedale. The resultant balloons were lettered in black either with the words "Vote for Mother" or "Votes for Women" on bright yellow, and, when blown up, were eighteen inches in diameter. Mrs. Lucy

Johnson, the Association's president, directed every state district and county officer to recruit young people to sell them to the public on that day.[2] The response to her suggestion encouraged Clark to form a company called the "Votes for Women Toy Balloon Company," and she subsequently sold the balloons from her home in Rosedale for ten cents each, after advertising them in the *Woman's Journal*.[3] Presumably all profits from sales were turned over to the cause.

Balloons were popular elsewhere as well. They were included in a large rally in New York on October 29, 1915, as part of the Empire State campaign. Suffragists riding on a "Baby Truck," decorated with Kewpie dolls and suffrage balloons, gave out little brooms, balloons, and small trumpets to the children who came to "Mothers' Meetings," of which the truck was a feature.[4] Dancers at the Suffrage Ball held by the Boston Equal Suffrage Association in August of 1915 did the "suffrage glide" in which they all carried yellow balloons bearing the movement slogan, "Votes for Women."[5] Balloons, supplied from the merchant stock of "Colonel" Ida Craft, who, along with "General" Rosalie Jones, was one of hikers who marched to Washington preceding Woodrow Wilson's inauguration in 1913, were also a featured item, along with "babies ... bears, bread and bon bons" at a fête in 1914 held at the 71st Regiment Armory in New York City.[6] They attracted especial attention at "Suffrage Day" at the Alaska-Yukon-Pacific Exposition, which was held in Seattle in 1909.

Balloons did become an issue at a demonstration of the League of Self-Supporting Women led by Harriot Stanton Blatch and Inez Milholland in New York City in 1908. A milliner on Fifth Avenue was extremely annoyed when members of the League, who had installed themselves in a window above his head, let out two hundred balloons with the words "Votes for Women." The milliner thought that they were aimed at him, but they were designed for a "Republican Business Man"'s parade that was passing by. Because a crowd did congregate at the spot, the milliner complained that they were interfering with his business, so the League recalled the balloons and hung them on a line at a high enough altitude to ensure their safety. The milliner, however, still aggrieved, hired a boy with a ladder to puncture the balloons. The crowd became angry and hauled down both the ladder and the boy. Eventually the police had to intervene.[7]

Ballots and Ballot Boxes

Ballots or paper tickets that deal with voting rights for women fall roughly into three distinct categories: (1) Ballots on which the issue itself was present; (2) Women's ballots, designed for those particular states or municipalities in which women had partial suffrage prior to 1920; and (3) Those pre–1920 ballots on which the name of a female candidate actually appeared. Such tickets, if they were for any office other than a local school board, are generally quite rare and were not always officially authorized.

In the early years following the Revolutionary War, the right of women to vote was a theoretical possibility everywhere until the adoption of state constitutions that limited the franchise to white male voters who met various qualifications.[1] Unlike those of other states, however, the Constitution of New Jersey, adopted in 1796, did not specifically prohibit women from voting, and they did so sporadically throughout the state, until they lost all suffrage rights in 1807 through the actions of the legislature.[2] It was not until 1887 that New Jersey women gained once again even a limited right to vote, and that only for school board. They could not vote for president of the United States until 1920.

The right of women in various states to vote in presidential elections came about slowly. Wyoming in 1869 was the first full suffrage state or territory,[3] followed by Utah in 1870, Washington in 1883, and Colorado in 1893. Utah and Washington women, however, temporarily lost their right to vote through actions of Congress and the Supreme Court, not obtaining it again until 1896 and 1910, respectively.

Kentucky women were allowed to vote in school elections in 1838, as were Michigan and Minnesota women in 1875, and Arizona, Montana, and South Dakota women in 1887, along with their sisters in New Jersey. In that same year, Kansas' women were able to vote in municipal elections. Partial suffrage rights for women, generally in the form of local school

elections, came much more quickly than their right to vote in presidential contests. In 1909, for example, women could vote for president in only four states, Wyoming, Colorado, Utah, and Idaho, but they had some limited suffrage rights in 25 others.

The problem for officials in those states where women had partial franchise rights was to set up a structure that kept male and female voting separate, lest women attempt to cast ballots for offices other than those that they were restricted to. Generally, this involved not only separate lines at polling places, but also separate ballot boxes for women to place their specially labeled "woman's ballot" in so that any attempt on their part to cast ballots for other elctions could be discovered immediately once the ballots were subject to counting. The George D. Barnard Company of St. Louis manufactured a gold-on-black metal drum marked "Women's Votes" for this procedure. The 12½" × 14½" drum

Wyoming in 1869 was the first territory or state to grant women full suffrage.

had at its top a lid with both a lock and a slit through which a voter could cast her limited ticket.

The same company also issued a corresponding but unmarked piece for male voters, the absence of the word "male" pointing out the inherent inequality. Women were "marked" but men were not. Also known is a wooden box, measuring 22" × 15", with white lettering reading "Ballots for Women" made for the First district for an unknown state. The top of the box contains a slit for women to deposit their ballots.[4]

Women were given their ballots when they entered the polls, and these tickets were usually destroyed at a specified time after they had been counted. A few, however, still survive, generally those unused pieces that were left over after all women had voted. Many of these surviving ballots come from Boston, where women had the theoretical right in the mid 1870s to be elected as members of the "School Committee," but did not have the right to vote for themselves for that office until later in the decade. By 1888, they were able to participate in all municipal elections. To vote in Boston, a woman had to pay a poll tax of fifty cents, be able to read and write, be at least 21 years of age, and to have resided in the state for at least one year and in the city for six months prior to the election.[5]

This first municipal election in Boston in which women were allowed to vote attracted such notice that it was featured four days after the event in *Harper's Weekly* through a large engraving and a story. *Harper's* rival, *Frank Leslie's Weekly*, also illustrated the event based on a drawing by A.B. Schute.[6]

In order for women to have even partial voting privileges,

Special ballot boxes were designed for women to restrict their voting to lesser offices.

PLAIN INSTRUCTIONS

FOR THE

Assessment and Registration
OF WOMEN VOTERS.

Any woman over twenty-one years old, who resided in Boston, May 1st, 1888, can be assessed for a poll tax of FIFTY CENTS, by personal application to the Assessors, City Hall, from May 1st to September 29th inclusive.

Notice that tax is due will be sent by mail. After receiving her notice, payment should be made at the Collector's office, City Hall. The receipted tax bill must then be presented in person, to the Registrars of Voters, No. 12 Beacon Street; and if the person presenting it is found qualified as hereinafter stated, she can be registered on the voting list. Payment of tax and registration can be made at Ward Room (as specified on tax notice) if preferred.

A receipted tax bill, either for property or poll, for a tax assessed anwhere in the **STATE**, in May, **1887 or 1888**, is as good for the purpose of **REGISTRATION**, as a poll tax bill assessed May 1st of the current year in the City of Boston.

No person can be registered or qualified as a voter, unless she is able to read and write; is twenty-one years of age; shall have resided in the State one year, and in Boston for six months, preceding the day fixed for the City election, and shall have paid a tax assessed upon her, as of May 1st, 1887 or 1888.

The Collector's office is opened daily from 9 A.M. to 2 P.M.

Assessors' and Registrars' offices open daily from 9 A.M. to 5 P.M., except Saturday, when they close at 2 P.M.

N. B.—Assessors' and Collector's offices are at City Hall; Registrars' office at No. 12 Beacon Street.

Latest day for Registration, November 27, 1888.

The name must be correctly entered on the check list *before election day.* If not, go with tax bill to No. 12 Beacon Street, and have it corrected *before election day; (else you cannot vote).*

Date of Election Day, December 11, 1888.

Hours for Voting, 7 A.M. to 4 P.M.

To avoid mistakes, women should decide for *whom* they wish to vote *before* going to the Ward Rooms election day, and be SURE they deposit a ticket with names they have decided upon.

A list of proper candidates for School Committee will be found at Tremont Temple, Room 10, and in the BRITISH AMERICAN CITIZEN.

List of voting instructions for the first municipal election in Boston where women could vote.

however, men had to approve suffrage referenda. Sometimes the ballot question was incorporated within a general electoral ticket that also contained candidates' names for various offices, but more often it was printed on a separate sheet restricted to amendment options. A ballot from Maine in 1919, for example, lists the suffrage question along with three other proposed changes to the state constitution involving taxes, bonuses for soldiers and sailors, and the division of the towns into voting districts.

While many of these "suffrage ballots" were lengthy in wording and large in size, others could consist of nothing more than a three-inch square of paper on which the male voter was asked to mark his preference for or against the "Suffrage Amendment to the Constitution." Various suffrage organizations distributed cards to potential voters that they could take with them into the polling booth as guides to how to vote.

Some, such as Empire State Campaign Committee, the New Jersey Woman Suffrage Association, the Massachusetts Woman Suffrage Association, the Woman Suffrage Society of Greater Cleveland, and the New York State Woman Suffrage Party, distributed cards that often resembled ballots on which the recipient could indicate whether he or she favored woman suffrage. Since these cards also included a space for an address, they were probably used both as fundraisers and as follow-ups to ensure that sympathetic voters actually went to the polls.[7]

Perhaps, though, the most interesting ballots were those issued for early women candidates for offices other than school committees, such as for mayor, Congress, and even president. For obvious reasons, these ballots generally were not issued by governmental sources, but in many areas voters were allowed to bring to the polls with them either election tickets that had been printed in newspapers or ones that had been ordered by candidates and political parties and handed out prior to balloting day. Each party had its own ticket that listed the names of its candidates only. If a citizen wished to split his vote between parties, he could cross out a name on that ballot and write in the desired candidate, or he could use a paster, a preprinted label that he could glue over a rival's name for the same office. Pasters were often preferred by voters be-

cause hand-written misspelled names were usually cast aside by ballot counters as invalid votes, and, with pasters, both the spelling and the form of the name, down to whether or not the candidate was using a middle initial, could be assumed to be correct.

Probably the first election ballot ever made for a woman was a two-inch-square piece that was inscribed "For Representative for Congress, ELIZABETH CADY STANTON." Stanton ran for Congress in the Eighth District in New York in 1866 to test the constitutional right of a woman to run for office. Many people of the time were surprised to find out that while women could not vote, they could hold any office that their constituents might see fit to place them in that was not expressly prohibited by state law or constitution. In a public letter to voters, Stanton indicated that her platform was that of "free speech, free press, free men, and free trade." James Brooks, a Democrat, won the election with 13,816 votes, but Stanton did get 24. Her only regret about running was that she did not have photographs of her "two dozen unknown friends."[8] It is not known how many of these ballots, if any, survive today, but at one time an example was in the possession of Theodore Tilton, whose wife was involved in a scandalous affair with Henry Ward Beecher, the famous preacher and at one time titular head of the American Woman Suffrage Association.

Apart from the Stanton ballot, the most sought-after nineteenth-century piece is that issued for the 1884 presidential ticket of Belva Lockwood and Marietta L. Stow (**see Belva Lockwood and the Equal Rights Party**). It consists of engraved portraits of Lockwood and Stow, along with the names of candidates for electors from various districts in New York State. Even today, one actually votes not directly for the president, but for electors who are pledged to vote for that candidate if he or she is selected by a majority of voters in a state. No ballots survive, if any were ever made, from Lockwood's subsequent 1888 run. There are no known ballots either from Victoria Woodhull's notorious run for the presidency in 1872 or for her two later, less publicized attempts. Woodhull was famous for her persuasive rhetoric, but her campaigns often showed the lack of long-term structured

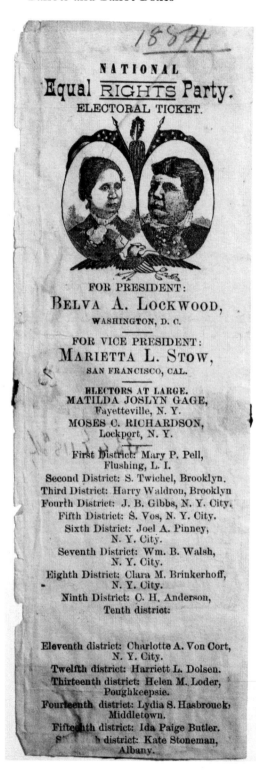

NATIONAL
Equal RIGHTS Party.
ELECTORAL TICKET.

FOR PRESIDENT:
BELVA A. LOCKWOOD,
WASHINGTON, D. C.

FOR VICE PRESIDENT:
MARIETTA L. STOW,
SAN FRANCISCO, CAL.

ELECTORS AT LARGE.
MATILDA JOSLYN GAGE,
Fayetteville, N. Y.
MOSES C. RICHARDSON,
Lockport, N. Y.

First District: Mary P. Pell,
Flushing, L. I.
Second District: S. Twichel, Brooklyn.
Third District: Harry Waldron, Brooklyn
Fourth District: J. B. Gibbs, N. Y. City.
Fifth District: S. Vos, N. Y. City.
Sixth District: Joel A. Pinney,
N. Y. City.
Seventh District: Wm. B. Walsh,
N. Y. City.
Eighth District: Clara M. Brinkerhoff,
N. Y. City.
Ninth District: C. H. Anderson,
Tenth district:

Eleventh district: Charlotte A. Von Cort,
N. Y. City.
Twelfth district: Harriett L. Dolsen.
Thirteenth district: Helen M. Loder,
Poughkeepsie.
Fourteenth district: Lydia S. Hasbrouck,
Middletown.
Fifteenth district: Ida Paige Butler.
S   h district: Kate Stoneman,
Albany.

First known printed presidential ballot for a woman picturing Belva Lockwood with her running mate.

political planning, and she probably never bothered to have ballots printed. Woodhull's sister, Tennie C. Claflin, apparently never produced any ballots either for her 1871 run for Congress in the largely German Eighth District of New York where Stanton previously had sought office. While Claflin gave an energetic announcement speech, there is no evidence that there was much of a subsequent campaign, although the speech itself was published in a dual-language edition.[9]

There were pasters made for Emma Beckwith when she ran for mayor of Brooklyn in 1889 under the standard of Lockwood's Equal Rights Party. Beckwith had announced her intention of printing up pink ballots for herself (the use of color in ballots is known, but extremely rare), but apparently settled on pasters instead as a matter of both practicality and expense (**see Belva Lockwood and the Equal Rights Party**). As more states came into the suffrage column, more women began to run for public office, even before 1920, causing additional ballots to be printed with their names. The most notable example is Montanan Jeannette Rankin, who successfully ran for the U.S. House of Representatives in 1916 as a Republican, the first woman to be elected to Congress.

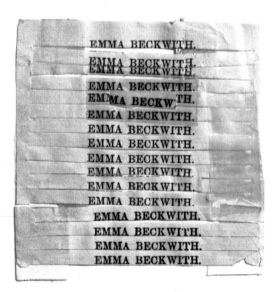

If a voter wished to substitute for a candidate's name on a printed ballot, he often used a preprinted paster, so that his vote would not be thrown out because of his inaccurate spelling.

Banks

There were several varieties of small, tin banks, all from official sources and emblazoned with suffrage slogans. Although these banks theoretically could be used for personal savings, they were given out with the intent that the suffragist would put aside her change for the movement. The earliest was produced by NAWSA in 1913, and was advertised as the "First Official National Suffrage Bank — A real bank in miniature — get one and start your suffrage account NOW."[1] The idea of a suffrage bank was not restricted to the national organization, however. Michigan activists distributed a rounded black-on-yellow celluloid-and-tin version. The top portion read "Give Your Dime For Liberty and Justice — Votes for Women." The bottom piece was more specific: "Your Dime will go toward $30,000.00, MICHIGAN'S SHARE of the MILLION DOLLAR SUFFRAGE FUND — When filled return to your COUNTY HEADQUARTERS."[2]

Belva Lockwood and the Equal Rights Party

Belva Ann Bennett Lockwood (October 24, 1830–May 19, 1917) was a lawyer, lecturer, women's rights activist, and public personality. Her tireless persistence resulted in her becoming the first woman allowed to argue before the U.S. Supreme Court. She also ran for president in 1884 and 1888, only the second woman to do so, Victoria Woodhull, with her 1872 campaign, being the first. One could argue, furthermore, that Lockwood was the first true legal female candidate. If Woodhull had won, she would have been only thirty-four years old at the time of her inauguration and, therefore, would have been ineligible to take office even if her gender had not been a constitutional issue.

Lockwood's run in 1884 was the result of an idea proposed by California activist Marietta Stow through the newspaper that she had started in 1881, *The Woman's Herald of Industry and Social Science Cooperator.* Stow believed that, however sympathetic a male political candidate might be to women's rights, women needed to be represented through their own party and by their own candidates. She also reasoned that the attention given to female office seekers would help in the cause of female emancipation. Accordingly, in the July issue of the *Herald,* she announced the formation of a new political party called "The Equal Rights Party" and selected Oregon suffrage leader Abigail Duniway as its presidential standard-bearer. She also included the name of attorney Clara Shortridge Foltz, her previous choice to run for governor of California, as a possible vice-presidential running mate. Duniway, who had not been consulted about her "nomination," wrote back immediately to Stow, asking for the removal of her name from the ballot. She felt, as did many in the movement, that the prospect of women running for office detracted from the larger issues involved with women's rights.

Lockwood, a subscriber to *The Woman's Herald,* had been following the exchange of letters between Stow and Duniway on the advisability of selecting a female candidate for president. She wrote a letter of support to Stow in which she argued, "Why not nominate women for important places?" Needing a new ticket with a female at its head, Stow now selected the sympathetic Lockwood as the party's presidential candidate with New Yorker Clemence S. Lozier as its vice-presidential token bearer. She wrote Lockwood a letter informing her of her "nomination" at the "Woman's National Equal-Rights Convention for President of the United States." Lockwood, taken by surprise at her selection, kept it secret for several days before she finally accepted. She sent a letter back to Stow outlining twelve platform points that she felt the party should run on. The elderly Lozier declined the party's nomination for vice president, and was ultimately replaced by Stow herself.

Lockwood ran a spirited campaign, setting up headquarters in her own home at 619 F Street in Washington, D.C., with her daughter Lura acting as her manager, and barnstorming throughout the country. She paid her expenses by charging admission for lectures along the way. When the election was over, she claimed that 4,711 of her votes had not been counted and that other ballots upon which her name had been inscribed had been awarded illegally to her opponents. Foltz, who had originally been listed as a vice-presidential possibility for the Equal Rights

Party, met privately with Lockwood in 1884, and informed her that "the true story" of her nomination had been a "prank," and that she and Stow had been surprised to find that the original story in the *Herald* about the "Equal Rights Party Convention" had been picked up by the Associated Press and distributed nationally.

Lockwood's loss in 1884 and the knowledge that there had not been a true party convention did not discourage her from running again in 1888, although her second campaign lacked the overall force of her first. Many in the movement, including Henry Blackwell and Matilda Gage, still opposed her efforts. She was once again "nominated" by the Equal Rights Party, and she chose Alfred Love, head of the Universal Peace Union, to be her ticket mate, without consulting with him beforehand. Love, who was a friend of Lockwood's, declined the nomination on the grounds that his ideology, which was based in part on anarchism, precluded his becoming involved in politics. Charles Stuart Wells replaced him, but while Lockwood still campaigned aggressively, no votes for her second run were ever recorded.[1]

Despite the enthusiastic support that Lockwood received from a number of activists throughout the country, the fears of some in the movement that Lockwood's campaign would become the subject of ridicule were certainly borne out. Hecklers throughout various parts of the country held mock Lockwood rallies, sometimes called "Mother Hubbard parades," in which men would dress up as women in a new type of freer garment that was considered improper for women to wear out of doors. In Binghamton, New York, in 1884, for example, a Belva Lockwood parade was conducted by high school students and was attended by 3,000 people along with 500–600 masqueraders dressed as washerwomen and ladies in parlor costumes. Mrs. Lockwood, "one of the best-looking young men in the city," gave a brief speech to those assembled. That same night in Amsterdam, New York, 100 members of the local mock Belva Lockwood Club took part in a Mother Hubbard parade.[2]

In 1885, the Sungerlust Society of New York inaugurated its new Prince Carnival at midnight, "assisted by the Belva Lockwood Guard."[3] In October of 1884, there was a Mother Hubbard

parade in Mystic, Connecticut, in which men attired in dresses carried torches and toted rag babies while marching to Williams and Dudley's Square, where a hand-drawn banner bearing a "portrait" of the candidate was raised on which the words "For President Belva Lockwood" were inscribed. There a speech was given by "Anna Dickinson," a caricature of the labor and suffrage activist portrayed by Oliver Hewitt, an obscure figure today who may have been the editor of an area newspaper. A poem was read and later distributed to the crowd by an anonymous "Sweet Singer of Lyme."[4] In both 1884 and 1888, militiamen in Davenport, Iowa, dressed up as women and paraded down the streets. A man named Harry Fulton played the part of Lockwood in the 1884 event.[5] In November 1888 in Chattanooga, 1,000 boys and men in women's dress paraded in mock honor of her in what *The New York Times* called "the most notable [demonstration] of the campaign in Tennessee."[6]

Mock demonstrations by Belva Lockwood Clubs also took place in Saratoga, New York and North Attleboro, Vermont.[7] *The New York Times* joined in the ridicule by publishing several tongue-in-cheek articles about Lockwood and her campaign. In one, the paper claimed that it had inside information that John St. John, the Prohibition Party candidate for president in 1884, had offered to withdraw from the race in favor of Lockwood, who did have temperance sympathies, for "a hogshead of rum, 2,000 choice cigars, and a season ticket to the bar of the Hoffman House," in addition to marrying him and selling her tricycle.[8] Lockwood had, indeed, purchased a tricycle in 1881 in order to conduct tasks associated with her law business more efficiently. She was criticized in the press for her female immodesty, and President Grover Cleveland told the wives of his cabinet ministers that he did not wish them to ride the machine.[9] The issue had been the subject of another mocking article in the *Times* in 1884, when the columnist said that he wished to end the "scandalous reports" that Mrs. Lockwood's back hair was not her own and that she rode a tricycle. He was convinced that it was a bicycle instead.[10]

The two Lockwood campaigns generated a fair amount of memorabilia, and, while many pieces were mocking, enough supportive artifacts

Front and back views of an official campaign card issued from Lockwood's home.

survive to show the extent of Lockwood's activities, her popularity with many segments of the population, the emerging strength of women for a variety of political offices, and some positive mainstream media acceptance of her candidacy. Lockwood revised the twelve points for her platform that she had outlined in her acceptance letter to Stow on September 3 into fifteen, and the new list appeared on campaign flyers under her portrait. *The Washington Star* made her candidacy front-page news, and reprinted the entire text of her acceptance letter. From her F Street home headquarters emerged a campaign card that contained Lockwood's engraved portrait on the front, and the replication on the rear of her campaign symbol, a globe of the earth, half-submerged in the ocean, with a flag at its top with the words "Our Country and Our Homes." This symbol appeared on the masthead of Stow's *Her-*

ald, when Lockwood became her co-editor at the end of the 1884 campaign and renamed the paper *National Equal Rights*. The card also announced that "Documents, information, and royal-size lithographs of the nominee" could be obtained from the Campaign Publishing Company of New York City. Other "official" items from Lockwood's candidacy include a small palm card for "'The Equal Rights Ticket,'" with engraved busts of Lockwood and Stow," and a New York State ballot for the "National Equal Rights Party Electoral Ticket" [**see Ballots and Ballot Boxes**]. Lockwood published several articles in popular magazines such as *The Illustrated American* and even lent her name to endorsement of commercial products such as "Fairbanks Fairy Soap" [**see Endorsements in Magazines**].

The W. Duke Tobacco Company of Durham, North Carolina, published a smoking

Paper edited by Lockwood following an 1884 campaign that indicated she would fight on.

tobacco insert card with Lockwood's photograph on it. While no mention was made on the card of her candidacy, Duke did issue cards for other presidential and vice-presidential hopefuls in 1884 and 1888, and this particular card was probably meant to be included in the series.[11] Such cards were also inserted later into cigarette packs in an effort to boost sales, and were one of the most popular of late nineteenth- and earlier twentieth-century collectibles. Subjects in addition to politicians included actresses, baseball players and other athletes, birds, and Native Americans.

Lockwood's campaign, though, while well received by many was unfortunately the subject of more anti- pieces of memorabilia than it was of pro-, particularly in her imagistic depictions in such social and political commentary magazines of the period as *Puck, Judge,* and *Wasp.* Satirical items mocking male candidates were commonplace, but the hostility directed towards

This card for Duke's Smoking Tobacco was probably part of a series of presidential candidates for 1884 or 1888.

Left: This ribbon with a grotesque image of Lockwood was probably worn during a Mother Hubbard parade; *right*: one of two known rebus ribbons for Lockwood — probably satirical.

probability that Lockwood would advertise either her candidacy or the cause through a rebus puzzle, the purpose behind these ribbons may have been comical rather than supportive.

Of less certain intent was a metal piece issued for the 1888 campaign. The top of the badge contained the name "Belva Lockwood" embossed in metal. Hanging from the bar by two chains was a metal disk on which the "1888" election date was imprinted. There is no known reference to such an item in existing Lockwood campaign records, but it conceivably could have been issued as a promotional piece and not as an accessory for a Mother Hubbard parade.

One of the more scurrilous of the attack pieces was a mechanical card that portrayed a full-length caricature of Lockwood in a long paper skirt that could be lifted up to reveal a hidden Benjamin Butler. The wording on the card was "Our Next President. Belvia [*sic*] Lockwood. But Do-n-t Give It Away." A similar theme appears on a stickpin satirizing Grover Cleveland in 1894.[15] Ben Butler, the Civil War general, was a leading progressive of the period, and the presidential nominee of the Greenback Party in 1884. Butler had previously helped Lockwood in 1874 by speaking on the floor of Congress on behalf of a petition that she had drawn up to permit women to be admitted to the Supreme Court bar. There was no known scandal between Lockwood and Butler, although Butler was often satirized in period media for his alleged wandering eye. There are two trade or advertising cards from 1888 that picture Lockwood with other presidential hopefuls. In one she is a barmaid serving alcohol to Clinton Fisk, the Prohibition candidate from that election. In the other, she is inspecting clothing, along with Fisk, from a leading store for boys and men. M.H. Rosenfield published in 1888 a satirical song titled "Belva, Dear, Belva, Dear!" which once again burlesqued the campaign.[16]

Somewhat akin to trade cards were "Salt River" tickets that, on occasion, alluded to Lock-

Lockwood's run, much of it undoubtedly a spin-off of the negative reaction to the concept of female suffrage in general on the part of its opponents, was proportionally high. The mock Belva Lockwood Clubs of Saratoga and North Attleboro both issued parade ribbons that still survive.[12] Another ribbon, undoubtedly a remnant from a Mother Hubbard parade, shows a rather portly woman dressed in the type of skirt for which the parade was named holding a sign proclaiming "Belva Lockwood." The entire image is under the letters "B.L."[13] There were two versions in 1888 of a rebus ribbon with the inscription "For President" with pictures of a bell, the letter "V," a padlock, and a block of wood. Sullivan and Fischer list this without comment in their comprehensive work on American political ribbons, as does Jill Norgren in her seminal study of Lockwood.[14] However, given the tradition of Lockwood-mocking parade ribbons and the im-

Mechanical card, note misspelling of "Belva" as "Belvia." Lift up the paper skirt and find Civil War general and presidential candidate, Ben Butler.

wood's candidacy. While the date of origin of the political term "Salt River" is obscure, its meaning is not — a party destined for defeat is said to be headed up "Salt River." The term first appeared in print in the 1830s, and by the 1870s and 1880s candidates were printing up mock sailing or excursion tickets for their opposition. Lockwood's name appears on occasion on these tickets along with other minor party figures that were destined for defeat. An elaborate anti–Grover Cleveland "C.D.H. Underground R.R." ticket, for example, contains tear-off portions for Fisk's Brook (Clinton Fisk, the Prohibition candidate in 1888) and for "Belva Dear." Another ticket, issued by supporters of Grover Cleveland in 1884, is for the "old Steamer Re-

publican," captained by James Blaine, headed up Salt River with John P. St. John, the Prohibition candidate, as barkeeper, Ben Butler as steward of the spoons, and Belva Lockwood as chambermaid. What may be significant in both trade cards and Salt River tickets is that, while the mocking of Lockwood may at times "feminize" her, it is placed in a context of the general satire of all opposition candidates, giving her campaign, ironically, a modicum of legitimacy from sources that may not have been inclined to accept her presidential run seriously. Victoria Woodhull's name also appeared on Salt River tickets, although, as is the case with Lockwood, always as a secondary rather than primary character.[17]

The 1884 campaign, from its inception, was illustrated in many of the news and political satire magazines of the period, much of it mocking. *Frank Leslie's Illustrated* in the beginning of November just prior to the election included an article on the Belva Lockwood Clubs that was accompanied by a lithograph of men dressed as women parading in a Rahway, New Jersey, demonstration.[18] The illustration was reprinted later in a German magazine called *Das Neue Blatt. Leslie's* article was gentler than most. The publisher of the magazine and, therefore, the one who controlled much of its editorial comment, was Miriam Leslie, Frank's wife, and a strong feminist, who often ran articles supportive of women candidates. *Puck* and *Judge,* however, were unabashed in their derision of Lockwood's campaign, a reflection, perhaps, of their lack of sympathy for the movement in general. On an 1884 *Judge* cover illustration, a mischievously aggressive Lockwood, waving a fan, is calling out "Peek-a-Boo" to an obviously frightened Uncle Sam, cowering behind a chair in a horse barn.[19] In another illustration, a lampooned image of Lockwood beating a drum for her candidacy at a carnival along with Greenback Party and Prohibition Party candidates, Butler and St. John, is captioned "The Neglected Side Show — Nobody Seems to Know That They Are in Existence." Still another from *Judge* displays an angry Lockwood pointing to Butler and St. John, who are in turn pointing to each other, all declaring "Your Fault I Was Not Elected."

Puck, a magazine that generally supported the candidates and policies of the Democratic Party in the same manner that *Judge* supported the Republicans, was equally dismissive. A famous cover illustration by Frederick Opper showed Lockwood bursting from the trapdoor on a public stage carrying her nomination from the "Women's Rights Party" to a disgruntled Ben Butler in a clown suit. The caption declared, "Now Let the Show Go On! Arrival of the Political Columbine to Join the Political Clown."[20] Opper later was to become famous for his comic strips, "Happy Hooligan" and "Alphonse and Gaston," among others. The satirical treatment of Lockwood's candidacy by both the Democratic

NEW JERSEY.—THE HUMORS OF THE POLITICAL CAMPAIGN—PARADE OF THE BELVA LOCKWOOD CLUB OF THE CITY OF RAHWAY.

A typical satirical Lockwood Mother Hubbard parade held in Rahway, New Jersey.

and Republican presses backed up Snow's original argument that the political parties then in place could not be trusted to advance the cause of women. One journal, *The Presidency—Sketches and Portraits of all the Candidates*, an ad hoc publication out of Pawtucket, Rhode Island, printed especially for the 1888 campaign, did take a neutral position towards Lockwood. It provided the engraved portraits of all candidates then running on the major and minor parties, including those of Lockwood and Love from the Equal Rights Party. Apparently either this issue was printed prior to Love's declining the nomination or the editors were unaware that he had.[21]

There are examples of other Lockwood memorabilia, more positive in nature, that survive, including the text of various speeches, advertisements for her lecture tours, at least one

One of many satiric cartoons involving Lockwood's presidential aspirations in humor magazines of the period.

carte de visite, and several cabinet photos, including one of Marietta Stow, that she signed, identifying herself as the equal rights candidate for vice president in 1884. Because of the derisive attitude that was taken towards her candidacy by many men, some suffragists, and most of the press, it is difficult to assess whether Lockwood's two runs at the presidency ultimately helped or hurt the cause of women's rights. One could argue that all press is good press, and that, despite the mocking reactions that surrounded her campaigns, she did foreground the struggle, indicating that it was one that would not be going away. The *Judge* cartoon that declared of the Equal Rights Party "Nobody Seems to Know of Their Existence" was contradictory in nature, for it would not have been published had that indeed been the case.

Moreover, it would be a mistake not to see the negative images of Lockwood in satirical magazines and novelty items in context. Mocking portraits of her typically emanated from those individuals who were hostile by nature to the idea of woman suffrage — the overriding issue for them, undoubtedly, was their opposition to equal rights for women as opposed to Lockwood's candidacy in and of itself. There was more support for Lockwood and other women office seekers in general than the satirical portraits that appeared in *Puck* and *Judge* might otherwise suggest. The website Her Hat Was in the Ring estimates that there were at least 3,500 female candidates for public office prior to 1920, with a surprising number running in the 19th century at the time that Lockwood sought to be president.[22] And there were examples of positive Lockwood memorabilia issued independently of her official campaign itself. Though limited in production, they probably reflected more enthusiasm for a woman candidate for president than suffragist opponents were willing to conceptualize.

Lockwood was not the only candidate to seek office under the banner of the Equal Rights Party. In 1889, Emma Beckwith ran for mayor of Brooklyn and re-

Mrs. BELVA A. LOCKWOOD.

949 BROADWAY, N

This rare cabinet photo of Lockwood may have been given out during one of her presidential campaigns.

ceived twenty-five recorded votes,[23] although Frances Willard and Mary Livermore claimed that the number was fifty with other votes discarded and uncounted.[24] The campaign was of but ten days' duration and had but two rallies. Beckwith, who was married to a wounded Civil War veteran, Edwin Beckwith, was the first president of the Rainy Day Club and involved with the Peace Circle.[25] She was nominated on October 28, 1889, at a hall in the Everett Assembly Rooms in Brooklyn that was rented from T. Charters for a fee of only twenty dollars.[26]

In a somewhat patronizing account, *The New York Times* described the music for the ratification convention as being provided by "two ladies, one at an aged but respectable piano, the other, embracing a fault finding fiddle, [which] evoked a rattling and screeching sound that fairly drowned the noise of the stamping overhead where a Democratic Committee meeting was in progress." Beckwith's platform included a prom-

ise to have "strong women" sweeping the streets because men knew nothing of sweeping, the appointment of women to the Board of Education, the selection of a woman to serve as coal inspector, and the inclusion of women on the police force.[27] In a later speech six years after the election, she called for closing doors on immigration and for the appearance of an American Joan of Arc because "I am tired of receptions, dinners, clothes and veils."[28] Although her campaign was brief, it was the subject of animosity and derision. "Bad Brooklyn boys" attempted to annoy her and keep her awake at night by singing a popular music hall song "Whoa, Emma!" in front of her house.[29]

The only general memorabilia that survives from this campaign are the aforementioned ballot "pasters," embossed with Beckwith's name. She later had printed up a petition that contested the election of John M. Clancy to Congress in the Second Congressional District of New York State in 1892 on the grounds that she, as a woman, was denied her constitutional right to vote.[30]

Bicycles

One of the more spectacular and unusual pieces created with the suffrage movement in mind was a special bicycle manufactured by Elswick Cycles and Manufacturing Company in Newcastle-on-Tyne in England for the Women's Social and Political Union. It was "enameled in the well-known Elswick Green, lined in the Colours of the union," with the gear case bearing the "Medallion of Freedom." An advertisement for the bicycle first appeared in the May 14, 1909, issue of the WSPU's paper, *Votes for Women,* and it was first shown at their famous "Women's Exhibition" at the Prince's Skating Rink in London on May 13 through May 26 in that same month. Like many of the advertisers in *Votes for Women,* Elswick entered into a special relationship with the WSPU, who carried full information at the Woman's Press about the bike for general distribution. They cost ten guineas each, with part of the profits of those bicycles that were ordered directly from the union itself going into their official funds.[1] Earlier in America, Belva Lockwood had been mocked for riding a tricycle [**see Belva**

Lockwood and the Equal Rights Party], for many in the nineteenth century thought it immodest of a woman to appear on such a machine. The reaction towards women and bicycles was one of many areas that were in flux in both countries, however, as the movement continued to evolve. Negative cartoon images of the period often correlated the concept of women riding bicycles with their desire to vote.

Blotters

One of the many new forms of advertising that roughly coincided with the rise of the 20th-century suffrage movement was that of the advertising or promotional ink blotter. With one side containing a rough surface to pick up inkblots, the other featured a design depicting all sorts of products and services. NAWSA was one of the first groups to see their value in terms of promoting a political message also, and, while they produced only a few varieties, those that were printed attracted both notice and popularity among suffrage supporters. In her secretary's report to the NAWSA National Convention in 1904, Elizabeth J. Hauser announced that the organization had blotters ready to send out two weeks before Christmas and by January 1 had already sold five hundred of them. The total cost for the lot was $81.44.[1] By the time of the next convention, the sales figure had risen to 885, and NAWSA had made a slight profit on the item.[2] Blotters along with suffrage stamps were the only novelties mentioned in Hauser's reports apart from souvenir items for the birthdays of Lucy Stone, Susan B. Anthony, and Elizabeth Cady Stanton. Other official blotters were issued by the Women's Political Union in their colors and by the 1915 Pennsylvania Liberty Bell Campaign.

The editors of the *Woman's Journal* were especially intrigued by a suffrage blotter created by Ella Kendrick ("always fertile in promoting ingenious ideas for promoting equal suffrage") of the Hartford Equal Rights Club. It consisted of a picture of the Connecticut State House along with a list of those who could vote and those who could not, using terms that today would be considered highly offensive.[3] The blotter was given out to each member of the Connecticut Legislature, and the Club also attempted to circulate the piece throughout city offices in Hartford. One month later, Jane Addams and three hundred suffragists from the Equal Suffrage League carried a similar blotter designed for a similar target audience aboard a special suffrage campaign train. They were on their way to Springfield, Ohio, to lobby the state legislators, where they were courteously received by the governor's wife.[4]

In England, suffrage blotters were rare. Farmer and Sons on Kensington High Street did advertise in *Votes for Women* advising women to "Be true to your colours and buy VOTES FOR WOMEN BLOTTERS — FORD'S Best Blotting, Purple, White, and Green." There was variation in the quality of these blotters as they sold anywhere from one to four pence each, depending on quality.[5]

Some advertisers, willing to spend a little more money to advertise their products, produced celluloid rather than cardboard blotters. These items consisted of a celluloid cover and a cardboard or celluloid back that enclosed several blotters inside. The use of celluloid not only protected the blotters themselves but allowed a brilliancy and depth to the colors of their images. The only known suffrage celluloid blotter depicts a photographic profile of Susan B. Anthony along with the message "Perfect equality of rights for women — civil and polit-

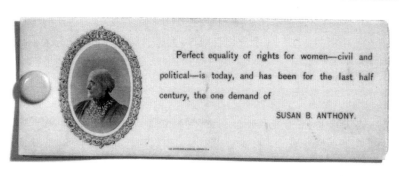

Celluloid blotters such as this were often kept as souvenirs rather than used.

ical — is today, and has been for the last half century, the one demand of SUSAN B. ANTHONY." The piece was made by the New Jersey firm of Whitehead and Hoag, one of the pioneer manufacturers of celluloid campaign and advertising buttons.

Even commercial interests picked up on use of blotters with suffrage themes to promote their products. A generic card, designed by Stuart Travis, depicts an ingénue draped in a "Votes for Women" sash reading a speech over the caption "Declaration of Independence." While her portrait is not necessarily negative, it lacks *gravitas*, and probably was intended to represent an artist's reflection of the contemporary scene rather than intentionally to make an ideological comment. One of the companies that used the design for its advertising was Sauers Milling Company of Evansville, Illinois, which presumably found the image neutral enough not to offend male customers who were still opposed to suffrage. Another advertising blotter that depicted a young woman with a "Votes for Women" banner driving a car was used to promote a play called "The Suffragettes" that was currently appearing at the New Grand Theater.

Blotters were among the items that a correspondent to the *Woman's Journal* from the Mississippi Valley Suffrage Conference recommended that activists print up for use and sale to promote the cause in their home districts. "Blotters, yellow printed with black, should bear sentences as 'Give the Woman a Square Deal,' 'Vote for the Woman Suffrage Amendment' and the date." She suggested that suffrage blotters, kept constantly in banks and post offices and distributed through schools and offices, were "good advertisements" for suffrage.[6]

Buttons and Badges — American

The period from 1908 to 1917, when the suffragists were producing much of their campaign and marching memorabilia, overlapped quite conveniently with what Edmund Sullivan terms "The Golden Age of Campaign Buttons,"[1] when, as Ted Hake notes, "button designing was at its peak."[2] Some form of lapel material had always been available for American presidential campaigns, from the clothing stud buttons worn to Washington's inaugural to the sulfide buttons of William Henry Harrison's campaign and ultimately to the ferrotype stickpins and portrait shell badges that graced elections from the 1860s to the mid–1890s. However, it was in 1896 that the newly invented, colorful, and inexpensive celluloid button was employed extensively for the first time.[3] The use of celluloid for campaign advertising had been tried in the 1876 election contest between Samuel Tilden and Rutherford B. Hayes. An image was struck right onto the plastic itself, but the celluloid proved to be too brittle for much use and was momentarily discarded. However, advances by the Baldwin and Gleason Company of New York in 1888 and by the Whitehead and Hoag Company of New Jersey in 1893 made the modern campaign button not only possible but also a desirable token. Beginning in 1896, it was to emerge as a mainstay of political elections for decades to come. The image was no longer embedded on the celluloid as was attempted in 1876; rather, it was printed on a piece of paper that was then coated with a thin layer of the new material and attached to a metal support.[4] By using the paper underneath the celluloid covering instead of the celluloid itself as a base upon which to do their printing, manufacturers were able to produce highly colorful and graphic products that became enormously popular with the public.

The use of the new lapel badge extended beyond political campaigns into advertising, and commercial manufacturers ordered and passed out to an eager public myriad buttons with various elaborate colorful designs to hawk their wares.[5] The suffragists, also, recognizing the graphic appeal of buttons, were among the first groups to employ these badges to promote a political cause rather than a political candidate; and, during the period from the beginning of the twentieth century to when the federal Suffrage Amendment was finally passed, they were responsible for distributing several hundred varieties of designs promoting the franchise for women. In addition to the two firms listed above, the main manufacturers of buttons during this period were American Art Works of Coshocton, Ohio, Bastian Brothers of Rochester, New York, the St. Louis Button Company of St.

Louis, Missouri, and Torsh and Franz of Baltimore, Maryland. Often these manufacturers inserted a paper disk in the back of their products that listed their company name, address, and the copyright date of their processes. In addition, there were also button "jobbers" that acted as middlemen between manufacturers and their customers. They suggested designs, took orders, and sometimes had their own names inserted onto the back papers of the finished product, but they did not actually manufacture the button. Suffrage groups did not have the capability and equipment to produce their own badges, and always had to rely on outside firms to make their products. But, like jobbers, they could have their own customized back papers inserted, which generally listed the name and address of their organization. These pins were sold at suffrage headquarters for as low as a penny each as well as distributed at meetings, bazaars, fairs, marches, and demonstrations. The popularity of buttons can be attested to by countless references to them in the memoirs of the suffragists, period newspapers, and official suffrage publications.

Suffragists such as Agnes Gay[6] and Alice Park collected suffrage pins, and Ella O. Guilford of New York even advertised in the *Woman's Journal* for additions to her collection.[7] Alice Park, a northern California worker, became intrigued with the message that buttons conveyed, and accumulated a collection of 178 varieties.[8] She saw much significance in these small objects and argued: "The wearing of the badge is significant of progress. Few are worn where the suffrage movement is unpopular. Many are worn as it grows in favor. Every badge, pin, or button is a help, arousing curiosity among strangers, stimulating conversation among acquaintances and discussion among friends and antis. Show your colors all day long — at home to the chance inquirer at the door, the caller and the tradesman; in the street and in the cars to the chance passerby; and in all meetings to all who attend. Until women have the courage of their convictions, how can they expect to win recognition and approval?"[9]

Park's arguments for the value of suffrage buttons had also been expressed a year earlier by an anonymous contributor to the *Woman's Journal*: "Let every suffragist, man or woman, wear daily and as conspicuously as possible a yellow badge with 'Votes for Women' printed in simple black letters. Not only would this advertise the cause from a visual standpoint, but it would promote conversation and questions on the part of those who are not interested and those who are only mildly interested."[10] These thoughts about the value of buttons in terms of initiating conversations were reiterated by Helen Loop, a suffrage supporter as well as a Women's Christian Temperance Union (WCTU) activist, who told of an incident with a saleswoman in an Indiana store. The saleswoman, seeing Loop's "Votes for Women" button, wanted to know where she could get one herself. Never really concerned about suffrage before, she had recently been let go from her previous position, where she had worked for nineteen years, because she was now considered "too old." She told Loop, "Your little button speaks a message to me that I would like to tell all women." Loop, of course, gave her own button to her.[11]

Nora Emerson Drew, advocating the promotion of suffrage in the manner of a commercial enterprise instead of a militant attack, saw much merit in the use and sale of buttons. Alluding to the suffrage parade along Pennsylvania Avenue that preceded Woodrow Wilson's inaugural in 1913, she noted, "If, I say, you had been selling suffrage buttons in those Washington crowds, for the sake of learning the temper of the populace, you would have been converted to the merits of advertising."[12] Prior to the parade, the sale of buttons had become an issue with the police, who warned the suffragists against distributing them on the street without a vendor's license. The police involved succumbed to the pleading of the suffragists, and not only granted them permission but also ended up wearing the buttons themselves.[13]

The Women's Political Union of New Jersey advised its members and affiliates to never conduct a suffrage meeting consisting of speakers alone. Instead, they urged that the message of orators should be supplemented with "literature, buttons, etc." and suggested that a table be set up at the back of the room where such items could be sold. Such merchandising not only provided money for the cause but also helped to convert people through a form separate from live speeches.[14]

Buttons proved enormously popular both as propaganda and as souvenirs. Their dual roles could, however, come into conflict on occasion. Reporting to the *Woman's Journal* about a train tour for suffrage in Illinois, Fanny Rastall, suffrage activist and Kansas WCTU president from 1884 to 1891, noted that the suffragists would stop en route to Springfield to address crowds and to distribute "our buttons, 'Votes for Women,' to those who would agree to wear them and vote in our favor, only men being privileged to receive them." At one stop, a policeman reached into the box to take a button, but was stopped by the woman in charge who told him the conditions that he had to agree to prior to obtaining one. He explained that he only wanted the pin as a "souvenir" for his wife. He was told, however, that the buttons were "not to be considered as souvenirs," only as promotional items for the cause. Finally a compromise was reached, and the policeman was allowed to take home the button for a week to see if he could meet the conditions of the suffragists by wearing it. If he could not, he was to return it.[15]

That buttons and badges could have a positive impact on the public at large is illustrated by another incident that occurred when Women's Social and Political Union (WSPU) founder Emmeline Pankhurst visited America in October 1909. She was escorted off the steamer by Deputy Collector Williams, who opened his coat and displayed to the press the "handsomest of her [Pankhurst's] badges." He had seen her wearing it, begged for it, and she gave it to him. Pankhurst told the crowd, "I find that my suffragette badge is always an incentive to courtesy." Kate Keegan, who had been imprisoned with Pankhurst at Holloway, agreed, recalling, "A man looked at my badge in the car the other day and then gave me a seat."[16]

English buttons in general had a considerable impact on the American suffragist movement. Organizations such as the Women's Political Union, the National Woman's Party, the Connecticut Woman Suffrage Party, and Maryland's Just Government League appropriated their slogans, their official colors, and their designs, and suffragists such as Alice Park collected them. Mrs. Alva Belmont, president of the Political Equality League, requested of her daughter

in England, the Duchess of Marlborough, that she send to her as many varieties of English badges that she could find. The duchess complied and mailed her mother a collection representing over twenty-five suffrage organizations, along with sashes and posters. Mrs. Belmont pinned the entire collection on a "Votes for Women" banner, and put it on display at League headquarters on East 41st Street in New York.[17]

What was one of the first if not the first of the suffrage buttons[18] was in the form of a small ⅝" stickpin that was issued in the mid 1890s by the National American Woman Suffrage Association, probably in 1896, to commemorate the first "Woman's Rights Convention" at Seneca Falls two years prior to its 50th anniversary. Curiously enough, it was not in the newly emerging celluloid format of political and advertising buttons of the period nor did it at all reflect NAWSA's "official" yellow color. It consisted instead of "a small silver sunflower ... the leaves gilded," with the numeral "1848," the date of Seneca Falls, set in gold on ruby glass, placed on top. It came in two versions, as a stickpin and as a badge with a hanger that contained the organization's acronym "NAWSA."[19] A copy of the badge was given to Carrie Chapman Catt.[20] Both versions sold for one dollar postpaid, a considerable amount considering that later buttons and badges were priced generally at a penny each or, at most, a nickel.

The long stem to this piece suggests it probably functioned as a hat pin and not as a lapel badge.

At the same time, NAWSA printed both letterheads and envelopes featuring the same Kansas-inspired image for "social correspondence."[21] Susan B. Anthony used this design for a period on her personal stationery, as did other suffragists.[22] It also appeared on the cover of the *Proceedings of the Thirtieth Annual Convention of the National American Woman Suffrage Association Held in Washington, D.C., Feb. 13–19, 1898.*[23] Sometime later, probably between 1910 and 1920, NAWSA commemorated the logo on a small ⅝" celluloid button, this time picturing the sunflower in yellow, not gold, with a brown center, similar to the design used by Alfred E. Landon, the Kansas Republican, in his presidential run against Franklin D. Roosevelt in 1938.

In general, many of the various button designs that NAWSA ordered tended to be only ⅝" in diameter, were understated in terms of color and graphics, and were printed in gold rather than the traditional yellow. The group's most famous celluloid, a simple "Votes for Women" slogan in black-on-gold, while it may have been lacking in design creativity, was issued in large numbers for distribution throughout the country and proved to be enormously popular. In 1912, Rosalie Livingston Jonas, an organizer for the New York State Suffrage Association, conducted a two-week sojourn throughout Nassau County with a pony and cart, from which she sold these simple buttons along with literature,

tea, and cake. Accompanying Jonas was Elizabeth Freeman, the American woman who had been sent to prison in London with other protesting suffragists.[24] In 1918, the National Organization gave to the campaigns of Michigan, South Dakota, and Oklahoma eighteen organizers, and supplied them with, among other materials, fifty thousand of these buttons.[25] In the successful New York effort of 1917, one million "Votes for Women" buttons were given out.[26] It was undoubtedly the NAWSA pin that was used in Evelyn Noragon's organized campaign in 1913 in Savannah, Georgia, to sell "Votes for Women" buttons.[27] The design was adopted by a number of NAWSA affiliates, and various versions were issued by the Massachusetts Woman's Suffrage Association of Boston, the New Jersey Woman's Suffrage Association, the 1911 Suffrage campaign in California, the Pennsylvania Woman Suffrage Association, and the Maryland campaign, among others. Both Bastian Brothers and Whitehead and Hoag manufactured the original NAWSA pin, but it is likely that groups throughout the country ordered the design from local manufacturers.[28]

It also was probably this simple "Votes for Women" pin that "General" Rosalie Jones and her ten suffrage followers attempted to pin on a reluctant Governor Martin Glynn after they had completed their 160-mile hike for the cause from New York to Albany on January 7, 1914. The women were received graciously by the governor and his secretary, Frank Tierney, who finally accepted the pins; however, they did not receive the hoped-for gubernatorial endorsement of suffrage in return.[29]

While NAWSA distributed pins with other slogans, for the most part they were issued in the same black-on-gold colors. One such pin proclaimed "Ballots for Both," the winning twenty-five-dollar slogan in a con-

Left: The most ubiquitous design of any American suffrage button; *right*: a variation of the "Votes for Women" slogan purposely framed to include men.

test sponsored by NAWSA. Dr. Eleanor M. Hi-estand-Moore of Philadelphia originated the phrase when she was campaigning in her home city in 1915. She had confronted an angry Italian immigrant, who, misinterpreting the cry of "Votes for Women," assumed that the suffragists were attempting to deny him the vote because he was a male. Her response to avoid such confusion in the future was the slogan "Ballots for Both,"[30] which was first used at the Pennsylvania State Suffrage Convention that began on November 25, 1916.

Another NAWSA slogan pin with a bit of history was one that proclaimed, "I'm a Voter." The idea for the pin originated with Jeannette Rankin of Montana, a state that had granted women the franchise in 1914 and then elected her to Congress as the first woman ever to hold that office. Rankin felt that the button would have special resonance at the Panama-Pacific Exposition in 1915 if worn by women from the western states where women could vote. The idea was "to make the visitors from the conservative Eastern States realize, through visual aid, there are thousands and thousands of well-groomed, happy, sensible women who actually vote, and the National Association has seized upon the Panama-Pacific Exposition as the best place in which to demonstrate the truth of their contention." The buttons also were distributed to women throughout the country through their local state suffrage organizations. Dr. Anna Howard Shaw observed that "Miss Rankin can wear the button ... thanks to the men of Montana, but I can't until the men of Pennsylvania give me the right next November."[31]

NAWSA was probably responsible also for a button that simply questioned "WHY." The message of this button may have been influenced by a series of articles on woman suffrage by Elizabeth Robins. The series started in December 1909 in the English publication *Votes*

for Women, after having first been advertised there on November 26.[32] Robins' initial article began with a series of questions all headlined with the word "why." Her follow-up articles each week also began with the "why" question. The series was bound up by the Women Writers' Suffrage League in 1910 and sold by the WSPU. The same antiphonal "why" structure then appeared on leaflets issued by various American suffrage organizations.

In 1911, in commemoration of Washington becoming the fifth suffrage state the previous year, NAWSA issued a memorial photo pin of Susan B. Anthony surrounded by a border of five stars. They also produced a portrait button of Anna Howard Shaw, one of the few times they promoted a current leader to the general public. Both pins were priced at five cents each and at $4.50 for 100.[33]

NAWSA found itself with a very fortunate problem when new states were being added to the suffrage map, for they had to rid themselves of earlier buttons which originally had but four stars to indicate the number of suffrage states. In July 1911, anticipating a win in California added to the win in Washington, they announced plans to produce a new six-star button, selling their now out-of-date stock of four-star pins at half price or two for a penny. There were two varieties available, one in red, white, and blue and the other in gold-on-white.[34] In 1912, upon victories in Arizona, Kansas, Oregon, and, os-

Left: A slogan designed to inspire women in non-suffrage states to fight on; *right*: one of the few portrait pins that the National American Woman Suffrage Association (NAWSA) issued of its leaders, although probably a memorial piece

tensibly, Michigan, NAWSA announced plans to issue a ten-star button. Unfortunately, the Michigan victory, challenged in court, turned out to be illusory, and the production of the proposed button had to be postponed.[35]

Surprisingly, there are very few other buttons that can be directly attributable to NAWSA, although it is quite probable that most black-on-gold pins of whatever suffrage slogan had a NAWSA connection. There were several buttons that were sold by headquarters, including a gold-on-white enamel pin in the shape of a flag at ten cents each, a "six stars" and "Votes for Women" pin in gold and white,[36] a "ten star" black-on-gold celluloid sold for a penny each,[37] and a perpetual calendar and paperweight for thirty-five cents that was intended for the 1916 Christmas market.[38]

The gold-on-white enamel flag pin was originally the idea of the Women's Freedom League (WFL) in England, which first produced flag pins. A quantity of the pins had been brought from overseas by Clara Colby, founder and publisher in 1883 of the *Woman's Tribune*, a suffrage newspaper, and sold at NAWSA's annual convention in Buffalo in 1908 for ten cents. Because "everyone fell in love with them," Colby's supply was soon exhausted. NAWSA, which had been "groping for a badge," decided to order a large quantity of this "official international badge" and sell it at national headquarters.[39] NAWSA's order was placed with an American manufacturer that modified slightly the "Votes for Women" lettering on the flag. In her personal account of the California campaign, Selina Solomons notes the popularity of the WFL badge there as well.[40]

Because NAWSA's headquarters in New York would sell on occasion items that were produced by other organizations, it is not always possible to determine what specifically was a NAWSA-issued button. But what can be noted is that this suffrage organization, criticized by others for its conservatism, typically avoided the flashy in its lapel memorabilia. Unlike the English WSPU, it generally did not produce pins with portraits of its leaders, although several photo pins of Susan B. Anthony did appear following her death in 1906 that may have been NAWSA related, including one worn by representatives of the six suffrage clubs of Minneapolis

in February 1911 when they went to St. Paul to march at the state capitol.[41]

NAWSA was responsible for a very intriguing medal issued to Boy Scouts who had assisted in the March 3, 1913, suffrage march in Washington, D.C. that preceded Woodrow Wilson's inaugural ceremonies, held the next day. The front of the medal, which is suspended from a hanger with the motto "Be Prepared," has the appearance of a typical Boy Scouts of America (BSA) piece, picturing two scouts and the scout insignia. The rear of the piece is inscribed: "Presented to _____ in Grateful Acknowledgement of Duty Well Done Washington D.C. Mar. 3, 1913 National American Woman Suffrage Association."[42] Prior to the suffrage march, Alice Paul, then affiliated with NAWSA, had tried to impress upon the local police that a huge crowd would be attending the event, but her efforts met with little success. Consequently, when the women began to march, the crowd began to press in, blocking their way. Reports differ as to whether the crowd was supportive or hostile,[43] and whether or not the police let in "rough characters" to break up the parade.[44] In desperation, Paul called upon Secretary of War Henry Lewis Stimson, who sent in the U.S. Cavalry for assistance, and the marchers were finally able to reach their destination. Also providing assistance were Boy Scouts,[45] for whom the medal was fashioned.

One of those organizations that could be critical at times of NAWSA for its conservatism was the Women's Political Union (WPU), founded by Harriot Stanton Blatch, the daughter of Elizabeth Cady Stanton. The buttons of the WPU, with their vibrant colors, extended graphics, and larger size, are reflective of the tactical differences between the two organizations, the latter known for its militancy (albeit nonviolent) and its aggressiveness. After living in England for 20 years and having married the Englishman William Blatch, Harriot Stanton Blatch returned to America in 1902, and joined several groups devoted to advancing the status of women, including the Women's Trade League and NAWSA. She founded the Equality League of Self-Supporting Women in 1907, which became the Women's Political Union in 1910, eventually merging with Alice Paul's Congressional Union, which ultimately in turn became the National Woman's Party. Blatch was strongly influenced by the assertive tactics and iconography of the English WSPU, formed by Emmeline Pankhurst, and she modified their name for her 1910 organization, borrowing their colors of purple, white, and green, and even using one of their slogans, "Deed not Words," for one of the WPU's buttons. In reframing the name of the WSPU to WPU, Blatch maintained the English practice of pluralizing "Woman" to "Women." Most other American suffrage associations used the singular form in their title.

The difference between the general appeal of the colorful WPU buttons and their NAWSA counterparts can be seen in a bit of street theater recorded by *The New York Times* in late May 1915. A stockbroker named Fritz W. Hoeninghaus "cornered the market" of a WPU button in the union's colors of purple, green, and white after he bought several from the WPU's Roving Shop for a penny each. He took his original purchase to "Curb Street" where he sold one for a dollar to Henry Barklay, causing a demand from other brokers for a copy. He went back to the van, bought out their remaining supply, and within "ten minutes every man was wearing a suffrage button." Hoeninghaus did the honorable thing and gave the profits from his speculative sales to the WPU. The *Times* commented that had this been an ordinary button [probably the common NAWSA pin] that was only the size of a nickel, "no man would wear it."[46]

The main symbol of the WPU, which appeared on its sheet music, postcards, meeting notices, playing cards, and buttons, was that of the Clarion figure, adapted from the English "Bugler Girl" poster, designed by Caroline Watts. The design was first published by the Artist's Suffrage League originally to advertise a procession of the National Union of Women Suffrage

Societies on June 13, 1908 (**see the Clarion Figure page A1**). WPU's first version of this pin substituted the red and white color scheme of the English design to their own purple, green, and white, at the same time adding five stars to the herald's banner. Later versions had six, ten, eleven, and twelve stars respectively, as the number of states that awarded women full suffrage began to increase. While there was a 1¹⁄₁₆" version of the Clarion pin produced, the rest were all 1¼" in size, which, combined with rich coloring, allowed for a far greater visual impact than that achieved by NAWSA's small black-on-gold buttons. The WPU also went to the 1¼" size when it issued a button picturing Elizabeth Cady Stanton on the hundredth anniversary of her birth along with another advertising the 1915 referendum in New York.

The design for the WPU New York pin served as a model for several pins issued by the Women's Political Union of New Jersey (WPUNJ). Mina C. Van Winkle originally established the WPUNJ as the Equality League for Self-Supporting Women of New Jersey, and it was affiliated with Harriot Stanton Blatch's organization with a similar name. Adopting the strategy of her friend Blatch, Van Winkle appealed to working women, both wage earners and professionals, attempting to draw them into the suffrage movement. The Equality League changed its name to the WPUNJ in 1912, fol-

Left: Because this badge is memorial, it was acceptable to use Stanton's image; *right*: the design for this Women's Political Union of New Jersey (WPUNJ) badge was borrowed from Blatch's New York-based Women's Political Union (WPU).

lowing the lead of Blatch's group, which had become the Women's Political Union in 1910. It retained its new name for the next four years until it merged with the larger New Jersey Woman's Suffrage Association in 1916. During the time that it was a WPU affiliate, it adopted the WPU's official colors, green, white, and purple (which it renamed "violet"). It was extremely active in the October 19, 1915, suffrage referendum, which was held on voter registration day, going down to defeat.

The WPUNJ produced a variety of ephemera, including other badges emblazoned with its colors, some in support of the October 19 referendum, as well as posters and stamps. The logo of the group, however, was not the Clarion figure of its New York counterpart, but rather a blindfolded Justice, which not only symbolized judicial fairness but also the fact that women had been kept ignorant of their rights. As was traditional with many suffrage images, rays of the rising sun behind the figure of Justice indicated hope for the future, an image that somehow was never depicted on its buttons. As was the case between the WPU and NAWSA, the buttons of the WPUNJ were far more colorful than those of its temporary rival, the New Jersey Woman's Suffrage Association, the NAWSA affiliate. One other New Jersey pin is worthy of mention, a 1¼"

There were many men's groups such as this actively supporting suffrage.

black-on-yellow celluloid issued by the New Jersey Men's League for Womens [*sic*] Suffrage, one of the few buttons issued by a men's franchise organization.

Alice Paul's National Woman's Party (NWP), formed in 1917 from her earlier organizations, the Congressional Union and the Woman's Party, was responsible for surprisingly few buttons despite what her biographers, Katherine H. Adams and Michael L. Keene, term her "dramatic visual campaign," which involved photographs, cartoons and other artwork, parades, boycotts, picketing the White House, train trips, and hunger strikes. Paul believed that NAWSA's program for change, which relied heavily upon writing and speaking, would never succeed. It needed to be combined with a new form of rhetoric that employed the visual impact of persuasive images and what would now be termed "street theater."[47]

The most interesting and historically significant of the pins that the NWP was responsible for, however, were not celluloid buttons. They were silver brooches that were given out to members who had been imprisoned for the cause and to those who had picketed the White House on behalf of suffrage, sometimes known as the "Silent Sentinels." In early June 1917, suffragists who were arrested for their demonstrations in front of the White House were sent to the District Jail or to the Occoquan Workhouse. At the District Jail, Alice Paul and Rose Winslow, a Polish born fundraiser and NWP organizer, responded by conducting a hunger strike, following the lead of their English counterparts. When word got out about their actions, fourteen other women, both at the jail and at the workhouse, joined them in a refusal to eat. Their jailers, in response, had them forcibly fed. Finally, frustrated by the various actions and refusals of the suffragists, Raymond Whittaker, superintendent of the workhouse, gave orders to as many as forty guards, who initiated a "Night of Terror," where women were grabbed, dragged, beaten, kicked, and choked.[48]

In December 1917, a mass meeting was held at the Belasco Theater in Washington to raise money for the party. Eighty-one women in white carried banners adorned with various slogans in the NWP colors of purple, white, and gold up to the stage, and many told of their prison ordeals. They were all presented with "Prison Pins," or "Jailed for Freedom Pins," tiny replicas of their prison doors. These pins were modeled after Sylvia Pankhurst's Holloway or portcullis pin, which was given out by the WSPU to its members who had been imprisoned for the cause. Later in 1919, when President Wilson, returning from Europe, arrived in Boston on February 24, he was greeted by a group of suffrage demonstrators, who were then arrested for speaking on the Boston Common without a permit and sentenced to ten days in jail. At a March meeting of an organized group of NWP volunteers called the "Prison Special Travelers," these arrested women were also given copies of the prison door replica, which the local press termed "a war cross."[49]

Those who picketed the White House were presented with another award, a silver "Silent Sentinel" pin in the shape of one of the banners that they had been carrying. The original demonstration banners contained various slogans, but the phrase engraved on this pin was "Without Extinction Is Liberty," the last words of the suffragist martyr Inez Milholland, who, in poor health, nevertheless carried on with her suffrage activities and died as a result. Inscribed on the back of these pins were the words "For Service in the Cause of Freedom of Women — Presented by the National Woman's Party." It is not known how many of these pins ultimately were given out, but since approximately 200 women were arrested for their picketing activities, a fair estimate would be somewhere between 150 to 200.[50]

Although avoiding some of the confrontational and many of the theatrical tactics of the NWP, the Woman Suffrage Party (WSP) of New York, formed in 1909 by Carrie Chapman Catt and others, was, at its height around 1915, quite forceful in its display of its official color of yellow, as seen on its surviving buttons, sashes, and other memorabilia. When Catt had been in England, she was impressed by the degree to which English women had made suffrage the outstanding political issue. While her focus back in the United States was on a federal suffrage amendment, she believed that in order to have any teeth, the push for such an amendment could occur only if enough of the larger states had already adopted suffrage. The Empire State was the jewel of the crown. But to carry New York State, the suffragists needed New York City. Catt, accordingly, brought the suffrage clubs of greater New York together in the Interurban Woman Suffrage Council, and discussed with their leaders the idea of organizing the five boroughs for suffrage, based upon party lines. They also needed to come up with a name for the group, and names were submitted on a piece of paper. Oreola Haskell sent up the name of the

Left: The "Jailed for Freedom" pin was modeled on an English counterpart by Sylvia Pankhurst, and given out only to National Woman's Party prisoners for the cause; *right*: this pin portrays one of the banners of the Silent Sentinels, who picketed the White House.

"Woman Suffrage Party." The delegates voted down all of the choices, but since "Woman Suffrage Party" was the last to go down, the delegates eventually chose it.[51]

The WSP issued numerous pins, most in black-on-yellow, and many were distributed during the Empire State campaign of 1915, when the organization joined forces with other suffrage groups across New York in an unsuccessful attempt to pass the suffrage referendum on the November 2 ballot. These buttons ranged in size from ½" to 1½" and came in several shapes, including oval varieties and stickpins, with one lithographed version cut in the shape of a flag. Several included the name of the party, others only the party's initials, so confident were the leaders apparently of the fame of the WSP that they felt that the letters did not need to be spelled out. Some pins departed from the simple color scheme and were printed in yellow, white, and blue, the last being one of the official colors of New York State.[52] One variety had a clicker instead of a pin attached to the back, so that when suffrage supporters could not wear the item, they could make noise to support their cause. Such clickers also were used occasionally in the manufacture of political campaign buttons of the period. So extensively did the WSP color its lapel material in yellow that almost any button or badge in yellow from the period that is not otherwise identifiable was probably produced by Catt's organization.

But the WSP, despite its avoidance of militancy, could be controversial, as seen in a group of its buttons that proclaimed "Suffrage First." These pins include an enameled flag pin that contained, along with the phrase, the party's name. Also issued were at least three oval pins expressing the same sentiment. One of the first public iterations of "Suffrage First" within the ranks of the WSP occurred on November 30, 1915, during a combined convention with the reorganized Empire State Committee at the Hotel Astor in New York. When Carrie Chapman Catt rose to speak, she criticized those who would ask women to take up other tasks before suffrage: "Have a printed card to give to people who ask you to do any other work, saying that on account of the deferred enfranchisement of women you must refuse. Let the card say further: 'We are obliged to give ourselves and our money to the suffrage work. Won't you help us so that the sooner we may help you?' Let us take this little button [according to *The New York Times*, pointing to the one she was wearing] and make its slogan our own: 'Suffrage first.'"[53] Mrs. James W. Wadsworth, who succeeded Mrs. Arthur Dodge as the president of the National Association Opposed to Woman Suffrage, was later to take Catt to task for her slogan, particularly because of its implications during wartime.[54] Alice Paul's Woman's Party, however, mirrored the sentiment

Left: Printed in yellow, white, and blue, this pin differed from the typical black and yellow color scheme of the Woman's Suffrage Party; *right:* the slogan "Suffrage First," shown here on a Woman Suffrage Party oval pin, was also used by Alice Paul's National Woman's Party.

and the phrase. On the cover of the 1916 convention issue of its official publication, *The Suffragist*, the words "Suffrage First" replaced the journal's title.

The confrontational slogan, however, did not originate with Catt or Paul or even in America; rather it derived from the Suffrage First Committee in England. In the December 5, 1913, issue of *Votes for Women*, edited by Frederick and Emmeline Pethick Lawrence, the following notice appeared:

Left: The manufacturer of the Harlem League pin borrowed an image of Elizabeth Cady Stanton used by both the Women's Political Union and the New York State Woman Suffrage Association. At the time this pin was made, the majority of Harlem's population was white; *right:* the 1908 Rochester, New York, march advertised here coincided with a suffrage convention held in that city.

"The 'Suffrage First' Committee reports that very great interest is being taken in their proposals, and that large numbers of letters are reaching the Home Secretary daily from electors pledging themselves to make the question of woman suffrage the supreme issue at the next election in their constituency."[55] The committee was first announced in the November 21 issue of the periodical and included a card for electors to pledge that they would at the next election, unless women had been already enfranchised, use their vote in such a way as to "put Woman Suffrage first."[56]

The WSP was the main driving force behind the Empire State campaign of 1915, a loose affiliation of various suffrage organizations. The core button of this combined group depicted, in gold, blue, and white, a rising sun coming out over the land along with the words "Votes for Women 1915." This logo also appeared on campaign stationery and on a paper cup, and was borrowed by the Pennsylvania suffragists for their referendum in the same year.[57] On August 16, members of the WSP, wearing the rising sun button along with "buttonhole bouquets of yellow flowers," passed out literature as well as blue-on-white buttons on "Car Barn Day."[58]

Other New York suffrage groups that produced buttons include Mrs. Alva Belmont's Political Equality Association, which also issued a 2¼" celluloid mirror in the Association's official color of dark blue, the Equal Franchise Society, and the Harlem Equal Rights League, which borrowed the image of Elizabeth Cady Stanton that Blatch's WPU had previously used on one of its buttons. The New York based Men's League for Woman Suffrage was responsible for a black-on-yellow ribbon, but no buttons are known. In a statement to the press that was issued in March 1910, Mrs. Belmont claimed that her Association had distributed 100,000 of their "Votes for Women" buttons at a cost of $500, all within the year of the Association's inception in 1909.[59]

The New York Woman Suffrage Association (NYWSA) issued a number of ribbons for its conventions throughout the years, some of which contained celluloid attachments of various national leaders, including Susan B. Anthony, Emma Willard, Elizabeth Cady Stanton, Anna Howard

Memorial badge of Elizabeth Cady Stanton, who died in 1902.

Shaw, and Carrie Chapman Catt. A celluloid is also known on which appears the photograph of Ella Hawley Crossett, who presided over the 1903 NYWSA convention in Buffalo when, because of illness, then President Mariana W. Chapman was unable to appear. Crossett was then elected president. She eventually wrote the New York campaign section for the *History of Woman Suffrage*.[60] The NYWSA differed from most suffrage organizations in that they typically honored both current and past suffrage heroines on their buttons, whereas others, if they pictured leaders at all, issued primarily memorial items.

The New England states, apart from New Hampshire and Vermont, were well represented by buttons. Even Maine was the source of three pins: (1) a ⅞" multicolored piece with a green pine tree, accompanied by the words "Votes for Women," along with the state motto, "Dirigo" ("I Direct" or "I Guide"), which, presumably, local suffragists hoped would be prophetic as far as their cause was concerned; (2) a convention delegate badge that featured a similar image set into a metal holder attached to a red, white, and blue ribbon; and (3) a small ½" gold-on-blue identification button for the Men's Equal Suffrage League. The initial meeting of the League took place in 1914 in a Portland hotel. Its first president was Robert Treat Whitehouse, a former U.S. district attorney and husband of Florence Brook Whitehouse, a suffragist activist.

The Connecticut Woman Suffrage Association (WSA) produced most of the suffrage pins in Connecticut. The organization was founded in 1869 primarily through the efforts of Isabella Beecher Hooker, the sister of Harriet Beecher Stowe and Henry Ward Beecher, who directed it for 36 years. In 1910, Katherine Houghton Hepburn, mother of the actress, took

The **Connecticut Woman Suffrage Association and the Just Government League of Maryland both borrowed the English chain link design.**

control of the CWSA, and, working with Alice Paul's NWP, concentrated on building support for a federal amendment. Like the WPU, the CWSA borrowed the English colors of purple, green, and white, not only for their buttons and sashes, but also for their campaign literature as well. Their most common button, which contained their initials set within a chain-link design, was taken directly from a WSPU pin.

Perhaps the most graphic of all American suffrage buttons was the CWSA issue of a 1¼" celluloid picturing a donkey along with the words "Votes for Women Plank." There is no reference to this pin in Annie G. Porritt's account of the CWSA activities in *The History of Woman Suffrage*, even though Porritt was the secretary of the Connecticut association. It was probably issued in 1916, however, at a time when the national Republican, Democratic, Progressive, Socialist, and Prohibition Parties all came out with platforms or "planks" endorsing suffrage, thereby providing encouragement for local suffragists to demand a similar pledge from state political organizations at their conventions. The CWSA, in their response to the challenge, planned two large parades, the first at Union Station in New Haven on September 5, the date of the opening of the Republican State Convention in that city, and the second, a similar demonstration on September 19, for the Democratic counterpart. The latter was considered by local suffragists to be "more picturesque and more impressive" than the Republican daylight parade. Marchers carried large paper lanterns suspended on the end of sticks and Mrs. O.H. Havelmeyer carried the Ship of State embedded with electric lights.[61] Although newspaper accounts of the day do not mention the "Votes for Women Plank" button, it probably was manufactured specifically for the parade. The fact that no Republican "mate" to this pin is known to exist may be due to the general lack of spectacle during that party's parade. The image of a donkey with a suffrage plank also appeared in an illustration by the St. Louis suffragists that appeared earlier in the *Woman's Journal*.[62]

Another group based in Connecticut that issued several pins was the National Junior Suffrage Corps. It had been organized in 1914 when Caroline Ruutz-Rees, principal of a flourishing girls' school in Greenwich, believed that the future of the movement was based on the success of attracting young women to the cause. To meet this objective, she started the Suffrage Corps, whose motto was "Youth Today, Tomorrow Power."[63]

A number of suffrage buttons were used in the various Massachusetts campaigns, but only a few specifically identify themselves with any state organization. The Massachusetts Woman Suffrage Association (MWSA) did distribute the common NAWSA "Votes for Women" black-on-gold button, but with their own name printed on the back paper. Lucy Stone, Henry Blackwell, Julia Ward Howe and others had founded the organization in 1870 within a year after they had helped form the American Woman Suffrage Association, and MWSA shared both the goals and activities of the national group. It later merged with the smaller National Suffrage Association of Massachusetts.

Two celluloid ribbons were later added to the Votes for Women pin advertising the "Victory Parade October 16, 1915," a major event designed to build support for the November 2 suffrage referendum. This parade, which included about 15,000 marchers with a substantial men's contingent, was attended by a half-million onlookers, and it was reviewed by Governor David I. Walsh in front of the statehouse and Mayor James Michael Curley in front of Boston City Hall. Despite the size of the parade and the participation of

The ***Woman's Journal***, founded by Lucy Stone and her husband, had the longest run of any suffrage paper.

prominent politicians, the referendum went down to defeat by a vote of 295,489 to 163,406, one of four such defeats in eastern states that year.[64] Many varieties of Massachusetts's pins were manufactured by the A.R. Lopez Company of School Street in Boston, including a set of three small red, white, and blue "star" pins that were modeled after those that had been designed originally by the National Equipment Company of New York. These pins, containing four, five, and six stars respectively, indicated the number of states at the time of their manufacture that allowed women to vote.

Although Pennsylvania was one of the eastern states that suffragists had targeted in the 1915 campaign, local organizations there issued very few buttons. One of the reasons for this lack of production may have been the desire of regional workers to avoid "sensationalism" included in the types of events where buttons were often distributed.[65] Apart from locally made versions of NAWSA's black-on-gold "Votes for Women" pins and those distributed as part of the Liberty Bell tour, the only notable pieces to emerge from Pennsylvania were two varieties of the universal suffrage slogan superimposed upon the state symbol of the Keystone. The Pennsylvania League of Women Citizens, formerly the Pennsylvania Woman Suffrage Association, circulated a pin in 1919 with a similar design that replaced the phrase "Votes for Women" with the name of their new organization. The members of the Association had voted to reorganize in November of that year, as NAWSA had done, and change the name of their group. Their new constitution provided for an additional name change, to "the Pennsylvania League of Women Voters," once the anticipated federal suffrage amendment was formally adopted, which it was the following year.[66]

Ohio was one of six states that had scheduled a suffrage referendum in 1912, and the Ohio Woman Suffrage Association drew attention to the upcoming vote on September 12 by organizing a huge woman suffrage parade in Columbus on August 27. California in 1911 had become the sixth state in the union to grant the franchise to women, and local suffragists were hoping that Ohio would immediately follow. Unfortunately, the referendum failed not only in Ohio but in two of the other five states as well.[67] Earlier, in 1911, local suffragists had even hoped to precede California in becoming the sixth state, and they issued a small blue-on-gold button, containing six stars and the slogan "Ohio Next,"[68] along with a pin similar in size and color with the words "Equal Suffrage." They were also responsible for several other imaginative pins from this campaign. One contained an outline of the state, along with the plea "Let Mother Vote," an obvious attempt to personalize the issue for men, reinforcing the idea that the vote was for the women in their lives, not the non-gendered harridans that the opposition had imaged them to be. It is the only known appearance on a button of the otherwise popular theme of giving one's mother the vote. Another pin contained a drawing of an allegorical woman holding arrows in one hand and a sheaf of wheat in the other along with the plea "Let Ohio Women Vote." This particular design emerged as the standard iconic image for the campaign, and it appeared on postcards, stationery, posters, and Cinderella stamps.

According to an Ohio suffrage worker reporting to the *Woman's Journal*, two of these pins helped to alleviate a situation in which the correspondent found an underage immigrant boy carrying a sign for the anti-suffragists during the 1912 campaign in violation of child labor laws. When questioned, the boy indicated that he worked for a dollar a day, from seven in the morning until six at night, with money deducted from his pay when he took time off to eat. When the sympathetic worker pinned an "Equal Suffrage" pin on one of his lapels and an "Ohio Next" on the other, he asked if he could carry one of her placards also.[69]

Suffragists in Kansas also had hoped to become the next suffrage state; they were responsible for a 7/8" celluloid that combined the traditional "Votes for Women" slogan with the date for the referendum, November 5, 1912. Wisconsin women issued a flat celluloid piece for their referendum held on the same day.

The Illinois Equal Suffrage Association issued three pins of different designs with borders of nine or ten stars each and sold them at ten cents a dozen. The first two, in blue-and-white and blue-and-yellow versions, urged "Equal Suffrage" and "Votes for Women." The third continued the star motif on a blue flag set against a yellow background.[70] The Association also produced for the campaign two black-on-yellow pins, one of which contained the name of the organization, each 2¼" in diameter. These pins are among the largest suffrage buttons known from the period. Suffrage pins in Maryland came from several sources: (1) local organizations such as the Just Government League; and (2) Maryland button manufacturers such as Lucky Badge and Buttons and Torsch and Franz.

The successful California campaign of 1911, which enabled the state to become the sixth star in the suffrage flag, produced a number of interesting pins, perhaps providing the incentive for the well-traveled Alice Park to begin her famous collection, the largest known among suffrage activists. San Francisco was the seat of the California Woman's Suffrage Movement, which had begun in 1868. There were two major campaigns in the state: that of 1896, when local suffragists worked hard but unsuccessfully to establish California as the fourth star or state at that time to approve the right of women to vote; and

Left: The suffrage appeal to men to give the vote to their mothers appears on buttons on only these two examples from Ohio; *right*: women in Ohio hoped in vain for Ohio to become the sixth state to grant suffrage, symbolized by the six stars on these pins.

One of the rarest buttons of the campaign, this California piece, which lists the date of the state referendum, was made in a metallic rather than celluloid format.

that of 1911, when voters on October 10 finally gave the franchise to women by a slim 3,587 majority. The suffrage plank was the eighth amendment on the ballot that year, a fact that was noted on one period poster,[71] along with a small 11/16" gold-on-white button manufactured by Brunt and Company of San Francisco that urged, "Vote for Amendment 8." It may have been this celluloid that Selina Solomons was alluding to in her *How We Won the Vote in California*: "A very neat button in white and gold was manufactured for the 'State,' of which nearly fifty thousand were disposed of, being sold at 5 cents each to individuals, and to organizations at cost, one cent each. We had previously worn the English flag pin [probably the gold-on-white enamel that was originally made by the WFL in England and reprinted in America by NAWSA], and all the different buttons we could get hold of."[72] The "Amendment 8" button was originally issued by the Votes for Women Club of Los Angeles, and it proved so popular that a second edition of 5,000 had to be ordered to satisfy the demand.[73]

Always fascinated by suffrage pins themselves along with the pragmatic lessons that they could convey, Solomons told the following anecdote: "The butcher with whom I had been dealing roared like a mad bull at the sight of my badge — a yellow, not a red flag! 'If my wife wanted to vote, I'd kick her out of the house,' he declared. 'A man of your sort will never know what his wife is thinking,' I replied, as calmly as I could to his outburst."[74] Towards the end of the campaign, she noted that the "glad-to-be martyrs" to the cause to gain attention even "adorned their dressy corsages with the white Votes for Women 'dinner plate,'"[75] this pin being a large 2¼" button made by Brunt and Company

that certainly must have drawn the attention of the anti-suffragists. For those "business girls and men, who did not care to be 'conspicuous,'" the California Votes for Women Club had made up a "special original design in poppies, a very dainty pin, similar in size and style to the popular fraternity pin" and sold it for twenty five cents."[76] In the aftermath of the victory in California, a triumphant delegate to the NAWSA convention in Louisville took note of this poppy pin and other state suffrage memorabilia: "We all have ... badges and pins, California poppies and six-star buttons on our dresses, coats and dainty votes for women butterflies on our shoulders, and as we go about in dozens or scores or hundreds the onlookers receive the fitting psychological impression and we find them thinking of us as victors and conquerors."[77]

One other California pin of note was a 1¼" red, green, and white celluloid pin that was issued by the Wage Earner's Suffrage League and included their initials along with the phrase "Votes for Women." Louise LaRue, head of Waitresses Local #48, started the League in San Francisco in 1908 when working women felt that middle-class women involved in the suffrage movement neither understood nor appreciated their situation. She was assisted in her efforts by Minna O'Donnell, who was able to tie in the vigorous support of labor to the suffrage movement when the union Labor Party's candidate, Patrick Murphy, was mayor of the city from 1909 to 1911. Maud Younger, who helped to heal the division between middle-class and working-class women, joined the two.[78]

While the production of suffrage buttons was more prevalent on the East Coast than in the West, other western states besides California issued pins. Perhaps the most spectacular was a

Button of the California Wage Earner's Suffrage League. The organization was one of a scant number nationally that had a direct labor connection.

badge made for the Alaska-Yukon-Pacific (AYP) Exposition held in Seattle, Washington, in 1909. Suffragists took the 1¼" multicolored art nouveau celluloid that was the official button of the fair, but was not related to the suffrage campaign, and attached it to a black-on-green ribbon that announced AYP "Suffrage Day," held on July 7. As Alice Stone Blackwell, daughter of Lucy Stone, described, "In the morning on arriving at the Exposition we found above the gate a big banner with the inscription 'Woman Suffrage Day.' Every person entering the fairgrounds was presented with a special button and a green-ribbon badge representing the Equal Suffrage Association of Washington, the Evergreen State. High in the air over the grounds floated a large 'Votes for Women' kite. All the toy balloons sold on the grounds that day were stamped with the words 'Votes for Women' and many of the delegates bought them and went around hovering over their heads like Japanese lanterns — yellow, red, white or green but predominantly green."[79] A correspondent from the Association writing to the *Woman's Journal* about the color scheme noted, "The color adopted by our National, State, and local organizations is yellow, but, in order to distinguish Washington women, and also to give prominence and a local touch to our campaign, we have selected green as a campaign badge, in honor of our Evergreen State." The green ribbon badges were given free to delegates, but could be purchased by anyone else from the Seattle headquarters for ten cents each. The organization also had made up a gold-on-green enamel pin in the form of a pennant upon which were inscribed the words "Votes for Women." These were available for twenty-five cents.[80]

Washington suffragists were responsible for another pin, this one a 1¼" celluloid with the initials "WWSA" for the Washington Woman Suffrage Association set within a stars and stripes

This white on green pin directly mocks the target design found on many anti-suffrage buttons.

background. This is one of the few suffrage buttons known with a stock design. Button salesmen carried with them catalogs and examples of such designs that featured a decorative border with blank space in the middle of the pin onto which the desired messages or images of their clients could be imprinted. Suffragists in Olympia, Washington, organized the WWSA in 1871 after a visit to the state by Susan B. Anthony and Abigail Scott Duniway as part of their ten-week, 2,000-mile lecture tour throughout the Pacific Northwest.[81]

Buttons from other states include examples from West Virginia, Indiana, Nevada, Minnesota, Iowa and Missouri, where a "Scratch No" design originated. The pin, which urged Missouri men to vote "yes" for the "Equal Suffrage Amendment 13" by scratching out the word "no" on the 1914 franchise referendum ballot, was produced by the newly formed State Woman Suffrage Association. In 1911 the old Missouri state organization ceased to exist. It was replaced when the St. Louis League with its various branches joined with the recently established Webster Groves Suffrage League on February 14 in St. Louis to work for passage of the amendment. Suffrage workers in the state also issued a rather curious "compromise button and ribbon" for the referendum that contained the Clarion design, so favored by the more militant WPU, in the yellow and black colors of the more conservative NAWSA organization with which the Missouri organization had an affiliation.[82] The amendment, which stated "Females shall have the same right, under the same conditions, to vote at all elections held in this State as males now have or may hereafter have," went down to defeat after a long and grueling campaign. Several pins came out of Indiana, including a ⅞" black-on-gold example from the Woman's Franchise League, which, having absorbed several other state organizations, formed around 1911.

While opposition forces throughout the country were generally less enamored of the value of pins than were the suffragists, they nevertheless did produce a dozen or so anti-suffrage buttons, virtually all of which were in the "official" anti- colors of red (or pink), black, and white. Most featured a target design where an inner circle in red or white was surrounded by the corresponding color. The slogans were simple: "Vote No on Woman Suffrage," "Anti Suffrage," and "Opposed to Woman Suffrage." There is no identification of any sort on these pins as to which organization was responsible for their distribution. Their back papers, however, indicated that they were manufactured in New York. Since two of the most influential opposition organizations came from the East Coast, it is most likely that one if not both were responsible for much of their production. These groups were the Massachusetts Association Opposed to the Further Extension of Suffrage to Women, and the National Association Opposed to Women Suffrage, formed in New York by Mrs. Arthur M. Dodge in 1911. The Massachusetts Association was founded in May 1895 and eventually changed its name to the Women's Anti-Suffrage Association of Massachusetts. By 1915, the Association numbered nearly 37,000 members, and had its headquarters in the Kensington Building, on Boylston Street in Boston. Harriot Stanton Blatch's WPU issued a black-on-green-on-white celluloid that was probably intended as an "answer" pin in a nascent war of buttons. The design was exactly the same as the "Vote No on Woman Suffrage" varieties, except that this version of the target design declared "Vote Yes on Woman Suffrage." Both pro- and anti-suffrage forces were definitely aware of each other, and this is not the only instance of one group mocking or criticizing the advertising of the other.

The only button that deviated appreciably from the general design of anti- pins was a small ½" blue-on-white celluloid with the warning "Suffrage Means Prohibition." Many of the early suffrage leaders were also involved in temperance societies. The liquor industry, fearing that female franchise would lead to restrictions on their products, strongly opposed suffrage and poured money and resources into defeating voting rights for women whenever the issue came up in a referendum. Although the anti- forces received significant funding from liquor interests, they typically denied any affiliation.

Left: Pink replaces the standard red as the official color on this most common of all of the anti-suffrage buttons; *right*: The liquor interests feared the outcome of a possible woman's vote because of the involvement of many suffragists in the Temperance movement.

The absence of significant and colorful anti-suffrage memorabilia such as buttons may have been the result of policy rather than lack of imagination. In a statement issued by the National Association Opposed to Woman Suffrage that preceded a pro-suffrage demonstration in Washington, D.C., on May 9, 1914, the anti-suffragists came out strongly against both street theater and the suffrage color scheme. They issued a statement that declared that the anti-suffragists "disapprove strongly of the street parades, hikes, and other spectacular and unwomanly tactics employed by suffragists." However, realizing that the absence of any visible sign of disapproval might be "misconstrued by on-lookers to be an acquiescence in the clamor of the streets," they issued instructions for the wearing of the red rose, "the badge of the anti-suffragists."[83] For the October 19, 1915, New Jersey referendum, the anti- forces took their campaign to the rural areas of the state. While the "ethics of their organization" prohibited them from outdoor campaigning, they did distribute anti-suffrage buttons rather than roses at county fairs.[84]

Despite their announced disapproval of street theater and its accompanying accouterments such as banners, ribbons, and sashes, along with the production of novelties as well, some anti-suffrage associations did pass out on occasion small collectible tokens, including matchbook covers, small pennants, a fan or two, as well as a measuring tape imprinted with anti-suffrage sentiments. The Women's Anti-Suffrage

League of Massachusetts of 687 Boylston Street in Boston gave away a small, flat celluloid stamp holder in black and red, the official colors of the opposition. The bold statement on the front of the piece admonished men to "Stick to the Women and Vote No on Woman Suffrage November 2, 1915"; the rear contained the League's address and the names of its two chief officers, Mrs. John Balch, President, and Mrs. Charles P. Strong, secretary.

Satirical swipes at woman suffrage also appear on buttons issued by the American Tobacco Company that were placed into packets of Hassan and Tokio Cigarettes. In one, labeled "Mr. Suffer-Yet," a man is doing the wash in a wooden tub, with a small child crying in the background. Another has the caricature of a woman attempting to sing opera along with the plea, "Don't Let It Suffer." A third pictures two women showing off their legs, labeling their attempt "Women's Rights." The American Tobacco Company also distributed a very popular series of buttons with cartoons by Rube Goldberg called "I'm the Guy." This series had nothing to do with suffrage itself, but it does indicate the interest that cartoon buttons contained for many smokers. The mocking approach that the American Tobacco Company took towards suffrage was probably done so in the belief that it was striking a responsive chord with its large overwhelmingly male audience, one that apparently felt that, if female suffrage succeeded, men would be forced to take on women's roles.

Buttons and Badges — English

Called "badges" or "pins" by their manufacturers and by suffragists, English "buttons" differ marginally from their American counterparts in several ways. First, English suffrage organizations were less reluctant to issue photographic pins depicting their current leaders. American suffragists, as a rule, did not distribute such pins to the public except as memorial items. Occasionally, they did authorize the printing of some images of leaders on buttons — Anna Howard Shaw and Carrie Chapman Catt come to mind — but these were, in general, convention pieces, not readily available to those who were not delegates. Second, a higher percentage of En-

glish pins than American were manufactured with an enamel rather than a celluloid coating. The enameling process was expensive, but it did result in a product that had a jewelry-like appearance. In addition, several of the primary manufactures of lapel material, such as Toye and Company, were known for producing medals of various types for different organizations, and had a wide variety of enameled products available for potential suffrage needs. Third, while there were notable exceptions, the focus of English pins was more on organizational identification than on upcoming demonstrations and referenda, although most did manage to incorporate "Votes for Women" and other suffrage messages in their designs. The fronts of many American buttons did not include the name of the group that authorized their issue; a goodly portion of English badges did.

But whatever slight differences there may have been between American and British buttons or badges, the English versions, from accounts written by correspondents to the WSPU periodical *Votes for Women*, drew considerable attention. Many English suffragists, as was the case with their American sisters, saw the button or badge to be more than a simple novelty; rather, they conceived of it as a significant device both to publicize the movement and to initiate conversation about women's rights. In a letter to *Votes for Women* in March 1909, Mary L. Parr advocated always wearing a "Votes for Women" badge over and above simply wearing a dress in the colors. Her argument was that the "wearing of a badge invariably attracts attention, whereas to dress in the colours is not yet sufficiently distinctive, as one frequently happens on wearers of the correct Union colours who are totally unaware of their significance."[85]

One activist, writing from the "North East Corner of Yorkshire," noted, "As for the 'Votes for Women' buttons, one sees them everywhere — on men, women, and children; and early in the campaign, some of our organizers were rung up, when they reached after an evening meeting, by a band of youths, armed with pennies, who wanted to buy what they called, 'our medals.'"[86] A certain Miss Phillips, accompanying Annie Kenney in a campaign in Cornwall in 1909, noted that each town vied "in the eagerness of the demand for ... badges."[87] Mrs. East was also champion of the button: "This year I have never once appeared anywhere without my badge, and it has been the means of opening conversation, putting the 'word in season.'"[88]

Even in France, one worker, handing the key to her trunk to a customs official, found it returned quickly after he caught sight of her badge, and insisted, "Mais non! Madame est Suffragette."[89] And E. Katharine Todd proclaimed "I always wear my WSPU badge in a conspicuous position, and find it acts as 'a thorn in the flesh' to the anti-suffragists — as a staff of strength to the wobblers, a bond of sympathy to fellow workers for Votes for Women, and it is always a scatterer of seed for propaganda."[90]

While suffrage pins begin appearing in some quantity in England in 1908, it is not known when the first pin was made, but it was sometime after 1892. Elizabeth Crawford notes that in that year Laura Morgan-Browne published the words to a song called "Franchise Ballad III" in the *Woman's Herald*, pointing out that there were badges for the Primrose League, temperance, the Irish cause, and Scottish nationalism, but none for "Our fight 'gainst Freedom's Foemen." She suggested, therefore, that women wear "a little badge" with "supersubscription Vote!" Her suggestion was endorsed in the same paper about a month later by a writer who believed that "a little brooch" would be useful in "showing that there are many more women in favour of it [suffrage for women] than is generally supposed." In 1904, the National Union of Women's Suffrage Societies (NUWSS) proposed that either a sketch or a specimen for a badge should be circulated to its constituent organizations for consideration, but the general idea of a badge met with some resistance from a few of those groups, and apparently the plan was temporarily dropped.[91] How-

ever, the minutes of the Cambridge Association in 1909 indicate that badges were being ordered for a meeting at which NUWSS president Millicent Fawcett was expected to attend, so the group was producing buttons at least by that date, if not, as is most likely, in the prior year.[92] NUWSS's rival, Emmeline Pankhurst's WSPU, was already solidly committed to the use of suffrage pins in their campaign. A 1909 advertisement in their newspaper, *Votes for Women,* from the Merchants' Portrait Company touted the firm as "Makers of the WSPU badge."[93] A year later, in 1910, in the same journal, Toye and Company noted that they, likewise, were "Makers to the NWSPU."[94]

The WSPU actually was selling its own buttons by 1908. A notice about a brooch that they had issued appeared, for example, in *Votes for Women* in that year, and the badge probably consisted of a circular enamel piece in purple, white, and green with the initials WSPU boldly emblazoned on it. The Women's Freedom League issued a white enamel flag pin also in 1908, which was carried to America and distributed at NAWSA's national convention that year.[95] Motivation for the idea of wearing a brooch or a badge may have come from NAWSA in America, which was placing orders for pins by 1896, and possibly from the Primrose League, alluded to in Morgan-Browne's ballad, which was issuing metal and enamel badges in the late nineteenth century.[96]

The Primrose League, named after the fa-

Left: **This may be the first pin issued by the Women's Social and Political Union, a variation exists where the purple and green colors are interchanged;** *right*: **The white flag design was more popular in America than in England, where it first appeared.**

vorite flower of Benjamin Disraeli, was formed in 1883 by a group of men that included Sir Henry Drummond Wolff and Lord Randolph Churchill who wanted an agency to obtain support from the people for Conservative principles. Women were allowed into the League, and a separate Ladies Branch and Grand Council was formed in March 1885. It was possible, however, for a local Habitation (lodge) to be served by a woman or "Dame President." Regarded by some as a forerunner to the suffrage movement, the Grand Council was not; its members were prohibited from involvement with the suffrage campaign.[97] Emmeline Pankhurst characterized the Council as an organization of women who adhered to Conservative Party principles and did not have "woman suffrage for ... [its] object." It "came into existence to uphold party ideas and to work for the election of party candidates."[98]

The Primrose League issued many badges for both men and women. League badges that hang from a ribbon or bar are sometimes called "jewels" and generally contain the group's initials, "PL," often set into an enameled yellow primrose. Some also contain the League's motto, "Imperium et Libertas," or "Empire and Liberty." Various types of badges were issued for different levels of membership.[99] Men were known as "Knights" and women as "Dames." Simple badges, with the plain primrose and yellow enamel over which the PL monogram was superimposed, were given to associate members. Men and women wore badges that were similar in design, but differed in terms of their clasps. The versions for men generally had a stud back for fastening to a buttonhole. Women's badges had a pin-brooch clasp. Star medals were awarded to both men and women who had made outstanding contributions to furthering the principles of the League.[100] The very act of women wearing a type of political badge, even in a Conservative context, could very well have provided later suffragists with some context for the use of lapel material.[101] The Grand Council, while not directly advancing the cause for equal franchise, ironically undercut a major argument set forth by the anti-suffragists, that politics was too dirty and ugly a world for women to become involved with. Working for the Conservative Party put council members directly in that world, even if they could not vote for the party or the candidates that they were so industriously campaigning for.

Of the various English suffrage associations, the WSPU, enabled by sales outlets at their numerous suffrage shops throughout the country, was undoubtedly the most prolific in terms of the production of badges and pins. Sylvia Pankhurst, daughter of WSPU founder Emmeline Pankhurst, was quite an accomplished artist, and her colorful designs appeared on several buttons of note. One, manufactured by Pellett of London, portrayed, in the WSPU colors of purple, green, and white, a woman emerging from her prison cell, stepping over broken chains. Another, in enameled relief, showed an angel trumpeter with a "Freedom" banner above her and the "Votes for Women" logo beneath. This particular image was used also for a tea set, a pendant made by the Birmingham firm of Joseph Fray,[102] the cover of bound volumes of *Votes for Women*, and for posters advertising the famous suffrage exhibition and sale at the Prince's Skating Rink in Knightsbridge in London May 13 through 26, 1909. A third Pankhurst image that also appeared on a variety of objects was that of a woman sowing the seeds of suffrage.[103]

The "Votes for Women" phrase imprinted on several of these buttons originated in 1905

Left: **One of three designs attributed to Sylvia Pankhurst that appeared on Women's Social and Political Union badges;** *right*: **the Women's Social and Political Union chain link design above was borrowed by other groups in both England and America.**

when a group of women, headed by Mrs. Pankhurst, tried to obtain pledges from leaders of the new government that they would make women's suffrage part of their reforms. They fashioned a banner with the words "Will the Liberal Party Give Votes for Women?" that they hoped to unfurl when Sir Edward Grey, the principal speaker at a meeting to be held at Free Trade Hall in Manchester, arose to give his address. When they had not been able to obtain the gallery seats that they wanted, they realized that they could not use their large banner. Late in the afternoon of the scheduled meeting, they cut the banner down to the three words "Votes for Women," which was to become a rallying cry both in England and America.[104] The phrase also appears on buttons produced by such WSPU breakaway organizations as the Women's Freedom League and the Votes for Women Fellowship, but not on those from the National Union of Women's Suffrage Societies, which had been formally constituted on October 14, 1897, and which was later to serve as a non-militant counterpart to the WSPU.

The WSPU also led other suffrage organizations in the number of photo buttons that were made depicting its leaders. In the December 24, 1909, issue of *Votes for Women,* the WSPU advertised a "photo button of Mrs. Pankhurst" and indicated that it would shortly have available similar pieces for Christabel Pankhurst and Mrs. Pethick Lawrence. These pins were in black and white with a celluloid covering and measured ⅞".[105] They sold for a penny each, and were probably made by the Merchants' Portrait Company even though their name does not appear on the pins. A larger and different image of Mrs. Pankhurst, hanging from purple, green, and white ribbons, sold for five pence.[106] These

The Women's Social and Political Union was not bashful in picturing its leaders, such as Mrs. Pankhurst shown here, on its buttons and postcards.

relatively inexpensive pins correspond to the numerous postcards that came out under the WSPU imprint picturing their various leaders. The low price enabled shopgirls and women whose budgets in general were limited to buy a piece of the movement. Mrs. Pankhurst was celebrated also on a non-photo button that simply contained her initials, "E.P." The button was set against a rosette of purple, green, and white ribbons.

The WSPU was not the only group to honor its leaders on buttons. The Men's Political Union for Women's Enfranchisement (MPUWE) issued a photo badge of Victor Duval, who had organized the union in 1910 as a male counterpart to the WSPU. The MPUWE also borrowed the linked chain design used by the WSPU for several of its badges and substituted its own initials on the pin for those of Pankhurst's group.

Other WSPU badges were primarily in metal or enamel, but one 1⅛" celluloid button, manufactured by the Merchants' Portrait Gallery in two reverse purple-and-green color varieties and a third in magenta, was adapted by the Connecticut Woman's Suffrage Association and the Just Government League of Maryland in America. Printed in WSPU colors, it featured two concentric circles, with the phrase "Votes for Women" in the outside circle and the initials "WSPU" and a four-link chain in the inner.

One of the more spectacular pieces was a molded metal stickpin showing Joan of Arc carrying a sword and holding the WSPU banner aloft. Hilda Dallas incorporated this design in a poster in 1912 for Christabel Pankhurst's militant paper, *The Suffragette,* which she started up after the Pethick Lawrences had been expelled from the WSPU and had taken *Votes for Women* along with them. Other non-celluloid WSPU pins include a "Boadicea" brooch, honoring the Celtic warrior queen, which was first advertised in *Votes for Women* on November 19, 1908, and periodically for the next few years at three shillings and nine pence.[107] Mrs. Pankhurst herself is seen wearing this pin in a photograph taken by Elliott and Fry. Annie Kenney gave one to Mary Blathwayt on December 10.[108]

The WSPU was also responsible for silver and silver-plated stickpins that copied the pointed arrow design worn by Holloway prisoners. These pins were sometimes attached to ribbons with the WSPU colors. They were priced at one shilling and six pence and one shilling, respectively, along with shamrocks at 6d.[109] Enamel pins included a $^{15}/_{16}$" × $1^{1}/_{16}$" rectangular piece with "Votes for Women" in gold letters set against the colors (a piece of fabric in the same design exists), a shield with the same phrase along with the WSPU initials, another shield pin with only the initials, two reversed color varieties of a $1^{3}/_{8}$" round WSPU identification badge, and a purple, green, and white "Votes for Women" flag pin that was made by Toye and Company and reprinted in 2004 by Portrayer Publishers to be sold in museums.

The two items issued by the WSPU that probably have commanded the most attention, though, are the Holloway, or portcullis, badge, designed by Sylvia Pankhurst, and the hunger strike medal. In an article that appeared in *Votes for Women* on April 16, 1909, there was an announcement about a forthcoming meeting on April 29 at Albert Hall, the purpose of which was to show "the triumphant exposition of the militant methods." At that meeting, all members of the WSPU who had been imprisoned for their

suffrage activities were to be presented with the Victoria Cross of the union, or the Holloway brooch, along with an illuminated address, also designed by Sylvia Pankhurst, to commemorate "their bravery and sacrifice."[110] The illuminated address was first presented to five women released in September 1908. The brooch, whose design was adapted from the portcullis symbol of the House of Commons, featured a prison gate on which was superimposed an enameled "prisoner's arrow" in purple, green, and white. The Albert Hall gathering was designed to coincide with a meeting in London of the International Woman Suffrage Alliance, and to draw world attention to the struggles of suffrage prisoners. In America, Alice Paul's National Woman's Party adopted the design for their "Jailed for Freedom" pin. In 1959, a plaque with the Holloway design was placed on the left pylon of the Pankhurst memorial in Victoria Tower Gardens.

Theresa Garnett's copy of the Holloway brooch became the center of attention when she was brought before a magistrate, accused of biting the hand of the wardress who was in charge of her in prison. Garnett's defense was that she had not bitten the woman, but rather she herself had been the subject of attack when the wardress ripped her dress. Garnett explained that she had been wearing her portcullis brooch, and it was this and not her teeth that had caused the obvious injury to her jailer's finger. The magistrate was skeptical that the Holloway piece had been the cause of the wound, but nevertheless dismissed the charge against her, believing that the wardress' injury had been sustained accidentally when her hand brushed against Garnett's teeth.[111]

Hunger strike medals were first given out in early August 1909. They had been preceded in 1908 by the Honour for Imprisonment Medal, of which only three are known. One bar of this earlier medal bore the word "Holloway," while the other was engraved with "October 8th 08," the date of an incident which led to the imprisonment of Emmeline and Christabel Pankhurst along with Flora Drummond. The medal that was given to Mrs. Pankhurst has her name on one side and the symbols H.2.4 on the other. "H" stood for "hospital wing," "2" for second floor, and "4" was the number of her cell in Holloway.

The Holloway or Portcullis brooch, designed by Sylvia Pankhurst, was given to Women's Social and Political Union prisoners, even to those who had not gone on a hunger strike.

The Medal for Valour, or Hunger Strike Medal, that followed came in a purple box with green lining. On the lining itself were inscribed the words "Presented to [name of recipient] by the Women's Social and Political Union in recognition of a gallant action, whereby through endurance to the last extremity of hunger and hardship a great principle of political justice was vindicated." The medal, manufactured by Toye of London, was attached to a purple, green, and white ribbon that hung from a silver bar. On the bar were inscribed the words "For Valour." On one side of the medal itself were the words "Hunger Strike," on the reverse was inscribed the name of the recipient. Just above the medal was an enameled bar in the colors, the back of which included the date when the recipient was force-fed. If the ribbon terminated in a silver bar instead of an enameled bar, the inscription included the date of arrest. When hunger strikers were released from prison, they were reminded to return their medals to headquarters so that additional bars could be added when they were incarcerated again. The medal that was awarded to Canadian-born militant Mary Richardson is believed to contain the greatest number of award bars given out by the WSPU. It contained four enamel bars and five silver ones, probably an indication that she was force-fed four of the nine times that she was imprisoned. Richardson was famous for slashing the "Rokeby" Venus with an axe at the National Gallery in protest over the arrest of Mrs. Pankhurst in March 1914, the act satirized on a period postcard. Her medal was auctioned off by London's Dix Noonan Webb on December 16, 2005, for £19,000 plus a 15 percent buyer's premium to a collector who expressed a desire to lend it to a museum.[112]

In 1912, the WSPU authorized the manufacture of a silver brooch in the shape of a toffee hammer upon which were inscribed the words "Votes for Women" on the handle. These were given to women who had taken part in the window smashing campaign of 1912 in which they used toffee hammers to break the glass of windows in shops and other businesses and government offices. The protest was designed to send a message to the government that without a suffrage bill, daily life could not proceed as normal. Two hundred women were ultimately arrested in the protest. Additionally, there is a medal dated 1914 that portrays Emmeline Pankhurst on one side and a force-feeding scene with the wording "Sacrifice for Women's Rights" on the other. However, the origin of the piece may be American, not British, and one was struck in this design to commemorate Pankhurst's visit in that year.[113]

The National Union of Women's Suffrage Societies also issued a variety of buttons and presentation pieces, although none with the "Votes for Women" slogan that was the creation of the more militant WSPU. Perhaps the most spectacular piece is "the Bugler Girl" badge, given to organizers and organizing secretaries, that was based on the design by Caroline Watts for a June 13, 1908, demonstration. The pin may very well have been issued for display on that occasion. Regular marchers in the same demonstration also wore red and white badges, while carrying red and white bouquets.[114] In 1914, NUWSS gave a badge to members of its Active Service League that consisted of a paper-covered metal disk with a green circle, with, in white, the words "Pilgrimage 1913." A previous badge for the associates had been given out in 1912.[115] Most of the general distribution pins produced by NUWSS were enamel pins in the red, white, and green colors of the organization, and were made by W.O. Lewis of Howard Street in Birmingham or by W. Mark of Campden, Gloucester. Many of the enameled pins feature a five-petal red rose. There exists a somewhat common small celluloid pin in NUWSS colors that identifies the name of the organization. Because none of these pins really does more than identify the group or its event organizers, their main purpose appears to have been that of identification and support, with proselytizing serving as a secondary function.

A typical National Union of Women's Suffrage Societies (NUWSS) enamel badge in the red, white, and green colors of the organization."

The Women's Freedom League (WFL), formed in the fall of 1907 by dissident members of the WSPU who believed that the original organization was not following democratic principles, also issued a variety of badges and medals. Their own version of an "imprisonment badge," which featured a stylized image of Holloway in relief, was engraved on the back with the name or initials of the prisoner and the date of her imprisonment.[116] Mrs. Despard, one of the founding members of the WFL, presented copies of these badges to Muriel Matters and Emily Duval in December 1908, predating the WSPU Holloway or Portcullis pin by at least four months.[117] These badges came with and without loops and chains, and, based upon the limited number of examples that have surfaced, were probably produced in even smaller quantities than the counterpart WSPU prison pin. Other WFL pins include a 1" round enamel pin in the group's official colors of green and white that carried the League's name along with the phrase "Votes for Women." It was made by Toye and Company, manufacturers also of medallic pieces for the WSPU. Their lack of hesitation to use the "Votes for Women" slogan that emanated originally from their rival group probably derives from the fact that the WFL considered itself for a while to be the true WSPU, which itself underwent a name change to the National Women's Social and Political Union at the time of the split.

Other WFL items include a 1½" celluloid pin that contained the group's initials along with "Votes for Women" and a flag brooch that was issued in 1908. A quantity of the flag brooch was brought back to America by Clara Colby, who sold it for ten cents at the NAWSA National Convention in Buffalo, New York, that year. NAWSA was so pleased with this "official international badge" that they reproduced it and advertised it for sale at their national headquarters.[118] Elizabeth Crawford believes that a 1½" white on grey and black celluloid that protested the upcoming census ("No Vote/No Census/Census Resisted") and was made by Merchants' Portrait Company was a WFL issue.[119] The census resistance badge was one of the few English pins that specifically mentioned a cause or demonstration.

Many other English suffrage organizations also issued buttons, but these also were primarily identification pieces. The one exception to this was a pin made by the Tax Resistance League that was designed by Mary Sargant Florence. It was a 1½" black, brown, and white celluloid on a stickpin that pictured a ship on stormy waves with the slogan "No Vote — No Tax."[120] The Men's League for Women's Suffrage was responsible for at least two pins, a simple badge in yellow with the League's name in black, and a 1½" celluloid that added a three-petal flower to the overall design. One of these buttons was involved, however, in a very unfortunate incident that took place during the Downing Street battle of

Left: The Women's Freedom League prison badge above was given to Elsie Cummin, whose name is inscribed on the back, upon her release from Holloway Prison in July 1909; *middle*: the tax resistance badge designed by Mary Sargent Florence was one of a handful of English pins to use a slogan other than "Votes for Women"; *right*: several English men's suffrage organizations, such as the Men's League, issued promotional pins.

November 22, 1910. An American woman, Elizabeth Freeman, participated in the demonstration. Roughly handled by rowdies, she spotted a man wearing a Men's League button, and she appealed to him to assist her to find a breathing spot. He turned out to be a detective who had resorted to wearing the button to do "dirty, insulting work" on the women demonstrators. He put his hand on Freeman's face and shoved her back into the crowd, where she suffered "two dislocated toes, a badly-sprained wrist and three sprained fingers, but not a sprained conscience."[121]

The Liberal Woman's Suffrage Union produced a small celluloid in green and gold that contained its initials set against a stylized background. The Catholic Women's Suffrage Society was represented by a 1¼" gold, powder blue, and white button that contained the Society's name around the edge along with a fleur-de-lys in the center. When the Society later became the St. Joan's Social and Political Alliance, another button was issued in a similar design that reflected the name change. Sometime in the 1960s, probably for her retirement dinner, this pin was reprinted in an enamel version on a gilded gold frame with a clasp back and inscribed on the reverse to Christine Spender, who had served as the editor of *The Catholic Citizen* from 1934 to 1943 and 1945 to 1961.[122]

Around 1908, members of the Actresses' Franchise League (AFL) wore a pin with the initials "AFL" and the "Votes for Women" slogan. When the Pethick Lawrences broke with the WSPU on November 1, 1912, they took with them the rights to the *Votes for Women* paper and formed the Votes for Women Fellowship (VFWF). This group put out a red, white, and gold enamel stud that contained the Fellowship's name and a red cross. They were first offered for sale at four pence each on July 18, 1913, following a delay in delivery from the manufacturer.[123] Despite their insistence that supplies of the badge were moving rapidly, the VFWF still had a supply on hand in December, when they offered for sale at six pence a new enameled bar badge that "is a great improvement in many ways on the cheaper article." The motto "Votes for Women" had been added to the word "Fellowship." A final VFWF badge, fashioned as both a stud and a brooch "in the

colours," was made available for a rally at Kingsway Hall on February 26, 1914, and sold for a shilling.[124] Finally, the Church League for Women's Suffrage issued at least five pins in various sizes, the most common design being that of a gold quartered circle with each of the initials CLWS placed in a separate quarter.

The opposition also produced buttons. The National League for Opposing Woman Suffrage issued a ⅞" black, pink, and white celluloid that contained their name around the outer edge and pictured a plant in the center containing three different flowers, a Scottish thistle, an English rose, and an Irish shamrock. These were the official flower symbols of three of the constituent elements of Great Britain and had appeared originally in WSPU designs.[125] Their use here was, in all probability, a statement on the part of the League designed to mock the appropriation of these national flowers by the suffrage militants and to show that it was they, the "antis," who truly represented the British people. The league was also responsible for a metal enameled disk with a similar image. The Merchants' Portrait Company, which manufactured many of the WSPU badges, was responsible for producing

Groups opposed to suffrage in England printed only a few badges, such as this example, which exists in similar metallic and celluloid varieties.

the "anti" celluloid, indicating that where profit was involved, it took no sides.

A pin put out hastily by the Anti-Suffrage Society, which was organized "to combat the tactics of the militant suffragettes," became an object of controversy when the majority of the Society's members refused to wear it because of the ridicule to which it exposed them. The item in question, which was promoted by Mrs. Humphry Ward and the Countess of Jersey, consisted of a white button on which there was a figure of a particularly forlorn-looking woman grasping a ponderous infant. The *Woman's Journal*, paraphrasing a London dispatch to a New York paper about the button, noted that the idea behind it was that "woman's place is the home but the members of the Anti-Suffrage Society, many of whom are spinsters, firmly decline to wear the button." The society also exposed itself to further ridicule from suffrage supporters in its unfortunate choice of official colors, which were black and blue. The suffragists let it be known that these were the tints that the anti-suffragettes expected to have when their husbands beat them.[126]

Buttons and badges were the one area of memorabilia where American suffragists outproduced the English. But at least one American, Mrs. George Lowell, was impressed by the apparent willingness of many more English men than American men to pin them to their lapels. Reporting on the Earl's Court Exhibition just prior to sailing home to America, Lowell noted, "It was a pretty sight to see men and women wearing the badge of the three colors, with the words 'Votes for Women.' Do you suppose our men will ever wear such emblems for us?"[127]

For a further discussion of suffrage buttons, see **Women's Oversea Hospitals and Suffrage War Efforts.**

Calendars

One of the first types of suffrage memorabilia to appear was the calendar, examples of which can be found as early as the 1880s in England and the 1890s in America. They came from a variety of sources. Some were published by suffrage supporters acting as independents, some by suffrage organizations themselves, and a few

others by commercial enterprises. While there is variation in their form and appearance, the majority consisted of thin cardboard pages strung together by a ribbon, contained quotations arguing for suffrage and the nobility of women, and often provided space for diary entries.

The publication of one of the first American calendars, "The Equal Suffrage Calendar for 1896," by E. Scott and Company, was announced in the August 17, 1895, edition of *Publishers Weekly*. The calendar was to be mounted to a "tastefully decorated board 7 × 7 inches" and contained "extracts for each day on the subject of equal suffrage selected from the writings of the best authors."[1] It sold for thirty-five cents.

In Washington, D.C., in 1900, Catherine M. Fleming published for 1901 "The Anthony Home Calendar — With Selections from the Letters and Speeches of Miss Anthony." The piece contained photographs by Frances Benjamin Johnston, which could be purchased separately. The calendar cost fifty cents, and all proceeds were "to be devoted to the enfranchisement of women." Fleming must have proceeded not only with the authorization but also with the encouragement of Anthony herself, as a presentation copy, signed by Anthony, is known.[2]

One of the features of the 1909 Convention of the Equal Franchise Society of New York at Carnegie Hall was the sale of a new suffrage calendar for 1910, which Mrs. Clarence Mackay and Alice Duer Miller of the Collegiate Equal Suffrage League had spent several months preparing together. It contained separate leaves for each week of the year, along with 450 "pertinent quotations" in its sixty-six pages, selling for a dollar and a half.[3] The *Woman's Journal* offered it free to anyone who could obtain three new subscribers to its publication.[4] The Chicago Political Equality League also published for 1910 a calendar compiled by Helen W. Affeld in the same format as MacKay and Miller's version, with numerous quotations for each week of the year. The Equal Suffrage League of Virginia printed in Philadelphia a calendar for 1912 featuring drawings by Josephine W. Neall. The cover illustrated a suffragist addressing a crowd. The calendar included quotations from suffrage literature supporting the argument that women, while homemakers,

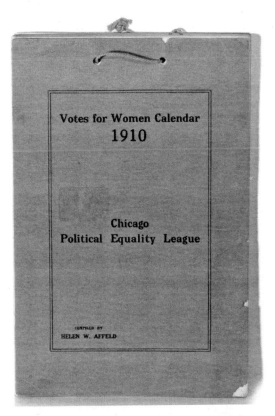

The non-descript cover of this 1910 calendar was typical of that of many put out by local groups.

had the responsibility to be politically active. A map on the last page showed Virginia with "man suffrage only."[5] The Woman Suffrage Party of Ohio sold for thirty-five cents a 7" × 9" calendar for 1916 that contained suffrage quotations from famous people and included space on which to write engagements.[6] The Suffrage Referendum League of Maine distributed a small calendar for 1917, which featured on its cover an illustration of a 1776 "Minute Woman," enclosed in a circular design.[7]

The National American Woman Suffrage Association (NAWSA) was very active in producing a variety of calendars. The first, printed for 1913, contained six cards that were "mounted in a neat standing frame," with quotations from a "world-famous person" for each month. It sold for fifteen cents.[8] For 1914, they distributed a calendar by Edwin Walter Guyol, the poet. Each month featured not only one of Guyol's poems but also a quotation from a noted suffragist. The frontispiece contained an illustration, called "No

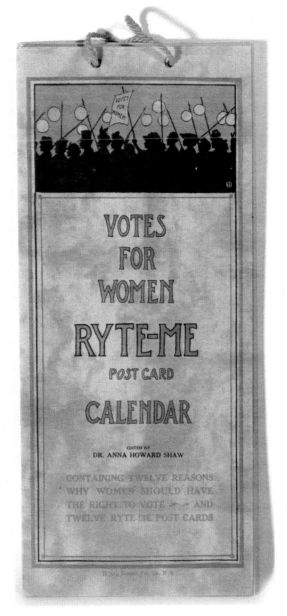

The fact that this calendar of tear-off postcards generally was used for its intended purpose can be evidenced by the missing cards on most surviving examples.

Longer Blind," of Justice removing a bandage from her eyes.[9] For 1915 and 1916, NAWSA simplified matters and printed a light card with a calendar on one side and a suffrage map on the other that sold for ten cents a dozen.[10] They also distributed a 3½" mechanical celluloid "combination calendar and paper-weight with mirror back." It covered the years from 1916 to 1926, was priced at thirty-five cents, and was promoted as a Christmas gift.[11] Probably, though, their most widely distributed calendar was the multicolored "Ryte-Me" postcard calendar for 1914, which was produced by the Stewart Publishing Company. Edited by Anna Howard Shaw, the cover illustrated against an orange background the silhouettes of men and women marching in a suffrage procession, with banner and lanterns. All twelve inside leaves consisted of a suffrage sentiment from some distinguished person, such as Mark Twain, Luther Burbank, and Louis D. Brandeis. Each of the leaves also contained a tear-off pale yellow postcard, picturing two ballot boxes and the words "Votes for Women," for supporters to send to their friends. The calendar was promoted heavily in the *Woman's Journal*, including a large endorsement from Alva Belmont, who sold them at her organization's headquarters.[12]

Other calendars, produced by individual activists and commercial establishments, included: a boxed, generic "Suffragists' Calendar" with a multicolored art nouveau cover, published by P.F. Volland Company of New York, Toronto, and Chicago; a boxed "Susan B. Anthony Calendar for 1918," with quotations from her life and speeches, compiled by Grace Hoffman White, printed in New York by Barse and Hopkins; and a single mount cardboard with a small attached paper calendar for 1918 that illustrated five smiling babies proclaiming "We Should Worry—We Should Fret—Mother Aint No Suffragette." A suffrage calendar was published in the Philippines in 1936, when in that year a special plebiscite gave Filipina women the right to vote.

The anti-suffrage forces also distributed several calendars, which often pictured a single rose on their covers. In 1911, Mrs. John Clinton Gray attempted to convert Alva E. Belmont, president of the Political Equality Association, to the other side by sending her the latest anticalendar, filled with supportive quotations, along with a brief note that said: "After you have read this for 365 days perhaps you will change your mind." The indignant Belmont returned the piece, replying: "It is strange that the antis will give us 365 days in which to be converted—

Why we suffragists can take a prejudiced anti and make a convert in a single meeting."[13] The calendar in question was issued by the New York State Association Opposed to Woman Suffrage, and was compiled by Lilian B.T. Kiliani, daughter of the poet Bayard Taylor. Containing quotations about women from Herbert Spencer and Nietzsche to Artemus Ward and Mr. Dooley, it sold for one dollar at the Association headquarters in New York.[14]

Suffrage calendars in England preceded their appearance in America by about ten years, beginning with the fourteen-year run of "The Woman's Suffrage Calendar," edited by Helen Blackburn, from 1889 to 1902. Blackburn, born in Ireland in 1842, moved to London in 1859, where she became active in several suffrage societies, and served as editor of *The Englishwoman's Review*.[15] Her calendar, which was small in size, featured an illustration of Queen Victoria on its cover, surrounded by the legend "Strength and Honour are her clothing." It included a compendium of landmark events in women's history from 1800 to 1898, a calendar of important dates for 1899, information about suffrage societies, and statistics about women in local government. The 1893 edition was reviewed favorably by *The Nation*, and notice of the 1895 version appeared as far away as India in the *Timaru Herald*.[16]

The Common Cause, the official journal of the National Union of Women's Suffrage Societies, promoted several other calendars. One for 1910 could be purchased from "Miss Tanner" of Bristol, and was printed in black and red-on-yellow boards with "an appropriate quotation for each month from some great thinker."[17] The second for 1911 was issued by the London Society and featured a cover of a woman holding a lamp, under which were the words "More Light, More Power." The inside contained quotations from such luminaries as George Bernard Shaw, Abraham Lincoln, Plato, and John Stuart Mill.[18] The Artists' Suffrage League also issued calendars as well as the WSPU, which produced a four-panel card for 1913, with circular die-cuts of its initials at the top. Previously, they had published a "Shelley Calendar," arranged by Miss Kerr, for 1909 and two calendars for 1910. The first, priced at a shilling, was designed by a "Miss Whitaker," and contained a color portrait of Christabel

Pankhurst, along with a quarterly calendar with mottoes. Christabel's artist sister, Sylvia, designed the second, and V.H. Friedlander provided mottoes for every day of the year.[19] Frielander's calendar was duplicated for 1911 and was sold alongside a companion piece that contained "mottoes selected by Miss Lelacheur."[20] For 1912, the Woman's Press, the literature department of the WSPU, advertised a "great variety" of calendars "printed in the colours," including one called "Keats," a daily tear-off, and a folding almanac.[21] A few years earlier, in 1906, Dora Montefiore published "The Woman's Calendar," which contained quotations for every day of the year from activists and famous people such as Mary Wollstonecraft, George Meredith, Mrs. Jameson, "Ellis Ethelmer" (pseudonym of suffragist Elizabeth Wolstenholme Elmy), Charlotte Perkins Gilman, and Margaret Fuller. Her foreword, dated October 31, 1906, was written shortly after she had been released from prison for her part in a WSPU demonstration in the lobby of the House of Commons.

One of the earliest calendars in England issued by a suffrage group rather than by an individual was that of the Women's Freedom League in 1908. It gave a suffrage quotation for each day, with "a striking design as headpiece and artistically finished." Promoted in part through the *Woman's Journal*, it was available to women in the United States.[22] In response to these calendars, the anti-suffragists in England put together an "Ideal Woman Calendar," as an "offset" to suffrage propaganda.[23]

The early popularity and form of the suffrage calendar may have resulted in part in America from the almanac tradition, which began in 1639 with the publication of *Almanack Calculated for New England*, developing from a genre that had been introduced several hundred years earlier in other countries. The first American almanacs focused on predictions, astrology, public schedules, and nautical subjects. Later they were to include home remedies, humor, and entertainment reading. The earliest known almanac designed especially for women was *The Lady's Almanac in 1856*. It was followed two years later by *The Woman's Rights Almanac for 1858*, which was published in Worcester, Massachusetts, and printed by E. Baker of Main Street. In

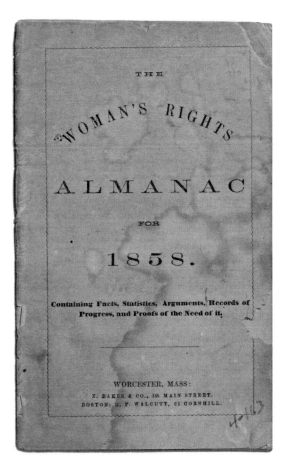

This small almanac, published for 1858, was probably the first such publication of this type that dealt with the rights of women.

addition to the usual information about the monthly phases of the moon, it included statistical data on women in the workforce, the progress of women "and Proofs of the Need of it," and the status of suffrage laws in 1857. Lucy Stone may have been involved in its production, along with the Rev. Thomas Wentworth Higginson, the Unitarian minister and abolitionist.[24]

Beginning about two decades prior to the Civil War, patent medicine promoters gave out health almanacs free to households to advertise their various concoctions. Included in advertisements for their products were testimonials, a precursor to the use of statements of support for women's rights in suffrage calendars. Most of these almanacs also featured some form of calendar for their daily weather predictions, giving a structure that could be easily modified by suffrage supporters. Much of the manufacture of suffrage memorabilia resulted from the development of new forms of products in the late nineteenth century, such as the souvenir spoon, the postcard, and the celluloid button or badge. But suffrage calendars evolved from a long historical tradition of both the household almanac and calendar.

Campaign Biographies

The campaign biography, an attempt to persuade the electorate to support a particular presidential candidate through a positively skewed account of his life, was a major form of political advertising throughout much of the nineteenth century and on into the twentieth. William Miles believes the first true such biog-

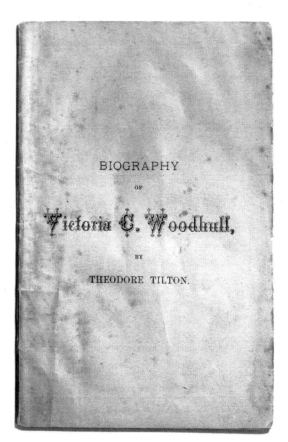

Tilton's campaign biography of Woodhull was the only such item for a woman candidate for president in the 19th century.

raphy was a revised edition of John Henry Eaton's panegyric on Andrew Jackson for the 1824 campaign, although he acknowledges an antecedent for the genre in John Gardner's life of the Federalist John Adams, published in 1796.[1] There is a sameness to many of these biographies in that they emphasize a candidate's humble beginnings (whether or not he was actually born in poverty is beside the point), his industriousness, his commonplace education, his family, and his connection to the people. Edmund Sullivan notes other commonalities, including a focus on patriotism, a playing down of things intellectual, a de-emphasis on business ties and friends, especially with regard to those who might be termed "cronies," and an acknowledgment of faith, with only vagaries expressed about a specific religious denomination.[2] Campaign biographies were mythic rather than real, for their purpose was not to examine objectively a person's life including his warts, but rather to promote his candidacy. They created a symbol that combined the features that the author believed to be the most appealing to the American electorate. William Burlie Brown notes that they evolved "out of the raw material of the candidate's life the biography of the ideal citizen of the Republic."[3] Despite James B. Hart's recognition that the campaign biography was "generally a hastily and poorly written bundle of paradoxes loosely tied by platitudes,"[4] a number of prominent authors and statesmen tried their hand at the genre. Some of the more notable attempts were Nathaniel Hawthorne's account of his college roommate Franklin Pierce, William Dean Howells' promotion of both Abraham Lincoln and Rutherford B. Hayes, Lew Wallace's book on Benjamin Harrison, and Franklin D. Roosevelt's life of Al Smith.[5]

Of the two major women candidates for president prior to 1920, Belva Lockwood and Victoria Woodhull, only one campaign biography is known, Theodore Tilton's hymn of praise to Victoria Woodhull.[6] Perhaps because of the circumstances behind its composition, Miles does not list this work in his bibliography of campaign biographies. The biography was written at Woodhull's insistence, not because she needed a campaign tract but because she wanted in part a defense against her mother's accusation of "scandalous acts" in a recent court action.[7] But the pamphlet went far beyond an attempt to salvage her public image and delved into her spiritualism and her political beliefs. It noted, for example, that she was a "downright democrat" who advocated abolishing the gold standard and promoted "the free love doctrine." That this pamphlet owes much to the conventions of the campaign biography is indicated, not only by Tilton's unabashed praise for his subject's political acumen as well as her position on certain issues, but also by the tag line "Mrs. Woodhull ... is now a candidate for the Presidency of the United States," a defining phrase that generally appears in some form throughout the genre.[8] Because of Woodhull's notorious public image, critics publicly condemned Tilton's attempt to whitewash her character. Lucretia Mott's niece, for example, questioned whether "anything but infatuation or aberration explain its absurdities," and Julia Ward Howe proclaimed "Such a book is a tomb from which no author again rises.... It would have sunk any man's reputation anywhere for common sense."[9] Undoubtedly, these women saw the work not in the context of a campaign biography, where uncritical praise was conventional, but more as an unethical attempt to defend the morally indefensible.

While the Tilton study, which was based in part on notes written by Woodhull's former husband, Colonel Blood, is the only pre–1920 presidential biography of a woman candidate, there is an 1840 book on William Henry Harrison's campaign that contains an intriguing and early suffrage reference. Entitled *Hero of Tippecanoe or the Life of William Henry Harrison* it is the only known children's campaign biography and was written by a "Captain Miller" to his boys. The work takes the form of a dialogue between the "author" and his sons William, Andrew, and Jose, with the mother having an occasional speaking part. When the father and his sons decide to have a mock ballot involving the entire family, the mother points out that "ladies don't vote." When she is given special dispensation to do so, son Andrew fears that she will cast her ballot for Van Buren, for he was "quite a lady's man," but the mother assures him that she is more interested in someone who would govern well than a person who is expert on knowing "how to bow and simper in a drawing-room."[10] Apparently, Harrison's leadership qualities were so obvious to the author that even a woman, who otherwise was incapable of making a responsible choice at the polling booth, could recognize them.

Cartes de Visite and Cabinet Photos

Among the first examples of suffrage memorabilia known are the photographic portraits of movement leaders that appeared on *cartes de visite* and cabinet photos when these new photographic forms became popular in America from about 1860 to 1920. Because both types of photography were cheap and easy to produce, they quickly replaced the earlier daguerreotype and the ambrotype as preferred formats for individual and group portraits and made possible the development of the family album during the latter half of the 19th century.

The *carte de visite*, which had preceded the cabinet photo for use in family portraiture by about fifteen years, consisted of an albumen print on thin paper attached to a 2½" × 4" cardboard mount. André Eugène Disdéri patented the *carte* originally in Paris in 1854. His process entailed the use of both a sliding plate holder and a camera with four lenses, resulting in eight negatives every time a picture was taken. Thus multiple images from a single picture could be made quickly and inexpensively, allowing for exchanges of portraits between families and friends. The *carte* was brought over to America in 1859, where it gained quick acceptance, particularly during the Civil War, when people were eager to have a photographic record of family members going off to the battlefield.

The *carte* also had its roots in the calling card, hence the French term *carte de visite*, which was a small piece of cardboard that visitors left when they called on people socially. The card contained the visitor's name along with a design that could, at times, be quite elaborate. The *carte* was the approximate size of the calling card, and visitors could theoretically leave their portraits now instead of their names, although most *cartes* appear to have been intended for the family album rather than for the receiving basket or tray. In addition to providing portraits for families, photographic studios also sold *cartes* with images of famous people. Theoretically one could purchase a photograph of a national hero such as a Civil War general and claim that he had been a visitor to one's house, but most probably such *cartes* were bought instead as collector's items. It was not until the end of the century that the technology was available to reproduce photographs in newspapers and magazines. In order for suffrage supporters at home to see what their heroines looked like, they had to rely on engravings and commercially produced photographs.

Cartes were popular in America from about 1860 to around 1880, although they began to be replaced gradually as the photographic format of choice in the mid 1870s by the cabinet photo, which was larger and therefore more spectacular in appearance. Cabinet portraits grew out of the earlier scenic view and typically measured 6½" × 4½" and were mounted on thicker card stock than *cartes*. As was the case with the earlier format, photographers generally included their names on the back of the mount, sometimes with their addresses. It is sometimes possible to date a cabinet by matching the city of the photographer with the known itinerary of a famous person. Cabinet cards of Tennie C. Claflin, Victoria Woodhull, and Woodhull's daughter, Zulu Maude, were produced by Bradley and Rulofson, for instance, when all three were in California. Cabinets, like *cartes,* were generally sepia in tone, although in the 1890s black became an increasingly popular alternative. In the beginning, they were intended primarily for display, not for the album, and wooden mounts allowed them to be visible from all parts of the room. Later, larger album pages appeared, allowing cabinets also to be placed in albums along with *cartes.* Although cabinets still were made as late as the early 1920s, they were on the decline after 1920, when they were gradually replaced by family snapshots made from the Kodak Brownie and other privately owned cameras.[1]

There are either *cartes de visite* or cabinet photos available, and sometimes both, for all of the major suffrage leaders of the nineteenth century and many of the minor figures. The list includes such luminaries as Susan B. Anthony, Elizabeth Cady Stanton, Mary Livermore, Belva Lockwood, Isabella Beecher Hooker, Anna Dickinson, Lucretia Mott, Lucy Stone, and Victoria Woodhull. There are also *cartes de visite* available for George Francis Train, who helped fund, albeit inadequately, early publication of Susan B. Anthony's *The Revolution*, and who ran a quixotic campaign for the presidency in 1872 with female suffrage as one of the items on his platform.

The number of suffragists whose image is on cards is not at all unusual as most people of the period had their pictures taken at least once. The problem lies in distinguishing between family photos and items that were intended pri-

This *carte de visite* of Belva Lockwood, taken when she was headmistress at Lockport, is probably her earliest known photograph. It was made about a year after the *c.d.v.* had been introduced in America as a popular and inexpensive form of photography for the family album.

marily for the collectors' market.[2] It is also not clear what the financial arrangement, if any, was between a suffragist subject and the photographer who sold her portrait to the public. On the rear of a *carte de visite* for Abigail Bush, who organized the second women's rights convention in Rochester, also in 1848 as was Seneca Falls, the photographer, J.H. Kent of Brockport, New York, advertised that "duplicates of this Picture can be had at any time." There are a number of extant views of Sojourner Truth, most of which consist of various poses of her sitting in a chair with her knitting above the phrase "I sell the Shadow to Support the Substance," an acknowledgment that Truth herself sold her own portraits as a source of income. A period broadside advertised a free lecture by Truth with a note that "at the close of her discourse, she will offer for sale her photograph and a few of her choice songs."[3] Photographs of Victoria Woodhull were

sold through *Woodhull and Claflin's Weekly* and at her lectures to raise money for her defense against federal obscenity charges and for a state libel suit.[4] These photographs probably were in the form of a *carte de visite*. Many photographers also essentially "stole" portraits from other photographers, redrawing images in such a fashion as to claim them as their own. Such was the case with most views of Lucretia Mott, Anna Dickinson, and, to a certain extent, those of Victoria Woodhull and her sister, Tennie C. Claflin. It is clear under such circumstances that the subject of the photo was unlikely to receive any compensation. Redrawn photo cards seldom come with any identification on the back as to publisher or studio.

Two of the most popular figures who appear in early photography were Susan B. Anthony and Elizabeth Cady Stanton. In one image that was made into both a *carte de visite* and a

I Sell the Shadow to Support the Substance.
SOJOURNER TRUTH.

VICTORIA CLAFLIN WOODHULL,
now Mrs. John Biddulph Martin. 133 REGENT STREET
(COPYRIGHT.)   LONDON W.

Left: One of many variations of *cartes* and cabinet photos that Sojourner Truth sold to support herself; *right*: Woodhull's notoriety accompanied her to England where this photo was taken.

cabinet photo, they appear together. Again, it is not clear what the circumstances were behind the production of these cards. Suffrage organizations did not advertise much in the way of memorabilia until the mid–1890s. *The Revolution*, the suffrage paper originally edited by Elizabeth Cady Stanton and Parker Pillsbury, an American minister and advocate for abolition and women's rights, and over which Susan B. Anthony served as proprietor, gave away "likenesses" in 1869 of either Mary Wollstonecraft, Frances Wright, Lucretia Mott, Elizabeth Cady Stanton, Anna E. Dickinson or Susan B. Anthony to those who renewed their subscriptions.[5] Whatever form these likenesses took, they were among the first collectibles ever issued by a suffrage-related paper or organization. By 1896, NAWSA was selling "Cabinet Photographs of Leading Suffragists at 25 cents each."[6] It is cer-

tainly possible that Anthony and Stanton both made up extra family photos in response to requests. Several cards were autographed by Anthony and Stanton, indicating some sort of connection between the suffragists and their supplicants. Two of the *cartes de visite* picturing Victoria Woodhull and Tennie C. Claflin identify the pair as stockbrokers, not as suffrage leaders, probably to the relief of many period suffragists for whom the pair was anathema to the movement.

The *Woman's Journal* published a cabinet photo of Henry Browne Blackwell, husband of Lucy Stone, not long after his death on September 7, 1909. It was taken from the memorial number of that periodical and sold for fifty cents or given free to anyone who had obtained a new subscriber at a dollar and a half. The *Woman's Journal* also offered several photographs of Black-

Left: This Susan Anthony card was a give-away by the firm of William Sumner Appleton of Boston, whose name is printed on the back; *right*: cabinet of Stanton of unknown origin with an interesting comment by the owner on front.

well taken on his eightieth birthday for three dollars each or free to anyone who had obtained six new subscriptions to the paper. The first showed him sitting down reading, and it was taken from a photographic portrait that hung at both the journal office and at National Suffrage Headquarters. A second pictured him with his hat on, and a third without his hat.[7] In 1911, the national headquarters also sold "The last Photograph of Julia Ward Howe" and "Pictures of Miss Anthony — all sizes and prices," without identifying of what particular type these memorial pieces were.[8]

Not all *cartes de visite* and cabinet cards were photos. Some were illustrations and cartoons that could serve as critical commentary on issues of the day. Perhaps the most famous of these was a card entitled "American Woman and Her Political Peers" that Henrietta Briggs-Wall distributed at the World's Columbian Exposition of Chicago in 1893. It was taken from a 58" × 48" pastel that Briggs, of Hutchinson, Reno County, Kansas, and active in the Kansas Equal Suffrage Association, had commissioned Mr. W.A. Ford, also of Hutchinson, Kansas, to execute. Pictured at the center was Frances E. Willard, temperance leader and suffragist, surrounded by a mentally disabled man, a convict, a Native American, and a madman draped in branches. The theme of those who were prohibited by law from voting, which helped to initiate a series of later images on the same subject, was obviously designed to arouse people to a sense of injustice, although modern sympathies would not allow that type of appeal today. Briggs sold the cards, which she termed a "postcard" and not a cabinet photo, in the *Woman's Journal* for five cents each. She also sold a collection of eight suffrage songs entitled "A True Republic and Other Songs" through the same advertisement.[9]

A less ideological and more satirical group of cartoon cards commented on the sexual proclivities of Henry Ward Beecher and Benjamin Butler, both of whom had some connection to the American suffrage movement, Beecher serving for a term as titular head of the American Woman Suffrage Association. The card for Beecher pictures him sitting with a woman's head on his lap, perhaps that of Victoria Woodhull.

The Women's Social and Political Union advertised in *Votes for Women* "beautifully finished Cabinet Photos of the Leaders of the union" at prices ranging from one to two shillings and six pence each. They also promoted a "Special Photo of Mrs. Pankhurst, taken in Boston," for two shillings each.[10] In 1912, when many of its leaders were being arrested for militant activities and the WSPU was moving away from the marketing of novelty items, the organization was still advertising photographs of the Pethick Lawrences, Emmeline and Christabel Pankhurst, and Mabel Tuke at various prices.[11] There are very few American cabinet cards for suffragists who made their mark essentially in the twentieth century rather than the nineteenth, although there certainly are an abundance of newspaper photos and studio portraits. But the fascination for collecting cabinet photos and *cartes de visite* was now over. Postcards in America, which could have provided a more contemporary forum for suffrage photos, focused more on message and not on personality.

Ceramic Figures

Small bisque and porcelain figures and statues with suffrage themes were quite common both in England and America. Most of the figures were commercially produced and most had an anti- or at best a neutral statement to make about the movement. Still, because these figures constituted a "collectible" and could be displayed alongside non-suffrage items in a cabinet or on a wall shelf, American merchants often favored the "cute" over the "ugly." Thus images of children and of animals such as geese, dogs, and cats rather than those of the harridan were frequently used to convey an anti-suffrage sentiment. Still, the depiction of the suffragist is less than flattering in many figurines, particularly those produced for sale in England. A good proportion of suffrage ceramic statues were made in Germany, many by the firm of Schafer and Vater, and shipped to both England and the United States. Established English firms such as Royal Doulton also provided pieces for the emerging market in suffrage collectibles. In addition to purely decorative items, suffrage ceramic figures were also made in the form of bells, ashtrays, match holders, bud vases, tobacco jars, candy dishes, stoppers, and inkwells.

One of the oldest known ceramic pieces alluding to suffrage is an ashtray that includes the figure of a gargoyle in a red cape holding out in his extended arms a sign that demands "Give Us Votes." A product of the English firm of Bratby Pottery, its mint mark, that of a sun rising over the name "ENGLAND," indicates that the figure was cast sometime between 1891 and 1900, before the coinage of the phrase "Votes for Women." Leslie Harridan designed two inkwells for Royal Doulton that were registered in July 1909 and are sometimes referred to today as "Virago and Baby." The first is that of a dour harridan with arms folded and the phrase "Votes for Women" incised in her apron. The matching bald-headed baby with rounded eyes wears a dress with pleated shoulders. The firm reissued the Virago inkwell as part of a salt and pepper set in 1977. The baby was replaced, however, with the image of a long-suffering man, whose motto "Toil for Men" was a response to the harridan's "Votes for Women" demand. Four years later, in 1981, the firm produced a positive figure of a standing suffragette designed by W.K. Harper.

Particularly popular in England were crested china items issued by Arcadian, Carlton, and Swan China for the bazaar trade. In the form of a hand bell or candle-snuffer, they were generally two-sided pieces, one side of which portrayed a harridan figure, sometimes identified as "Mrs. Gamp," with "Votes for Women" written on her hat. The other side pictured an elegantly dressed woman, along with such phrases as "She Shall Have Votes" and "Nature has endowed woman with so much power that the law gives them very little." Colorful crests of the various towns in which these pieces were sold appeared on the harridan portion. Thus, while these pieces were seemingly issued as neutral commentary on the suffrage issue, the placement of the crest would suggest that manufacturers assumed that it would be the harridan side that would be put on display in the home. Crested china stalls were a feature of the Edwardian seaside promenade. It is also likely that suffrage novelty items appeared in those holiday towns in concert with WSPU demonstrations,[1] although, obviously, the suffragists were not connected in any way with their sale or distribution.

There were a number of other suffrage ceramic pieces sold in England, but most of these were issued without a manufacturer's mark, and were often made in Germany. One was a porcelain figure of a woman with an umbrella and a suffrage sign trampling on a bobby. The ongoing engagement between police and suffragists was a constant theme on ceramic images. Another was a bust of a woman dressed in purple, white, and green, proclaiming: "I Say Down with Their Trousers." The colors of the WSPU had become so identified with the movement that no other sign or symbol was necessary for purchasers to understand the suffrage connection. The piece, which came in both 5" and 6½" sizes, had a removable top portion to enable storage of either tobacco or small biscuits. A third was a red-ribboned puppy dog that carried a "Votes for Women" satchel under one shoulder and a hammer in

This souvenir porcelain bell with a crest of Matlock Bath has two sides that display both positive and negative images of the suffragist, leaving it up to the purchaser to decide which to display.

Left: A satirical tobacco or biscuit jar draped n the colors of Mrs. Pankhurst's suffrage union; *right*: This porcelain cat, which came in three different colors and two inscriptions, was the most common of all suffrage ceramics.

her right hand. The allusion was to those suffragists who used hammers to break store windows on behalf of the cause. The same image of the puppy appears on an English postcard of the period.

The most common of all ceramic pieces that was distributed in both England and America was that of a 3¼" cat. It came in several versions, none of which identify the manufacturer, including that of a bud vase, and contained one of two phrases at its base: "I Want My Vote" or "Votes for Women." Varieties in blue, brown, and white are known. There is a corresponding dog that was of more limited issue. The distribution of the latter may have been limited to England.

An extremely prolific manufacturer of ceramic suffrage items was the German firm of Schafer and Vater, whose style was so distinctive that its suffrage designs are easily identifiable even though they generally exist without any markings except for mold numbers. The company was located in Rudolstadt, Thuringia, in the southwestern portion of Germany, and produced various products from about 1860 to 1962.[2] They apparently even manufactured a few

pieces in a Kewpie design, although, perhaps, without an apparent suffrage association. Schafer and Vater suffrage ceramics were sold in both England and America; however, the nature of extant designs, which often feature English bobbies, suggests that distribution of their products did not always occur on both sides of the Atlantic. Perhaps their most popular item is what is most commonly referred to, albeit mistakenly, as the "Sojourner Truth" statue. Produced in sizes of 6" and 7½", this hand-painted bisque portrays an African woman dressed in only a corset and panties with a club in her right hand and a "Votes for Women" sign in her left. Her mouth is wide open in a shriek. The word "suffragette" appears on the base. This piece was distributed primarily in America.

Other popular Schafer and Vater items involved animals. There are two varieties of match holders with geese demanding "We want our Votes," a kitten with an erect tail meowing "I want my vote," a fierce-looking dog whose head nods back and forth with the same demand at the base of the piece, and a dog with his head stuck in a fence post proclaiming to a cat, "Who says: 'Votes for Women!'" Some pieces have

Left: Dogs and cats were quite common images in suffrage ceramic collectibles as illustrated by this German piece exported for the English market; *right*: Nodding or moveable heads were often a feature in bisque figures of the period.

moving parts, including a statue of a frantic woman running about with wire spirals instead of arms, and two women sitting down to tea with nodding heads, proud that "We Got the Vote!" In another, a bobby sits astride a large head of a woman, attempting to keep a muzzle on her. Threads extend from the sides of the muzzle into his hands.

There are a number of other Schafer and Vater items that involve policemen, often interacting with little girls and always attempting to prevent the vote. One piece has a bobby with his arm extended upward. The base of the statue contains the words "Stop the Vote." The hand is actually a stopper, which can be removed for a small amount of liquid to be poured in. In another piece, a bobby is writing up a ticket on which the words "No Vote for Women" appear. The same slogan is at the base of another statue on which a bobby's huge coat covers what is presumably a future suffragist. Still another bobby is covering his ears while a tiny girl is wailing, "I want a vote."

One of the most imaginative ceramic pieces known is a 6" brown-on-white whiskey flask issued by an unknown manufacturer that portrays Theodore Roosevelt dressed as a "Suffer-E'Get," carrying an umbrella. Curiously enough, while suffrage figurines were popular in America, no known piece, including the Roosevelt flask, possessed an American imprint, and the majority of surviving ceramic pieces are probably the result of either German or English import.

China and Dinnerware

Unlike the English, American suffragists, apart from Mrs. Alva Belmont, produced very little in the way of china or stoneware. Perhaps the best example was the teacup (more of a demitasse) and saucer set that NAWSA sold for fifty cents each and five dollars for a dozen. Both cup and saucer were embellished with a small, elegant gold rim design on which was inscribed "Votes for Women,"[1] and marked on the bottom of the cup "Hutschenreuther Selb Bavaria — The Art China New York Import Co." In the J. Doyle Dewitt collection at the University of Hartford there is a small dinner plate on which the phrase "Votes for Women" is inscribed in the center. There also exists a saucer on which the ubiquitous phrase is written in small gold script and which is identified on its reverse as "Colonial vitreous china." While at least four copies of the saucer are known, no corresponding teacup has been found, although one doubtless exists or existed. At the St. Louis World's Fair in 1904, a group called the Madison County Chapter 8439 PHK gave out a cup inscribed in gold "Women's Sufferage [*sic*] Committee." Because of the misspelling, it is unlikely that this had any connection to an actual suffrage group, and the piece was probably intended as a joke.

The most celebrated of all American suffrage dinnerware, though, consists of a collection commissioned from England by Mrs. Alva Belmont, founder of the Political Equality Associ-

Left: **Suffrage cup and saucer ordered by Mrs. Alva Belmont for a 1914 celebration at her Newport, Rhode Island, estate; right: the small creamer and celery dish were probably ordered separately from the other pieces of this design and sold at Mrs. Belmont's New York City suffrage shop.**

ation and prominent Newport, Rhode Island, socialite. Each piece from the set of stoneware includes the phrase "Votes for Women" written in cobalt blue script on a clear white background. There are at least eight different examples known in this design, including a cup and saucer, a lunch or dinner plate, a salad or bread plate, a berry bowl, a soup bowl, a celery dish, and a small creamer.

There has been some confusion, however, as to the date, circumstances, and place or places where the stoneware was distributed originally, or even whether all eight pieces were ever ordered together. Because Marble House, Mrs. Belmont's Newport estate, does not have examples of the celery dish, the berry bowl, and creamer in its inventory and because the manufacturer's marks on the back of both differ slightly from those of the remainder of the set, it is possible that these were ordered at a later time. Mrs. Belmont sold the creamer for twenty-five cents at the suffrage shop connected with her lunchroom at the Political Equality Association headquarters in New York City, suggesting, perhaps, that it was sold separately as a fundraiser.[2]

The present gift shop at Marble House has a hand-lettered sign next to reproductions of some of these pieces, including the plate and cup and saucer, indicating that the originals had been ordered from Minton Manufacturing Company in England for an open house that Mrs. Belmont arranged at the estate in 1909 to raise funds for the suffrage cause. Guests were charged five dollars to tour the grounds for that event and listen to a suffrage lecture. The admission fee was not unsubstantial then, and was the object of some controversy that Ida Husted Harper addressed in an article in that year for *The Independent*. A printed card put out by Newport Historic Reproductions to accompany the reproduction Marble House set also assumes the 1909 date and occasion to be correct. However, the manufacturer's mark on the back of several of the original pieces (the manufacturer was John Maddock and not Minton) indicates that they were made in 1913, not 1909, so they could not have been available for the famous open house.[3]

The service may have been made instead for the Council of Great Women Conference, which Mrs. Belmont hosted on July 8 and 9, 1914, to celebrate the opening of a new Chinese teahouse on her estate and the return of her daughter, Consuelo, from England. Woman suffrage was the unifying subject of the eight speeches given at the conference, although each of the speakers approached the subject from an entirely different perspective. When Mrs. Belmont sold the house in 1932, only residual elements of the service escaped dispersal and what the Society now has in its possession is not necessarily complete. Belmont inventory records were destroyed in a fire that occurred sometime prior to 1933.[4]

English china, although somewhat more plentiful than American, consisted primarily of various pieces from at least four tea sets along with white glazed earthenware produced by the Women's Freedom League for meals at its Min-

The cup and saucer pictured here are from a larger tea service first sold in 1909 at a Women's Social and Political Union suffrage bazaar and exhibition.

erva Club. Three of the English tea sets were imprinted with designs created by Sylvia Pankhurst. The first, drawn in 1908, consisted of an image of an angel, facing left, blowing a curved horn. In the background are prison bars and the initials of the WSPU. Above her is a banner upon which the word "freedom" is inscribed. Known pieces from this set, which was made by the firm of Williamsons of Longton, Staffordshire, England, include a teacup and saucer, a small plate, a teapot, a small milk jug, and a sugar basin. Various size versions of the plate, the cup and saucer, the teapot, and the milk jug or creamer are known. The china was originally manufactured for use in the refreshment room at the Prince's Skating Rink Exhibition at Knightsbridge, London, held from May 13 to 26, 1909. After the suffrage exhibition was over, a tea set consisting of thirteen pieces, including four small cups and saucers, four plates, and the teapot, was made up and sold to the public. The milk jug or creamer and the sugar basin appear to have been sold separately.[5] In 1911, the WSPU expanded the set to twenty-two pieces and sold it for ten shillings and six pence at its Woman's Press Office on Charing Cross Road in London. Individual items were also made available.[6]

Sylvia Pankhurst was likewise responsible for a similar design of an angel facing right that graced the cover of the program for the Prince's Exhibition. This image appears on a transfer for the tea set that was commissioned by the WSPU from the Diamond China Company for their refreshment stall at the Scottish WSPU Exhibition held in Glasgow in April 1910. While the cup portrayed Pankhurst's angel design, the saucer contained images of the Scottish thistle. A note in the May 13, 1910, issue of *Votes for Women* indicated that some of the china "in the colours"was still for sale from Mrs. White, who was in charge of the refreshment stall: "a breakfast set for two, 11s. [shillings]; a small tea set 15 s.; whole tea set, 1 pound, or pieces may be bought singly."[7] A third tea design, undoubtedly the rarest, was that of the Sylvia Pankhurst's Holloway badge, with the prison gates drawn in green and the prison arrow in dark purple. The lip of the cup is edged in green. It was probably made by Williamsons. Only a cup and saucer and a creamer are currently known. It is unknown whether or not these pieces were made for a specific occasion.

The Women's Freedom League (WFL), the breakaway organization from the Pankhurst-dominated WSPU, also produced a full service in white china. The sole decoration was the WFL shield, which contained within it the phrase "Votes for Women,"the WFL initials in gold, white, and green, and the exhortation "Dare to Be Free"underneath. There is no manufacturer's name inscribed on any of the pieces, but some bear the mark of the retailer, J. Abrahams.[8] There was also china available for the Minerva Club, a residential club that was started up by the WFL

Another Women's Social and Political Union tea cup and saucer, this one using Sylvia Pankhurst's Holloway Prison image.

in 1920 as an outgrowth of its Minerva Cafe, used for luncheons and lectures during the war. Pieces in the set contain a rim in green and gold. The small medallion transfer includes an image of the Roman war goddess Minerva (counterpart to the Greek Athena) in full helmet and the words "Women's Freedom League — Minerva Club."

At least one foreign piece of china is known, that of an 8.4" plate made by the Arnhemse Fayence Factory of Arnhem, Holland, in 1919 for the International Woman Suffrage Alliance. In blue, yellow, and white, it pictures the alliance's symbol of Justice holding her scales, with the words "Jus Suffragii" in the background. Surrounding the image are four yellow stars.

Because surviving examples of suffrage-related china and stoneware in both England and America are typically found in very good condition with little signs of wear, it is likely that most people purchased these items intending them for display or to bring out for special occasions and not for everyday use.

Chocolates

There were at least two firms that produced "Votes for Women" chocolates. It is not clear whether either product was essentially a commercial venture or had formal tie-ins to the movement, but at least one was advertised as a possible fundraiser. *Printer's Ink* makes note of

an unnamed Cleveland manufacturer who gave five cents to the cause for every pound of suffrage chocolate that he sold, presumably keeping any additional profit for himself.[1] The Roach Tisdale Corporation of Minneapolis prepared a special box for their "Votes for Women Chocolates." Printed in the colors of yellow and black, it pictured five well-dressed women all seated together.[2] While there is no record of this also being used as a fundraiser, it could have been. Whatever the case, the product illustrates the increasing buying power of women and the need for large commercial manufacturers, which Roach Tisdale was, to respond to their interests.

Mrs. Arthur Dilkes of Milton Road, Eastbourne, advertised her handmade candies in the WSPU paper *Votes for Women* with the slogan "Buy Your Chocolates from Suffragette Who Makes Them Herself." Since none of Mrs. Dilkes' original packaging apparently survives, it is not known if there was anything that specifically tied her chocolates directly to the movement apart from her ads and her political sympathies.[3] The WSPU itself opened a Christmas bazaar for the 1910 holiday season on November 14 of that year, and sold boxes of "daintily packed chocolates" in boxes with pictures of either Emmeline Pankhurst or her daughter Christabel on the lid, along with homemade sweets in boxes ornamented with the WSPU medallion.[4]

Christmas Cards

NAWSA in America and the WSPU in England both recognized the appeal of tying in suffrage merchandise with the holiday season, including the printing of Christmas cards. Because the medium of the postcard could also be employed to extend yuletide cheer, the number of actual Christmas cards printed, however, was not all that extensive. The first two such cards to be advertised in the *Woman's Journal* were related to a subscription drive held in 1911. One was described as "an attractive Christmas card to send when offering the *Journal* as a present." The second contained a "telling suffrage motto and picture," for the reader who could obtain two new yearly subscriptions to the paper.[1]

In the following year, NAWSA advertised

a full line of suffrage products for Christmas, including six cards and booklets. Among these were "The Christmas Babes," a hand-colored card that sold for twenty cents each, a Christmas greeting card with a calendar for the coming year, an item that proclaimed," Peace on Earth-Good Will to Men and Votes for Women," and a "Santa Claus Postcard,"[2] probably the one that had been issued originally by the Just Government League of Maryland. For whatever reason, NAWSA was not as prolific in producing Christmas items in the following years. In 1913, the only new cards advertised in the *Woman's Journal* consisted of "Suffrage Holiday Cards," issued by Mabel Powers of East Aurora, New York. They included "Beatitudes of a Suffragist," a desk card with envelope "in the colors," and a postcard in a "Holly Design." Powers claimed endorsements by "World-Leaders" (presumably prominent suffragists) and the *Woman's Journal*.[3]

The WSPU first featured a "special Christmas card" to its readers in 1907. Selling for one and one half pence each, it offered "Greetings and Good Wishes for 1908," along with a lengthy quotation from *Neale's Egypt*.[4] In 1908, the organization produced two designs, one a plain Christmas card in the colors of the union, the other a more elaborate piece adapted from Laurence Housman's famous banner that was constructed for the Hyde Park demonstration held on June 21, 1908.[5] While the WSPU continued to advertise the sale of seasonal cards at its stall, no new designs were announced for the following year, although the Kensington branch, always noted for its merchandising efforts, did print a special "Kensington Shop" card in addition to selling the WSPU issues of the previous year.[6] In 1910, the WSPU began advertising its own issues again, this time with three varieties priced at one, two, and three pence each.[7] When the Pethick Lawrences split from the WSPU in 1912 and regained control of the periodical *Votes for Women*, they did attempt to revive on a modest basis a few of the novelties that they had sold when they were with the Pankhurst organization. Accordingly, they issued for the 1913 Christmas season a greeting card, with the motto of their newly formed "Votes for Women Fellowship" in their own organizational colors, along with a book of labels.[8] For the same Christmas season,

the Women Writers' Suffrage League produced a series of cards bearing the portraits of what they highlighted as "well-known women writers," including "Mrs. Flora Annie Steel and Miss Beatrice Harraden."[9]

Cigarettes and Tobacco

On August 26, 1910, an ad appeared in *Votes for Women* promoting "Votes for Women Cigarettes." Manufactured by Vallora and Company of 170 Piccadilly, W, the cigarettes came in several varieties of Virginia, Egyptian, and Turkish tobaccos and were packaged in containers printed in "the colours of the union."[1] This was not the first reference to a suffrage-related tobacco product in the paper, but the other had been for the male-oriented "Pethick Tobacco Pouch."[2] By spring 1911, the WSPU Charing Cross shop was also carrying "Women's Suffrage Cigarettes" of "exquisite flavour and aroma," handmade by Fredk. Pinto Company, likewise located in Piccadilly.[3]

The concept of women smoking cigarettes had been a controversial one ever since the introduction of the product in the late 1890s. The issue went to the forefront of the question of what was the purpose of suffrage. Did granting the franchise to women allow them to perform their traditional duties as wives and mothers more effectively, or was it a harbinger of things to come that would eventually revolutionize and, perhaps, even reverse gender images and roles? It may be relevant to note here that a commercial brand for women called "Eve," independent of any suffrage connection, appeared on the market in England in 1922.

The association of the suffrage movement with the idea of women as smokers came to a head in America with the opening of the Women's Political Union (WPU) Shop in New York in December 1910. Press releases sent as far away as Utah indicated that the shop would sell a variety of suffrage merchandise in time for Christmas, including "Votes for Women" cigarettes made of "genuine Egyptian tobacco daintily rolled in a white and gold wrapper with a slogan of the seekers of the ballot emblazoned in gilt letters."[4] There was so much publicity about these cigarettes, in fact, that Lucy Gaston Page, head of the Anti-Cigarette League but a friend of the WPU, came all the way from Chicago to see whether her "good friends, the suffragists" would actually sell cigarettes. She was offered a cigarette, but refused it on the principle that "it would break the symphony of the even row of the box." The cigarettes turned out to be made of chocolate, and one assumes that the "joke" was played in the hopes that the ensuing controversy would generate publicity for the opening.[5]

Two years later, however, another incident involving the WPU and "Votes for Women" cigarettes occurred that did not end so happily. On September 12, 1912, for its day of "Suffrage Week," the WPU had taken over at the Victoria Theater in New York. During intermission of the afternoon performance of the vaudeville show then running, two officers of the WPU sold "Votes for Women" cigarettes in the lobby, having "adopted some of the English methods and cigarettes ... [were] one of these." The women quickly sold out their stock, adding, "What a nice time to introduce our cigarettes at a theater where smoking is allowed during the performance." However, many suffragists were shocked by the incident and soon began wearing yellow bands encircled in black on their arms in protest. Suffrage supporters from the more conservative organizations feared that WPU's activities in breaking a gender barrier would reflect against them: "And suffragists are just suffragists to the people, and they will never know that we didn't do it." In its reporting of the incident, the *New York Times* sympathized with their situation, noting that "the yellow suffragists did not have anything to do with it. That means the National, the State, and the Woman Suffrage Party."[6]

To prevent further such incidents, the Hammerstein family, which owned the Victoria, banned all suffragists, whether they were members of the WPU or not, from selling anything at all around the theater in the future. For the Woman Suffrage Party, which had preceded the WPU at the Victoria that same week and which had "the prettiest young girls" come down from the stage and sell badges, banners, pins, and pencils, this was an economic blow.[7] Mrs. James Laidlaw of the Woman Suffrage Party commented that "'Votes for Women' means purity of life, manners and morals" and that she did not like to see the phrase marking a brand of cigarettes. Harriet May Mills, cofounder of the Political Equality Club, added that while she would not criticize any person who smoked, she decidedly disapproved of "women selling cigarettes in the street." Dr. Pease of the Men's League for Equal Suffrage and head of the Anti-Cigarette League also noted his disapproval.[8]

Despite the controversy at the Victoria, representatives of the WPU sold "Votes for Women" cigarettes as well as "buttons, pencils, and other trinkets" at a benefit performance several days later of Aristophanes' play *Lysistrata* at Martia Leonard's Brookside Theater in Mount Kisco, New York. This time there did not appear to be any outcry, and the controversy subsided.[9]

The aversion that some of the non-militant organizations had towards tobacco did not necessarily extend to ancillary products. During the Empire State campaign in 1915 in New York, for instance, the Equal Franchise Society, which had been in charge of literature, distributed 200,000 matchbooks with "Vote Yes on the Suffrage Amendment" on the back cover. Matches, obviously, had functions other than the lighting of cigarettes, and the majority of these covers probably were handed out to men. Still, the amount of match covers involved did show some flexibility on the issue.[10]

The anti-suffrage forces in New York also distributed matchbooks, all with a pejorative statement about the franchise. One suffrage leader in 1915, on entering a restaurant in the city, saw that a suffrage poster had been turned upside down on the table. She proceeded to admonish the waitress that the poster in this position did not show to its advantage. The waitress smiled gently, and lifted up the poster to show a number of anti-suffrage matchbooks that she had been instructed to pass on to male patrons for their afternoon cigars. She then gave them all to the leader, telling her, "If you don't take them, they may fall into the hands of somebody who won't know which way he is going to vote and perhaps they'd just put it into his head to vote against us."[11]

Some men apparently feared that the suffrage movement was a threat to their love of tobacco just as they perceived it previously to be hostile to their fondness for beer and alcohol. A song published by Arthur B. Eastman of New York City with words by Ardell Haddad in 1921, just after women had obtained the vote, pleaded "Please, Oh! Please, Little Suffragette, Don't Take Away My Cigarette."[12]

A Parisian manufacturer produced a silver cigarette case on which was affixed a photograph of a woman in revealing dress. Inside the case were four thick cigarettes, stamped with the words "Vote pour les Femmes" along with an image of a pharaoh, presumably indicating that the tobacco was of Egyptian variety.[13] It is not known in what context the case and cigarettes were made, but obviously they were not ordered by French pro-suffrage activists.

Nine years after passage of the Suffrage Amendment, a previously obscure Bertha Hunt with nine other women marched down Fifth Avenue in New York as part of the Easter Parade, all smoking Lucky Strike cigarettes. The press came out in full force, having been alerted by a release indicating that these women would be

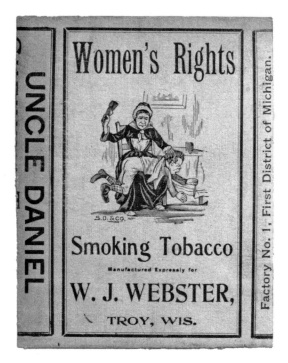

This satiric unassembled tobacco box reduces the concept of "Women's Rights" to that of child discipline.

lighting up "torches of freedom" in the interests of sexual equality. Their actions had been orchestrated by Eddie Bernays, who had been given a retainer by the American Tobacco Company the year before to promote cigarette smoking among women. Bernays was a fervent feminist, and his wife was a member of the Lucy Stone League, which argued that women should be able to keep their own names after marriage. But the "torches of freedom" parade was not about further female emancipation; it was a cynical attempt to capture suffragist energies, still riding high, to sell a product. And Bertha Hunt was Bernays' secretary. From this incident, Bernays became known as the "father of modern public relations."[14] Obviously, the WPU would not have approved of the attempt by American business to manipulate women in the name of sexual equality to make a profit.

The W.J. Webster Company of Troy, Wisconsin, sold packages of "Women's Rights Smoking Tobacco." That the product name was intended as satire can be seen by the cover illustration on the box of a woman spanking a boy with her shoe. In the same vein, there is an extant box circa 1872–1882 for "Women's Rights" cigars that pictures two men with election-day placards. One man in a top hat urges voters to "rally women — the independent Woman's Rights Ticket." A woman in bloomers is attempting to convert the supporter of the "Regular Democratic Ticket" by passing out a cigar. Given the probable age of manufacture of the box, the naming of the brand perhaps was in response to Victoria Woodhull's campaign for the presidency, although the female suffragist depicted is not specifically identified as her.

Clarion Figure

Suffragists frequently used a number of icons, including those of the scales of justice, the bursting sunrise, Joan of Arc, the map of the suffrage states, and the prison gate. One of the most frequently utilized, however, was that of the woman trumpeter, generally referred to as "the Clarion." The design of the Clarion figure, which stands out so boldly on the buttons and stationery of the Women's Political Union, is ultimately English and not American in origin, and it had a fascinating history before being borrowed by Harriot Stanton Blatch for the WPU. The figure was the creation of Caroline Watts, and was originally titled "The Bugler Girl." It was first published by the Artists' Suffrage League to advertise a procession by the National Union of Women's Suffrage Societies that took place on June 13, 1908. A spokesperson for the Artists' Suffrage League in an article in the *Manchester Guardian* explained the symbolism of the image was that "the Amazon who stands on the battlements of the fort may be said to be heralding the new day of which the sun is just seen rising."[1]

The National Union of Women's Suffrage Societies (NUWSS) was formally constituted on October 14, 1897. The intent was to bring together under one organization the various district organizations that had made women's suffrage their sole object in parliamentary elections. Its official colors were originally red and white, as reflected in the 1908 Bugler Girl poster. Green was added to the NUWSS official colors in November 1909, after Watts' original poster had been published.[2] While not as well known today, NUWSS actually had more members than the Women's Social and Political Union (WSPU), founded by Emmeline Pankhurst. Although NUWSS and the WSPU did share a common purpose and occasionally worked together, there was generally distrust and sometimes acrimony between the two suffrage societies. NUWSS was the more conservative of the two, and its leadership believed that the militant acts of Pankhurst's followers were hurting, not helping, the cause of woman's suffrage.

The Artists' Suffrage League, of which Caroline Watts was a member, was formed in January 1907 to assist the NUWSS in a demonstration in that year that was later termed the "Mud March." The league consisted of a group of professional women artists who utilized their talents for the NUWSS by designing posters, postcards, and other ephemera. Unlike the members of a comparable group, the Suffrage Atelier, league artists never received any income from the sale of their works.

Watts' design, while used for several other NUWSS events, was not without its controversy within the organization. The

image of the militant woman was more in keeping with the activities and philosophy of Pankhurst's WSPU than that of the non-confrontational NUWSS, and several officers of the NUWSS were inclined to repress the design. In 1913, Maud Royden, the editor of the NUWSS's official paper, *The Common Cause,* decided to abandon the image for that very reason, but she was overruled by the governing council of the organization. In the November 1913 issue of *The Common Cause,* the Council glossed Watts' design with a quotation from one of Elizabeth Barrett Browning's poems, "Now press the clarion to thy woman's lip," resulting in another term for the image, that of the Clarion figure. One council member, sensitive to the organization's stance against militant acts, called the image instead a reflection of "constitutional militancy." She further went on to argue: "Does she represent Joan of Arc? No — except as far as Joan of Arc herself embodies for women the spirit of courage and love.... Our Bugler Girl carries her bugle and her banner; her sword is sheathed by her side; it is there, but not drawn, and if it were drawn, it would not be the sword of the flesh, but of the spirit. For ours is not a warfare against men, but against evil; a war in which women and men fight together.... We are militant in the sense that the Christian Church is militant.... We are against wrong, but we inflict none."[3]

Two versions of the Clarion, a joker from an American playing card deck and an English postcard.

When Harriot Stanton Blatch, the daughter of Elizabeth Cady Stanton, returned to the United States in 1902 from England after approximately a twenty-year absence, she felt the need to reinvigorate the American suffrage movement, which appeared to many to have become tired after a lack of major successes. She formed in 1907 the Equality League of Self-Supporting Women, which later became the Women's Political Union (WPU), an organization that merged with Alice Paul's Congressional Union in 1915. Although no longer in England, Blatch followed the activities of various suffrage organizations in that country with considerable interest and was impressed especially by those that were confrontational. Her WPU was based largely on Emmeline Pankhurst's WSPU, modifying not only its name in her own organization, but borrowing its official colors of purple, green, and white, and one of its slogans, "Deeds Not Words."[4] Yet she saw in the iconography of Pankhurst's rival organization, the NUWSS, a figure that she had to adopt, that of Caroline Watts' Bugler Girl. Watts' image was modified; her original colors were changed from red and white to purple, green, and white, and the revamped design appeared not only on posters but also on at least six different celluloid buttons, as well as on stationery, postcards, and broadsides. NAWSA borrowed the image from the WPU to post on the front page of what served temporarily as its official publication, the *Woman's Journal*, for its May 6, 1911, issue. The Bugler Girl or the Clarion even graced the front cover of a piece of sheet music entitled "Marching on to Victory," by Schuyler Greene and Otto Motzan.

In adapting the Clarion figure, Blatch did not appear to be apprehensive about the militancy that the image portended to some. Rather, it probably was in keeping with her own aggressive inclinations, inclinations that at times were at odds with the approach of the more conservative NAWSA. And while some Americans may tend to see the Clarion figure as one of their country's own, it is important to realize that it was one of a series of icons that was borrowed from the English movement and also a pivotal piece in the bridge of women's rights between the two countries.

Clocks and Watches

The May 6, 1910 edition of the WSPU paper *Votes for Women* announced that a "Votes for Women" clock would be placed outside the new shop of the Woman's Press at 156 Charing Cross Road on Whit Monday. The clock was to be made and erected by the Synchronome Company, whose timepieces were already in use at WSPU headquarters at Clements Inn. Accompanying the announcement was a drawing of the clock, which had the words "votes" and "women" along with two diamond-like designs that all replaced the usual numbers on a clock's face to indicate the time. The middle word of the traditional Votes for Women phrase, "for," was placed in the center of the design. The purpose of the shop to which the clock was being attached was to increase the sale of newspapers, postcards, pamphlets, and other literature, and to help with the distribution of these materials throughout the country.[1] Pictures of the shop with its famous clock appear on real photo postcards of the period. In a follow-up article on May 13, the editors of *Votes for Women* included a tongue-in-cheek response to the news from a columnist from *The Daily Chronicle*: "The Suffragists' new depot in Charing Cross Road is to have a clock, the figures of which will be Votes for Women. But that will never do — thirteen hours to the day.... Possibly the papers are wrong, inconceivable as this may seem, and the first word will read, not Votes, but Vote — which is more to the point still."[2]

It is not possible to say whether or not the new adornment of the Woman's Press influenced the production of pro- and anti-suffrage watches, but "Votes for Women" timepieces subsequently did become a popular period item. Three or four different designs are known, including one with several variants of yellow flowers with green leaves, another of red flowers, and still a third of a disgruntled man holding two babies. All known watches respond to the problem of replacing 12 numerals with 13 letters by following the *Chronicle*'s suggestion of leaving out the "s" in "Votes." The resulting phrase, "Vote for Women," is often written backwards. All of these watches appear to be of private manufacture and many may or may not be period items. Reprints of the backwards "Vote for Women" watch face design are known and have been inserted into later, post-suffrage pieces, including wristwatches.

A comic clock, made in England, features a normal clock face placed in an embossed copper setting that portrays a woman wearing a "Votes for Women" banner, shouting her message across a bridge, with both a bobby and Big Ben in the background.[3]

Coffee and Tea

Several suffrage organizations in both America and England packaged coffee and tea with a suffrage label to sell to supporters. F.L. Lent of the Massachusetts Woman Suffrage Association advertised "Suffrage Fund Coffee" in the *Woman's Journal*, primarily to suffrage clubs to use as a fundraiser.[1] The Woman Suffrage Party distributed "Equality Tea" throughout the country for suffrage groups also to use as a fundraiser. It was sold, for example, by the Oakland Amendment League at a cherry festival in San Leandro, California, as part of the 1911 campaign in that state.[2] The Pennsylvania Woman Suffrage Association advertised "Suffrage Tea in a Special Box" for fifty cents.[3] Tea parties were a common method employed by suffragists to promote the cause, as evidenced in the reports of various state committees throughout Volume VI of the official history of the American movement. Whether the tea served was always "official" is not known. In England, the WSPU began selling "Votes for Women" tea in 1910 through its publishing arm, the Woman's Press. Described as of "Superior Quality," the tea was sold in half-pound and one-pound packets.[4]

Colors

Most of the major and many of the subsidiary suffrage organizations in both America and England had "official colors" of sorts, the most noted being the yellow (and black) of NAWSA and the purple, green, and white of the WSPU.

But the process by which yellow emerged as the representational color of NAWSA and its affiliates was more of a folk development as opposed to a single idea and plan that was developed by an individual or a committee. It began with the failed Kansas campaign of 1867, which attracted among other suffragists Olympia Brown, Lucy Stone, Susan B. Anthony, Elizabeth Cady Stanton, and various members of the Hutchinson Family singing group. The state flower and symbol of Kansas was the sunflower, whose petals could be represented as either gold or yellow. Loyal Kansas supporters during the campaign wore, accordingly, homemade yellow ribbons, a practice that quickly moved on to gain acceptance as part of the iconography of the suffrage movement in general. In 1876, for example, Marie Le Baron took the tune of "Wearing of the Green" for the words of her song "The Yellow Ribbon," whose chorus appears to assume a familiarity with the new suffrage symbol: "Oh, we wear a yellow ribbon upon our woman's breast,/We are prouder of its sunny hue than of a royal crest;/' Twas God's own primal color, born of purity and light,/We wear it now for liberty, for justice and for Right."[1] The color was formally adopted in 1876 at the suggestion of Laura Johns of Kansas at the American Woman Suffrage Convention of Philadelphia during the nation's centennial celebration. The words to "Yellow Ribbon" were reprinted by NAWSA in 1896 in its manual for political equality clubs.[2]

By 1887, the time of the second Kansas campaign, both the yellow ribbon and the sunflower were relatively well established, at least in the midwest, as suffrage symbols. Anna Howard Shaw wrote, "during the second Kansas campaign, yellow was adopted as the suffrage color."[3] In the same year as this campaign, the pro-suffrage journal *Justicia* pointed out "It has remained ... for the 'Equality before the law' agitators to don an emblematic color. Yellow, the color of sunflower petals, has been adopted as the distinguishing badge of the woman suffrage army; ... The sunflower seems an appropriate flower, as it always turns its face to the light and follows the course of the sun, seemingly worshipping the type of righteousness. Let us all don the yellow ribbon, and fling our banners to the breeze. By this sign let us be known, and the more who wear it the greater our strength will be." *Justicia*'s account of the 37th convention of the Indiana American Woman Suffrage Society also observed that "the ladies and gentlemen present all donned the 'sunflower' ribbon of the suffrage cause."[4]

In 1891, Shaw, along with Alice Stone Blackwell and Lucy Elmina Anthony, Susan B. Anthony's niece, compiled a series of suffrage readings and recitations entitled *The Yellow Ribbon Speaker*.[5] Mary Livermore helped to introduce the symbolism of the color yellow to suffrage supporters in her home state of Massachusetts, and in 1894 she urged, "Let every matron wear a knot of yellow ribbon on the left breast; every girl a bow of yellow ribbon on the left shoulder.... Let's have change, and show our colors."[6] In 1896, NAWSA began selling stickpins or hat pins, along with stationery, incorporating the sunflower design.[7] Curiously enough, however, the stickpins were not cast in yellow or gold, but made with ruby red glass placed in a copper sunflower setting, and the stationery, which Susan B. Anthony and Harriet Taylor Upton overprinted for their own use, was in blue.[8] It wasn't all that long after, however, that yellow became standard in suffrage events. In 1908 in Oakland, California, for example, 300 women marched in the first suffrage parade in the State "behind a yellow silk banner, embroidered with the State coat of arms by Mrs. Theodore Pinther."[9] In 1916, NAWSA funded a group of women who traveled by a car called the "Yellow Flier" to draw attention to the cause.[10] In 1911, during the California campaign, a Mrs. Balentine published at her own expense the first suffrage paper on the Pacific Coast, which she called *The Yellow Ribbon*.[11] In the decade between 1910 and 1920, just prior to the passage of the Federal Franchise Amendment, virtually every parade, every bazaar, and every gathering sponsored by NAWSA or one of its affiliates featured in one fashion or another a display of yellow in the form of banners, ribbons, sashes, or pennants.

At the Indiana State Convention of 1912, every "business house" in Logansport was draped in the yellow suffrage colors[12]; in 1914 in a suffrage section in a parade that marked the opening of the state fair, six women marched "wearing yellow silk Votes for Women badges"[13]; at a reception in April 1910 for Anna Howard Shaw at the McAlpin Ballroom in New York City, the event was decorated with "suffrage yellow"[14]; at the National Democratic Convention in St. Louis in 1916, there was a "walkless-talkless" parade in which 7,000 women were arranged in rows alongside the main street, "all dressed in white with yellow sashes and each one carrying a yellow parasol"[15]; in a march organized by "General" Rosalie Jones that began at the Hudson Terminal in New York on February 12, 1913, Elizabeth Freeman drove a "little yellow wagon with the good horse 'Meg'"[16]; in a parade in the same state in 1915, the affiliated Woman Suffrage Party of New York made an appeal to firemen by offering a ten-dollar gold piece to the first of their number who "made a daring rescue of a yellow-sashed dummy—a suffrage lady."[17]

So common had the color become at the events of NAWSA and its affiliates by even 1910, that Harriot Stanton Blatch of the Equality League and later of the Women's Political Union, both societies aggressive rivals to the mainstream suffrage organizations, felt that she could use "yellow" as a subtle metonymy for what she considered to be her more cautious counterparts. In describing the Woman Suffrage League's (WSL) hesitancy to participate in the New York's true suffrage march in that year, which she had organized, a march that the other suffrage groups could not afford to stay away from despite their reservations, Blatch observed that the WSL participants "climbed into automobiles, and rushing down the avenue, gave the onlookers one flash of yellow and were gone."[18] The anti-suffragist Helen F. Lovett was so concerned about the sense of power and solidarity that the wearing of yellow in suffrage parades conveyed that she suggested to the *New York Times* an oppositional alternative, blue or light blue, and that those against the franchise "be willing to wear a bit of it on suffrage parade days."[19]

But while the connection of yellow to the movement was firmly embedded in the minds of most suffragists, militant or otherwise, and doubtless in the minds of many of the general public as well, the color did have a problem in terms of promoting the franchise. Yellow is ubiquitous, and outside the immediate context of a suffrage event, did not necessarily suggest women's voting rights to the average person. In England, on the other hand, the WSPU colors of purple, white, and green were so distinctive that such firms as Mappin and Webb and such retailers as Annie Steen could advertise movement jewelry "in the colours" of purple, white, and green, without any other identifying factors tying these pieces to the suffrage cause.[20] Such an association allowed WSPU members and their sympathizers to promote suffrage in their daily lives, even when they were not attending demonstrations, by simply wearing jewelry, dresses, and hats in the color scheme of the organization. No comparable advertisements for decorative NAWSA jewelry all in yellow are known.

Other American suffrage organizations, typically those associated with more aggressive and even militant tactics, had their own official colors, generally modeled directly after or adapted from the purple, green, and white symbolism of the WSPU. Such borrowing allowed these organizations not only to separate themselves from NAWSA in the minds of the general public but also to reflect their more assertive approach towards achieving ballot equality. Among the groups that directly or indirectly borrowed their color scheme from the English WSPU were:

1. Women's Political Union — Founded by Harriot Stanton Blatch, the daughter of Elizabeth Cady Stanton, out of her Equality League of Self-Supporting Women in 1910. It lasted until 1915, when it merged with Alice Paul's Congressional Union, later the National Woman's Party. Blatch was obviously strongly influenced by both the nature and the iconography of Pankhurst's WSPU, as she adopted not only her own variant of their name but also their colors and even, on occasion, their slogan "Deeds Not Words," for one of the organization's badges.[21] The color scheme of purple, white, and green did not always meet with the approval of sartorial critics. When Alfred H. Brown was about to embark on a suffrage lecture tour of New York State in 1913 following his visit to the offices of the WPU, a reporter for *The New York Times* critiqued, "He was festooned with all the colors that made the peacock the proudest fowl in the barnyard."[22]

2. Women's Political Union of New Jersey — Originally established as the Equality League for Self-Supporting Women of New Jersey by Mina C. Van Winkle, it was affiliated with Harriot Stanton Blatch's early organization with a similar name. Adopting the strategy of her friend Blatch, Van Winkle appealed to working women, both wage earners and professionals, attempting to draw them into the suffrage movement. The Equality League changed its name to the Women's Political Union of New Jersey (WPUNJ) in 1912, following the lead of Blatch's group, which had become the Women's Political Union in 1910. It retained its new name for the next four years until it merged with the mainstream New Jersey Woman's Suffrage Association in 1916. Even though the WPUNJ borrowed their color scheme from Blatch's group, they referred to the WPU's "purple" as "violet" in order to create the acronym "GWV" for "Give Women Votes."[23]

3. The Just Government League (Maryland) — Formed in 1909 by Edith Houghton Hooker, it consisted of 17,000 members at its peak in 1915. Although the JGL eventually became affiliated with NAWSA, its colors of purple, white, and green indicated its connections also with the more aggressive wing of the movement. In fact, Hooker, who edited the *Maryland Suffrage News* from 1912 to 1920, also served beginning in 1917 as editor of *The Suffragist*, the official publication of Alice Paul's National Woman's Party. Hooker had previously been a member of the executive group of Paul's Congressional Union in 1914.[24]

4. The Connecticut Woman Suffrage Association — Founded in 1869, it was directed for thirty-six years by Isabella Beecher Hooker, sister to Harriet Beecher Stowe. Although it had achieved some minor success, it eventually became a tired organization, one of limited membership, until it was revived in 1910 by a group of young middle-class women, including Katherine Houghton Hepburn, mother of the actress. Much of the group's new leadership worked closely with Alice Paul's Connecticut affiliate of the National Woman's Party in 1916, but the CWSA adopted the colors of the WSPU and not those of the NWP.

Although purple was generally associated with the more militant suffrage organizations in America, no suffrage group wanted to be linked with the violence that sometimes accompanied the tactics of the WSPU in England, from which the color scheme originated. Alice Stone Blackwell, Lucy Stone's daughter, became especially indignant when a Mrs. George said that Inez Milholland wore the colors of Mrs. Pankhurst's society. Blackwell pointed out that while the Women's Political Union, of which Milholland was a member, had chosen purple, green, and white as its official colors, the same as Pankhurst's WSPU, those colors had been worn "for years" by thousands of women "engaged in perfectly peaceful propaganda" and not in violent activities. Blackwell, though, in her defense of both Milholland and the nonviolent tactics of American suffragists, mistook the WSPU's purple for violet and assumed that the symbolism of the resultant acronym "GWV" was understood to mean "Give Women Votes."[25] As Emmeline Pethick Lawrence, who first proposed the official symbolism, explained, the colors actually had the following meaning: "Purple is the royal color. It stands for the royal blood that flows through the veins of every suffragette, the instinct of freedom and dignity ... white stands for purity in private and public life ... green is the color of hope."[26]

Perhaps the most militant, albeit nonviolent, of the American suffrage organizations was Alice Paul's National Woman's Party (NWP), whose colors were modified from those of the WSPU to purple, white, and gold.[27] The NWP grew out of what was originally NAWSA'S congressional committee on suffrage that Paul and Lucy Burns had formed in 1912. Dissatisfied with what they perceived to be NAWSA's lack of aggressiveness, Paul and Burns left the organization in 1914, bringing with them the Congressional Union (CU) for Woman Suffrage and using the color scheme of purple, white, and gold instead of NAWSA's standard yellow. In 1916, the CU merged with other militant organizations to become the NWP. Purple, white, and gold were likewise designated as the NWP's official colors, and were proclaimed as such on the masthead of its newspaper, *The Suffragist.* Just as NAWSA on occasion substituted gold for its official color of

yellow, however, the NWP could sometimes employ yellow for gold on its badges and buttons.[28] During the period of picketing the White House by the "Silent Sentinels" of the NWP, the administration became increasingly frustrated by the amount of publicity that the suffragists were achieving. Recognizing in part the impact of the NWP's color scheme, the Committee on Public Information published a daily official bulletin under the direction of the president, which urged newspapers not to print their attacks on Wilson even when "flaunted on a pretty little purple and gold banner."[29]

Blue was the official color of the Equal Franchise Society of New York. When its members participated in a May 4, 1912, march up Fifth Avenue that was attended by 20,000 women, they all wore a square badge in blue with the name of the Society on it.[30] The society also issued a button for the 1915 Empire State Campaign in two color variations, one using the official blue, the other printed in the unofficial colors of green and gold. A deep blue was likewise the color of Alva Belmont's Political Equality Association. However, Belmont refused to "wear the colors" of her own organization. For the same May 4 parade, she expressed her intention to wear instead a white gown with a hat trimmed in black even though her Association for the occasion planned to sell for seventy-five cents a standard parade hat, trimmed in blue, with a big bow in front.[31]

The anti-suffragists also had a general color scheme of red, usually combined with white and black. This combination was often used on their plentiful "Vote No" buttons and for their several anti-suffrage poster stamps. They often used the red rose as their symbol, as illustrated on the cover of a piece of sheet music, Phil Hanna's "The Anti-Suffrage Rose," issued by a Boston organization. Since suffragists often displayed their "official yellow" through jonquils, one could term their ideological confrontations with suffragists a "War of the Flowers, " if not one of the Roses. Indeed, their animosities often were symbolized through a clash of the colors. Anna Howard Shaw, incensed by the distribution of anti-suffragist literature just prior to a suffrage demonstration in Brooklyn in 1913, lashed out at the anti-suffrage forces through a mockery of their iconography: "The antis have taken for their colors the red of anarchy and the black of piracy. I don't know why they have done it unless they wanted to represent themselves literally."[32] Alice Edith Abel, responding for the opposition several days later, noted that the yellow of the suffragists represented the sun to ancient people and hence to "idolators," and that red, on the other hand, symbolized "love." She further argued, "Black can mean an absence of light or obscurity, as well as death, and is offset in the anti-suffrage tricolor by the white, which signifies both light and purity."[33] Later during the Empire State Campaign of 1915, suffragists staged a rescue of a drowning dummy they termed "Aunty Anti-Suffrage." The figure wore a "red sash" upon which her "principles" were printed in "big, black letters." One of the spokespersons for the suffragists, noting that women wearing yellow sashes had rescued the mock figure, observed, "Our yellow sashes inspired her with courage, I am sure."[34]

In an editorial in the *Woman's Journal,* Alice Stone Blackwell also lashed out against the antis' choice of an official emblem, the American beauty rose, from which their official color derived. She declared that the "flower that bears this pretty name is a perversion of nature. It is produced by denying the right to life to every blossom on the bush but one.... It is the exact type of the woman who does not care how many of her fellow creatures are sacrificed to her ease and pleasure.... The American Beauty rose is the perfect type of special privilege. It is a negation of democracy, and the personification of selfishness."[35]

The concept of official suffrage colors came later to England than it did to the United States, one of the few instances in which English suffragists appear to have borrowed from America rather than the other way around. The number of various color combinations that shaded the iconography of English suffrage groups, though, did exceed those in use in America, and, unlike the yellow symbolism of NAWSA, those combinations were the result of conscious choice and not of gradual and, to a degree, unplanned assimilation.

One of the first of the English suffrage organizations to have official colors was the National Union of Women Suffrage Societies (NUWSS), which adopted the combination of red and black as early as 1906. Green was added in November 1909, following an exhortation by Helen Fraser in the organization's official journal, *The Common Cause,* to make these, as constitutional colors, separate and distinct from the purple, white, and green adapted by the WSPU in 1908. Fraser argued, "Every member can help to ensure that 20,000 red, white, and green badges and ribbons all over the country are being stared at, being talked about, are bringing in more and more supporters every day.... Let us put forth our greatest endeavours to have the colours known everywhere."[36] In a follow-up article in 1910, *The Common Cause* glossed the NUWSS color scheme as the standard of the Italian Risorgimento, and therefore it was used in memory of Garibaldi and Mazzini.[37]

The WSPU in its early days did issue flags in red and white, although it is unclear as to whether these colors constituted any sort of official organization standard. In May 1908, when Emmeline Pethick Lawrence, treasurer and co-editor of the WSPU's newspaper, *Votes for Women,* introduced publicly the new color scheme of purple, green, and white along with her glosses, it was soon evident that color was to be a central feature of the campaign. When the WSPU held its first major national demonstration at Hyde Park on June 21, 1908, the program announced that there would be 700 banners in green, white, and purple, all bearing such inscriptions as "Rise, go forth and conquer," "Working women demand the vote," and "Taxation without representation is tyranny."[38] Christabel Pankhurst, Emmeline Pankhurst's daughter, lauded the instant success of the WSPU's new color scheme in an article for *Votes for Women* in May 1909, and looked forward to the upcoming suffrage exhibition at the Prince's Skating Rink, where there would be myriad suffrage items for sale in the official colors. Pankhurst urged women to not only buy but to wear the colors. In so doing, she wrote, "every member of the union will become an advertiser for the exhibition," and, by bringing men and women of their acquaintance to the exhibition, will allow them to "appreciate for the first time the strength of the woman's movement."[39] Reginald Potts wrote words and music for the June 18, 1910, procession in a piece entitled "Chorus of the Purple, White, and Green March," that included in its lyrics Mrs. Pethick Lawrence's glosses.[40]

Advertisements from both merchants and manufacturers in a variety of issues of *Votes for Women* in the period following the Hyde Park demonstration pointed out products for sale in "the colours," including jewelry, "hats for sale for the Procession," "Procession Corsets," "floral displays," "home-made cakes," and "Christmas gifts." Anna Howard Shaw, returning from abroad, noted: "The colors of Mrs. Pankhurst's party, purple, white and green, are so popular in London that enterprising shopkeepers are adopting them for their advertisements. You see a purple, white and green placard, and you see [a display of] 'Father's Rolled Barley,' or of the newest thing in soap."[41] So effective had the WSPU's campaign of promoting the colors become that even when anti-suffragists ridiculed the movement on postcards, tobacco jars, and ceramic pieces, they often portrayed suffragists in purple, green, and white in such an allusive fashion that it is obvious that they assumed the meaning of the colors was familiar to all members of the public, not only to suffrage supporters.

Other English suffrage societies had their official colors, but none were as universally recognized as those of the WSPU. These include:

1. The Actresses Franchise League — pink and green
2. Artists' Suffrage League — blue and silver
3. The Catholic Women's Suffrage Society — pale blue, white, and gold
4. The Church League for Women's Suffrage — yellow (gold) and white
5. Conservative and Unionist Women's Franchise Association — pale blue, white, and gold
6. East London Federation of Suffragettes — purple, white, green, and red[42]
7. Free Church League for Woman Suffrage — buff, blue, and green
8. The International Woman Suffrage Alliance — white and gold
9. Men's League for Woman Suffrage — black and gold[43]
10. The Men's Political Union for Women's Enfranchisement — purple, green, and white

11. New Constitutional Society for Women's Suffrage — white and green
12. Suffrage Atelier — blue, black, and yellow
13. Tax Resistance League — black, white, and gray
14. United Suffragists — purple, white, and orange
15. Votes for Women Fellowship — purple, white, and red (originally green)
16. West Essex Women's Suffrage Society — white and green
17. Women's Freedom League — green, white, and gold
18. Women's Tax Resistance League — black, white and gray on copper ground
19. Women Writer's Suffrage League — black, white, and gold.[44]

So numerous were the various English suffrage organizations and so popular was the concept of official colors that when the Pethick Lawrences broke away from the WSPU in 1912 to form the Votes for Women Fellowship they found that "almost every colour combination has been adopted." They were unable to drop white for "White must enter into every combination wherever large effects are necessary."[45] They ended up adding purple from the WSPU and red from the NUWSS, which placed them halfway between the militants and the constitutionalists.[46] Prior to adopting the new colors, the Fellowship had borrowed the scheme of the WSPU, using green rather than red.[47]

Those Englishmen and Englishwomen opposed to suffrage also had their official colors, although at times their choice of hues was not always fortunate. Writing in the American publication the *Woman's Journal*, Alice Stone Blackwell noted the ridicule that English suffragists had bestowed on the black and blue colors of the English Anti-Suffrage League. These activists remarked that the choice was "appropriate, since they are the color of bruises, and all the men who beat their wives are opposed to votes for women."[48]

Cookbooks

Special suffrage cookbooks designed to promote the cause and to make it more acceptable to the average housewife appeared on both sides of the Atlantic, although such publications were more prevalent in America than they were in Great Britain. What had to have been a concern among many suffragists was the mythic image that anti-suffragists had created of the would-be woman voter as a harridan, a non-gendered other, whose desire for the ballot was a freak of nature and outside the world of the respectable mother and wife. Whatever else their intent may have been, suffrage cookbooks allowed potential supporters to respond to a desire to vote without necessarily having to abandon their traditional roles or images. Often packed with household hints as well as with recipes for fish, poultry, salads, puddings, cakes, and breads, these cookbooks offered the response that suffrage was concomitant with the concerns of a woman to be a dedicated mother and wife.[1] Perhaps in this spirit, one such publication contained on its title page a quotation from Dr. Harvey W. Wiley, first chief of the U.S. Bureau of Chemistry, later known as the U.S. Food and Drug Administration, who fought hard for passage in Congress of the Pure Food and Drug Act of 1906. Wiley observed, "If the members of women's clubs of this nation could vote, it would not be so difficult to secure food and drug legislation."[2]

The primary suffrage cookbook in England, which went through several editions, was compiled by Mrs. Aubrey Dowson and entitled *The Women's Suffrage Cookery Book*. As was the case with similar publications in America, it sought to humanize the movement by soliciting recipes from various suffrage workers throughout the country and publishing their names under their submissions. In addition to recipes, the book also included a section on such household hints as how to deal with moths and how to cook for invalids. It was not until the end of the book that a specific suffrage message appeared, in a piece entitled "Menus for Meals for Suffrage Workers," where it was pointed out that "it is not always easy to provide suitable food for workers who have to get their meals as best they can during a day's hard and exacting work often lasting for 12 hours or more."[3] No organizational name was attached to this cookbook, but it was likely associated with the National Union of Women Suffrage Societies, the largest of the English suffrage associations and one that prided itself on

its non-militancy. The cover of one of the editions is in the red, white, and green colors of the NUWSS, and its contributors included "Mrs. Philip [Ethel] Snowdon, London," both an active member of the organization and married to an M.P. who supported equal franchise in Parliament, and "Mrs. [Millicent Garrett] Fawcett," president of NUWSS and one of the leaders of the famous February 1907 "Mud March" through London. This cover shows an illustration of an allegorical figure carrying the lamp of truth standing over a female scholar and a woman feeding an infant out of a bowl. Another version of the same book, with white printing on red, portrays two children standing under a tree.

The first American publication of this type was the 1886 *The Woman Suffrage Cook Book*, edited by Hattie Burr. It was printed "in aid of the Festival and Bazaar" that was held in Boston of that year from December 13 to 19.[4] Mary Livermore served as president of this festival, and Julia Ward Howe was the editor of its official publication, *The Bazar [sic] Journal*. The event, including sales of the cookbook, cleared $6,000 for the cause.[5] The list of contributors of recipes for the volume contained a number of prominent suffragists such as Livermore, Howe, Lucy Stone, Frances Willard, Anna Howard Shaw, Matilda Joslyn Gage, Abigail Scott Duniway, and Alice Stone Blackwell, along with other distinguished professional women and wives of politicians, most notably Mrs. Oliver Ames, whose husband was governor of Massachusetts from 1887 to 1890.[6] As was the case with the NUWSS cookbook, this work also provided a section on both cooking and caring for invalids, with recipes and advice coming from women doctors and physicians such as S. Adelaide Hall, Vesta D. Miller, and Anna B. Taylor. It, too, contained household hints such as how to maintain a "pretty bedroom." There was no explicit suffrage message to any of its contents until the final pages where a section titled "Eminent Opinions on Woman Suffrage" appeared. The total effect was to reinforce the idea that suffrage and a woman's traditional role were not necessarily antithetical concepts.

Other and later American suffrage cookbooks included the *Washington Women's Cook Book*, printed in 1909,[7] *The Suffrage Cookbook*, published by the Equal Franchise Federation of Western Pennsylvania in 1915,[8] and the softbound "Choice Recipes Compiled for the Busy Housewife 1916,"[9] a fundraiser for the Clinton, New York, Political Equality Club. In addition, food manufacturers often distributed to women free booklets with a suffrage tie-in that contained recipes for meals that could be made with their products. Karo Syrup came out with a special "Votes for Women" version in 1913 that included such " "suffrage recipes" as "Mary Livermore Gingerbread," "Lucy Stone Boston Brown Bread," "Lucretia Mott Tea Biscuits," "Aunt Susan [B. Anthony] Marble Cake," and "Julia Ward Howe Crumpets." A number of these small booklets were distributed by the Political Equality Club of Rochester, Anthony's home base, and the organization's stamped imprint appears on the inside cover of many copies.[10] It was clear to many a merchant and manufacturer by

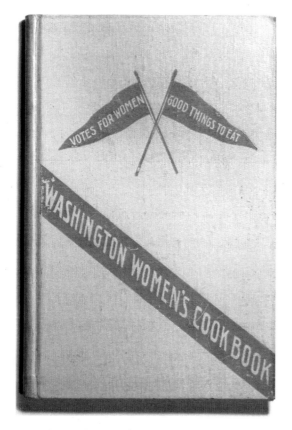

The Washington Women's Cookbook was distributed widely throughout the state in 1910 as a campaign device.

this time that while women did not have the vote, they did buy household products, and it was to their interest to at least give lip service if not outright support to the aims of the movement.

Perhaps the most aggressive and imaginative use of a cookbook to promote the cause of suffrage was that of the Washington State Equal Suffrage Association under the leadership of Emma Smith Devoe. In their campaign to achieve the franchise in the state in 1910, the Washington Committee avoided all use of "spectacular methods" of other state organizations, fearing that too public an effort would mobilize the anti-suffragists and their huge war chests. Instead, they placed emphasis on the campaign roles of wives, mothers and sisters of men who were to decide the issue at the polls. Big demonstrations, parades, and large suffrage meetings were studiously avoided, and the intensity of the strength of the effort "was never revealed to the enemy," who did not awake until election day, when it was too late.[11]

The Association published and sold 3,000 copies of its cookbook, with many workers going out into the field with a package of them under their arms in their efforts to influence potential sympathizers. The ultimate aim of the campaign was to encourage women to solicit their neighbors, their doctors, their grocers, their laundry men, and even their garbage collectors on behalf of the franchise for women. The "suffrage department" of the *Tacoma News* aided by conducting a "kitchen contest" in which 250-word essays on household subjects were published and a $75 prize was awarded. Various suffrage clubs throughout the state gave programs on "pure food" and discussed and exhibited "model menus," perhaps from the cookbook itself. Suffragists also rented booths at state and county fairs, where they sold the cookbooks along with "Votes for Women" pins and pennants.[12] Their efforts succeeded and Washington women earned the right to vote in 1910. The cookbook itself was relatively traditional, with the first part once again given over to recipes and household hints. It wasn't until the very end of the volume that pro-suffrage material appeared, including an essay by Adella M. Parker on how women were tricked out of the ballot in Washington on two previous occasions by hostile politicians, and also a sample election ballot containing those names of sympathetic candidates.

Despite the book's political success, however, its publication may not have been a profitable venture. In a financial statement printed in the *Woman's Journal* in 1909, the Washington Association listed the expense of printing the book as $769.46 but sales as only $366.[13] Alice Stone Blackwell, the editor of the journal, attempted to help by urging the periodical's readers to obtain a copy and by suggesting that the president of each suffrage organization buy a copy and show it at the next meeting as a sample, along with taking orders for additional books.[14] The Association itself took out small ads in the *Woman's Journal* to boost sales.

Recipes from the *Washington Woman Suffrage Cook Book* were a special feature of a "Votes for Women" grocery that was opened up in New York City in 1913. It was owned by the Suffrage Pure Foods Stores Company Incorporated, whose president was Sofia Kramer, its vice president Sarah Mayer and Alice Snitjer (or Snitzjer) Burke its secretary. These suffragists who conceived of the store were concerned about teaching women "how to cook properly," in part by using aluminum pans. Recipes from the cookbook, which was sold at the store, were prepared by a "domestic science expert."[15] The cookbook was reprinted in 2009 as a paperback by Createspace.

The cookbook issued in 1915 by the Equal Franchise Federation of Western Pennsylvania was perhaps the most diligent of all in terms of maintaining a traditional image. A figure of a supportive Uncle Sam graced the cover and an introductory essay by "Erasmus Wilson (The Quiet Observer)" argued that it was important for women, "being the housekeepers and guardians of their children," to be made familiar with culinary arts so that they "may be entirely competent to lead coming generations in the paths of health and happiness." Wilson added "So say the members of the Equal Franchise Associations throughout the length and breadth of our land."[16] One innovation to the suffrage cookbook genre, however, was the inclusion in the volume of thirty-six portraits of noted suffragists and their supporters, including men. Reviewing

the volume in the *Woman's Journal*, an anonymous critic noted that this book "ought to silence forever the slander that women who want to vote do not know how to cook," an argument that was reinforced by an advertisement that the Equal Franchise Federation took out in the periodical a few weeks later that was headlined "The Best Cooks Are Suffragists."[17]

The Wimodaughsis Club, while not organized specifically to promote suffrage, nevertheless had strong tangential relationships to the movement, and published its own cookbook, edited by Mrs. Ella M.S. Marble, in 1892.[18] "Wimodaughsis," an acronym for "Wives, Mothers, Daughters, and Sisters," was formed in Washington, D.C., in 1890. Its main goal was to "furnish educational advantages in practical, industrial, and educational work" for women of limited means, offering courses in stenography, dressmaking, and arithmetic. It also served as an arts, sciences, and literature club, opening its membership to all women regardless of race or class. An early president of the Club was Anna Howard Shaw, who later was to become president of the National American Woman Suffrage Association. One of the Club's first acts was to raise money for a building in Washington to house the National Woman Suffrage Association prior to its merger with the American Woman Suffrage Association.[19] Its lofty goal of uniting women of all classes and races suffered a serious setback when a woman of color was denied membership in a Kentucky affiliate and Shaw threatened to resign over the affair.[20]

The cookbook that the organization published was only sixty-four pages in length, but included recipes from many prominent suffragists and important women of the time including Caroline Scott Harrison (wife of President Benjamin Harrison), Mrs. Senator Dolph, Isabella Beecher Hooker (sister to Harriet Beecher Stowe and founder of the Connecticut Woman Suffrage Association), the Rev. Anna Howard Shaw, Hannah Bassett Sperry (whose original printing press was once situated in Susan B. Anthony's basement), and Bessie Boone Cheshire (a descendant of Daniel Boone). Susan B. Anthony wrote a brief prefatory note for the book, noting that it takes "common sense" to put ingredients together and "eternal vigilance" to cook them. The *Wimodaughsis Cook-Book* did not include an overt suffrage message, although that message easily could be inferred by the presence of its activist contributors. Local chapters of the original club still exist today in such sates as New York and Pennsylvania. A Canadian counterpart of the group, "Wimodausis," published its own cookbook around 1912 with subsequent and expanded editions in 1922 and 1934.[21]

By including recipes by noted suffragists alongside those of ordinary housewives, suffrage cookbooks appeared on the surface to be nonthreatening and nonconfrontational and promoted an image of suffrage leaders as typical neighborly housewives. Perhaps it is for this reason that the more militant organizations in both England and America, such as the WSPU, the WPU, and the National Woman's Party, did not publish their own versions.

Cosmetics

Although one might assume otherwise, suffragists produced very little in the way of offical suffrage cosmetics. Alva Belmont's Political Equality Association did have a "Department of Hygiene" at its New York headquarters where it sold various "Victory Toilet Preparations," but based upon a price list, these all appear to have been commercial products with no special suffrage packaging.[1] The Department of Hygiene was actually a beauty salon designed primarily for working-class women. Belmont felt that good grooming was a concomitant prerequisite with the franchise for gender empowerment.[2] The one example of a suffrage related cosmetic that is known to exist is "Votes for Women Face Powder," contained in a small 1¾" round yellow and

This small box of face powder may have been the only suffrage-related cosmetic produced by American activists.

white cardboard container. The top of the box displays the phrase "Votes for Women" and the bottom label indicates that the item was produced by the National Woman Suffrage Publishing Company of 171 Madison Avenue, in New York City.

Counterstamps

Counterstamps, sometimes termed "countermarks" or "defaced coins," are those coins on which an impression is made after they leave the mint. In the United States, the practice began in the late 18th century when coins were impressed by punch and hammer to bear the imprint of a merchant, jeweler, patent medicine vendor, or a political party. In essence, coins became traveling billboards for anyone with patience to punch out one letter at a time to make a slogan on their faces. In America, one of the first political messages to appear was "Vote the Land Free," produced by supporters of the Free-Soil Party, which fielded presidential candidates in 1848 and 1852, and was opposed to legalizing slavery in the western expansion of the country. Counterstamps with the message of "Votes for Women" are known in both America and England. Because they were generally hand-punched, the lettering is often crude and off center. The message could appear on any denomination of coin, but generally larger size coins were preferred in order to make the slogan "Votes for Women" more distinct. There is no record in any of the suffrage journals or catalogs of any worker offering them for sale, perhaps because of legal restrictions. Counterstamps technically involved defacing official coinage, and, while the practice was common enough for merchants, it could have led to criminal prosecution for suffrage supporters, particularly in England, where suffragist activities were generally under intense official scrutiny. Because counterstamped slogans are so easily reproduced today on early coins, collectors and historians need to ensure that items they procure are authentic period examples and not modern counterfeited pieces.[1] Genuine examples often show wear on the counterstamping. Coins whose imprint is crisp and clear have not necessarily been faked, but, unless they have been authenticated by an expert, it is best to avoid either studying or collecting them as period suffrage artifacts.

Dust Mops

While there does not appear to have been any suffrage reference on the product, the Beacon Manufacturing Company of Cleveland, Ohio, did produce both a mop holder and a chemical dust mop to "raise suffrage campaign funds."[1] Beacon was one of a number of companies that was faced with the problem of attempting to appeal to its suffragist customers while still producing products associated with women's traditionally accepted social roles.

Eggs

When suffragist activists Sofia Kramer, Sarah Meyer, Alice Snitjer (or Snitzjer) Burke, and Almee Hutchinson announced their plans in February 1913 to open up a grocery store in New York City, they also let it be known that they intended to stamp their eggs with the phrase "Votes for Women."[1] For obvious reasons, none of these eggs appears to have survived. While these grocery owners also planned to stamp other products with the same phrase, they may have been responding to a popular anti-suffrage cartoon involving roosters, hens, and the question of who was going to lay the eggs if women had the vote. A "suffrage" egg laid by "Rosa Bennett," a pure-blooded Rhode Island Red, was sold for 10 cents at a country store booth at the Woman Suffrage Party Cosmopolitan Fête held at the Seventy-First Regiment Armory in New York City on March 26, 1914. Even though the typical price for eggs at the time was forty cents a dozen, Rosa's egg brought a premium because it weighed four ounces. Described by *The New York Times* as a "lovely suffrage egg, a warm, yellow brown," it was one of many eggs that Rosa had laid that weighed a quarter pound or more.[2]

A novelty egg made of papier-mâché was produced by an unknown manufacturer. While subjecting suffragists to a certain amount of ridicule, it seemed intended more to record a cultural response to suffrage than it did to change minds. On one side of the 5½" piece is pictured a group of angry hens holding up "Votes for Women" signs. The reverse pictures a similar scene, albeit with rabbits. The piece opens up as a box.

Endorsements in Magazines

Among the many ads for commercial products such as Campbell's soups and Nabisco Shredded Wheat that were now appearing in both national magazines and suffrage periodicals were endorsements from suffragists. When activists associated themselves with cosmetics, soaps, and beauty products, they not only gave organizational sanction to those items, they also imaged themselves as traditional women whose concerns were the same as those whom they were attempting to enlist for the cause. Famous suffragists were not harridans whose faces frightened children but women who were attempting to look their best. Elizabeth Cady Stanton, for example, in an advertisement for

When suffrage was gaining widespread support, manufacturers began using famous activists to endorse their products.

Fairbanks Fairy Soap, noted that she had tried it and found it "delightful." She observed that "it leaves the skin soft and velvety, and I particularly like it because it is as free from odor as the air and sunshine." Belva Lockwood, in an endorsement for the same soap, declared that she had "used Fairbank's Fairy Soap and deem it unequaled for bathing purposes, for all sorts of toilet uses, and particularly adapted for the nursery; as it is pure and white and will not injure the skin of the most delicate babe."[1] The ad, ignoring Lockwood's presidential aspirations, identified her as "the most prominent woman lawyer in the world."[2] Mrs. Alva Belmont was so concerned with integrating female beauty with the woman suffrage movement that she opened up a "Department of Hygiene" in the offices of her Political Equality Association and sold various skin creams, shampoo, a dandruff remedy, and castile soap. She later gave her consent to an ad in which she endorsed Pond's face cream.

Agnes Morgenthau, a leader among the "Y.S.S." ("Younger Suffrage Set") felt the need for a "ready-to-wear-to-anything-and-not-at-all-expensive-suffrage-blouse" and had her recommendation acted upon by an unidentified commercial manufacturer, and an illustration of her in that blouse appeared in a June 1917 issue of *Woman Citizen*. Elizabeth Cady Stanton also endorsed an item of clothing, this time nightwear, the Lewis Union Suit: "I take great pleasure in recommending the Lewis Union Suits for women in all stations. Dress has much to do with health. Nothing could be more beautiful than the various materials of which the Lewis Union Suits are knitted." Even Emmeline Pankhurst, noted for her militancy, allowed an endorsing letter for Natureform Shoes that she had written to Holden Brothers in April 1892 to be published in a 1909 issue of *Votes for Women*. She had purchased the product for her "two little girls" (Christabel and Sylvia) and expressed pleasure "with the shoes and think they are of admirable shape."

The Quaker Lace Company of Philadelphia pictured Carrie Chapman Catt's residence, Juniper Ledge, in Briarcliff, New York, in a two-page advertisement for its curtains. Identifying Catt as a "world-wide suffrage leader and President of the International Suffrage Alliance," the ad noted how well the curtains from the outside of the house blended in with the sweeping lawns of the estate, reflecting credit not only on the company's product, but also on Catt's sense of harmony and aesthetics. No words from Catt were quoted in the text, but the implication was clear: This was not a woman outside the mainstream of American life![3]

Belva Lockwood, who had temperance sympathies, nevertheless endorsed Dr. Greene's Nervura, a nerve tonic that consisted of 17 percent alcohol. Greene promoted his product as one that would make aches disappear and bring "Vitality and Vigor to All." Lockwood concurred, arguing that her good health and strength were augmented through its use. Lockwood, like many women of her day, used nerve tonics, knowing of their alcoholic content, and in 1886 she attempted to form a medicine company herself. She established a partnership with homeopathic physician E.B. Rankin to create the Lockwood Improvement Syndicate and even issued stock certificates in the company embellished with an engraving of her portrait. The venture never went far — there are no records of incorporation, and only one stock certificate apparently has survived.[4]

Perhaps the most interesting endorsement along with being the most groundbreaking was that of Alice Snitjer (Snitzer) Burke and Nell Richardson for the Saxon Roadster car. In April 1916, the two left New York to embark on a nationwide tour to promote the suffrage cause. During the course of their journey, they traveled over 10,000 miles, driving through mountain ranges on both sides of the country, arid deserts in Nevada and California, and waste stretches in Utah. According to an advertisement featuring photographic portraits of both women, they had carefully considered "the merits of many makes of cars" and "finally selected Saxon Roadster as the ablest car for the long grueling itinerary." Their journey was widely promoted in newspa-

Opposite: One of the first magazine ads for an automobile ever published where the appeal was directed entirely to women.

Mrs. Burke

Miss Richardson

Two Noted Suffragists
Travel 10,000 Miles in Saxon Roadster

Last April Mrs. Alice Snitzer Burke and Miss Nell Richardson left New York to tour the U. S. A. in behalf of woman's suffrage.

After carefully considering the merits of many makes of cars they finally selected Saxon Roadster as the ablest car for the long gruelling itinerary.

For five months they sped from city to city, from town to town, following a definite schedule, covered 10,000 miles, and were never late once.

Over both the Eastern and Western mountain ranges, across the arid deserts of Nevada and California as well as the great waste stretches of Utah, and through mud hub deep, went Saxon Roadster surmounting every obstacle of road and weather. Today it is ready for another such trip.

Throughout the entire journey Mrs. Burke and Miss Richardson handled the wheel, changing tires when necessary, and personally gave all the slight service that was necessary to keep the car in perfect condition.

So that this trip furnishes not only convincing evidence of the remarkable endurance of Saxon Roadster, but also a striking testimonial to the ease with which it is handled.

You are urged to visit the nearest Saxon dealer and view the beautiful, new series Saxon Roadster which has a 2-unit starting and lighting system and 20 other fine-car improvements. Price $495 f. o. b., Detroit.
(732)

SAXON MOTOR CAR CORPORATION, DETROIT

pers throughout the country, and was pictured on a period postcard issued by NAWSA. Their endorsement was significant in that it was an appeal from women to women for a product that previously had been considered to be located exclusively within the male purview.[5] In England, several advertisements for cars appeared in *Votes for Women* that also linked an automobile directly or indirectly to an endorsement from a suffrage leader or prominent woman. The agents for the "La Ponette" car noted that they had supplied one to Frederick Pethick Lawrence, editor of *Votes for Women*, and that they were "specialists in bodies designed for ladies' driving." General Motors of Europe, advertising its Bedford Buick in another issue of the same publication, noted that it had been driven by Gladys de Havilland, who had no previous driving experience, from Land's End to John-o'Groats, and therefore was "admirably adapted for the use of the ladies."[6] Havilland was the sister of the airplane designer of the same name.

Margaret Finnegan and others have pointed out the strong correlation between the rise of the suffrage movement and the development of consumerism. Certainly suffragists were willing to take advantage in the twentieth century of the methods of merchandising developed by both merchants and manufacturers. The fact that these same merchants could turn to the movement itself for "celebrity endorsements" of their products was an indication that suffrage was now being recognized as an integral part of the American and British cultural fabric. Perhaps women did not have the vote as yet, but the movement was mainstream, one that advertisers could and did associate themselves with in order to sell their products.

Face Cloth

The Universal Suffrage Society of Philadelphia offered for sale a "Votes for Women" face cloth in 1911. The wrapping explained that women could vote in Colorado, Idaho, Utah, Wyoming, and Washington, and that "Taxation Without Representation Is Tyranny." This was the way that the Society "emphasized that cleanliness is next to godliness, and part of godliness is winning democracy."[1]

Fans

One of the more common ways that merchants and manufacturers could promote their goods and services in the late 19th and early 20th centuries was through advertising on a cardboard or paper fan, whether of the pleated, accordion style variety or the flat, circular version, which was held by a stick. These fans were given out free at churches, funeral homes, sporting events, theaters, and cafes, or almost any place else where people needed relief from the heat in an age that preceded air conditioning and even electric fans. Some fans contained generic illustrations on one side and advertising on the other, others conveyed promotional material on both sides. Fans of historical significance were given out at the 1876 Philadelphia Centennial, the World's Columbian Exposition of 1893, and the 1901 Pan-American Exposition.[1]

Most pro-suffrage fans were issued and distributed either by suffrage groups themselves or by individual supporters working in conjunction with those groups. Fans that were generic and not tied in with a specific demonstration or referendum were often advertised in the *Woman's Journal*. The Woman's Franchise League of Ohio, for example, offered at $19.50 per hundred a yellow variety with "Votes for Women" printed on both sides of the piece along with a "good Suffrage quotation." They were advertised as "good for advertising the Cause at Chautauquas, County Fairs, Reunions, Summer Resorts." A cheaper fan was sold by Sylvia Norrish of Beaver Falls, Pennsylvania at a $1.50 a hundred that was promoted as the "latest thing in Suffrage Propaganda," and contained "sentiments of noted suffragists, arguments, and information."[2] There are only two known pleated fans, one of which was produced by the suffrage forces in Michigan. A red, white, and blue label was glued to a blank white paper, to which two sticks were attached, and then folded. The label proclaimed, "Votes for Women in Michigan—Governments derive their just powers from the consent of the governed—Are Women Governed? How and to whom can they give their consent without the ballot?"[3] A version of this exists with an ad for Bissell carpet sweepers.

There are a number of extant varieties of

flat, non-pleated suffrage fans, both pro-and anti- many of which were printed originally during the eastern states campaigns of the period 1915–1917. They were given away at street corners and at rallies, and must have provided much relief during summer months at indoor meetings. The Woman Suffrage Party (WSP) of New York had printed up several different varieties for the Empire State campaign of 1915. One version that contained the legend, "Keep Cool. There will be nothing to worry about after we get VOTES FOR WOMEN Election Day, Nov. 2," was distributed by party workers at a Wall Street rally on September 15 of that year. According to period accounts, the rally consisted of two buglers, eight highly decorated automobiles, and speakers at every corner. The suffragists gave out various pieces of suffrage memorabilia during the course of the rally, including small whirligig rattles and pennants, but the most popular item was the fan. Dignified Wall Street brokers grabbed for them eagerly, exhausting the supply of several hundred that had been brought to the rally.[4] Other fans issued by the party include an Emily Chamberlain illustration of two children dressed in patriotic clothing, which also appeared on a suffrage postcard and a pennant. The girl is tapping the boy, dressed in an Uncle Sam costume, and announcing, "I want to speak for myself at the polls." Another, probably issued for Valentine's Day, features an outline of a heart with a brief verse that concludes, "We want the vote as well as you." The Massachusetts Woman Suffrage Association (MWSA) also issued several fans in black and yellow, similar in design to WSP varieties, that included a slogan on one side and a map of the suffrage states on the other. One example that may have been unique, however, to the MWSA pictured the two major candidates for president in 1916, Woodrow Wilson and Charles Evans Hughes, on one side and their positions on suffrage on the reverse.

Anti-suffrage societies tended not to distribute memorabilia to the extent that suffragists did, but fans were a partial exception. Surviving examples contain more text than those of their opposition, appear to have been printed in some haste, and lack a sense of professional design. One even contains a paper strip glued over a portion of the text in an attempt to revise or correct a mistake in the original message without having to go to the expense of printing another fan.

The Woman Suffrage Party of New York was especially prolific in producing fans for the 1915 and 1917 state campaigns.

Flyswatter

There was a wood and wire flyswatter put out for the 1915 campaign in New Jersey. One side of the swatter urges, "Swat the fly, give women the vote and be happy." The other side is more serious," Remember to vote on OCTOBER 19th for a square deal for New Jersey Women." New Jersey was one of the four eastern states to hold a referendum on the franchise for women in that year. The other three states, New York, Pennsylvania, and Massachusetts, held theirs on Election Day, November 2. New Jersey held its vote on October 19, which was Registration Day. Unfortunately, not many people made

One of many household novelties issued by various suffrage groups.

the extra effort to turn out to vote on this subject alone, and the ballot initiative went down to defeat. NAWSA also sold two varieties of swatters at twenty-five cents a dozen. One slogan proclaimed, "Swat the Flies and Save the Babies," the other simply "Votes for Women."[1] Wire swatters were far more lethal than later plastic varieties, although the awkward stapling of the stick to the top portion of most suffrage examples made them ineffective in achieving their desired aim, and most were probably obtained and kept for souvenir purposes only.

Garden Seeds and Sticks

An ad for "Suffrage Maiden Garden Sticks" sold by the Congressional Union appeared in a May 1916 issue of *The Suffragist*. Readers were informed that "the Glad Days are Here — Help make your friends glad. Use our 'Suffrage Maiden' garden sticks for personal gifts, luncheon and dinner favors, bridge prizes, etc. 50 cents each, $5.75 per dozen."[1] The Pennsylvania Woman Suffrage Association (PWSA) sold garden seeds, which they packaged in an illustrated mailer labeled "The Suffrage Garden." Each packet of seeds contained different varieties of yellow flowers, with such campaign names as "Persistence," "Conquest," and "Victory."[2] The idea came from an anonymous suffrage worker who announced her intentions to the PWSA to plant her entire garden in a variety of these flowers so that everyone in her "little town will see the suffrage colors and know that our campaign is on in earnest." The idea caught on, and many of the local affiliates of the League sponsored contests for the

most beautiful suffrage garden. In anticipation of the 1915 suffrage referendum in Pennsylvania, the League quickly designated May 1 as "Planting Day" for suffrage flower gardens. According to the *Woman's Journal*, in the sister campaign states of New York, New Jersey, and Massachusetts, where suffrage referenda were also to be held that year, "hundreds of waving yellow gardens will make their appeal to the men voters."[3]

In 1917, the Albany branch of the New York State Woman Suffrage Party (NYSWSP) distributed a "Garden Primer" that dealt with how to plant and care for a vegetable garden. The primer, however, was printed not by the group but by "Mayor Mitchel's Food Supply Committee" out of New York City as a response to the war in Europe. NYSWSP pasted its own organizational label over the pamphlet and participated in the effort as a public service.[4]

Somewhat loosely related was a "Suffrage Gardenia" manufactured and promoted by Katherine L. Potter of New York as "the most salable article for meetings and pageants." The petals of the gardenia were actually made of cloth. Accompanied by a small "Votes for Women" sticker, the piece sold for fifteen cents, and was one of six suffrage novelties sold by Potter in 1913.[5]

In England, a "Miss Smith" of Sussex advertised "Sweet Pea Seeds" in the colors of the WSPU. Varieties included "Dorothy Eckford" (large, white), "Lady Grisel Hamilton" (mauve) and "Mrs. Walter Wright" (violet, mauve).[6]

Handkerchiefs

There are several silk handkerchiefs from the period that are known. Because of the popularity of embroidery, however, it is not always easy to determine which of those were commercially produced. The most common design in purple, green, white, gold, and yellow shows a woman demonstrator holding up a "Votes for Women" banner. It is probably of English origin. L. Lanphear of Chicago advertised a "Full Suffrage" handkerchief for "club display and campaign work."[1] The firm of Robinson and Cleaver, located on Regent Street in London, promoted handkerchiefs "with pretty borders in Purple, Green, and White" as Christmas presents for the

Clockwise from top left: A generic design on which the name of the product, "Woman's Suffrage Stove Polish," has been imprinted; an advertising booklet that contains a manufacturer's attempt to appeal to the emerging women's rights market; the trumpeter image on this colorful pin is English in origin; this particular example of a hunger strike medal was awarded to Lavender Guthrie, whose name is inscribed on the back.

He may yet become President.

She may yet wed a President.

Pinkerton's Oriental Coffee.

Two future possibilities defined by gender.

Left to right: Ballot "boxes" were not always "boxes," as illustrated by this Women's Votes tin drum; the Congressional Union and its successor, the National Woman's Party, both preferred enameled pins to celluloid buttons.

Top: The colors purple, green, and white identify this as a product of the Women's Political Union; ***bottom left to right***: printed in yellow, white, and blue, this pin differed from the typical black and yellow color scheme of the Woman's Suffrage Party; "Carrie Chapman Catt"—the New York State Woman Suffrage Association was one of the few suffrage groups to picture famous leaders on its buttons.

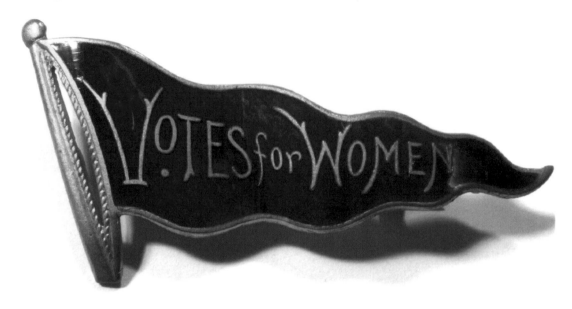

Top: Because of its expensive production costs, Washington suffragists charged 25 times more for this enamel than they did for a simple pin; *bottom left to right*: the Connecticut "Suffrage Plank" pin was one of only a few badges to use an illustration other than that of a trumpeter or herald; a delegate badge with hanger from a suffrage convention in Maine.

Top left to right: One of many badges designed for the conservative Primrose League, which was open to women — because this example has a brooch rather than a stud style back, it was probably intended for female members; when the Pethick Lawrences were "expelled" from the Women's Social and Political Union, they formed the "Votes for Women Fellowship" and produced several enamel badges; *bottom*: the firm Royal Doulton issued these two inkwells that reflect in their grotesque portrayals negative images of both present and future suffragists, typical for the period.

Clockwise from top: This Art Nouveau calendar featured quotations for every day of the year relevant to women and their struggle for equality; example of the Cargill postcard design used on a watch fob manufactured by Butler; perhaps because the opposition often complained about the "cackling of suffragettes," they were often portrayed as geese as in this Schafer and Vater example.

There are several small variations of this card, and the image was also used for poster stamps and stationery; *bottom left to right*: the figure of Joan of Arc was used as an iconic image by suffragists on both sides of the Atlantic; the Woman Suffrage Party also reproduced both the image and verse on this fan for a postcard.

Flagg, one of the most noted illustrators of the period, was responsible for several suffrage magazine covers; *bottom*: not even a change in policy to one that supported suffrage was to save *Puck* from declining sales.

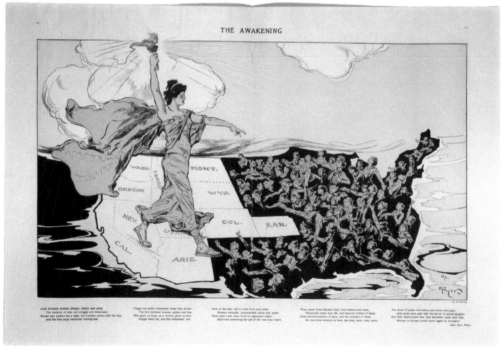

Suffragette Puzzle to Get Bill Through Parliament was a game in which it was virtually impossible for the player to master, symbolizing the difficulties facing the suffragist worker.

One of several versions of Buchanan's famous statue printed on a Woman Suffrage Party pennant.

Top: This *Life* cover, promoting suffrage, would not be considered acceptable today; *bottom*: the butterfly sticker was too large (2¼" × 4") to be used as a decoration on an envelope, and probably adorned luggage and the like instead.

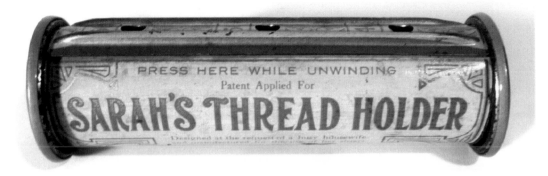

This novelty item not only helped in the 1915 suffrage campaign in Massachusetts, it also honored an early female labor leader.

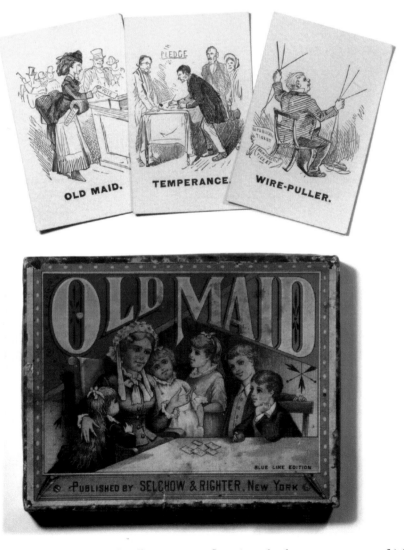

Although the image of the old maid suffragette is not flattering, she does not appear as a frightening hag as she does in other period versions of the game.

Left: A widely circulated poster by the artist Evelyn Rumsey Cary; *right*: typical example of an Artist Suffrage League poster.

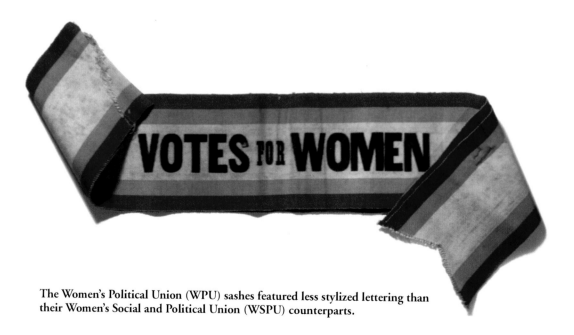

The Women's Political Union (WPU) sashes featured less stylized lettering than their Women's Social and Political Union (WSPU) counterparts.

Clockwise from top: Both the sheet music cover and the song appealed to men's consciences — how could they deny the vote to the mother of their children?; a very graphic ribbon for Kansas women created for one of their campaigns prior to their finally receiving full suffrage in 1912; the earliest official suffrage stamp, it features the design of a woman college graduate, a standard icon in later suffrage art.

Clockwise from top: Negative images of activists were typical on English cards; this one shows a suffragist chasing the devil; dolls were a very popular novelty in the suffrage campaign, but most, unlike this example, were probably handmade; one of the most colorful items produced for any of the four states in the 1915 Eastern campaign was this tin bird that was nailed up as a decorative advertisement for suffrage.

These six markers are often missing from surviving examples of the board game Pank-a-Squith.

There were several English board games, some from suffrage groups, some from commercial sources, that strikingly demonstrated the obstacles women faced in obtaining the vote.

While the majority of Valentine's Day cards sent by women denied that they were suffrage sympathizers, a significant minority, such as this example, indicated that love was conditional, relative to a man's attitude toward suffrage.

Left: This colorful button reflects the efforts of many suffragists to engage in the war effort; *right*: this umbrella, sold by the National American Woman Suffrage Association (NAWSA), was decorated for a parade celebrating states such as Idaho that had granted the vote to women;

This handkerchief was probably English in origin and was machine stitched. It features the colors of the Women's Social and Political Union.

season of 1909.[2] Later, in 1911, the firm was also selling a "Wrapo" fleece rug in the colors, an "Xmas Gift that any member of the WSPU would be delighted to possess."[3]

Jewelry

Given the numbers of buttons, badges, and ribbons that American suffragists authorized for the campaign, it would seem plausible that either they or commercial manufacturers would also have been involved heavily in the production of decorative jewelry with a suffrage theme. This, however, does not appear to be the case. Unless one becomes extremely inclusive in a definition of "decorative jewelry," one cannot find a single piece represented in the APIC suffrage project, a special triple issue of the American Political Items Conservators' organ, *The Keynoter*, that was devoted to publishing extensive images of suffragist artifacts. Moreover, apart from one significant exception, there appears to be an absence of any listing of these items in suffrage newspapers and catalogs. One primary explanation for the lack of production of American suffrage jewelry simply may have been a problem with official colors. The "yellow" of NAWSA was the most prominently displayed color symbol of the movement (**see Colors**), and, while it certainly resonated a message in the context of a demonstration, it carried little meaning when worn alone. Suffragists wore campaign material to make a statement, and buttons and ribbons with their worded messages made those statements emphatically, whereas brooches, pendants, and necklaces without accompanying text did not. This is undoubtedly why the one American manufacturer, the Butler Brothers Jewelry Company of Attleboro, Massachusetts, that did produce an extensive line of jewelry, used a design and slogan ("The Ballot Is Denied to Women — The Blot on the Escutcheon") that resembled a campaign button more than it did a piece of ornamental adornment. The situation was different in England, where the WSPU's official colors of purple, green and white did permeate public consciousness, but even there, as we shall see, there were some problems in transferring that consciousness into the commercial production of ornament jewelry.

The Butler Brothers suffrage jewelry line was first announced in a full-page advertisement in the *Woman's Journal*, not long after the publication had become NAWSA's official paper. The escutcheon design was taken from a set of thirty postcards recently issued by the Cargill Company of Michigan that was advertised concurrently with the Butler Brothers' jewelry in the same issue. The Butler Brothers' products, which consisted of the multicolor slogan on a shield on made-to-order belt buckles, hat pins, brooches, cuff links, scarf pins, barrettes, veil pins, sash pins, collar pins, and rings, were issued under license from Cargill. The only prices listed in the ad were for a ⅝" gold-filled pin at fifty cents each and versions in sterling and solid gold for seventy-five cents and two dollars respectively. As was the case with the postcard set from Cargill, Butler Brothers' jewelry line was authorized by NAWSA, which received a percentage of the profits, but this clearly was a commercial venture, even though "club rates" were available. Despite the large *Woman's Journal* ad and Butler's attempt to promote its line as fundraisers for suffrage clubs, sales appear to have been minimal. Examples of escutcheon jewelry, unlike those of Cargill postcards, are seldom seen in current auctions or in online sales today, and no other type of Butler Brothers' suffrage jewelry, other than its pins, is known.[1] Apart from one follow-up advertsement, the Butler company made no attempt to advertise its product line in any additional issue of NAWSA's paper.

It was undoubtedly the Butler jewelry line that the publishers of the *Woman's Journal* attempted to sell when they secured a booth at the National Style Show at the Horticultural Show in Boston, February 7–11, 1911. At the booth, "girls and women" secured subscriptions to the paper and sold suffrage stationery, books, pamphlets, postcards, and jewelry, including lockets, watch fobs, collar pins, cuff links, belt buckles, and veil and hat pins.[2] If Butler's jewelry pieces lacked the popularity of the Cargill postcard series, they nevertheless achieved mention in the British periodical *Votes for Women*, where the "Blot on the Escutcheon" ring and locket were cited as examples of items that were made popular by including the "Votes for Women" slogan.[3]

Jewelry, other than the Butler Brothers' line, did have its function in the American campaign, but not specifically suffrage jewelry. Personal unwanted items were often sold at suffrage bazaars as fundraisers. In 1914, for instance, the Campaign Committee of NAWSA sent out an appeal to women, signed by Dr. Anna Howard Shaw and Medill McCormick, to donate their old jewelry to help fund campaigns in Ohio, Missouri, Nebraska, Nevada, Montana, and the Dakotas. The committee had hoped to raise $50,000 through the sale of such donations.[4]

There were presentation pieces of jewelry, however, that were given to some of the American suffrage leaders to honor their service. Harriet Taylor Upton presented a star sapphire brooch to Carrie Chapman Catt at the February 15, 1920, Victory Convention of NAWSA immediately after Catt had presented other suffragists with service awards.[5] Certain western leaders thought that there would be no better way to make Carrie Chapman Catt into a household name than by initiating a program among schoolchildren to take part in raising funds for this brooch. Schoolteachers were enlisted to ask their students to bring in a penny to help honor the person who had accomplished so much for the women of the nation. One student, following his teacher's request, went home and asked his mother for the solicited penny, When the mother asked what it was for, the boy told her that it was for "Charlie Chaplin's cat!"[6]

The women of Wyoming gave Susan B. Anthony a jeweled flag on the occasion of her eightieth birthday. The four states that had enfranchised women were represented on this flag by diamonds, the others by silver enamel. At Anthony's funeral, the flag was pinned to her breast. Just before the lid to her coffin was closed, however, Mary Anthony, Susan's sister, removed the pin and gave it to Anna Howard Shaw. Accepting responsibility for the honor, Shaw made it a point to add a diamond to the flag every time a new state was won for suffrage.[7] So pleased was a Mr. Edwards when his home state of California had granted women the franchise in 1911 that he gave Shaw the money for the new diamond the following year.[8] At the close of her address to the NAWSA National Convention in 1915, Shaw held up the pin, and, giving a slightly different and less macabre version as to how she had obtained it, declared: "This is Miss Anthony's flag, which she gave me just before she died. It was the gift of Wyoming women and had four tiny diamonds in it for the four equal suffrage States; now it has thirteen. Who says 'suffrage is going and not coming'? We have as many stars now as there were original States when the government began."[9]

A cameo pin with image of Susan B. Anthony was cut by Pio Siotto of Rome and set in gold by the London jeweler George Blogg and Co. A copy, owned by the University of Rochester, is inscribed on verso to Mary S. Anthony. Presumably other copies were made.

In England, traditional decorative jewelry definitely was made and produced in the various colors of the movement. Elizabeth Goring, in her seminal article "Suffragette Jewellery in Britain," observes, "Thousands of examples must have been made and worn between 1908 and 1914." The problem is that "it can be difficult to identify."[10] This difficulty is caused by the fact that while the colors of purple, green, and white were strongly associated with the WSPU, which aggressively promoted them, "amethysts, pearls and demantoid garnets or emeralds were very commonly used in Edwardian jewellery."[11] Therefore, as Goring notes, "it is important to recognize that not all jewellery in purple, white and green was intended for the suffragettes."[12] This is not to say that such generic pieces were not incorporated into a suffrage context, for women, who had been exhorted by the WSPU to "wear the colours," may very well have purchased such items because of their coincidental color combination and not because they had been expressly manufactured for the movement.

There are advertisements in various suffrage newspapers from both commercial and arts and crafts sources promoting suffrage jewelry, much of which consisted of individually made-up items as opposed to mass-produced commercial pieces. The problem is that if such pieces were not advertised or somehow identified through other means, there is no way today to link them up directly with the suffrage cause. As Goring points out, "Many items presumably languish in jewelry boxes across Britain, their original meaning no longer recognized."[13] Even here, however, Elizabeth Crawford issues a cautionary note. Finding only one commercial manufacturer advertising jewellery in the entire run of the WSPU *Votes for Women*, she argues, "As it would have been an obvious place to have done so, one is tempted to conclude that little more was commercially manufactured." Her remarks are not intended to include the individual products of the arts and crafts marketplace, for there were many suffrage bazaars that clearly afforded manifold opportunities for purchasing hand-wrought pieces.[14] The most famous of these bazaars, an event so large that the term "bazaar" is perhaps inappropriate, was the Women's Exhibition and Sale of Work at the Prince's Skating Rink in Knightsbridge in May 1909, where there was much jewelry for sale, presumably crafted for the event and presumably at least some in the WSPU colors.

The one commercial advertisement in *Votes for Women* that Crawford alludes to first appeared in 1909 in time for the Christmas holiday. It was from the London firm of Mappin and Webb, which also had showrooms in Paris. The ad pictured five pieces of "suffragette jewellery in enamels and gems," including several brooches and pendants. Each item was set in gold with emeralds, pearls, and amethysts representing the colors of purple, green, and white.[15] Prices ranged between two and six pounds, and the pieces clearly were not intended for the working-class woman who had little in the way of disposable income. There is nothing to these pieces, apart from their color scheme, that would oth-

erwise suggest a connection to the WSPU or somehow set them apart from non-movement jewelry of the period in the same colors. An ad for arts and crafts as opposed to commercially made jewelry also appeared in *Votes for Women* from Annie Steen of Birmingham at about the same time promoting "Christmas Presents for Suffragettes! Hand Wrought Jewelry in Gold and Silver Set With Stones in the Colours."[16] Unfortunately, there were no illustrations to this ad, and no examples of Steen's work have been specifically identified, although reports indicate that some of her pieces were donated to the Birmingham stall at the exhibition at the Prince's Skating Rink. Birmingham was one of the country's centers for inexpensive silver work and jewelry.[17]

In 1913, the Wholesale Service Company of Birmingham placed several illustrated advertisements in two different suffrage publications for commercially produced jewelry that it was distributing. The first appeared in the January 3 issue of *Votes for Women*, when the paper was no longer serving as the official mouthpiece of the WSPU because of the fracture between the Pethick Lawrences and the Pankhursts. The ad featured a "pendant with necklet" and a "motor veil, brooch to match enameled in the colours: purple, green, and white."[18] The second was placed January 13 in the new WSPU publication, *The Suffragette*, edited by Christabel Pankhurst. It featured a differently designed pendant made by the Birmingham firm of Joseph Fray that the Wholesale Service Company also carried. The pendant was in the form of a double "S" shaped profile with a pendant drop. It was enameled in the colors of purple, green, and white, placed in a silver setting, and sold for 9 shillings. A matching brooch was also available.[19]

The WSPU itself sold jewelry, although these pieces contained a pronounced political theme that separated them from the ambiguity of the commercial items discussed above. In 1908, they merchandised Votes for Women "woven ribbon badges" along with "button badges" and "Boadicea brooches."[20] Emmeline Pankhurst is shown wearing this brooch on a postcard issued by J. Beagles. The various WSPU suffrage shops sold for the Christmas 1909 "an exhibition angel, set in a pendant," that had been designed by Sylvia Pankhurst, a silver hat pin in the shape of an arrow, the design on clothing worn by suffrage "convicts" and hunger strikers, "pretty brooches," badges, both in enamel and "precious stones," and "very dainty silver articles."[21] The various Holloway pins and hunger strike medals that were given to prisoners by the WSPU and the WFL were, obviously, jewelry pieces, but since these were not available to the general public and since they can be considered also as badges, they are described under the section English Buttons and Badges in **Buttons**.

English suffragists, like their American counterparts, also presented one-of-a-kind jewelry pieces in honor to their various contributors and leaders. One of the most elegant was an enameled pendant portraying the winged figure of Hope outside prison bars. It was fashioned by Ernestine Mills and presented to Louise Eates, and now is housed at the Museum of London as part of its suffrage collection. Mills also crafted an enameled pendant featuring a lily in the colors for Maggie Murphy. The reverse of the piece was engraved "Holloway Prison No. 15474, Maggie Murphy, 2 months hard labour, E.4 Cell 12, Hunger Strike 16th April 1912, Forcibly Fed."[22] Mills was vice president of the craft section of the Society of Women Artists, and produced much artwork, including jewelry, for the WSPU, some of which still survives,[23] as well as publishing several suffrage postcards. Recipients of other presentation pieces, made by various craftspeople, include Emmeline and Christabel Pankhurst, Flora Drummond, and Mrs. Pethick Lawrence. Black-and-white photographs of prominent suffragists from the period often show them wearing jewelry. While many of these pieces obviously were free of any association with the movement, had the pictures themselves been taken in color, it is quite probable that in some the purple, white, and green color scheme would have shown up, giving us more insight into what jewelry had been produced.

Thus, while there are records in English of jewelry being sold to the public and presented to prominent suffragists, the situation for the scholar of such objects is frustrating. What is a suffrage piece and what is not? Because of the enigma, a number of auctioneers and merchants are now selling period pieces as suffrage items because of their color scheme without having any evidence to support their claims. A myth has arisen that one of the colors on these items is not purple but violet, and that the resultant initials, "GWV," was a secret code for "Give Women the Vote." The explanation for the code is variously given, but generally it goes along the lines that women were afraid to announce openly their support of the movement, and so kept it hidden except to other sympathetic individuals who also knew the meaning of the "secret" letters. There has never been in any period record in any paper, journal, memoir, or letter the suggestion that the symbolism of the colors be kept hidden from the public, and one must assume that the existence of such a secret code is a myth. Obviously suffragists wanted women to be open, not secretive, about their support, and a hidden code, if it existed, would probably have drawn their disapproval, and even, perhaps, their scorn.[24] Still, this myth has been perpetuated by a number of dealers on the Internet who are trying to sell ordinary pieces as suffrage jewelry. It matters not that the piece in question is English or American. Suffrage scholars who wish to own period jewelry from the movement are generally very careful to ask for some form of period authentication before buying any item. In most cases such substantiation does not exist.

Magazine Covers and Illustrations

The approach or attitude towards woman suffrage and its leadership in American popular magazines over the years is certainly complex as reflected in their covers and featured illustrations. Depictions of aspects of the suffrage movement were influenced by a variety of factors, including popular conceptions regarding equal rights, the changing nature of magazine readership, growing pressure to increase readership, the emergence of women as consumers, concerns of advertisers that they not offend potential customers, and advances in printing techniques that led away from black and white engravings and towards full color reproductions. It would be tempting to say that the initial reaction towards suffrage in popular magazines was both hostile and satirical, but that this attitude softened and ultimately changed to supportive the closer that women came to attaining the franchise. And, to a large extent, this was indeed the case, but there were some interesting exceptions in a few magazines to prevailing pejorative views even relatively early in the campaign for equal rights.

One of the first significant illustrations of the suffrage movement appeared in the *Harper's Weekly* issue of June 11, 1859, roughly eleven years after the Seneca Falls Convention. A full-page cartoon pictures a group of dour-looking women, along with a few men, and is titled "Ye May Session of Ye Woman's Rights Convention—Ye Orator of Ye Day Denouncing Ye Lords of Creation."[1] The particular satire of this illustration, that of the horrors attendant to a public meeting of socially engaged women, was mirrored ten years later on May 15, 1869, when *Harper's* published a print by Charles W. Bush entitled "Sorosis—1869," in which a fierce-looking woman is banging a paddle inscribed "Women's Rights" on a table, attempting to maintain order before a group of women who are engaged in sundry activities while drinking tea, including reading Susan B. Anthony's suffrage paper, *The Revolution,* and signing petitions for suffrage.

Harper's, which had commenced publication but two years earlier, in 1857, was basically a cross between a newspaper and a magazine. It dealt with foreign and domestic news, but also printed fiction and essays. At a time when technology was as yet unable to reproduce photographs in mass print, it relied heavily on elaborately engraved pictures to illustrate its stories, engravings that were frequently colored in by magazine subscribers. In featuring engravings, *Harper's* was following a practice first established in England by the *Illustrated London News* and brought to America by Frank Leslie, whose *Frank Leslie's Illustrated Newspaper* appeared in 1855. *Harper's* was to outsell its rival, in part by hiring such famous illustrators as Thomas Nast, Winslow Homer, and Granville Perkins.

As a news publication, *Harper's* could approach the topic of suffrage somewhat objectively, but its attempt to be humorous at times could lead to gentle satire that could, on occasion, turn bitter. Perhaps its most famous comment on suffrage is Thomas Nast's lithograph of February

17, 1879, that depicted Victoria Woodhull as "Mrs. Satan," trying to promote her doctrine of "Free Love" to a poor woman carrying a burden of a drunken husband and two small children up a steep mountain. The response of the woman is "I'd rather travel the hardest path of matrimony than follow your footsteps." While Nast's satire may have been directed specifically against Woodhull, it did reflect an early criticism directed against the suffrage movement in general, that its activists were not only not interested in matrimony themselves, but were inclined, if they had their way, to eliminate it altogether. Other illustrations in *Harper's* were less hostile towards the movement and even towards Woodhull herself. One from November 25, 1871, shows her somewhat heroically attempting to cast a ballot. Several of these engravings are objective representations of either contemporary or historical events, without satirical overtones. Two

Nast's vicious attack on Victoria Woodhull reflected many contemporary reactions to her character.

such lithographs, which are often reproduced today, show Howard Pyle's drawing of women voting in colonial times in New Jersey, prior to later restrictions, and women voting in municipal elections in Boston on December 11, 1888. The magazine also reprinted on June 22, 1872, an illustration of a woman's rights meeting that was held in England at Hanover Square Rooms that was originally printed in *The Graphic,* an English newspaper-magazine, on May 25 of the same year. Absent are the satirical renditions of women meeting that *Harper's* had published but three years earlier. They are replaced by the fiercely determined but noble image of Rhoda Garrett making her point, accompanied by several attractive depictions of women, including those of Mrs. Fawcett and Mrs. Mark Garrison.

Harper's rival, *Frank Leslie's Illustrated Newspaper,* often referred to as *Frank Leslie's Weekly,* was begun by an Englishman, Henry Carter, who had changed his name to Leslie and moved to America in 1848. Leslie originally had been an illustrator for the *Illustrated London News* and he brought with him to the United States his experience with a type of publication that was new to America. At times the subject of gossip regarding libertine sexual habits, he married Miriam Florence Follin in 1874, a woman who was a genius at business and twice saved the Leslie publication empire from financial ruin. She took over control of *Leslie's Weekly* in 1880 upon the death of her husband, changed her name legally to Frank Leslie, and managed the publication until it changed hands in 1902, when it evolved into a more traditional magazine.

Because Follin was an ardent feminist who left much of her fortune at her death to Carrie Chapman Catt to use in support of the movement, *Leslie's Weekly* is sometimes seen as a pro-suffrage publication. Yet its depiction of the movement through its illustrations is often rather similar in attitude to its rival, *Harper's,* sometimes objective, sometimes flattering, but mixed in with occasional satire and derision. Perhaps its most reproduced lithograph today is its cover for the November 24, 1888, issue, based on a photograph by Kirkland, which positively portrays women at the polls at Cheyenne in Wyoming

Territory. A less flattering portrait of women voters, however, was the subject of an illustration in 1887 of "female suffrage in Kansas," where women activists are depicted as overweight, dour, and "spinsterish." Still, on April 21, 1888, *Leslie's* featured a story titled "A Revolution in Municipal Government — A Kansas Town Governed by Women," with flattering portraits of six such leaders, including Mayor Mary Lowman, Mrs. Carrie Johnson, and Mrs. Mittie Josephine Golden. A cartoon published on November 25, 1876, while the original Frank Leslie was still alive, pictures an overweight policeman dragging a weak and sick-looking man to the polls in front of a domineering wife, assuring her "I will take him to the polls, Madam, and see that he votes as you dictate." Nevertheless, an illustration that appeared on February 4, 1871, shows a "lady delegate reading her argument in favor of woman's voting" before the Judiciary Committee of the House of Representatives. That the woman pictured was Victoria Woodhull is not mentioned in the caption to the engraving, which may have been an attempt to deflect attention from Woodhull's notoriety to the legitimacy of her cause. Finally, what was perhaps the last appearance of the topic of suffrage on a cover of *Leslie's* while it was still under family control, was that of May 3, 1894, which contained a drawing by B. West Clinedinst entitled "The Woman-Suffrage Movement in New York City." It portrayed a group of sincere and determined society women securing signatures on behalf of suffrage to be presented to the Constitutional Convention.

When *Leslie's* moved to a magazine format in the twentieth century, still calling itself *Leslie's Illustrated Weekly Newspaper,* the style of its covers changed, no longer featuring carefully prepared black-and-white lithographs of contemporary events, but now using color drawings from famous artists and illustrators that were more decorative in nature and less focused on news. Among the three that stand out is P.J. Monahan's cover from November 2, 1912, which pictured an elegantly dressed young woman waving a "Votes for Women" banner from the back seat of an open automobile, while her companion in a feathered hat blows an accompanying horn. The final two were by James Montgomery Flagg, who began contributing artwork to magazines at the age of twelve, worked as an illustrator for *Life* at fourteen, and later produced the famous recruitment poster "Uncle Sam Wants You." Flagg's first suffrage *Leslie's* cover appeared on October 28, 1915, and portrayed a young woman dressed as a minuteman, holding a rifle, with the sign "Taxation Without Representation" along with the caption "As Her Father Fought, So Will She." Flagg's second cover was published on August 7, 1920, after passage of the suffrage amendment was assured. A young woman with a slightly worried look on her face is holding an official ballot. The caption questions, "What Will She Do with It?" While both Flagg covers appear positive, replacing the harridan image that often accompanied derogatory depictions of suffragists in the past, there still are indications that voting rights for women are not entirely respected. Both women pictured are young, pretty ingénues who seem out of place in the world of politics. The sharp

militancy that was depicted in earlier derogatory images had been replaced by that of an innocent naïveté, a suggestion, perhaps, that, while women should have the right to vote, many are not quite serious or ready enough to take on their new responsibilities.

Among other early popular magazines that covered the topic of suffrage in their covers included *Appleton's Journal of Literature, Science, and Art* which, on August 14, 1869, pictured a woman holding her baby with the caption "Will She Vote." To answer that question, the cover directs the reader to page 614, where a satirical poem by Edgar Fawcett attempts to isolate the wife and mother from the dogma of the suffrage zealot. The cover of a magazine published by J.M. Ivers of Fulton Street in New York called *Womens* [*sic*] *Rights* depicts a shouting woman proselytizing to a group of ruffians armed with pitchforks and knives. The inside contains many illustrations of women smoking, behaving like men, and asserting their rights in an aggressive, threatening way. The magazine, presumably re-

Left: Monahan's cover art involving a 1912 suffrage parade borrowed from images of a college football rally; *right*: cover of a one-issue magazine that viciously attacked the character of suffragists.

stricted to one issue, was probably published in response to Victoria Woodhull's presidential candidacy and advocacy of free love. One image shows women as stockbrokers physically assaulting a defenseless man and alludes to Woodhull as a "Dolly Varden politician," an obscure reference that may be to a character in Charles Dickens' *Barnaby Rudge*.[2]

Even magazines intended for youths could occasionally deal with the subject of suffrage. In the July 12, 1901, issue of the periodical *Work and Win, An Interesting Weekly for Young America,* the featured story is "Fred Fearnot in Debate or The Warmest Member of the House." The cover illustration pictures Fred among a group of women, proclaiming to one, "I have a mother and sister, and there's another fellow's sister, for whom I would do anything in the world necessary to their comfort and happiness, even to the laying down of my life, but I am opposed to their becoming voters." One wonders which of Fred's values would become paramount if he saw his

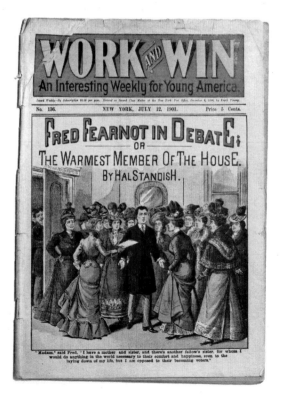

Even boys' magazines commented on the impact of suffrage, although not necessarily in a positive way.

mother being attacked while she was in the process of casting her ballot.

The late 1870s and early 1880s, several decades after the appearance of the newspaper-magazine such as *Harper's* and *Leslie's*, saw in America the rapid growth of the cartoon magazine, whose covers and inside illustrations frequently provided biting commentary on the suffrage movement and its leaders. The most influential of these were *Puck* (1877–1918), its main competitor in style and design, *Judge* (1881–1939), and, in its first format, *Life* (1883–1936). American cartoon magazines featured political humor and social commentary all augmented with illustrations that could be highly elaborate and colorful at times.[3]

The inspiration behind *Puck* was Joseph Keppler, an Austrian-born immigrant, who launched the first issues of his new magazine in German before adding a more popular edition in English several months later. *Puck* in its humor was highly political in nature, generally supporting the Democratic Party and its candidates. What caused the magazine to become popular, however, was Keppler's highly creative use of chromolithography to provide evocatively illustrated covers in full color as well as double-page centerfolds that often were removed and framed. Both covers and centerfolds typically consisted of allegorical representations of politicians and contemporary issues, with those individuals whom Keppler approved portrayed with saint-like imagery and those of whom he disapproved, including Republicans and the leading suffragists of his day, drawn pejoratively. The back cover of his magazine generally moved on to gentler social satire and commentary, with the topic of women's rights a frequent subject of attack.

When Kepler first arrived from Austria, he was a proponent of woman's suffrage, and one of his earliest cartoons for a publication called *Die Vehme* expresses a wish for, among other things, "suffrage" and "equal rights." However, his feelings on the subject soon changed, perhaps due in part to what he perceived to be radical pronouncements on the part of the movement's leaders.[4] Susan B. Anthony, Elizabeth Cady Stanton, and Belva Lockwood [see **Belva Lockwood and the Equal Rights Party**] were frequent targets of Keppler's wrath. In one early centerfold entitled "The New Tower of Babel," an angry Anthony is kicking the "one stone on the weary way to woman suffrage." In a later centerfold, Anthony, Elizabeth Cady Stanton, Belva Lockwood, and Dr. Mary Walker are pictured as wax figures in "a chamber of female horrors" for the upcoming Buffalo Exposition. An 1894 cartoon shows three suffragists, one of whom is drawn as an Anthony-like grotesque, ringing the bell of "Equal Rights" during the "Independence Day of the Future." In the cacophony of the background are two statues, one of a woman with a rolling pin "erected in the memory of the first woman who wore breeches," the other of an eagle dressed as a female over the inscription, "The American Bird Is a Hen Eagle and Lays Eggs."

Other generic attacks on the suffrage movement include a centerfold published on July 14, 1880, entitled "A Female Suffrage Fancy," which allegedly illustrated what activists were striving for, including a reversal of gender roles with women at bars and men minding babies, a woman dressed as a man with a preparation designed to make whiskers grow, and with "the political machine" superseding the sewing machine. An 1894 cover shows an unflattering portrait of a woman with a flowing dress attempting to enter a voting booth and asks the question "How can she vote, when the fashions are so wide, and the voting booths are so narrow?"

When Keppler died in 1894, the publication was taken over by his son, Joseph Jr., who appointed Harry Leon Wilson as the new editor. Wilson was replaced in 1904 by John K. Bangs, former editor of *Harper's Weekly*. The change in both ownership and editorship was reflected in the magazine's editorial position towards suffrage. Still, as late as 1913, *Puck* did print a cover that could be taken as satirical towards the movement. It portrayed a group of dowdy nymphs dragging John Bull, the English counterpart to Uncle Sam, into the water spring of woman suffrage.

Puck, however, was now faced with declining sales. That, along with a strategy to increase its readership by attempting to appeal more directly to women and a growing realization that suffrage was both popular and inevitable, caused the magazine to completely reverse its once-hos-

tile attitude towards the franchise and become a proponent for its aims. On February 20, 1915, it published a pro-suffrage issue that was prepared under the official editorial direction of the Empire State Campaign Committee, the New York State Woman Suffrage Association, the Woman Suffrage Party, the Equal Franchise Society, the Collegiate League for Woman Suffrage, and the Men's League for Woman Suffrage of the National Woman Suffrage Association. The cover of the issue featured a drawing by Rolf Armstrong of the magazine's mascot, Puck, draped in a "Votes for Women" sash, alongside a suffrage activist. The centerfold, by Hy Mayer, portrayed a female torchbearer bringing the promise of votes for women to desperate women across America. *Puck* promised that its commitment to the cause was anything but fleeting: "We shall have something interesting to say about the cause next week, and the week after, and so on, until certain short-sighted gentlemen now enjoying a brief sojourn in Washington awaken to their plain duty./And as long as *Puck* pursues its course on behalf of equal franchise, it merits the continued support of every woman who believes she is entitled to a voice at the polls./From now until the battle for woman suffrage is won, *Puck* will have some very pointed things to say about the matter./Every issue will be worth watching. The skilled 'campaigner' has learned the enormous value of a clever cartoon, a pithy editorial, used immediately and with chilling effect."

To further promote sales of the special issue, *Puck* took out a half-page ad on the back cover of the *Woman's Journal* for February 13, 1915, declaring, "Never before have so many brilliant minds of such diverse attainments been grouped in one magazine. Here, indeed, is a feast of satire, wit and brilliancy in prose, poetry, and caricature." Unfortunately for *Puck,* its deathbed conversion, while undoubtedly sincere enough, did not save the magazine, and it ceased publication three years later.

Puck's main competition in its early years, *Judge,* was founded by a former artist from *Puck,* James A. Wales, who reportedly had a disagreement with management. Buttressed by artists such as Bernard Gilliam and Grant Hamilton, who had previously illustrated for *Puck, Judge* followed a similar format with brilliantly well-executed chromolithographed covers, a center-fold, and a back page with social commentary. It became a vehicle for Republican propaganda in 1884, when Republicans saw the need to counteract *Puck's* attacks on James Blaine and offered to back the magazine financially.

Judge was as hostile towards suffrage in its political cartoons and satire as Keppler had been. An 1887 cover by an artist who signed himself "Victor" portrays a determined Uncle Sam disgustingly rejecting a group of tailors, including Susan B. Anthony, Belva Lockwood, an anarchist dynamiter, a communist, a socialist, and a Mormon, seeking to "repair" his coat. A centerfold by Hamilton shows two groups of women, the first consisting of dour-looking females labeled "dyspeptic," "old spinster," and "unhappily married," the second a happily married woman with her cute daughter and a winsome female attracting the attention of men, and asks "Find the group in favor of woman's suffrage." A back page pictures a carnival scene with Susan B. Anthony, Elizabeth Cady Stanton, and Belva Lockwood as a "neglected side show" that "nobody seems to know" exists. Another centerfold shows a pathetic toboggan slide with Anthony, Stanton, and Lockwood on the sleigh of "women's rights," and another back page illustrates the increased power of the ward heeler with a teeter-totter of four "ignorant" women voters weighing down the influence of one "intelligent" male voter.

Like *Puck, Judge* did have a conversion of sorts on January 29, 1910, when it issued its own "Suffragette Number." This particular issue, however, was not produced in conjunction with suffrage workers, and was extremely guarded and circumspect in presenting its views, which still included the satirical. It announced that its official position towards suffrage was the same as that once expressed by President Taft: "I am in favor of woman suffrage [pause] when all the women are." One of the inside color plates, though, did show a caring Mrs. Alva Belmont bringing "aid and comfort to less fortunate sisters" accompanied with the caption "This Kind of Woman Suffrage Looks Good to *Judge.*" By 1912, though, the magazine underwent a sea change when it published James Montgomery Flagg's cover art of an attractive woman casting a ballot with the caption "Independence Day."

Life, the other major humor magazine that started soon after the appearance of Keppler's *Puck,* was not known for its cover artwork until the twentieth century, when it produced several significant pro-suffrage illustrations during the movement's final decade prior to the passage of the federal franchise amendment. These included the "Pro-Suffrage" number of October 12, 1912, which pictured an attractive woman dressed in the purity of white, standing amid a knife-wielding member of the Black Hand, a drunken laborer with a beer belly, a black man dressed as a dandy, and a confidence man, all over the caption of "Four Voters." For July 1, 1915, *Life* published Paul Stahr's illustration of a modern woman adding "and women" to the phrase "all men are created equal" to the Declaration of Independence. When the suffrage amendment was finally ratified, *Life* celebrated with a cover by Charles Dana Gibson showing Miss Columbia offering her congratulations to a figure representing American womanhood. *Life* was relaunched as a newsmagazine by Henry Luce in 1936. Later editors, though, were still so proud of the classic Gibson illustration that they reprinted it in 1970 in celebration of the fiftieth anniversary of the passage of woman's franchise.

There were a number of other pro-suffrage covers on American popular magazines from 1910 on, several done by famous illustrators of the period such as James Montgomery Flagg and Joseph Christian Leyendecker. Flagg, in addition to the covers previously noted, also drew one for the *Collier's* issue of November 4, 1916, portraying a woman clutching a large, official ballot in front of a glass ballot box. Leyendecker's contribution was for the December 30, 1911, *Saturday Evening Post,* where the baby for the new year is seen clutching a "Votes for Women" sign. B. Gary Kilvert created a cover for *Everybody's* special suffrage issue of July 1915 of a young girl lighting a "Votes for Women" firecracker that the magazine described as "chucklesome" in its advertisements.

By 1915, virtually every popular magazine in America that either had a special suffrage number or illustrated the issue on its cover took a decidedly positive stance in its editorial comments. To a degree, they were in all probability aware of the inevitability of passage of the

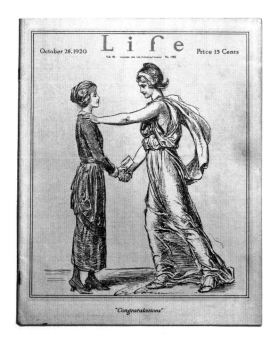

Life's famous cover celebrating the passage of the suffrage amendment.

amendment and wished to take the side of the angels. But they may have also been influenced by a publishing event that took place on November 1, 1910, with the appearance of Richard Barry's article "What Women Have Actually Done Where They Vote" in *The Ladies' Home Journal.* The journal's editor, the Dutch-born Edward Bok, had sent Barry out to visit the four states where women were then allowed to vote, Colorado, Idaho, Utah, and Wyoming, to determine the franchise's impact on society.

Unfortunately the venture, as far as suffragists were concerned, was doomed from the start. Barry had previously written several articles for *Pearson's Magazine* that had been perceived to be critical to the cause. Moreover, Bok, a publishing genius who considered himself a progressive on most social issues,[5] took a paternalistic attitude towards suffrage. In an interview with *The New York Times* he had declared that "women as a whole do not seem interested" in the subject and that many suffragists emerged from a "dangerous type of woman who, misunderstanding the modern current of thought, has believed that her work in the world lay outside of the home, or who for some reason or other has developed a positive aversion to motherhood."[6] Barry's re-

sultant article was negative about suffrage and was soon reprinted and distributed by anti-suffrage organizations in New York, Massachusetts, and elsewhere.[7] NAWSA quickly responded with a pamphlet of its own, "The Truth Versus Richard Barry,"[8] and the pages of the *Woman's Journal* were quick to denounce both Barry and Bok.

The resultant controversy did not seem to have affected sales figures for the *Ladies' Home Journal,* which was the first American magazine to reach a circulation of 1,000,000. By 1920, the year of the passage of the Federal Suffrage Amendment, that figure had escalated to 2,000,000. But the editors and business managers of other magazines of the period, along with their advertisers, undoubtedly realized the number of potential female subscribers and that they risked alienating them at their own peril. Moreover, a magazine with a graphically illustrated and colorful pro-suffrage cover was often saved and provided in itself a compelling advertisement for future issues.

In addition to their appearance in popular magazines, illustrative covers about the theme of suffrage were also an essential feature of suffrage publications themselves. Beginning around 1907, the cartoon, generally editorial in nature, became a weekly staple on the front page of many of the more prominent suffrage papers, such as the *Woman's Journal* and *The Suffragist* in America and *Votes for Women* and *The Suffragette* in England. While these cartoons could comment on a variety of topics, Elisabeth Israels Perry sees them as employing two basic approaches: (1) to present the franchise as a way of ending women's oppression; and, the more common argument, (2) to point out that civilization had lost ground by denying women the full rights of citizenship.[9] The works of selected movement artists such as Nina E. Allender, Annie "Lou" Rogers, Ida Sedgwick Proper, Katherine Milhaus, Blanche Ames, Marietta Andrews, C.D. Batchelor, Harriet Park (daughter of activist Alice Park of California), Frederikke Palmer, and Alfred Pearse, who signed himself "A. Patriot," appeared most often in suffrage journals, along with the efforts of many others.

The editors of suffrage journals were fascinated by cartoons. They often reprinted illustrations that appeared in other suffrage periodicals and on newspapers, postcards, and posters. The *Woman's Journal* on more than one occasion would announce the publication of what it felt to be an interesting cartoon from another source, describing it with the same excitement that it would when it heard about an especially intriguing new postcard, button, or Cinderella stamp. It recommended that activists seek out cartoons not only from the *Journal* itself but also from other publications in their attempt to publicize the movement. In 1911, the Woman's Press held a special exhibition at its offices on Charing Cross Road in London of all the original drawings that had appeared in *Votes for Women* over the past two years. *Votes for Women* for several years republished in December the entirety of the drawings that had graced its front pages that year.

Millinery and Accessories

Costumes or uniform modes of dress were a standard feature of most large-scale and even some smaller parades and demonstrations. Often the style consisted of white apparel covered with a sash or other accessories in the official colors of the sponsoring organization, generally yellow for NAWSA and its affiliates and purple, green, and white for the WSPU in England. It is not known how many of these white dresses were commercially produced and how many were the products of individual dressmakers and parade participants. In any event, while "parade regalia" such as ribbons, sashes, and trimmings for apparel were often advertised in suffrage catalogs and newspaper advertisements, the basic demonstration dress, with some exceptions, was not. In England, where WSPU supporters were asked to "wear the colors," many dressmakers trimmed their products in purple, white, and green for everyday wear, often advertising the fact that they were able to add the colors to parts of a customer's existing wardrobe. In America, where the official yellow of NAWSA was not nearly as distinctive as the English scheme, such trimming would not have attracted quite the public notice, and suffrage dresses, apart from those that were put together by suffragists to be worn in parades and demonstrations, are virtually unknown.

American women did not have a distinctive suffrage dress for their everyday wear. Still, even in America, suffrage fashion accessories such as hats, gloves, and purses, if not dresses, were produced, advertised, and sold by the major suffrage organizations.

In the May 13, 1916, issue of *The Suffragist*, a large ad announced that the Congressional Union (CU) had recognized a hat produced by Gage and Brothers of Chicago as "The Official Hat of the Woman's Party." Known as "Liberty Gage," it was priced at five dollars and was to be sold by "the leading retailers all over the country."[1] In a follow-up story the next week, *The Suffragist* pictured Mrs. J.A.H. Hopkins, chair of the New Jersey Congressional Union, wearing the hat, and provided more details, indicating that it was designed for the delegates of the upcoming Woman's Party Convention to be held in Chicago that June. It was a straw sailor hat trimmed on the left side of the brim with a ribbon in the purple, white, and gold colors of the party. The CU was to receive a royalty from the sale of each hat, provided that purchasers filled out a detachable slip and sent it to the NWP. The hat had earlier figured in the demonstration at the Capitol steps in Washington, D.C., when the envoys from the Salt Lake City Conference presented a resolution of that conference to both the House and Senate. The article emphasized, however, that this was not to be considered a parade hat, but one that women could wear year-round on all occasions, a concept that represented a departure for most American women's suffrage wearing apparel.[2] Gage took out a full-page advertisement for the hat in the June 3 *Suffragist*, just in time for the Woman's Party Convention, which included a drawing of a smartly dressed woman wearing both the hat and a Woman's Party sash.[3] Florence Harmon of Alva Belmont's Political Equality Association made up a parade hat for a May 4, 1912, demonstration that sold for seventy-five cents. It featured trim in the Association's color of dark blue along with a large bow in front. However, the suffrage aspect of the generic hat appears to have been entirely handmade.[4]

NAWSA did not have an official hat, but they did sell "Votes for Women" glove purses at ten cents each. Quantity discounts were available from the retail store at national headquarters. Each purse came with a six-star "Votes for Women" button attached.[5] In England, one of the first advertisements in the WSPU paper *Votes for Women* was for leather tricolor purses and wrist bags in purple, green, and white.[6]

Special suffrage editions of *The Detroit Times* and *The Chicago Examiner* contained suffrage-related clothing ads that were probably reflective of similar ads placed in the many suffrage numbers of popular newspapers throughout the country. Fashion manufacturers and clothing outlets had much to lose if the franchise movement caused women to turn away from traditional concerns with dress, so rather than fight the emerging political tide, they chose to incorporate themselves within it. But generally the suffrage clothing products they offered had nothing particularly suffrage about them except for the product's name or the manner in which they were promoted, not even an inclusion of official suffrage colors in their design. Huetter's Shoes for Women of Michigan called one of their products "The Suffragist" because "it is most popular among the Suffragists in Detroit today." At the same time, Crowley-Milner promoted its June white sale by proclaiming, "It must be said that suffragists are progressive — and all progressive women will be interested" in the sale at its store.[7] Crowley-Milner was simply following a trend. As the suffrage movement was becoming more and more popular, ads for fashions that appeared in suffrage-related papers were addressed to suffragists but, likewise, were not necessarily suffrage specific. D.B. Fisk proclaimed, "Women are Voting their approval of Fisk Hats and Fisk Millinery the Country over." The Sahlin Company exclaimed, "At the Polls — not all the well-dressed women you see at the polls wear Madame Moraine corsets, but all those who do are well-dressed."[8] One could fight for political equality, but one still had to be well dressed in the process!

The Illustrated Milliner featured in its pictorial supplements for its September and October 1915 issues sixteen prominent and professional suffragist women arrayed in the latest fashions, indicating that all of them were "very interested in beautiful millinery." Rose O'Neill drew a special Kewpie cartoon for the *Hats from*

Paris & New York supplement, and the hat that she selected to be photographed in was designed by an artist friend of hers, Edna Hume. Ida Proper, chair of the Art Committee of the Woman's Suffrage Campaign, wore "a smart sailor of cameo pink beaver." Also wearing a sailor hat was Alice Morgan Wright, "Chairman of the Professional Group in the committee of the Suffrage Parade."[9] Activist suffragist social leaders who were sketched and photographed in the September issue included Mrs. Alva Belmont, founder of the Political Equality League in New York, Mrs. James Laidlaw, Suffrage Borough President of Manhattan, and Mrs. Norman de R. Whitehouse, who was to become chair of the New York State Woman Suffrage Party in 1916.[10] Again, however, there was nothing distinguishably "suffrage" about the hats these women were photographed wearing.

In England, the situation was slightly different because of the identifiable nature of the official colors of purple, white, and green. While the WSPU itself did produce a small amount of clothing,[11] the union generally left it up to private enterprise to supply women with symbolic suffrage apparel. And while some milliners and dressmakers fashioned items whose design and colors indicated that they were directly intended for the suffrage market, other manufacturers, as was the case with many of their counterparts in America, simply attempted to sell their clothes to suffragists by implying that they were in solidarity with their aims. Two ads in the May 26, 1911, issue of *Votes for Women* show both strategies. In advertising clothes for "The Procession" and "Great Demonstration" scheduled to take place on June 17, both Peter Robinson and William Owen illustrate fashions that could be worn at the demonstration but had no specific WSPU tie-in. However, Annette Jacobs and Caprina Fahey of New Street announced that "they wish to draw attention to the members of the WSPU to the fact that they are making a specialité of Procession Hats and Toques in the Colours of the union."[12] Beatrice, an "expert French fitter from Dover Street," made Quaker Girl Bonnets in "colors of all the Suffrage Societies"; and Clara Strong fashioned hats in WSPU purple, white and green for the same event.[13] A year earlier, Roberta Mills of Brixton sold "Emmeline and Christabel Leather Shopping Bags," proclaiming "Nothing like leather for Suffragettes Wear."[14]

Votes for Women showed an especial editorial interest in the topic of everyday women's dress, both suffrage and non–suffrage related, and ran several articles on the subject with such titles as "Concerning Dress," "Suffragettes and the Dress Problem," "Dress in the Colours," and "Some Hints About Dress." In 1908, the periodical considered the "full dress uniform" to consist of "the white frock with regalia and colours," letting women know that the color of the dress was very important; therefore, it was essential "that we have at least one white frock in our winter wardrobe." The editors also pointed out, with apparent pride, that women's shops throughout Bond Street featured items in the colors for fall and winter fashions. It was common in these articles about dress to promote the efforts of such dressmakers and merchants as Mrs. Oliver of Bond Street, Elspeth Phelps of Molton Street, Charles Lee and Son, who had showrooms on Wigmore Street, Madame Rebecca Gordon of Belgrave Road, and Thelma, of Southampton Row, providing not only detailed descriptions of their suffrage-related millinery and dress but also prices. It was probably not coincidental that these same dressmakers also advertised heavily in *Votes for Women*, and Mrs. Oliver was singled out especially for being "one of the best friends of the movement." In asking its readers to patronize these establishments, the editors emphasized that by dressing in the colors, they "will help to make it understood that women are standing together and supporting one another in the great fight in which we are engaged."[15] Krista Lysack points out also that the WSPU was especially sensitive to the image of the suffragist as "frump" that appeared in *Punch* and other satirical journals of the time. In attempting to manage what they felt to be a "crisis in public perception," they included these columns dealing with fashionable dress in several issues of *Votes for Women*. The Women's Franchise League (WFL), the breakaway group from the WSPU, also carried fashion columns in its paper, *The Vote*. The journal of the National Union of Women's Suffrage Societies (NUWSS), *The Common Cause*, included shopping directories,

but the NUWSS decided against fashion columns because they were "frivolous." [16]

In addition to those merchants who received special treatment in *Votes for Women*, two anonymous "suffragettes" advertised that they made, trimmed, and renovated hats "in the colours of the union" at special, "moderate prices." Their advertisement responded to a WSPU concern that, while women should dress up in purple, green, and white to promote the cause, many supporters lacked sufficient funds to buy new wardrobes or add extravagant items to their present dress.[17] One shoe company, Holden Brothers of London, while not specifically advertising a suffrage product, did publish a purported endorsement from 1892 by Emmeline Pankhurst for their Natureform shoe, which she had purchased for "my two little girls," Christabel and Sylvia.[18]

Anti-suffrage forces did not emphasize costume to the degree that pro-suffrage forces did, and there is scant mention in period newspapers of any type of clothing produced for their cause. For an afternoon tea dance at the Hotel Gramatan in Bronxville, New York, the anti-forces, however, did sell an anti-suffrage summer hat in the color of white with pink roses drooping over the brim. The pink rose was the anti-suffrage emblem.[19]

What ultimately emerges from all of this was that suffrage dress fell into two different areas. The first was a parade "uniform," which generally consisted of a white dress, handmade or purchased, that could be trimmed with the colors of the group sponsoring the demonstration. The second was suffrage-related apparel designed for everyday wear. In America, such apparel, apart from a few pieces, generally was suffrage in name only, there being nothing readily identifiable at least in terms of color to suggest that a dress or any other article of clothing was linked somehow to the suffrage movement, despite a dressmaker's advertising it as such. In England, a woman could show her support for the WSPU by wearing dresses trimmed in purple, white, and green, but not every British suffragist was comfortable with the militancy of the union, and, while all the major organizations did have their own colors, most were not distinctive enough to suggest "suffrage" to the general public when applied to everyday wearing apparel.

Miniature Bissell Carpet Sweepers

What may have been the first woman suffrage convention favor was a miniature Bissell carpet sweeper that was given out to all 150 delegates at the 1899 NAWSA gathering by the factory president, Mrs. M.R. Bissell. Each was marked in gilt "National American Woman Suffrage Association." There were other souvenirs distributed at the convention, but this was the only one with a distinctive suffrage tie-in.[1] The Bissell Company later imprinted an ad on a pleated suffrage fan that was distributed by the Michigan campaign.[2]

Paper Bags

The suffragists of Brooklyn distributed 30,000 white bags, the size of which was suitable to hold a pound of coffee or flour. They cost little more than a flyer, and were given out to grocers who expressed a willingness to use them. On the bags were printed: "Woman Suffrage Party — WANTED: Every woman in Brooklyn to join the Woman Suffrage Party, and help us get votes for women. We want to elect wise and honest officials, who will give us lower taxes, less rent, a clean and happy city, and full time in school for every child. Get a postcard, write on it 'I believe in Woman Suffrage,' sign your name and address and mail it to Mrs. Robert H. Elder, 80 Willow St., Brooklyn. You will then be invited to our next meeting in your district. No money dues."[1] While it is probable that other organizations also printed up their own version of the Brooklyn bag, reference to them in suffrage periodicals is virtually nonexistent.

Paper Napkins

Several varieties of paper napkins with a suffrage motif were available. Perhaps the one most widely circulated was that issued by NAWSA in 1911, which was printed with a "Votes for Women" border in blue and sold for thirty-

One of two different napkins that Mrs. Burgess designed for the June 17, 1911, coronation demonstration, this one in the Women's Social and Political Union colors.

five cents per hundred.[1] Mary Ware Dennet, the recording secretary for the *Woman's Journal*, felt compelled to offer a profuse apology to the periodical's readers when the manufacturer of the napkins failed to deliver them on time. According to Ware, who contacted the manufacturer, "They blandly answer that special rollers are required, and after the manner of our Congressmen, assure us that the matter will be given their 'most careful consideration.'"[2] In New Jersey, at a meeting of the Civic Club of Arington, Eric Laddey, the son of the hostess, provided "white Japanese napkins bearing the strange device 'Votes for Women,' in gilt."[3]

The most spectacular napkins, however, were the souvenir issues of Mrs. S. Burgess of London, who created items for various historical and period events. One of her first suffrage napkins was printed for the 1908 Hyde Park demonstration. Labeled as the "Official Program of the Great Demonstration," it featured engravings of the WSPU leaders, a list of the major events, and a border of violets in purple, green, and white. She used essentially the same design for her efforts for the June 29, 1909, march to the House of Commons, during which the suffragists smashed Whitehall office windows after Prime Minister Asquith refused to see them, and for the June 17, 1911, Suffrage Coronation Demonstration. Burgess also produced souvenir napkins for Emily Wilding Davison's internment in Morpeth on June 14, 1913, and for the June 13, 1908, National Union of Women's Suffrage Societies' procession, when 13,000 people marched from the Embankment to attend a rally at Albert Hall. The WSPU had mixed feelings about her efforts. Disturbed by her producing an "unauthorized 'official programme'" for the June 29 event, they nevertheless pointed it out as an example of "how the movement interests the public."[4] Mrs. Burgess' products demonstrated quite clearly how important the concept of a suffrage "souvenir" or collectible had become to suffrage sympathizers, who wanted to retain a tangible memory of a major event that they might have participated in.

Pencils

There were numerous wooden lead pencils both given out and sold by various suffrage organizations during the campaign. A few bear the name of their issuing organization, such as the Women's Political Union of New Jersey, but most simply were imprinted with "Votes for Women" in various styles. Pencils proved to be an especially popular novelty because they were both useful and cheap to produce. NAWSA, through one of its New York affiliates, sold them for five cents each.[1]

At least one manufacturer, Burton S. Osborne of Camden, New York, who may or may not have had connections to the movement, advertised suffrage pencils and pen holders beginning in 1913 in the *Woman's Journal*. Recognizing the profit potential for activists, he directed his appeal to suffrage organizations, suggesting that they hold a "Pencil Day Sale" in their city and "gather in the cash and a lot of it." He assured readers that he had just shipped 20,000 pencils to one suffrage organization for a sale in September.[2] The idea of a special "Pencil Day" appears to have caught on with the Woman Suffrage Society of the County of Philadelphia. Led by their president, Mrs. J.D. Thomas, twenty-five members of the group hawked pencils in the downtown streets of the city in February 1914. They reportedly sold 10,000 of the product, and, after

expenses, cleared $5,000. They received five cents or more for each pencil, and, if permitted, tagged the purchaser with a little yellow tag bearing the words "Thank you. V for W Pencil Day."[3] Given the Society's final sales figures, either they wee exaggerated or a number of purchasers must have offered considerably more than the asking price to obtain one.

The Woman Suffrage Party (WSP) of New York also took an especially active role in the distribution and sale of pencils. In late June 1916, they were one of "many useful trinkets" that included calendars and drinking cups with the suffrage map on them that the WSP gave to soldiers departing for Mexico.[4] If reports in *The New York Times* for the period are to be believed, however, and the paper did, at times, reflect an anti-suffrage bias, the WSP was not above using the sex appeal of some of its volunteers to sell these pencils to men. During Vaudeville Week at the Victoria Theater in New York in September 1912, the WSP prepared "the prettiest of young girls with golden hair that is almost a suffrage color" to march down from the stage to hawk pencils and other suffrage articles.[5] In July 1913, an outraged R.A. Lawrence wrote a letter to the paper complaining of the "strange method of raising funds now being practiced by the suffragists." He related the story of a commuter he knew who, possessing anti-suffrage sentiments, nevertheless purchased one of these "Votes for Women" pencils. When he asked his friend why he was supporting financially a cause that he did not believe in, the friend responded, "What are you going to do when a pretty girl comes up to you in the street and asks you to buy one?" Lawrence himself bought a pencil from "a pretty girl of good class" on Broadway in New York, but admonished her in the process: "It seemed a shame if there was no better way to raise funds than placing pretty girls at such work."[6] Whether or not the WSP specifically chose attractive "girls" to sell some of their products is a question of perception. From the complaints of some men, it appears that they were disconcerted more by the assertiveness of women who were moving away from a socially expected passiveness to support the cause than by their looks.

While most suffragist organizations distributed pencils rather than pens because they were cheaper to produce, a few of the latter are known. The Woman Suffrage Party of New York put out a dip pen with a nib inserted into a black-on-yellow plastic holder, also issued in wood, that was imprinted with the phrase "Votes for Women" and the party's address at 48 East 34th Street in New York. In England, the Lewis Pen Company offered a "Lewis Pen" with a 14-carat gold nib for three shilling and six pence post free to members of the WSPU or "a friend of one." There were no special markings on the pen, however, to indicate that it was a suffrage pen or distinguished in any way from products that the company sold to the general public.[7] When the Pethick Lawrences, editors of *Votes for Women*, were expelled from the WSPU, they formed the Votes for Women Fellowship and contracted with "one of the largest fountain pen manufacturing firms" in England to produce a special suffrage pen. This particular pen, which sold for five shillings and nine pence, did have "Votes for Women" inscribed on the barrel. The anonymous pen company, which had agreed to donate a "substantial portion of the profits"[8] to the cause, may or may not have been the Lewis Company, which previously had entered into an arrangement with the WSPU.

Pennants

It is not clear when the first pennant was issued in America to support a political candidate. Herbert Ridgeway Collins and Theodore L. Hake in their respective studies do not record any political pennants prior to the 1908 presidential race between William Howard Taft and William Jennings Bryan. Edmund Sullivan, however, speculates that pennants were probably first used during the 1896–1904 campaign period. A piece that features a color portrait of Theodore Roosevelt's head along with the words "Our Next President" is known and probably from 1904, when he ran under the Republican Party banner, and not from 1912, when he campaigned as the Bull Moose candidate.[1] Whatever the case, most suffrage pennants appear roughly about the same time as their presidential candidate counterparts, during the period from 1908 to 1917 when movement parades and marches came into fashion. Their variety and abundance

suggest that suffrage pennants were not so much an outgrowth of the tradition of the political campaign pennant but rather a parallel development.

Suffrage pennants were generally made of felt, but varieties in wool, linen, gauze, and even paper are known. Most simply consisted of printed or felt lettering over a color background, which was generally yellow, but a few contained spectacular multicolor images and were probably intended as much for display as they were for carrying in parades. Pennants were advertised in suffrage papers, movement literature, and price lists, but these ads generally gave few specifics in terms of designs and colors. The Congressional Union grouped its offerings generically with buttons and regalia.[2] After the 1911 California campaign, the New Woman Publishing Company sold "Votes for Women" pennants as "souvenirs" of that struggle that could "also be useful for general suffrage work in other states."[3] NAWSA sold a variety of nondescript banners through its headquarters in New York, including a yellow felt version that measured 8" × 18" with the "Votes for Women" slogan printed in black and priced at fifteen cents apiece, a larger 12" × 30" copy with the lettering stitched instead of printed for fifty cents, and a yellow cambric item, again for fifteen cents.[4] NAWSA also listed quantity prices for each of the above, indicating that sales were intended for organizational events as well as for individual needs.

In her account of the California campaign, Selina Solomons noted: "We had pennants likewise to suit all tastes, from the hand-some handmade ones in black felt letters" that were designed for home and office and sold for seventy-five cents each to commercially produced yellow felt varieties that sold for only thirty-five cents, and cambric items for automobiles that cost five cents. "When carried 'accidentally' through the streets from one headquarters to the other, or for some other ostensible reason, those pretty pennants and bannerettes attracted just the right kind and amount of attention." For a mass meeting, Mrs. Mary T. Gamage carried a large silk pennant through the entire length of Fillmore Street.[5]

Unlike buttons, the majority of pennants do not list either the names of the organizations that put them out or the specific events that they were intended for. Some exceptions to this practice were pennants produced by the Woman Suffrage Party (WSP) of New York and by Harriot Stanton Blatch's Women's Political Union (WPU). Simple varieties of the former consisted of the party's encircled initials, "WSP," in a stylized format along with the words "Votes for Women." More elaborate pennants included an image of Ella Buchanan's 1911 statuette "The Suffragist Arousing Her Sisters," which portrayed the suffragist blowing her clarion over the female figures of Degradation, Vanity, Conventionality, and Wage Earner. A variety of this pennant exists with a purple rather than yellow background, unusual in the fact that Carrie Chapman Catt generally attempted to dissociate the WSP from many of the more militant acts of the WPU and Alice Paul's National Woman's Party (NWP), both of which employed purple as one of their official colors. The NWP was perhaps also responsible for a pennant that featured a full-color image of an allegorical figure holding up a sign urging "Equal Rights," although no party name is attached to the item. This design appears on pennants with both purple and yellow backgrounds. The Women's Political Union distributed several varieties of pennants with the Clarion figure of a woman blowing a trumpet that they also featured on their buttons and stationery. A 7.5" × 17" black-on-yellow pennant with the words "Votes for New Jersey Women" was probably issued by the New Jersey Woman's Suffrage Association as these were their colors.[6]

There were other examples of pennants that demonstrated some distinctive quality that set them apart from the traditional black-on-yellow design. For a parade in New York on May 4, 1912, Mrs. Alva Belmont's Political Equality As-

sociation carried blue pennants with six stars and the words "Votes for Women" emblazoned upon them.[7] This is the only known pennant attributed to her organization. For the suffrage demonstration in Washington, D.C., in March 1913 that preceded Woodrow Wilson's inauguration, a pennant was made with white lettering and design on gauze. Along with the words "Votes for Women," it contained images of a sunburst behind the Capitol dome, an eagle, and the date and place of the event. At the Alaska-Yukon-Pacific Exposition in Washington in 1909, where suffragists were particularly active, pennants and banners were part of elaborate displays. On the special Suffrage Day, a dirigible balloon, a feature of the exposition, carried a large silken banner inscribed with the words "Votes for Women." Later a pennant with this motto was carried by a member of the Mountainers' Club to the summit of Mount Rainier, near Tacoma. It was fastened to the staff of the larger "A.Y.P." pennant of the exposition, and the staff was planted in the snows of Columbia Crest.[8]

One of the more creative displays of a pennant occurred at the state fair in Huron, South Dakota, in 1914. Native American women from the reservation did their native dance while waving suffrage banners. A snake charmer on the midway carried a "Votes for Women" pennant while a large serpent was curled around her body.[9] At an agricultural fair in Rochester, New Hampshire, in 1911, suffragists distributed 10,000 leaflets and sold "hundreds of buttons and pennants."[10]

Sashes rather than pennants are more typically associated with the huge suffrage parades and rallies that were in evidence in the period just prior to the passage of the national suffrage amendment. However, more pennants than sashes appear to have survived the period, an indication of their popularity among suffragists at these campaign events.

Carrie Chapman Catt's Woman Suffrage Party came to rely more and more on display items as the campaign went on.

Pennsylvania Liberty Bell Campaign

At the 46th annual convention of the Pennsylvania Woman Suffrage Association, which was held in Scranton November 19–24, 1914, suffragists enthusiastically engaged in planning for the upcoming 1915 campaign, which was part of a drive in four eastern states that year to achieve full ballot rights. There were strong indications that the next legislature would approve a constitutional amendment subject to voter ratification giving women the right to vote. As part of the publicity for that campaign, Katharine Wentworth Ruschenberger of Strafford announced that she planned to have a replica cast of the Liberty Bell, to be known as the "Woman's Liberty Bell." This bell, also referred to as "the Justice Bell," was one of the few examples of visual rhetoric approved by the publicity department of the convention, which, in general, wished to avoid "sensationalism."[1] The only change in the replica from the original Liberty Bell, "which announced the freedom of the men," was an addition to the inscription to include the phrase "establish justice."[2] The intent was to bind the bronze clapper of the proposed bell to keep it silent until November 2, the day that suffragists hoped the voters of the state would pass the suffrage amendment "to complete our nation."[3]

The actual casting of the bell, which took place at the Meneely Bell Works of Troy, New York, on March 31, was preceded by much ceremony. A delegation of Pennsylvania suffragists, led by Ruschenberger and Jennie Bradley Roessing, president of the Pennsylvania Woman Suffrage Association, was met at the train station in New York the day before by representatives of the Woman Suffrage Party in "gaily decorated automobiles," who took them to party headquarters for a luncheon. Once there, Ruschenberger told the assembled crowd that just as the "original Liberty Bell announced the creation of democracy, the Women's Liberty Bell will announce the completion of democracy."[4] The delegation then left for Grand Central Station, accompanied by Carrie Chapman Catt, who addressed a mass meeting in Troy later that evening.[5] The ceremonies for casting the "New Liberty Bell," a ticketed event, took place at the Meneely Street Foundry on River Street in Troy at 10 A.M. the next day. Catt was once again

the main speaker.[6] The event included a street parade of suffragists, the placement of a chain of white daisies by six little girls around the mold, and the pulling of a lever by Ruschenberger, which released the hot metal for casting.[7]

Once brought back to Pennsylvania, the bell was recognized as "the best and main publicity feature" of the Pennsylvania association's 1915 efforts. Carried on a specially reinforced truck that criss-crossed all of the sixty-seven counties of the state, the bell traveled a total of 3,935 miles before the end of the campaign on November 2. Hundreds of suffragists used the truck as a platform on which they addressed rural audiences, who received the bell "with almost as much reverence and ceremony as would have been accorded the original bell." A "Woman's Liberty Bell" leaflet was passed out to the crowd by participating suffragists, who also sold novelties in the likeness of the bell to defray the heavy expenses of operating the truck, paying speakers, and providing literature.[8]

Despite an energetic campaign on its behalf, however, the Pennsylvania suffrage amendment went down to defeat on Election Day. Ruschenberger had originally assumed victory and hoped that "the bell [could be] ... taken to Washington and hung in a campanile so beautiful that all the world will come to see it."[9] But the bell was not given a permanent home at that time; instead it was used for other campaigns throughout the country, most notably the "famous rainy day suffrage parade" on June 7, 1916,

Ticket to ceremonies of the casting of the Suffrage Liberty Bell in Troy, New York.

in Chicago when the Republican National Convention was in session.[10] The bell's clapper was finally unchained at a ceremony in held in Independence Square in Philadelphia in September 1920 after the 19th Amendment had been ratified the previous August. It now does have a permanent home, not in Washington, D.C., as Ruschenberger had planned, but in the Tower Room of the Washington Memorial National Bell Tower at the Washington Memorial Chapel in Valley Forge, Pennsylvania.

Among the various memorabilia that survive the Liberty Bell Campaign are:

(1) a 1½" × 4¾" gold-on-yellow silk delegate ribbon for the 1914 convention of the Pennsylvania Woman Suffrage Association, where the proposal for the bell was first made

(2) a 2½" × 4" admission ticket to the ceremonies surrounding the casting of the bell at the Meneely Foundry

(3) a souvenir replica bell, which was sold during the campaign to defray expenses. This bell was actually in the form of a watch fob with an attached strap. On the back of the fob are the words "Woman's Liberty Bell — Justice — Equality 1915 Pennsylvania."

(4) a black-on-yellow blotter that pictured the Liberty Bell, accompanied by the words, "Women Being Called Upon to Obey the Laws Should Have a Voice in Making Them"

(5) a colorful 1¼" celluloid pin picturing the Liberty Bell along with the words "Liberty Justice 1776–1915." Hanging from this pin are a small American flag and a black-on-yellow ribbon with the words "Votes for Women"

(6) a ⅞" blue-and-white button with four stars and the phrase "Justice and Equality." Blue is one of the official colors of the state of Pennsylvania, and the combination of blue and white was used on at least three other pins authorized by state suffragists.

(7) the aforementioned "Woman's Liberty Bell" flier that was distributed by suffragists travelling with the bell[11]

(8) a number of real photo postcards [see **Postcards**] that depict the bell at various rallies in Pennsylvania along with its truck and the speakers who accompanied it.

Pillow Tops

Fay Aldrich of Lowell, Massachusetts advertised for sale an embroidered pillow top, made of Irish linen, size 18" × 18" and stamped "Votes for Women," for a dollar. For five dollars, she would embroider the entire pillow. Because her ad appeared in the *Woman's Journal*, most, if not all profits from sales likely went to support the cause.[1]

Playing Cards and Card Games

"Votes for Women" playing cards were especially popular among suffrage supporters, and at least three organizations issued decks on the

The Liberty Bell watch fob was probably the most common all of souvenirs from this campaign.

Left: Based on the number of extant copies, these cards were extremely popular with Women's Social and Political Union supporters; **right**: the conservative National American Woman Suffrage Association for some reason printed a version of this deck in purple, a color associated more with the militancy of Alice Paul.

figure of Justice holding her scales that was first used by suffragists in America as a seal for NAWSA's 1911 convention in Louisville and also as an emblem for the International Woman Suffrage Alliance. Although the faces of the cards themselves were primarily traditional, both the joker and the ace of spades contained suffrage designs. The Association of NAWSA with an item that conceivably could be used for gambling may have come as a surprise to some supporters who were aware of the group's policy against games of chance at suffrage fairs.[2]

theme in various designs and colors. These cards, along with various other card games designed and sold by activists, served a role as a way of introducing the suffrage issue into the household in a nonconfrontational and, perhaps, more socially accepted manner than street rallies and mass meetings.

In England, Emmeline Pankhurst's WSPU was responsible for a conventional deck, published by DeLarue and Company, whose face cards were indistinguishable from those of a typical pack. The back of each card, however, reflected its true intent by carrying the slogan "Votes for Women" surrounded by prison arrows, all printed in the group's traditional colors of purple, green, and white.

In America both the National American Woman Suffrage Association and Harriot Stanton Blatch's Women's Political Union (WPU) issued decks. NAWSA's version, printed by the National Woman Suffrage Publishing Company, its publishing arm, came in two distinct colors, yellow and purple, although a blue variation is known.[1] The back of each card contained the slogan "Votes for Women" encased in a ribbon design above and below the symbol of an allegorical

When one male supporter stopped by the Woman Suffrage Party's (WSP) Manhattan headquarters at 48 East 34th Street prior to his lecture tour, he spied "a box of playing cards" for twenty-five cents that had NAWSA's Justice design. Someone in the crowd urged the suffragists to give him one of "those poker decks," but one of the suffragists responded, perhaps half humorously, "Oh no, there must be no immoral influences."[3]

In July of 1913, the *Woman's Journal* nevertheless attempted to promote sales of these cards by referring to a note from Mrs. Raymond Brown, who found them to be "the easiest kind of suffrage goods to sell." She advised that "if every suffragist would put a box or two in her trunk," when she goes away for the summer, "and not only sell them herself, but try to place them on sale at the various hotels and shops, she would make money for the cause and do valuable propaganda work at the same time."[4]

The most common suffrage cards were the decks issued by the Women's Political Union, and they came with either a green or yellow back. The design on both featured conjoining V's with the traditional "Votes for Women" slogan repeated four times. There are slight variations in shading and size to some of these decks, indicating that they were so popular several editions had to be published. As was the case in the WSP's version, the faces of the cards were conventional, except for the joker and the ace of spades. The joker contained the Clarion design that the WPU had adapted from the National Union of Women's Suffrage Societies (NUWSS) for use on its buttons and stationery. In some decks, but not all, this Clarion figure was printed in the WPU's official colors of purple, green, and white. A contemporary newspaper account notes that among various suffrage trinkets of the day, they were the "best sellers." Women used them primarily to play bridge with and often presented each of their guests a deck to take home.[5]

In addition to playing cards, several card games were sold, although not always with official authorization and not always pro-suffrage. In England, the most popular game was that of "Panko," whose name was an allusion to the efforts of Mrs. Pankhurst. It was manufac-

tured by Peter Gurney of the Breams Buildings in London, although it was distributed in part by the WSPU as well as by a number of stationers throughout the country. It contained forty-eight cards divided into six different categories and featured cartoons by E.T. Reed of *Punch* magazine. It was first advertised in the December 3, 1909, edition of the WSPU's *Votes for Women*. The manufacturer gushed, "[The pictures] form a portrait gallery of the leading figures in the movement. Not only is each picture in itself an interesting memento, but the game produces intense excitement without the slightest taste of bitterness. Are your friends interested in the cause? If so there is no better way to please them than to buy a pack of 'PANKO.'"[6]

Panko had been preceded by another card game in November of 1908 called "Holloway, or Votes for Women," which Elizabeth Crawford characterizes as "a slightly more complicated version of 'Panko.'"[7] She also calls attention to another card game, "Suffragette," which was created by the Kensington Branch of the WSPU,

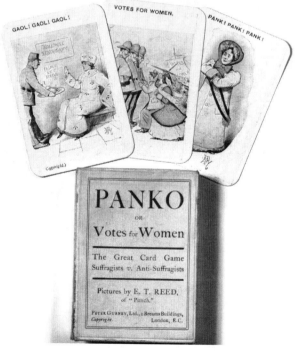

Left: There are a number of small design variants to this National Woman's Party deck, indicating its wide popularity; *right*: Panko was extensively advertised by the Women's Social and Political Union and sold both by them and by private merchants as well.

probably in the summer of 1907 and first described in *Votes for Women* in November 1907.[8] This game featured photographs and questions about prominent suffragists and came in a purple box.[9] One other English card game, which went through several editions, was called "Snap" and had a mildly anti-suffrage flavor. The object was to pair up sets of cards of various scenes of contemporary life. The suffragette card pictured a woman smashing a mirror with a hammer while shouting "I want a vote."

Apart from various sets of the standard playing card deck, American activists also produced a few pro-suffrage card games. Anna Cadogan Etz developed a "Votes for Women" card game for the New York State Woman Suffrage Association to be used both as a fundraiser and as a method to obtain converts to the cause. It sold for thirty-five cents. The object of the game, as in "Authors," was to arrange cards in groups called "Doubling the Vote," "Woman Suffrage and the Home," "Two Cardinals," and so on. Each card in the group bore a question about suffrage and provided the answer.[10] W.M. Ford copyrighted a set of "Progressive Chautauqua Cards" in 1897 that featured among its 140 portraits and character sketches such celebrities as Elizabeth Cady Stanton, Lucretia Mott, Julia Ward Howe, Lucy Stone, and Mary Livermore. The Chautauqua schools were part of an adult education movement that began in New York State in the mid 1870s and spread to the rest of the country before essentially dying out in the late 1920s. Although for the most part apolitical in nature, they were utilized by the suffragists to educate women and, perhaps, some men about the movement. The purpose of Ford's game was essentially pedagogical but with a progressive focus.

Mrs. Charles Fremont Pond, a suffrage activist and wife of Rear Admiral Pond of the Atlantic squadron, originated a card game called "Constitution," which, though it focused on elections and the electoral vote for each state, had a decided suffrage message. Cards of states where women were allowed to vote counted for double their electoral vote. Pond anxiously awaited the outcome of the ballot initiative in California in 1911, because she wanted to include its thirteen electoral votes in the suffrage camp.

Thirteen was a "magical number" in the game.[11]

The only other noteworthy appearance of the suffrage issue in American card decks was in the popular game of "Old Maid," where the old maid was invariably a suffragist. Selchow and Righter, now best known for Scrabble, produced a set of cards in the late nineteenth century in a colorful box, where the "Old Maid" is pictured casting a ballot. The Affinity Card Company of Portland, Oregon issued an Old Maid–type game called "Affinity" in which the "suffragette" card was the only one without a match, although her portrait was surprisingly traditional and fashionable, and not at all the old hag figure that was so typical of the genre.

Postcards — American

The golden age of the postcard, the period from 1902 to 1915 when "the accumulating of picture postcards was a major pastime in almost every household,"[1] dovetailed for the most part with the final push to achieve a national suffrage amendment. Suffragist learned early to exploit the popularity of the new form of communication, and the movement in both America and England as well as internationally was directly or indirectly responsible for the appearance of thousands of different varieties.

The first true postcard of any type, suffrage or not, that was sent through the mails probably was the issue of the H. Lipman Company of Philadelphia in 1870. Once the commercial aspects of the new format were appreciated, advertisements for a wide variety of products, often accompanied by black-and-white illustrations, appeared on postcards throughout the remainder of the century. Advances in printing technology in the 1890s resulted in the addition of both color and photography to the new format, along with a further expansion of its possibilities. Because many people did not possess their own cameras, the commercial photo or view card became a popular way to preserve memories of a trip or a local event. Moreover, as long as a postcard was mailed locally, it was generally delivered on the same day that it was sent out, making it a rapid and inexpensive way to announce a meeting or event such as a suffrage gathering.[2]

In 1903, Kodak developed the No. 3A

Folding Pocket Kodak designed with postcard-size film, which allowed photographs to be applied directly to a card. In 1907, they offered a service to the public to print postcards from any photograph that an individual sent in, hoping to create a larger market for their cameras. Kodak was not the only manufacturer to develop for the general public cameras that could take pictures capable of convenient transformation into postcards, but they were responsible for the term for the resultant product, "Real Photo." Although sometimes confused with their commercial counterparts such as the souvenir photo card, "Real Photo" postcards can be described as those photographic cards that come, not from large-scale commercial sources that were often printed using dot pixels, but generally from individuals seeking to preserve memories and from local groups attempting to raise funds.[3] Many cards depicting suffrage marches, demonstrations, and other events thus are "Real Photo," although commercial studios employing more sophisticated printing techniques for their products could also photograph the same event and sell the resulting product.

In a brief article entitled "Get Out Your Cameras," the *Woman's Journal* recognized the potential of the Real Photo postcard both as a fundraiser and as a propaganda device. Noting the example of some Washington suffragists who had photographed for a postcard a little girl who held out her arms entwined horizontally along a staff of a "Votes for Women" pennant, the periodical urged that "those of our readers who have cameras and artistic taste try it." It further argued, "There is money, and, what is better, useful propaganda work for the person or club that can evolve a really bewitching postcard along this line. It would be bought by thousands of suffragists for a Christmas card."[4]

For the most part, though, cards that were printed or ordered by suffrage organizations or by activists affiliated with those groups fall into three main categories: meeting notices, which constituted the bulk of the first official suffrage cards, propaganda or message cards, and commercial photo and Real Photo cards of local or national events.

One of the earliest American suffrage cards known was a meeting notice issued in 1874 by the Young Men's Women Suffrage League and sent out by J.K.H. Willcox, League President, soliciting letters of support for the franchise of women to be read at a gathering on June 15 of that year. Another early card was sent out for a meeting on December 15, 1886, by the Ladies' Suffrage Committee of New York at Hoffman House in New York City in "Celebration of the Vote of Mrs. Lucy S. Barber."[5] Among those scheduled to give speeches were Isabella Beecher Hooker and Kate Palmer Stearns. Barber was soon to be arrested in her home in Alfred Centre by Deputy Marshal Hubertne for voting in the previous general election. She actually was able to cast a ballot despite threats of prosecution at the time.[6]

In general, meeting notice postcards are more interesting for their historic as opposed to graphic content. Apart from the WPU, which, on occasion, included its Clarion image along with an announcement of upcoming events, very few of these cards had any accompanying pictorial representation. Most were printed in a standard, unelaborated font, some simply in typewriter face. In context, however, they do give us a more complete picture of the activities of many suffrage groups, providing information about officers and events that may not necessarily be readily available elsewhere, particularly with respect to smaller organizations and spurs from larger state or national groups. The

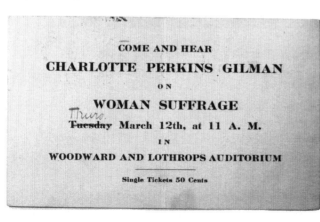

This card announces an address by the famous author of *Herland* and "The Yellow Wallpaper."

THE JUST GOVERNMENT LEAGUE
PRESENTS

The
Maryland
Players

In
Elizabeth
Robins'
Great Play

THE
CONVERT
(Votes for Women)
Arranged for this
Performance
and produced by
HARRY B. WEEKS

Albaugh's
Theatre

Tuesday,
October 29,
8:15 P. M.

Reserved Seats 25c. to $1.50, on sale at
Albaugh's Ticket Office,
2 E. Fayette St.

One of many cards using Marjorie Hamilton's English design of "A Woman with a Placard" to announce a suffrage event.

New York City Woman Suffrage League, for example, sent out a notice of an address by "Harriet [sic] Stanton Blatch" at one of its meetings that were held on the first Thursday of the month, and the Political Equality Club of Rochester invited members to a reception for Christabel Pankhurst at the Hotel Seneca on Saturday, November 13, 1909; announcements for various events were also sent out by such organizations as the Woman Suffrage Society of the County of Philadelphia (Mrs. N.S. Mason was the corresponding secretary), the City Point Woman Suffrage League, the Women Workers' Suffrage League, the Cambridge Political Equality Club, the Colorado Equal Suffrage Association, the Equal Suffrage League of New York (Mary Garrett Hay, President), and the Political Equality Club of New Haven (Mrs. T.S. McDermott, President), among others. The larger organizations such as the New York State

Woman Suffrage Association, the National American Woman Suffrage Association, the New York State Woman Suffrage Party, the Congressional Union, and the National Woman's Party also made frequent use of the postcard for meeting and event announcements.

One exception to the lack of graphics on meeting notices was the American appropriation of Marjorie Hamilton's "woman with a placard" design that had originally been made for the June 21, 1911, WSPU demonstration in London. It showed a woman in purple and green carrying a large sign on which information about the demonstration was included. American suffragists liked the image so much that they used it on handbills for their own events, such as Mrs. Pankhurst's farewell meeting at Carnegie Hall on January 5, 1912. The design fit perfectly on postcards and was used by a variety of organizations to announce meetings and events, including a production of the suffrage play "The Convert," sponsored by the Just Government League of Maryland; a meeting of the Connecticut Woman Suffrage Association at the Hebron Town Hall on October 16, 1916; and an appearance of Mrs. Pankhurst at the Symphony Auditorium in Newark under the auspices of the New Jersey Suffrage Association.[7]

Anti-suffrage groups, while often making a point to eschew public demonstrations and parades nevertheless did meet frequently to plan strategy and listen to opposition speakers, and many of these activities are also well recorded on postcards. Among the groups who gave notice of their events on cards were the Connecticut Association Opposed to Woman Suffrage, the Jamaica Plain Anti-Suffrage Association, the Anti-Suffrage Current Events Class, the Cambridge Anti-Suffrage Association, and the Lexington branch of the Massachusetts Society Opposed to the Further Extension of Suffrage to Women.

It was the second category of the message or propaganda card that proved to be an extremely effective form of advertising and persuasion to the general public. In these cards, suffragists could articulate in bullet form their core arguments, counter the negative claims of the antis, and help frame the public image of the potential woman voter. Women who desired to vote were not the degendered harridans that the opposition portrayed them to be, but rather were wives and mothers who would use the franchise to strengthen their traditional roles, not overturn them.

Suffrage "message" postcards were circulated widely with the help of advertisements in suffrage papers, through direct sales at suffrage shops and headquarters, through mail order, and through distribution at bazaars and rallies. The College League of California held a "Postcard Day" in 1911 where "prettily costumed young saleswomen" sold 10,000 cards that had been printed especially to promote the upcoming state suffrage amendment, while at the same time distributing "a large number of other campaign cards."[8] In the same year on February 22, Harriot Stanton Blatch delivered a "speech by postcard" on "Suffrage Day" before a Joint Judiciary Committee meeting of the New York State Assembly and Senate. She brought with her a stack of postcards, which portrayed the map of suffrage states, and handed them to all of the members of the committee. She observed, "I'm glad that you all want one.... You will see that they are all together. It is never a State at a distance that gives the vote to women, but one adjoining, which has seen how well it worked."[9]

Message postcards were so effective that at times the opposition felt compelled to denounce them publicly. Mrs. Arthur Dodge, while president of the National Association Opposed to Woman Suffrage, charged, on at least one occasion, that two "anonymous" pro-suffrage cards were part of a "cowardly" poison-pen plot to link the anti- forces with the liquor industry. She declared, "These cards are being mailed to all parts of the country and tell the recipient that 'for positive proof the anti-suffragists are working with the liquor industry and receive financial assistance from them send 10 cents to the National Woman Suffrage Publishing Company.'" Dodge vehemently denied that there was any connection. She also objected to a companion card that directed the recipient to write for two copies of the official suffrage paper.[10] At least one of the cards that Dodge alleged was part of the plot was readily available for sale at three cents each both at NAWSA headquarters and by mail. It was printed in yellow and black and carried the warning, "Antis — Beware Your Friends."[11]

But the anti- forces were also involved themselves with negative postcards, at least one of which was ultimately linked to the liquor industry. In discussing the role of liquor interests in Oregon to defeat suffrage, the *Woman's Journal* noted, "These vicious interests [including the liquor industry] were a unit against equal rights for women. A vulgar card, bearing a picture of a woman's undergarment, with a coarse remark aimed against equal suffrage, was mailed to the voters throughout the State." The treasurer of the Oregon Association Opposed to the Further Extension of Suffrage to Women later acknowledged responsibility for sending these out.[12]

The quality and design of message cards varied considerably. Some featured colorful designs by famous artists who were sympathetic to the movement, others graced the front pages of such publications as the *Woman's Journal* and *The Suffragist*, and still others were issued in series format, allowing the sender to postcards on a periodic basis to potential supporters. Some, however, were printed on cheap cardboard, with little more than a crudely printed suffrage argument. An interesting example of the latter was a set of six cards distributed by the Woman Suffrage Headquarters of Philadelphia and published by the "Printery in the Single Tax Village of Arden, Delaware."[13] Arden, Delaware, was a socialist utopian community founded in 1900 by sculptor Frank Stephens and architect Will Price, based partly on ideas formulated by Henry George and William Morris. Advocates of the "single tax" believed that all property should be taxed at a single rate, no matter what improvements or buildings had been added to it.

Although most major suffrage organizations and many of the lesser-known groups published cards, it was the National Woman Suffrage Association that most fully exploited their potential. Perhaps the most attractive was a set of six cards consisting of five illustrations by Emily Hall Chamberlin, a noted artist of children's books, and one by Rose O'Neill, creator of the Kewpies.

Chamberlin's drawings were of young boys and girls playing peacefully, with the girl sometimes admonishing the boy, declaring, "I want to speak for myself at the polls," and "Suffrage First." The innocence of the illustrations em-

This card, designed by Emily Hall Chamberlin, takes the overtly sexual implications of the *Lysistrata* theme from classic Greek comedy, and reduces it to one of innocence.

phasized that equal suffrage was really a cooperative and engaging enterprise, not at all an embodiment of the threatening revolutionary overtones suggested by the anti- forces. The suffrage issue depicted through drawings of children was quite common among commercial cards also. O'Neill's contribution to the set consisted of the design of three Kewpies marching in "Spirit of '76" style, carrying a "Votes for Women" banner instead of the American flag. O'Neill also illustrated another card for NAWSA outside of this set that depicted four Kewpie-like figures carrying a banner that requested "Votes for Our Mothers," a continuation of the argument sometimes reflected in NAWSA literature that women needed the vote, not to overturn traditional gender roles in society, but rather to augment them. A woman could be a better mother, for example, if she had the right to vote on certain issues that

affected the family, such as regulation of the purity of the milk that she was feeding her children.

Chamberlin and O'Neill were among many illustrators to contribute their work to the movement. Other women artists represented on suffrage cards included Katherine Millhaus, Henrietta Briggs-Wall, May Wilson Preston, and Augusta Fleming. Not all suffrage card artists were female. Examples of male illustrators included C.D. Batchelor, Pulitzer Prize–winning artist for *The New York Daily News* and *The New York Tribune*, Ralph Wilder, Herbert Johnson, Stanley Lisby Arthur, Clifford K. Berryman, who was famous for his Theodore Roosevelt "Teddy Bear" cartoons, and Charles Twelvetrees. Some of this postcard art also found its way onto posters, particularly the work of Briggs-Wall, O'Neill, and Berryman. Not quite a famous artist, Elmer Wise drew a design for a postcard for the California campaign entitled "The New Woman Voter — Purifying the Political Pool." Wise first came to the attention of California suffragists when, at the age of 15, he contributed an entry in a suffrage poster contest that was described by Selina Solomons as "full of spirit and spirituality." She later used Wise's design in 1912 for the cover of her book on how women won the vote in California.[14] Surprisingly, no postcard has apparently surfaced with any art by Nina Allender, whose intriguing illustrations were featured on the cover of many an issue of the *Suffragist*, even though this publication was the official organ of the Congressional Union (later, National Woman's Party), which did publish some cards. In England postcard and poster art were even more than in America significant adjuncts to the movement. Both the Artists' Suffrage League and the Suffrage Atelier organized artists, professional and non-professional, for the cause. Artwork from these two organizations is found on a profusion of English postcards and posters, as well as in color inserts for *The Vote*.

Many NAWSA cards published after 1913 bear the imprint of the National Woman Suffrage Publishing Company. That company was established at the NAWSA convention of 1913 when suffragists realized that literature, presumably including postcards, had "become so large a feature that it was decided to form a company to publish it." In 1916, Esther G. Ogden, who was then the head of the publishing company, noted that the publishing house existed "for two purposes — to serve the suffrage cause throughout the country and to prove that we can serve the cause, and also develop a successful business." By 1917 suffragists had proved so successful in their efforts to advance that cause that Ogden joked to the convention attendees that the company was "bankrupted" trying to keep the "suffrage maps" up to date. A popular icon for NAWSA was a map of the United States depicting shaded those states that had granted women the right to vote in presidential and municipal elections. As soon as literature with a suffrage map was printed, another state was added to the suffrage fold, and

Votes for Women a Success
North America Proves It

Yellow- Ballots for Both
Black- Male Suffrage Only

The Canadian provinces of British Columbia, Alberta, Saskatchewan and Manitoba extended full suffrage to their women in 1916. Ontario gave them full suffrage in March, 1917.
How long will the Republic of the United States lag behind the Monarchy of Canada?

An extremely popular image on postcards and handbills was the map of those suffrage states where women could vote in presidential elections.

thousands of pieces of pamphlets and leaflets would have to be scrapped.[15] The publishing company printed several updates of the map design on postcards and may have been responsible for a similar card that was distributed by the NAWSA affiliate, the New York State Woman Suffrage Party, for its successful 1917 campaign. The California suffragist Alice Park borrowed one version of the NAWSA map for a postcard that bears her imprint.

NAWSA did not promote its leadership through postcards the way that its English counterparts such as the WSPU and the WFL had. In England, supporters could not only purchase photo cards from party headquarters and shops of the central figures of the movement, including the Pankhursts, but also of many of the less prominent leaders such as Marguerite Sidley, Ethel Annakin Snowden, Alice Schofield, Isabel Seymour, Bessie Semple, Lady Frances Balfour, and Isabella Ford. At its 38th annual convention in Baltimore in 1906, NAWSA did circulate three cards in honor of Susan B. Anthony, Elizabeth Cady Stanton, and Carrie Chapman Catt, but these appear to have been issued to delegates only as a tribute to these women and not as a promotional device to the general public. Stanton had passed away four years earlier in 1902, and Anthony, who attended the convention at the age of 86, was in frail health and died one month later. Two other famous suffragists who made brief photographic appearances on American cards were Charlotte Perkins Gilman, author of "The Yellow Wallpaper" and the feminist novel *Herland*, and Anna Howard Shaw, Anthony's close friend and ultimate successor as president of NAWSA.[16]

It was perhaps this impulse to avoid too much focus on current suffrage leaders that caused Harriot Stanton Blatch in 1930 to have mixed feelings about a plan of the League of Women Voters to establish a "Suffrage honor roll." She was influenced in part by a "larger feminist ethic of selfless service" that led her "to deprecate the idea of honoring individuals at all," and to credit instead the "vast suffrage army."[17] In any event, period suffrage cards of any leader of any American organization are rare except for the occasional memorial or convention piece.

The most popular set of suffrage message

postcards associated with NAWSA was not actually printed by them but rather by a commercial publisher, the Cargill Company of Grand Rapids, Michigan, in 1910. Although NAWSA did not issue the set, they "endorsed and approved" it, and received a portion of the sales for their participation. The set consisted of thirty cards, most of which were "aphorisms," which, the Cargill Company assured potential buyers, when judiciously taught to "the rising generation of both sexes, will secure for WOMAN the right of "EQUAL SUFFRAGE in every State of the union not later than 1916."[18] The thirty cards were divided into two packs of fifteen, individually wrapped and sealed, selling for thirty-five cents each or sixty-five cents for both, plus postage. Each pack also contained a circular from the Butler Brothers Jewelry Company of Attleboro, Massachusetts, for its line of jewelry products that used the same escutcheon image along with the slogan "The Ballot is denied to Women — The Blot on the Escutcheon" that appeared on Cargill's cards. The shield design was Cargill's, but they licensed its use to Butler Brothers, and both companies announced their new lines in concurrent full-page ads that appeared in October 15, 1910, issue of the *Woman's Journal*.[19] Although both Cargill and Butler Brothers spent considerable resources advertising their products initially, judging by current auction and online listings, the postcards appear to have been quite popular but the jewelry line was not.

Cargill was extremely aggressive in its attempt to move its product line, its advertising suggesting that its postcards were an inherent part of the movement. In the issue of the *Woman's Journal* that followed its unveiling of the escutcheon postcard set, the company urged suffragists to support Equal Suffrage Week, which in their math lasted from October 31 to November 8, 1910, by requesting retailers of postcards, stationery, and jewelry to make full window displays of suffrage products. Their

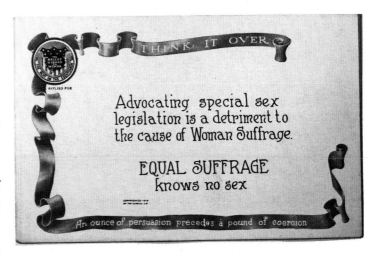

The rarest card of the Cargill set, numbered 111, may have been withdrawn from sale because many suffragists disagreed with its argument.

main target was the "100,000 stores that carry postcards." Cargill was careful not to mention their own set, but the implication was clear, particularly since the *Woman's Journal* that week carried news of Equal Suffrage Week, along with praise from Agnes E. Ryan, the periodical's business manager, for Cargill. Ads from Cargill for the distribution of promotional materials during Equal Suffrage Week also appeared in *Novelty News, Pharmaceutical Era, National Druggist,* and *Walden's Stationer,* as well in as other trade publications.[20] Cargill continued to promote the set through a number of smaller ads in the *Woman's Journal* over the next year and advertised for agents willing to sell its movement products, including not only the postcards but also suffragist stationery.[21]

When the "message" of a suffragist postcard was accompanied by a photograph, a lithographed drawing, or a cartoon, the image of that card could also show up on the cover of a suffrage publication. Thus, a drawing for a card by Katherine Milhous entitled "A Moving Picture" appeared on the front of a 1916 issue of the *Woman's Journal*.[22] The card portrayed several women involved in such occupations as cleaning lady, nurse, waitress, and factory worker and noted: "This doesn't 'unsex' her," but "this is another story [picture of a woman voting]." The lithograph cartoon of "Blind Justice," which illustrated a group of rowdy men voting while

When Milhous' drawing, featured on the front page of the *Woman's Journal*, later appeared in this postcard version, its original title "A Moving Picture" was removed.

FIRST MUNITION OF WAR
SHOULD WAR BE WITHOUT THE CONSENT OF THE
MOTHERS?

1331 NEWTON STREET N. E.
WASHINGTON. D. C.

This card addressed the suffrage argument that if women were responsible for the safety of their children, they had the right to vote on matters relating to warfare.

women were denied the ballot, appeared on the front page of the March 27, 1909, edition of the same journal and was advertised for sale in September, two for five cents, by the Massachusetts Woman Suffrage Association.[23] A cartoon by "Briggs" (Henrietta Briggs-Wall), that originally appeared in *The New York Tribune* picturing a young boy confronting his father with a ballot box and proclaiming, "A vote for Mother is a vote for a better world for me Dad," was reprinted on the front cover of the November 16, 1916, issue of the *Woman's Journal* as well as on a postcard issued by the Suffrage Department of the Women's Christian Temperance Union (WCTU) of Iowa.

The Suffragist, the official paper of Alice Paul's NWP, likewise featured on occasion illustrations of postcards on its front covers, including a reproduction of an English card and

poster "the Appeal of Womanhood — Our Message to Women of All Nations 'Dare to be Free,'"[24] and a photo of a baby with the caption "The First Munition of War."[25] The card's subcaption, "Should war be without the consent of the mothers?," buttressed the suffragist argument that, if children's safety is the responsibility of mothers, then those very same mothers needed the vote to support legislation that would protect that safety. This particular card was advertised later in the paper as being for sale at the Congressional Union headquarters in Washington, D.C., for five cents each. A Clifford Berryman cartoon depicting Theodore Roosevelt declaring, "Let the People Rule" that also portrays a group of women responding by holding up a sign wondering "We're What?" was used by the New York State Woman Suffrage Association not only for a black-and-white postcard but also for the cover illustration of its April 1912 newsletter. The design earlier appeared on a poster commissioned by the Men's League for Equal Suffrage and on the front page of the *Woman's Journal* for June 10, 1911.

There were several themes that reoccurred over and over on the message cards issued by official suffrage sources. The first was that of motherhood, and the approach was to elicit from men a sense of guilt. How could a man possibly deny the right to vote to either his own mother or to his wife, the mother of his children? One card contains a photo of a small boy holding up a sign that reads, "I wish Mother could vote"[26]; another card, issued by the Socialist Party of America, noted in its contrasting images of a drunk with a mother and baby that the former could vote while the latter could not. Another shows a child captured by the machine of child labor holding out her arms for the protection of her mother who is imprisoned by the chains of "woman's political restrictions." The caption reads, "Give women the vote, and let the mothers protect their children." Recognizing the need to undermine the emotional appeal inherent in such messages, the New York State Association Opposed to Woman Suffrage issued a card depicting a young mother in a rocking chair holding a rolled ballot instead of a child, noting that she was "hugging a delusion."

Another common theme was that of those

The Socialist Party was quite active in publishing postcards, pamphlets, and leaflets supporting suffrage.

groups who could vote and those who couldn't, with the message often having questionable social, racial, or ethnic implications. One card, in response to the question "Who Can't Vote?" answered "children, insane, idiots, aliens, criminals, and women." Another depicted the disenfranchised, including women, with "the Indian, the idiot, the convict, the lunatic." A third portrayed a woman linked by the chains of law to both a convict and a mentally disturbed man. No American card of the period pointed out that black men could vote while women could not, but that racist message did appear on an English card in 1910 designed by Edwyn Llewellyn that was produced without a printed imprimatur from any suffrage organization.[27] The resentment of some suffrage supporters in America over the fact that black men could vote and white women could not, while not a topic per se on postcards, does show up on a cover of *Life*[28] and on at least one cabinet card of the period.

It is unfortunate that production numbers of postcards are nearly impossible to come by. However, the popularity of "official" cards can be easily demonstrated by the variety that was issued. Even a number of the smaller suffrage or-

ganizations and local affiliates published cards, including the Just Government League of Maryland, the Woman Suffrage Party of New York City, the Ohio Equal Franchise Association, the Equal Suffrage League of Virginia, the Delaware County Equal Suffrage League, the Brooklyn Woman Suffrage Party, the Suffrage Department of the WCTU of Iowa, the Votes for Women Club of San Francisco, the Berkeley Club, the Political Equality League of Los Angeles, and the Massachusetts Woman Suffrage Association. Many were quite graphic, often displaying the seal of the issuing organization along with a finely drawn illustration, and, in addition to promoting a message, could be used as fundraisers. Some groups, such as the Chicago Woman Suffrage Organization, would take a generic design used by others, such as that of a woman dressed in a yellow hat and gown holding out a streamer with the words "Votes for Women," and add their own imprint, sometimes attempting to elicit national sales in the process.[29]

The *Woman's Journal* was probably the most influential American source in terms of encouraging and promoting the use of pro-suffrage postcards. On more than one occasion it pictured imaginative new arrivals on its front pages; it also announced with a fair degree of frequency the printing and availability of other new cards in columns with such headings as "Notes and News," "A Suffrage Postcard," "More Suffrage Postcards," "The California Matinee," and "Easter Postcards." Its emphasis on postcards undoubtedly provided the incentive for even small local organizations and individual activists to advertise their efforts through small display ads and classified appeals in the periodical's pages. On April 27, 1912, the *Woman's Journal* added an advertising section that was labeled "Local Suffrage Supplies" that not only provided a convenient spot for state chapters to advertise their newest postcards but also their uniquely designed hat pins, rubber stamps, napkins, sashes, and other materials as well.

To help with the four-state eastern campaign of 1915, the *Woman's Journal* produced a set of eighteen postcards, reprinted from its own pages, that was available for fifteen cents. The cards were in response to a question as to what the supporter could do "as an individual to help win." The cards were headed with such titles as "If you are a working man," "If you are a doctor," "If you are a policeman," "If you are a minister," and "If you are an educator," and the journal advised suffragists to divide their male acquaintances into various occupational categories and send them the most appropriate card.[30]

In addition to both the meeting notice and the message card, a third type of card that suffrage groups produced was the Real Photo card, which, while potentially of great value to historians, does present problems when questions arise involving identification of both maker and event depicted. Because Real Photo cards typically do not bear the imprint on their address side of either their photographer or distributor as was the general practice for their commercially produced counterparts, it is often quite difficult to know who issued them, and what demonstration they were recording. With some exceptions, suffrage journals and papers provide at best tantalizing, oblique references to such cards. Moreover, many of these cards were printed up by individuals and itinerant photographers and not by suffrage organizations themselves, so little, if any, publicity was attached to their production.

Real Photo cards were not made in large quantities and were often used to record small local festivities that provided little financial incentive for national commercial publishers to record. They were quick to produce, however; thus they could be sold or distributed within a day or so of the event, when the desire for a souvenir was still high. While there are occasional clues that do tie in some Real Photo cards with official sources and not independent photographers or individuals, attempts to clarify their origin can be an exasperating endeavor.

One Real Photo card that probably did have an official imprimatur from a local group shows a woman with two children holding up a large banner with the words "Connecticut — Votes for Women." The same photograph appears in the program of the Connecticut Woman Suffrage Association (WSA) for a demonstration in Hartford in May 1914, where the woman in the picture is identified as Mrs. M. Toscan Bennett, treasurer of the organization.[31] Mrs. Bennett, also a member of Alice Paul's National Woman's Party, left the CWSA in 1917 along with the group's president, Mrs. Thomas N. Hepburn (mother of the actress Katharine Hepburn), both feeling that the state organization was "not aggressive enough" in its pursuit of the franchise.[32]

It is fortunate here that another source exists to identify the otherwise anonymous Bennett on the card, for, much to the disappointment of suffrage historians, too often individuals and events depicted on Real Photos remain obscure. The process for the production of Real Photos did allow captions to be engraved directly onto the photographic plate, showing up on cards most often in the form of white lettering, but the practice was not universal. At times there may appear an identifying notation from the period on the back of the card, presumably written by someone who was either the original photographer or who had personally attended the event in question. One such notated card depicts a diminutive woman addressing an unidentified suffrage rally. The name "Maud Ballington Booth" is inscribed on the back of the card in pencil; comparisons with published photos of Booth indicate that the attribution is likely an accurate one.[33] Maud Booth, born in England,

Mrs. Toscan Bennett, pictured here with her children, was a neighbor of Mrs. Thomas (Katherine) Hepburn and her ally in the Connecticut Woman Suffrage Association.

came to the United States in 1887 with her husband, Ballington, the son of William Booth, the founder of the Salvation Army. Together they established the Volunteers of America in 1896. While Booth was involved with many progressive causes, this appears to be her sole appearance on a postcard in support of suffrage, and it is fortunate that someone from the period made the identification even though he or she neglected to include additional information about the demonstration.

Another Real Photo card by a photographer identified only as McElroy is lettered on the front identifying Grace Wilbur Trout as the main speaker at a Chautauqua event in Pana, Illinois. Trout is seen in a group shot with eighteen other women. Trout was president of the Chicago Political Equality League and a central figure in securing passage of the suffrage bill in Illinois in 1913. The Chautauqua was a lecture circuit and study school held throughout the United States, and Trout was one of the official speakers. What makes this particular card especially interesting is that someone has identified in pencil on the back of the card each of the women depicted, suggesting, perhaps, that the card was at one time owned by a person who was present at the event. It is not known how many copies of this card exist, but the number is probably quite low, perhaps restricted to the participants at the Chautauqua.

Despite the number of extant photographic cards, Real Photo or otherwise, American suffragists were not quite as focused as their English counterparts were on the potential of the postcard to record history. It is far easier to trace most of the major events in the English suffrage movement through postcards than it is in the American struggle, perhaps because English suffragists maintained closer relationships with both individual photographers and commercial studios. The Bexleyheath firm of F. Kehrhahn, for example, is sometimes regarded as the semi-official photographer of the WSPU, commissioned by them to capture their activities, processions, and related happenings, and many of their resultant photos appeared on WSPU cards.[34] Other photographers and firms involved with the production of postcards included Mrs. Albert Broom, Lizzie Caswell Smith, Graham of Morpeth, Emeny of Felixstowe, and Allworth Brothers of Tonbridge.[35]

There were, nevertheless, American suffrage demonstrations that attracted their share of cameras, including the Pennsylvania Liberty Bell campaign, "General" Rosalie Jones' march to Washington, the suffrage parade at President Wilson's 1913 inaugural along with the accompanying pageant on the steps of the Treasury, and, to a limited degree, the activities of the "Silent Sentinels," who demonstrated outside the White House gates around the time of the First World War.

As part of her strategy to generate publicity for the 1915 suffrage campaign in Pennsylvania, Katharine Wentworth Ruschenberger developed plans to "recast" the Liberty Bell (**see Pennsylvania Liberty Bell Campaign**). The resultant bell, carried on a specially reinforced truck, crisscrossed all sixty-seven counties of the state, traveling a total of 3,935 miles, before the campaign ended on Election Day, November 2. There are Real Photo cards that follow the journey of the 2,000-pound bell, from the time that it was first presented to the Pennsylvania state organization on June 23, 1915, through several of its many stops along the way, to its triumphant ceremonial ringing in Independence Square in Philadelphia on September 25, 1920, in celebration of the passage of the National Suffrage Amendment. During the campaign, the truck that carried the bell was used as a speaker's stand, not only in urban centers, but also in rural areas, a fact recorded in extant Real Photo cards. The September event attracted a crowd large enough that a commercial publisher, Ernest B. Orr of Philadelphia, saw enough potential for profit to produce a set of two cards to sell to the public at five cents a pair.

Another suffragist, the socialite Rosalie Gardiner Jones, also knew how to generate publicity for the cause, in her case by organizing a series of highly publicized suffrage hikes. She recruited a small army of volunteers, of which she was the "General" and Ida Craft of Brooklyn was the "Colonel," to march from New York City to Albany starting on December 16, 1912, to press Governor William Sulzer for his support in passing a state suffrage amendment. Even though no such amendment came about, the march was regarded as such a success that Jones and Craft,

The card illustrates the Suffrage Liberty Bell on its official truck making a stop at a rural community.

"General" Rosalie Jones and her suffrage pilgrims stopping along the way of their march to Washington.

reinforced by the "little Corporal," Martha Klatschken of New York, initiated another from New York, where the "army" was mustered, to Washington, D.C., in February 1913 to deliver a message to President Taft. The intent was to stay in Washington to participate in the large suffrage parade that was to be held there on March 3, the day preceding Woodrow Wilson's inauguration as president.

The sixteen-day journey was attended at various times by forty-five press correspondents, most of whom had cameras, and by enthusiastic crowds. Among the many hikers who participated in one fashion or another, fourteen women, dressed as pilgrims, walked the entire distance from Newark, New Jersey, the actual start of the march, to the final destination. It is quite probable that members of Jones' army may have been at least partly responsible for the series of Real Photo cards that depicted the march, for Jones was quite cognizant of the propaganda value of souvenirs and memorabilia, passing out suffrage buttons, flags, and leaflets along the way of the hike.[36] A reporter for the *Bay City Times* who was covering the hike was approached by one of the marchers who attempted successfully to sell her a dozen postcards and buttons, arguing that she could "charge them up to your paper."[37] Several Real Photo cards show the triumphant group entering Washington, D.C., on February 28. Others depict the beginning of the march, and still others a stop or two along the way. One contrasting pair of the same scene in an unidentified wooded area, a Real Photo card and its commercial equivalent, is an interesting and stark example of the retouching techniques that were available to professional reproductions but not to the Real Photo process. The commercial card adds eight marchers to the twelve depicted on the Real Photo by superimposing their heads onto the image. The integration was not flawless, as the added heads are larger than those of the women who were in the original photo.

The largest group of both commercially produced photo cards and Real Photo cards that was produced for any suffrage event was associated with the March 3, 1913, Washington, D.C., parade and demonstration that preceded Woodrow Wilson's inauguration as president. The event was first conceived by Alice Paul to

invigorate "the lifeless campaign to seek a federal amendment." She had the help of a number of volunteers, including Helen Gardener, who handled publicity, and Hazel MacKaye, an experienced pageant director, who was in charge of the tableau on the steps of the Treasury Building that was to follow the parade. But the ideas behind the event were largely Paul's, who wanted, among other priorities: to ensure the beauty of the marchers in an effort to symbolize the "Ideals and Virtues of American Womanhood"; to keep the event memorable and ensure press coverage through elaborate staging and floats; and to celebrate women of different occupations and organizations by having them march in separate divisions, with all wearing or carrying banners.[38] With respect to the latter, she may have been influenced by the structure and symbolism of the massive march of 40,000 suffragists in England on June 17, 1911, that had preceded the coronation of King George V, and which had also been extensively pictured on postcards.

Not all of the various contingents of women who participated appear on cards of the march, but enough of them do to allow a sense of the parade's scope. Real Photo cards show groups billed as Home Makers, Students from Radcliffe, Cornell and Bryn Mawr, Women in Government Service, and Women from Other Lands, all marching down Pennsylvania Avenue. A six-card commercial set issued in a blue envelope by Leet Brothers of Washington, D.C., captures other aspects of the procession, including the appearance of Inez Milholland, who led the parade all dressed in white riding on a white horse; a contingent of women from Sweden, "One of the Countries Where Women Vote"; a group of trained nurses carrying the banner of Florence Nightingale; a procession of small girls, also dressed in white and carrying balloons passing by the NAWSA reviewing stand; and a picture of the crowd that later was to surround the marchers, preventing them from making progress. There are also a number of cards that portray the suffrage tableau that took place on the steps of the Treasury. At least one other commercial photographer, I. & M. Ottenheimer, from nearby Baltimore, produced and sold a number of cards portraying the festivities, including Hazel MacKaye's tableau.

THE SUFFRAGE WATCHFIRE BEFORE THE WHITE HOUSE.

One of the few cards issued by the National Woman's Party that pictured the protestors known as "the Silent Sentinels" in front of the White House gates.

One of Paul's later events, the demonstration of the "Silent Sentinels," party members and sympathizers who, with large suffrage banners, picketed in front of the White House gates, achieved a great deal of notoriety, but, given its historic importance, was, unfortunately, under-depicted in period postcards. Her National Woman's Party issued and sold several commercial-type photo cards of these suffragists marching near the White House and holding a watch fire in front of it, but very few other cards from any source picture this famous demonstration. In general, though, the NWP, for all of its concern with what is now termed "visual rhetoric," did not produce many postcard souvenirs of its activities.

There are many additional existing Real Photo cards that depict a variety of suffrage events throughout the country, including several marches in New York City, a depiction of the delegates at the 1915 NAWSA annual convention, a group shot of the New Jersey delegation at the White House on November 17, 1913, and local demonstrations from Connecticut to Oregon.

But the number of cards for each of these other events is generally limited, a sometimes frustrating state of affairs for the suffrage historian who wishes to research aspects of some of the lesser-known parades and demonstrations.

If the number of postcards of various types issued by suffrage associations was high, the quantity issued by commercial firms was even higher. While these outside firms did issue photographic views of suffrage events, more often than not their products consisted of humorous images that commented on the perceived consequences of the extension of the franchise to women. Some cards contained overt pro- or anti-suffrage propaganda, and, based on the signatures attached to their handwritten messages, were often purchased and sent by suffragists themselves. But most cards, even those with an edge, can be best seen not as direct propaganda for either side but as a reflection of varying cultural attitudes and concerns of the day towards suffrage, the fear that the franchise could overturn the roles of men and women in the household, the gentle ridicule of women attempting to take over the occupations of men, and the image of the pretty ingénue who was somehow out of her element when she was engaged with any activity other than her appearance. Although occasionally the attempt at humor could be vicious, for the most part it was gentle on American cards, with children often depicted as arguing with each other on the subject to downplay any potential acrimony that the card might generate with potential customers.

The most popular commercial cards were those issued in sets; while no figures of actual production are known, their popularity is attested to by the number of surviving examples still for sale on the Internet and at postcard shows. Most notable among these sets are sixteen cards collectively called "The Suffragette," copyrighted in 1909 by Walter Wellman; a set of twelve called "Suffragette Series," by the Dunston-Weiler

Lithograph Company, also published in 1909; twelve cards drawn by Dr. Bernhardt Wall, half of which proclaim "Votes for Women," the other half with the same image but a different inscription advocating "Votes for ~~Wo~~men" with the "Wo" crossed out; twelve cards of children published by the T.P. Company of New York and illustrated by Cobb Shinn, an Indiana artist who started his career as a newspaper illustrator who drew "doughboy" cartoons during World War I; and a group of twelve cards issued by the firm of Barton and Spooner, more noted for their Halloween themes than suffrage, featuring children engaged in various pro- and anti- activities and arguments. That some of these series, though commercial products, could be popular with suffragists can be seen by the fact that they were occasionally pictured in movement journals as amusing and positive cartoons.[39]

These two popular cards, from widely circulated sets, attempted to set an innocent framework for a controversial issue.

The Wellman and the Dunston-Weiler sets in general portray a topsy-turvy world in which women, as the result of the vote, were now taking over the roles of men with various disasters accompanying the switch. The Wellman cards, for example, show a nosy female letter carrier reading everyone's mail, a woman bartender replacing beer and whiskey with pretzels and ice cream, the war department under a "presidentress" ordering rolling pins and flatirons for weapons, and a female Teddy Roosevelt who is wielding a broom as her "big stick." The Dunston-Weiler set also portrays women in traditional male roles, but focuses also on what was obviously a fear of many men at the time, that they would have to take over the duties of child care, washing the clothes, and general housework. While the men are obviously harried and rather

inept at handling the new situation that has been thrust upon them, the harshness of the situation is undercut by the general attractiveness and youth of the women pictured. The effect is not vicious satire but soft ridicule. The topsy-turvy world with young, attractive women in male roles is also seen in a six-card set called "The Suffragette Ticket" in which various women, sometimes scantily dressed, ask such questions as "Would you vote for me as Mayor?" and "Would you vote for me as Mail Man?"

The children in the Cobb Shinn, Wall, and Barton and Spooner series of cards ultimately do not take one collective position for or against suffrage, but reflect in an innocent way the various issues, situations, fears, and responses raised by the movement and its opponents. A Cobb Shinn boy who proclaims, "If I ever had a vote and you wanted it, you sure would get it," offsets another, who comments, "I'd rather kiss her, than hear her talk." A Barton and Spooner girl who is holding a rolling pin and demanding of a frightened boy, "You believe in women's suffrage, don't you?" has a more positive counterpart in a tiny blond girl who is sweetly pinning a banner on a small boy, noting, "We want you men to be with us." Another card in this series with the caption "I'm a militant suffragette" has a frightened girl running away from an angry storekeeper after she has broken his window in the fashion of the militant British suffragists. In a Bernhardt Wall illustration, a girl dressed in pink with a large bonnet on her head declares, under the caption of "Votes for Women," that "I want to speak for myself at the polls." The counterpart image with the opposing caption of "Votes for ~~Women~~" has the same girl pointing out less defiantly, "I've a dandy hubby who works and votes for me. I should worry?"

Suffrage was also a popular issue depicted on holiday cards. A number of postcards that contained suffragist messages were issued for St. Valentine's Day, Christmas, Easter, Thanksgiving, leap year, and New Year's Day, but not, interestingly enough, for Mother's Day, even though a suffragist theme was "Votes for Mother." While a few such holiday cards did evolve from sanctioned suffrage sources, the majority were printed by independent publishers, although their images and messages could be at times di-

The images of children playing out the issue of suffrage was quite common to American postcards of the period.

rectly in line with movement thought and strategy. Many of these cards, picking up on the conventions established in other commercial cards, pictured children with cherubic faces. That, along with associating enfranchisement with traditional holidays, provided a powerful imagistic comment that woman suffrage was a nonthreatening and obvious addition to the social tapestry.

Suffrage Valentine postcards were especially popular. Over and over the message was repeated, "Love Me. Love My Vote," as it was on a popular card by the famous illustrator equinely named Ellen Clapsaddle. Another Valentine card pictured a sad-looking boy trying to win the affections of a standoffish girl, who responds, "I may look like a demure little miss/But this I'll say, 'No vote, no kiss.'" A third little girl proclaims," Love me, Love my vote." And a small girl is depicted giving a heart to a young boy carrying a "Votes for Women" placard, calling him "My Hero!" The use of images of children was especially effective in this context to avoid the implications of granting voting rights with sexual solicitation. Christmas postcards were less common than Valentine's Day cards, but they were known. One popular card featured Santa Claus bringing with him "Votes for Women" in his pack of Yuletide presents. Another portrays a confused Santa bending over the bed of a modern little girl, whose Christmas list requests not only the traditional "dollies," but also a "flag" with "Votes for Wimen" on it. Not all holiday cards were pro-suffrage. On one Valentine's Day card, obviously intended for a male purchaser, contains the rhyme, "The Suffragettes can rule, they say,/And splendid they may be,/But the girl who can rule the kitchen,/Oh, that's the girl for me." A Thanksgiving card featuring a drawing of two turkeys assures the recipient, "This is not a suffragette lecture but a kind greeting."

Commercial publishers were concerned with profit, obviously, and, in order to appeal to as broad an audience as they could, often couched anti-suffrage sentiments in benign settings. The intent seemed to be in part to avoid offending the woman, who, while she might not necessarily be favorably disposed towards the concept of political enfranchisement, might still

Suffrage Valentine post cards, often with images of children, were very popular.

be inclined to react negatively to male attacks. Perhaps this is why images of cherubic children, similar to those appearing in Valentine's Day greetings and in the suffrage sets produced or illustrated by Cobb Shinn, Wall, and Barton and Spooner, made frequent appearances on commercial postcards dealing with suffrage themes. Their innocent features served to temper the positions that they were advocating and made them far less threatening. While caricatures of the suffrage harridan are known on American cards, her appearance is far less common than that of her English counterpart.

Other typical images or themes on American cards include those of the bespectacled old country gentleman confused by the social revolution going on about him, chickens, cats, and dogs enacting the roles of men and women in the debate, and double entendre cards, allegedly containing excerpts from "actual" suffrage speeches, in which the speaker boldly declares, "We will have what the men have.... I say up with the Petticoats and down with the Pants."[40] The theme that suffragists literally want to wear pants is also common to cards of the period, as are cards dealing with the harem skirt.[41] Unlike their English counterparts, American cards seldom lampooned actual suffragists, such as the Pankhursts, or specific events, such as the destruction of mailboxes and golf courses. For while the movement was often ridiculed on American cards, there was also a sense of compromise and conciliation.

Both the quantity and variety of types of postcards with suffrage related themes are testimony to the impact that the movement had on American popular culture. Since all suffrage postcards, even those that were officially sanctioned, had cultural overtones that broadsheets and pamphlets did not, a close study of these cards provides important clues as to what texts and subtexts were embedded in the American consciousness about the franchise. They also provide at times a glimpse into the strategies and concerns of the suffragists themselves, giving us interesting contrasts to their English counterparts along the way. To study "Votes for Women" as a cultural movement from its artifacts, one must also look at other suffrage ephemera such as buttons and badges, banners, clothing, phonograph records and cylinders, newspapers and popular magazines, sheet music, ceramics, and children's toys. Still, the popularity of the postcard during the final phases of the movement along with the number and variety of cards that were issued makes it an especially valuable source for scholarly inquiry.

Postcards — English

There were more cards produced in England with suffrage themes than even in America, where they were plentiful indeed. English suffragists were generally more aware than their overseas counterparts of the potential of the sale of memorabilia to both help with expenses and to promote the cause. Among the many items featured in their various shops throughout London and England as a whole were postcards and postcard albums. Sylvia Pankhurst even de-

signed a special album for the Women's Social and Political Union (WSPU) that featured on the cover in "the colours" her design of an allegorical woman figure blowing the trumpet horn of "Freedom." There are several period photographs of suffrage shops that show multiple shelves displaying her album. Both the WSPU and the Women's Freedom League (WFL) sold cards that featured photographs of their organizers and leaders. Their low sales price, generally for sale at one English penny each, allowed women with very little money to still purchase a piece of the movement and to bond with their heroines. The fact that these cards were often kept as souvenirs and not always sent through the mails can be seen by the fact that many were autographed by the leaders so depicted. There were also several photographers, such as Mrs. Albert Broom and F. Kehrhahn, who made it their business to photograph major suffrage events, their efforts not only producing many resultant postcards but also providing for a solid photographic record of suffrage history. The WFL and the National Union of Woman Suffrage Societies (NUWSS) were, in addition, connected directly or indirectly to several organizations of suffrage artists, principally the Artists' Suffrage League and the Suffrage Atelier, whose members produced numerous posters and postcards, sometimes of the same design. The militant activities of some of the suffragists resulted in a strong response from the public, and commercial firms took advantage of these reactions by issuing a large number of cartoon cards depicting suffrage themes, many of which were not only highly unflattering to the movement but, at their extreme, could also be vicious in their conception of suffragists.

The WSPU advertised its postcards not only in its paper *Votes for Women* but also in the back of its pamphlets and in other literature. Elizabeth Crawford notes that the first card that can be directly attributed to the WSPU bears the caption "Votes for Women! The Price We Pay for Demanding Our Rights," and contains a photograph of a woman, perhaps Irene Miller, being marched down the street by two policemen. It probably was issued around 1906.[42] But generally the cards that bear the imprint of the WSPU (later NWSPU) are those that depict its leaders. Typically, these cards contain a rectangular or oval photographic portrait of the honored suffragist under the caption "Votes for Women," with her name below along with her role in the union (organizer, officer, etc.). The Women's Freedom League (WFL) also produced a number of cards picturing its organizers and officers, and it is a fascinating but sometimes futile venture to attempt to read into these "leader" cards a history of the development of both organizations, a study of the movement towards what Elizabeth Crawford terms "a cult of leadership,"[43] and the nature of the relationship between the two organizations.

The WFL was formed in September 1907 when dissident members of the WSPU, including Charlotte Despard, Teresa Billington-Grieg, Edith How Martyn, and Caroline Hodgson, believing the earlier organization had become too despotic under the leadership of the Pankhursts and the Pethick Lawrences, formed a breakaway group. Because they felt that they represented the "true" WSPU, they retained the name of the original organization for a while, but decided to change it to the Women's Freedom League in November of that year. The Pankhurst faction renamed itself the National Women's Social and Political Union (NWSPU). It is possible to see the aftermath of the split on postcards, because so many "leader" cards were produced around this time. Edith How Martyn, for example, appears in a two-scene card wearing both cap and gown and prison dress that identifies her as the honorable secretary of the Women's Political and Social Union when it was located at 4 Clement's Inn, Strand. However, two other photo cards with her portrait in oval, issued very soon after, identify her now as the secretary of the WFL. The first includes the original WFL 18 Buckingham address and the second lists the League's

later location at 1 Robert Street. Charlotte Despard, first treasurer and then president of the WFL, is identified on an early card as treasurer of the WSPU, but, on a later card that is virtually identical to the first, her affiliation is now listed with the WFL. Since both cards show the WFL address on Buckingham Street, they were obviously issued after the split, but the first still shows the WFL's brief use of the WSPU name. Preceding the hostilities, the original WSPU did publish a card in honor of Despard. A card for Teresa Billington-Grieg identifies her as the "Organising Secretary of the WSPU," but with the WFL Buckingham address. Someone has crossed out WSPU and overwritten it with WFL. Since the same card also appears with a Women's Freedom League caption, the first version also probably came out just after the split when the WFL was known as the WSPU.

Notices for "leader" cards appear throughout many issues of the WSPU paper *Votes for Women*. Perhaps the most extensive listing was in a February 1910 issue, where postcards for the following were advertised for sale at 1 d. each: "Mrs. Pankhurst, Mrs. Pethick Lawrence, Christabel Pankhurst, 'General' Drummond, Mary E. Gawthorpe, Adela Pankhurst, Gladice Keevil, Mrs. Baines, Mary Leigh, Mrs. Massy."[44] Elizabeth Crawford, noting the absence of such WSPU luminaries as Annie Keeney and Lady

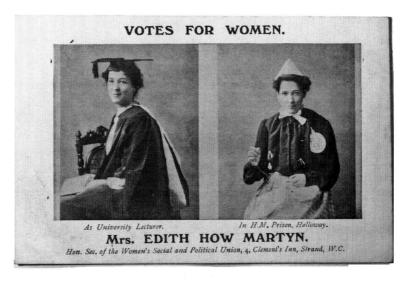

Card of Edith How Martyn staged in prison dress when she was still with the Women's Social and Political Union.

Constance Lytton from a similar 1909 notice and the correspondingly large number of cards available for both Emmeline and Christabel Pankhurst, speculates on shifts within the leadership core. This shift would reflect in part a consolidation of power on the part of the Pankhursts that was reflected in the postcards that the union had for sale.[45] Lytton appears on a 1910 WSPU card, but alongside Mrs. Pankhurst and not by herself.

It is difficult to tell how many of the cards depicting WSPU leaders were actually published by the WSPU and how many by commercial firms that may or may not have had any ties to the union. Some cards of leaders such as Charlotte Marsh did not always list their suffrage affiliation, although presumably they were in-

tended for the suffrage market. Other WSPU leaders who are represented on postcards with their union affiliation listed include S. Ada Flatman, Helen Fraser, Edith New, Isabel Seymour, Mabel Tuke, Elizabeth Clarke Wolstenholme Elmy, and Patricia Woodlock, the last-named photographed wearing a "Votes for Women" button or badge on her tie. Among the large number of WFL members similarly honored were Sarah Benett, Countess Russell, Margaret Milne Farquharson, Lilian Hicks, Madame Aino Malberg, Muriel Matters, Dorothy Molony, Alison Neilans, Bessie Semple, Alice Schofield, and Marguerite Sidley. On a series of numbered WFL cards labeled "Suffragettes at Home," activists are depicted performing duties of everyday women. Mrs. Despard, for example, is shown

Left: One of many official Women's Social and Political Union photo cards of Mrs. Pankhurst, reflective of her dominance in the organization; *right*: Muriel Matters (1877–1969) was an Australian-born suffragist, journalist, and lecturer. In February 1909 she hired a dirigible in an unsuccessful attempt to shower Parliament and the king with Women's Freedom League handbills.

knitting, Mrs. How Martyn is making jam, Alison Neilans is cleaning the stove, Mrs. Joseph McCabe is bathing her baby, and Mrs. Snow is making pastry.[46] These domestic impressions were intended to offset the negative image created by the opposition of suffrage activists as "the other," genderless creatures who had little or no relation to women's daily lives.[47]

Additional organizations also celebrated their leaders on cards, but to a far less extent. Millicent Fawcett appears on two varieties where she is identified as president of the National Union of Women's Suffrage Societies (NUWSS). Other NUWSS members who appear on cards, though without any identifying affiliation, include Isabella O. Ford, Lady Frances Balfour, and Margaret Ashton. The NUWSS actually had more members than either the WSPU or the WFL, and the organization did not always eschew memorabilia, as the number of buttons or badges that they produced can attest. However, the relative absence of postcards portraying their leaders appears to indicate both a general lack of interest in the medium as well as an avoidance

of the "cult of leadership" that characterized some rival English suffrage organizations. A photo card also exists for Victor D. Duval, who founded the Men's Political Union for Women's Enfranchisement in 1910, and several for Hugh A. Franklin, who was a prominent member. A commercial photo card pictures the arrest of Captain C.M. Gonne of the union on November 18, 1910. The Women Writer's Suffrage League and the Tax Resistance League also issued at least one card each.

Even more numerous than leader cards were Real Photo cards with their glossy fronts and the more technologically advanced rotary photograph cards favored by some large commercial firms, both types of which depicted WSPU offices and suffrage events such as demonstrations, marches, carnivals, and exhibitions. Independent merchants produced most of these cards, although several of these photographers appear to have had a working relationship with suffrage associations, and many of their products were probably available through suffrage shops. The WSPU advertised some

A Mrs. Albert Broom photo card of Sylvia Pankhurst carrying the portcullis image that she designed to a Hyde Park demonstration.

photo cards in their publications, including three cards each for demonstrations at Hyde Park and Trafalgar Square, the arrest of Mrs. Pankhurst, and a photo card of "Mrs. Pankhurst, Miss Kenney, and Mrs. Lawrence in Motor."[48] However, it is apparent that they sold many more varieties than they advertised, as can be seen by the number of cards displayed in period photographs of WSPU storefronts.

Perhaps the most prominent of the "semi-official" suffrage photographers was Mrs. Albert (Christina) Broom, whose freelance photographs captured events not only of the WSPU but also of the NUWSS and the WFL during a period from 1908 to the start of the First World War. Broom began her career at the age of forty when her husband was permanently injured in an accident and she needed to bring in an income for the family. While known for her images of the suffrage movement, she also photographed the Oxford and Cambridge boat crews, the funeral of King Edward VII, the coronation of King George V, and the first women police.[49]

Among the suffrage events that Mrs. Broom covered, in addition to scenes of suffrage life in London, were:

(1) The July 23, 1910, WSPU demonstration that ended in Hyde Park. Her photographs of the marchers include Sylvia Pankhurst wearing a large portcullis symbol, which she had designed to celebrate the dedication of suffrage prisoners. Estimates were that approximately a 250,000 people assembled around the forty platforms that had been erected for the demonstration.

(2) the NUWSS "Land's End" Pilgrimage, which began on June 18, 1913, when a large group of marchers left the Market Cross in Carlisle, walking all the way to London and arriving on July 26

(3) various pictures of a car that was given to Mrs. Pankhurst by Mary Dodge, an American suffrage supporter

(4) a summer bazaar at the headquarters of the Women's Freedom League in London

(5) the International Suffrage Fair at the Chelsea Town Hall in November 1912.

One of Broom's most extensive groupings

A Mrs. Albert Broom photo card of the National Union of Women's Suffrage Societies "Land's End Pilgrimage" from the west to the east of England on July 23, 1910.

of suffrage real photo cards involves the WSPU's exhibition and sale of work at the Prince's Skating Rink in Knightsbridge from May 13 to 26, 1909. The exhibition featured over fifty stalls, all decorated in purple, green, and white, where merchandise was sold, many pieces of which were suffrage related. Sylvia Pankhurst's magnificent banners decorated the hall, and there were "tea girls," who sold tea in special china that Pankhurst had also designed. These china suffrage tea sets could be purchased at the exhibit, and later through the WSPU paper *Votes for Women*. Prominent exhibits included "Political Peepshows (Political Cartoons in Model)," a series of twelve individually designed scenes dealing with suffrage issues,[50] and a prison show, where, three times a day, an inmate of Holloway, represented by an actual ex-prisoner, was seen in a mock cell performing those duties forced on her such as scrubbing the floors, scouring pans, sewing shirts, and knitting stockings. One such card without the Broom imprint but probably published by her portrays Mary Brackenberry in prison dress engaged in sewing. Mrs. Broom also

photographed the WSPU fife and drum band that had been formed in 1909 to advertise the exhibition. The drum major of the band was Mary Leigh, who, along with Edith New, threw stones at a window at the prime minister's residence at 10 Downing Street on June 30, 1908, generally regarded as the first suffrage act involving physical violence. Other photographers captured many of these same scenes, but most of Mrs. Broom's cards, but not all, bear her stamp on the rear, along with her address at 38 Burnfoot Avenue, Fulham, London, so they are identifiable.

Some of the suffrage events and scenes that were photographed by F. Kehrhahn, who was commissioned by the WSPU to record many of their activities, include

(1) a "poster parade" of Ealing activists all wearing sandwich boards that were printed in purple, white and green, the suffrage colors, to advertise a demonstration to be held on Ealing Common on June 1, 1912. Unfortunately, Kehrhahn captured this picture in black and white, so the effect of the colors did not come through.

Mrs. Albert Broom's photo card of the Women's Social and Political Union band that advertised the suffrage exhibition and sale at the Prince's Exhibition Hall in 1909.

(2) a scene of Holloway prison, where many suffrage activists served sentences

(3) the WSPU Christmas bazaar of 1911

(4) an image of two suffragettes in replica clothing as warder and prisoner, in front of a mock cell

(5) scenes of participants at the June 21, 1908, Hyde Park demonstrations

(6) the funeral of suffrage martyr Emily Davison at Morpeth.

H. Searjeant published cards of the June 18, 1910, "Prison to Citizenship" procession, the funeral of Emily Davison, and a large number of cards related to the procession of June 17, 1911 that preceded the coronation of King George V. The procession involved extensive pageantry, and was headed by Marjorie Annan Bryce, dressed as Joan of Arc, the patron saint of the suffrage movement. Bryce led a procession of at least twenty-eight different suffrage organizations, a group of 700 released suffrage prisoners holding a "From Prison to Citizenship" banner, a parade of suffragists dressed as famous women of the past, and the "Car of the Empire" float, representing the symbol of unity of the British Empire.

Local firms photographed many of the events that took place outside London. Harvey Barton and Son of Bristol covered the Bournemouth Centenary Carnival. H. Walters and Son photographed a scene outside of the WSPU offices in Ipswich. Graham's of Morpeth was one of many firms that published cards related to the funeral of Emily Wilding Davison in that town. Davison, a suffrage activist, jumped onto the track at the Derby racecourse one June 4, 1913, and attempted to hold the bridle of Anmer, the king's horse, as a social protest. In the process, she was seriously injured by the horse's hooves, and died four days later. She was considered to be the first martyr of the suffrage movement, and her funeral procession drew national attention along with a large contingent of mourners.

What appeared to fascinate many English were scenes of suffrage destruction, such as the burning of Roughwood House, the fire at Hurst Park, which destroyed the grandstand, the attack on the Nevill Cricket Ground in Tunbridge Wells, the conflagration at the prime minister's house at Levitleigh, St. Leonards, and the destruction of several churches, including War-

F. Kehrhahn's card of the Women's Social and Political Union Christmas Bazaar in December 1911.

FIRE AT M.R DU CROS, M.P. RESIDENCE LEVIT LEIGH S.T LEONARDS.

A postcard view of the still smoldering fire that was started by suffragists at the prime minister's house.

grave, Breadshall, and St. Catherine's. Anti-suffragists took revenge, and their actions can be seen on several cards depicting the wreckage of the suffrage headquarters in Bristol. None of these cards, for obvious reasons, contains any overt connection to a suffrage source.

While photo cards of various types could, through their images, convey a message, the main English suffrage associations, such as the WSPU, the WFL, and the NUWSS, relied more on the artist-drawn propaganda cards to make their appeals. These cards consisted primarily of black-and-white line drawings, although a few were in color, of realistic figures in allegorical or semi-allegorical scenes that served either as statements of the suffrage argument or as a reference to a specific contemporary suffrage event. These artist cards were produced either directly by the suffrage organizations themselves or by artist groups such as the Artists' Suffrage League and the Suffrage Atelier, with which they were loosely affiliated.

The Artists' Suffrage League (ASL) was founded in 1907 by Mary Lowndes, who, along with other professional women artists, helped promote the first large-scale demonstration held by the NUWSS, the infamous "Mud March." The ASL did not appear to have had a formal structure, and no constitution or membership lists are known. Nevertheless, it hoped to further the cause of the franchise by engaging the help of professional artists who would donate their efforts to keep before the public in an appealing manner the long-standing demand for the vote. League members embroidered banners, and created designs for posters, Christmas cards, and postcards. All of this was done without compensation, although the League, beginning in 1907, did sponsor competitions for poster designs. In 1909, they awarded a prize of four pounds (later increased to five) for the best poster "suitable for elections."[51] In that same year, they also awarded a prize of two pounds "for a design for a picture postcard suitable for furthering the cause of woman suffrage." The picture was to be in black and white, and the League reserved the right to purchase any image not awarded the top prize for 10 shillings.[52] While the known members of the ASL were all professional artists, their competitions were open to anyone, including men and amateurs.

The league was responsible for at least twenty-four different postcard designs, all of which sold for one English penny at various suffrage shops throughout the country.[53] While several of their posters were offered on occasion for sale in America, the specific allusions reflected on the images on the cards made their use marginal outside of England. Still, an attempt was made by NAWSA to sell a selection of them at their headquarters in New York, where one could obtain a sample set of ten for twenty-five cents.[54] Most of the postcards were signed by the artist, either with full names or initials. These artists included C. Headley Charlton, Joan Harvey Drew ("JHD"), K.F. Powell, H.S. Adkins, E.J. Harding Andrews, Dora Meeson Coates, Mary

Lowndes ("M.L.") and Emily Ford, who was the vice-chairman of the ASL. One of the League's earliest cards was entitled "Taxation Without Representation," and portrays a woman taxpayer before the chancellor of the exchequer, H.H. Asquith, demanding a say in how her money was to be spent. The card, while undated, must have been printed prior to April 1908, when Asquith became prime minister.[55] Other scenes include that of the Mad Hatter's Tea Party, entitled "Men Only," a picture of a mother feeding her son but denying her daughters that is captioned "Everything for him — nothing at all for her," another of an earnest young man called "the Supporter," who is determined to vote for suffrage because his mother was taxed when his father died, and of a group of young girls holding up signs, demanding "Votes for Mammies." One of its cards, depicting a schoolgirl named "Miss Jane Bull"

Left: An Artists' Suffrage League version of the Mad Hatter's tea party; *right*: an artist's appeal to men to provide the vote for the women important in their lives, their wives and mothers.

requesting a piece of the "Franchise Cake" from a boy named "Johnny Bull," was featured on the front page of the American suffrage publication the *Woman's Journal*, despite its English topicality.[56]

The Suffrage Atelier, formed in February 1909 by Laurence and Clemence Housman as a nonaffiliated organization whose products would be available to all suffrage associations, nevertheless had loose ties with the Women's Freedom League, just as its counterpart, the Artists' Suffrage League, did much of its work for the National Union of Women's Suffrage Societies. The Atelier, however, did stock the art stall at the WSPU's Prince's Skating Rink exhibition in May 1909. Sharing many similar aims, it differed from the ASL in several ways. It had its own handpress, allowing the Atelier to publish its own work, much of which was done in block prints with wood or linocuts. It permitted amateurs to take part in the organization, allowing enterprising women to develop a profession. It permitted its artists to take a percentage of the profits arising from the sale of their work, and it had a formal constitution.[57]

As is the case with the ASL, the exact number of postcards that the Atelier produced is not known, although Lisa Tickner notes that around fifty varieties survive today. Not all of the Atelier's postcards come with the Association's name imprinted on them, making identification at times difficult. However, there are three surviving broadsheets that reproduce in miniature twenty-nine of those cards from which potential customers could make a selection. These sheets do help to authenticate and date Atelier cards.[58] Many are produced with the same type of sophisticated line drawings that characterize ASL products, and they are virtually interchangeable except for the imprint of the organization. Some of its most memorable cartoons along this line are a series of cards portraying the "Anti-Suffrage" society as a jackass, a woman labeled "The Modern Shirley" holding the banner of "Political Power," an image by Gladys Letcher of Prime Minister Asquith dressed as a young girl picking the petals off the daisy of woman suffrage while saying "This Year, Next Year, Sometime," and "King Asquith Canute" attempting to keep back the surging tide line of

"Woman Suffrage." Other artists whose names appear on these cards include G. Watson, Isobel Pocock, Poyntz Wright, and Catherine Courtauld ("C.C."). Cards that were printed from wood blocks were less likely to include the League's name.

So popular were the designs on many of these cards that the *Woman's Journal* reproduced them on occasion, either on its front page or as part of a column called "Last Laughs." The famous design that originally appeared in *The Vote* called "The Appeal of Womanhood," for example, graced the cover of the July 13, 1912, issue of the *Woman's Journal*. It portrays an allegorical figure of a woman holding up a sign that explains, "We want the vote to stop the white slave traffic, sweated labor, and to save the children." Cards produced by the Suffrage Atelier entitled "The Vote Girl," in which a girl is struggling with a boy for the ballot, and "The Anti-Suffrage

Gladys Letcher's design for the Suffrage Atelier of Prime Minister Asquith delaying the vote.

Society as Dressmaker," in which a jackass is attempting to dress a woman, were pictured also.

Because the NUWSS relied so extensively on the Artists' Suffrage League for its artwork, it produced but a few illustrated propaganda cards on its own. One depicts a version of an Aesop's fable with a crow in a tree holding the bill of "Limited Franchise," and a fox urging her to say "Adult Franchise." The second reprints a cartoon from the January 23, 1918, issue of *Punch* showing Joan of Arc holding up the banner of "Woman's Franchise" to the caption of "At Last."

The WSPU, except for occasional help from the Atelier, relied internally to meet its needs for artwork for symbols and banners, particularly favoring the brush of Sylvia Pankhurst. It produced a number of postcards, which it sold at its various shops and through the mail, but these were essentially "leader" and Real Photo cards. The handful of artist cards that it printed were primarily the work not of Pankhurst but of Alfred Pease, who, playing on his initials, signed his name "A Patriot." One of his efforts, an illustration entitled "The Two Asquiths," appeared on the November 19, 1909, cover of *Votes for Women*, and was soon made into both a poster and a postcard. The title of his drawing alludes to Asquith's zeal in attempting to reform the House of Lords, while at the same time refusing to support the suffragists' desire to achieve political equality. An advertisement for the poster in two sizes appeared in the December 10, 1909, issue of the same journal, and a notice for the postcard version appeared two weeks later.[59] The December 10 issue also featured on its cover another of Pease's designs that was made into a postcard. Under the caption of "Votes for Women," it portrays the king writing on a poster the words "The People *Not* the Commons Must Decide the Taxes." A commoner is writing on the back of the king, "The Commons as Representative of the People must decide the TAXES," and a woman is writing on his back "Women are half the people and demand a voice in deciding the TAXES."

Artist cards were sometimes printed and sold by individuals independent of any of the major organizations. The best known of these are two cards designed by Ernestine Mills, who also produced suffrage jewelry. The first of these

depicts Mrs. Paddington of the Anti-Suffrage Society attempting to sweep away the tide of emerging suffrage forces. The second of Mills' cards illustrates a spray of roses set against a distant landscape and a glimpse of the sea. A butterfly is attempting to make its way back into the chrysalis, and below is an adaptation of stanzas from Charlotte Perkins Gilman's poem "A Conservative," entitled here "The Anti-Suffragist." The first of Mills' efforts had a decidedly English allusion, but the second could theoretically be applied to a suffrage message in any land. Mills accordingly tried to promote them through the *Woman's Journal* in America, selling them at a dollar and a quarter per hundred in color and sixty-two cents in black and white. Individual cards could be obtained for two and four cents, depending on the version. Despite the promotion and the tie-in to Gilman, there is not much evidence that the cards were popular in America.[60]

Official anti-suffrage artist cards are virtually unknown. Perhaps one of the reasons that the anti-suffrage forces felt little need to enter the propaganda wars through postcards is that commercial publishers were stating their case for them in a far more graphic and extreme way than might have been comfortable for the antis' public image. Commercial comic cards in both England and America often employed similar themes, but in general the imagery on English cards reflected a sharper and more hostile attitude towards suffrage. Suffragists are often seen in combat with police, frequently jumping on their prostrate bodies and shouting, "Votes for Women." While not all suffragists are portrayed as "ugly," many of them are: some are fat, others are thin, with sharp, harsh features and exaggerated noses. One card, linking ideology to physical development, shows the transformation of an attractive young girl into a grotesque suffragette. Often suffragettes are depicted carrying hammers with which to break windows (one activist is drawn in the shape of a female hammer), and sometimes their weapon of choice is a hatchet. Frightened devils run from suffragists as they attempt to chase them down with "Votes for Women" broadsides in their hands. On occasion, strident women are shown muzzled, and in one card, a suffragist's tongue is nailed down to keep her quiet.

There are gentler images, to be sure. Sometimes children are depicted in the role of suffragettes, but to a lesser degree than on American cards. There are Valentine cards, but frequently these contain comic images of female prisoners, and the majority, with their grotesque depiction of women, could be classified as "Vinegar Valentines," an unflattering and definitely unromantic genre of greeting card that was popular in the late nineteenth and early twentieth centuries.

One gentler and rather common card depicts a kitten set against a background of the WSPU's color scheme of purple, green and white, mewing, "I want my vote." A suffrage supporter, attempting to test the fame of Carrie Chapman Catt, sent this card to her from England addressed, "Suffragette, New York, U.S.A." The local post office in America simply forwarded it to suffrage headquarters at the Hotel Martha Washington, where it managed to reach Catt.[61]

English commercial comic cards were far more likely than their American counterparts to allude to specific events and personalities in the unfolding suffrage saga. In a set of six cards signed A.M. (Arthur Moreland) and published by C.W. Faulkner of London, several women are wearing Tyrolean hats, an allusion to the early suffragist Lydia Becker, who wore such apparel. In the same set, a woman at the docket declares, "I protest against Man-Made laws," a reference to the trial of Teresa Billington-Grieg in 1906, where she made the same pronouncement. A card distributed by the North British Rubber Company shows a suffragist pouring acid on a golf course to ruin the green. This is a reference to a series of similar incidents that occurred around Birmingham in 1913, and the card was made by the company to illustrate the durability of their golf balls.[62] In February 1909 Muriel Matters hired an airship, painted with "Votes for Women" on its side, to

A "STRIKING" SCENE AT A SUFFRAGETTES DEMONSTRATION.

Philco Series.

A typical negative image of activists on English cards, featuring a suffragist beating a policeman.

DON'T BE SURPRISED IF IT'S YOUR WIFE WHO DOCTORS THE GREENS!

One of the acts of destruction that militant suffragettes in England were famous for was the pouring of acid on golf greens.

drop approximately six pounds of WFL leaflets over the House of Commons on the opening day of Parliament. The event was satirized on several cards, including one by an unidentified commercial company that depicts two suffragists spinning like helicopters, and asks, "Do You Aviate?"

Christabel Pankhurst, daughter of Emmeline Pankhurst of the WSPU, was affectionately known to some supporters to whom she lectured as "Chrissy." Several resultant cards punningly portray a goose called "Miss Hissy" debating before the "Goose's Social and Political Union." In another card, a female bear, carrying a "Votes for Women" sign, is escorted away by a teddy bear policeman, who tells her, "Come Along, Christabear." Emmeline Pankhurst is caricatured as "Miss Ortobee Spankfurst" on an anonymous card published in Germany. Many other cards lampoon either mildly or viciously women destroying contents of letterboxes and shop windows. At least three cards mock force-feeding by having sympathetic but often harried jailers attempting to pour food through a gigantic funnel or shoot it through a large syringe into a resisting harridan. A set of twelve cards, six pro- and six anti-, labeled the B.B. London series, depicts numerous references to contemporary events, including women holding up a "From Prison to Citizenship" banner, which suffrage ex-prisoners bore in the coronation procession of 1911; a suffragette about to throw a brick through the prime minister's window, as Mrs. Pankhurst did on March 1, 1912; and another in prison after a failed attempt to enter a meeting of Parliament. English commercial publishers were obviously confident that customers not only understood their allusions but were fascinated enough by them to purchase their products.

In all probability, at least some of the hostile tone reflected in commercial cards derives from a response to the violent acts on the part of suffrage militants. Some suffrage associations such as the NUWSS attempted to distance themselves from these acts of violence, and they drew up posters and banners, which are often depicted on postcards, in which they describe their members as "law abiding." But, if the evidence from commercial cards is to be believed, the typical English person, man or woman, imagined the suffragist as a property-destroying militant whose ugly features rendered her genderless. While the ubiquitous implication of the stereotype may not have been accurate, postcards of the period do reflect at least both a partial and a hostile response to a social movement. The number of commercial cards with a suffrage theme, larger even than those published in America, shows the force and immediacy the issue had for the English public.

Posters — Art and Propaganda

The direct antecedent of the activist art poster of the 20th century was the worded suffrage broadside of the 19th, although both the political and advertising poster were of considerable influence in its development, as were in-

THE AGE OF BRASS.

The hostility toward suffrage in early prints, such as this Currier and Ives example, was intense.

Rights Convention at Cooper Union in 1856 that addresses by Susan B. Anthony and Lucott and for the Eighth Woman's Rights tion at the Mozart Hall on Broadway in ork in 1858. Sojourner Truth advertised ree Lectures" on broadsides (noting that would offer for sale her photograph and her s), and appearances by such suffragists as y Stone and Olympia Brown were similarly omoted. Susan B. Anthony's broadsides often ve us the titles of her speeches, such as Woman Wants the Bread and Not the Ballot" and "The New Situation As Women Already Voters Under the Constitution."[1] Unfortunately, we are frequently left with little more than these titles as Anthony never wrote out her speeches and no stenographic reports were ever made. Brief and inadequate newspaper accounts are sometimes all that remain,[2] apart from whatever clues about her speeches can be gleaned from the broadsides themselves.

Except for standard decorative borders and dividers, designs and illustrations were rare in all early broadsides, and did not really become standard features until later. As a result, the first suffrage broadsides are devoid of the artwork that does appear with some frequency in later handbills. Nineteenth-century printers, however, could convey visual appeal through an imaginative array of font shapes and sizes. The more creative a printer was with his or her use of typeface (there were women printers, and suffragists did employ them when available), the more likely the broadside was to attract attention. But it was not until the development of the suffrage art poster that the "message" of the design was inherently as important if not more important than the "message" of its accompanying text.

As aesthetically pleasing as most art posters were, however, they never really replaced the broadside, which continued as an essential source to announce events and to articulate pro-suffrage positions. Moreover, American suffragists published far fewer designer posters than did their English counterparts, and too few examples of those that were produced survive today. The English movement had two organizations that devoted themselves to suffrage art, the Suffrage Atelier and the Artists' Suffrage League. The result was that the English campaign was able to rely

di
ri
l

broadsides on to convey a message or sen appeared with some regularity in the arter of the nineteenth century when new printing techniques allowed for both the use of color and more efficient means of reproducing illustrative graphics. The earlier form of the broadside consisting primarily of a worded announcement was never really supplanted, however, by the use of suffrage art posters in the 20th century, because simple text messages remained both cheaper and quicker to produce. Additionally, they often carried a textual argument for the franchise that would have conflicted with the sometimes spectacularly rendered imagery on the art poster, where symbol rather than words drove home the message. Whatever the case, though, the word "broadside" gradually fell out of fashion in the early twentieth century and was ultimately supplemented by the term "poster," which was applied indiscriminately to any form of printed message, with a design or not or with color or not, that could be displayed in some fashion.

Suffrage broadsides without accompanying graphic illustrations first appeared in the 1850s, not long after Seneca Falls, typically for the promotion of conventions or to advertise upcoming rallies and the appearance of speakers. There are extant broadsides, for example, for the Woman's more on elaborate artwork than was its American counterpart. NAWSA did import and sell some of these English posters in its catalogs to help respond to the need for graphic propaganda, and period photographs of suffrage headquarters sometimes show examples. Still, despite this unfortunate paucity of native pieces, there are important American art posters. This fact was apparently recognized by a Mrs. Harvey, who was head of the press Department of the Women's Freedom League in England, when in 1912 she solicited through the *Woman's Journal* for some of "the smartest American suffrage posters" for a poster parade to be held at the International Suffrage Fair from November 13 to 15 of that year.[3]

One illustrator whose art on behalf of suffrage appeared in magazines, leaflets, postcards, and on posters was Rose Cecil O'Neill, originator of the Kewpies. O'Neill began her professional artistic career in 1893 when she went to New York and became an illustrator for *Cosmopolitan, Good Housekeeping, Truth,* and *Ladies' Home Journal* as well as the satirical political publication *Puck.* She later became very active in the suffrage movement, lending her time, her name, and her Kewpies, particularly during the New York State campaigns of 1915 and 1917.[4]

Among O'Neill's contributions to the movement include a series of pro-suffrage cartoons called the "Kewpie Korner Kewpiegrams," which were distributed through newspapers throughout the United States in 1917 and 1918,[5] and at least four posters, one of which probably served as a trolley car placard. O'Neill's posters were conservative in theme, generally promoting the argument that women needed the vote to augment their traditional roles as wives and mothers. Two of O'Neill's posters, for example, feature Kewpie-like children carrying signs urging, "Give Mother the Vote," noting that "Our Food, Our Health, Our Play, Our Homes, Our Schools, Our Work are all regulated by Men's Votes, Think it Over." A more realistically drawn poster for "Suffrage Sacrifice Week," shows a young mother, with babe in arms, depositing a coin into a bank in the shape of a house, highlighting the plea, "Won't you give us just a mite? Some small coin or other? Won't you help us win our fight Vote for Home and Mother?" A fourth

poster, used in the New York campaigns of 1915 and 1917, shows a happy couple walking arm in arm under the legend "Together for Home and Family." There are other unpublished examples of original O'Neill artwork promoting suffrage[6] that indicate the intent, at least, if not the actual production of additional suffrage posters.

While the suffrage movement in America lacked the organized collectives of activist artists that were a feature of the English campaign, they did borrow at least one idea from these groups, that of the poster competition as a source for new designs. The California campaign of 1911 featured at least three such contests. One, conducted by the San Francisco College Equal Suffrage League, offered a $50 prize for the best design, and it was won by Bertha M. Boye for her poster of a Spanish-American California woman clad in Native American–style draperies holding up a "Votes for Women" sign. She is standing against a background of the Golden Gate with the setting sun serving as a halo around her head. This design was also issued as a postcard, probably by the League, although there was no listed affiliation on the piece. The Political Equality League of Los Angeles held a competition that was won by Julia Bracken Wendt for her piece entitled "Liberty, Equality, Justice." Elmer Wise, who was only fifteen at the time, presented to the Votes for Women Club a "poster full of spirit and spirituality" of an allegorical female figure holding up the sixth suffrage state star. In the California campaign, these and other local designs were supplemented by English posters published by the Artists' Suffrage League, including "Factory Acts" and "Justice Demands the Vote."[7]

Poster competitions were a prominent part of the Empire State campaign in New York in 1915. The campaign committee advertised a first prize of $50 for the winning design, which they intended to display on over 300 billboards throughout the state. The judges were John Sloan, May Wilson Preston, and Luis Mora. The contest's guidelines called for a poster that would "persuade the passerby to vote for suffrage when the question is to be submitted to the voters." The restrictions on the design were that it be 13" by 28½" in size and capable of being enlarged to a twenty-four-sheet stand. The color scheme was to be "in suffrage yellow (the color of a ripe orange) and black," although white could also be used if desired.[8] The entire competition, including $10,000 a month in billboard rental, was funded by a $60,000 gift to the campaign. The first prize was awarded to Ruben R. Purcell, whose design, entitled simply "Votes," depicted a "struggling mass of fighters, rearing horses and desperate men in the mad rush of a bayonet charge." Unfortunately, although Purcell's entry was the unanimous first choice of the judges, it was not permitted to work for the cause, for the advertising company in charge would not allow any references to war on the billboards that it controlled. Other entries in the competition, whose designs were regarded as more acceptable for posting, included Anne Morrison Peck's "Oyez! Oyez!," which depicted a trumpet girl clad in black and white against an orange background. The anti-suffragists began a campaign of ridicule against this poster, proclaiming that the Clarion figure was a "striped hussy, blowing into her trumpet so loudly that they could not get a word of protest in." In part because of the ridicule, Peck's poster was replaced on billboards throughout the state by Nathalie Matson's image of St. George rescuing a woman in chains. A fourth poster from the competition, and one that finally took over from "St. George," was Alice Boyd's "Shoulder to Shoulder," which illustrated a resolute man and woman holding up a banner that requested, "Vote for the Woman Suffrage Amendment."[9]

In October 1915, another poster competition was held in New York, this one under the auspices of the School Art League. Twenty-two high school girls took part in a two-hour free drawing contest, which was won by Irene Forrest of Bay Ridge High School. Entitled "The Ballott [sic] Box Closed to Women," it showed a typical ward politician dropping his ballot into a box, while a refined-looking woman is denied access to the polling booth.[10] There is no record that the winning entry was ever redone and published as a movement poster, but the mere fact that *The New York Times* saw fit to cover the results of the contest is an indication of the interest that such visual productions had for suffrage activists and perhaps for many in the general public as well.

Mrs. Alva Belmont awarded $300 in prizes to five members of the Artists' League of the Po-

litical Equality Association, of which she was president. The money was awarded to the best posters and statuettes representing the cause and the intent was to use the winning designs for future propaganda. The original models were put on display at the League's headquarters at 140 East 24th Street in New York,[11] but there is no evidence that they were ever put into production. The Artists' League, somewhat obscure, was probably modeled after the Artists' Suffrage League in England, which produced posters and other artwork for the campaign.

The Votes for Women Club of San Francisco was so attracted to posters developed by Emmeline Pankhurst's WSPU in England that they held a special exhibition of them as part of their suffrage bazaar that began on December 12, 1910, to help raise funds for the 1911 campaign. Included were posters that "cannot be seen elsewhere." Shortly after the start of the California bazaar, Sylvia Pankhurst, Mrs. Pankhurst's artist daughter, visited New York and gave a lecture at the Carnegie Lyceum on January 6. She was introduced by Harriot Stanton Blatch, who, along with several members of her WPU, had been engaged in a "poster bee" during Christmas week. The city was plastered with suffrage posters, and the police reportedly turned their backs on their activities and chose not to make arrests for littering and defacement of public property.[12]

One of the most attractive of all American posters was that painted by a native of Buffalo, New York, Evelyn Rumsey Carey, and generally referred to as the "Give Her of the Fruit" design. Using a verse from Proverbs 31:31 ("Give her of the fruit in her hands, and let her own works praise her in the gates."), it depicts an ethereal woman emerging from the earth like a tree. Behind her is an image of the White House. The original painting from which the poster was taken is now on display at the Wolfsonian Museum at Florida International University in Miami. Carey's design reflects a tendency in American suffrage posters to feature allegorical or semi-allegorical figures, as opposed to the political cartoon images that often characterized English productions. Moreover, while home, children, and motherhood were prominent themes in the surviving Rose O'Neill posters, many American artists were more inclined to depict trumpet blowers, earth goddesses, and art nouveau women draped in gossamer. One other artist, however, who also focused on the home in her illustrations for suffrage, was Blanche Ames. In her sentimental poster "Double the Power of the Home — Two Good Votes Are Better Than One," for example, a loving mother holds her baby while surrounded by her young blond daughter and her studious son.[13] Ames was secretary of the Massachusetts Woman Suffrage League, and her cartoons on behalf of the movement appeared in *Woman's Journal* and *The Boston Transcript*. Her father was Oliver Ames, Republican former governor of Massachusetts.

Other attractive posters that were printed during the campaign include

(1) "Political Responsibility," a 12" × 36" multicolored piece that portrays a man burdened by a heavy load on top of which is a woman tied down. The image contains the legend "A Load Too Great for Man Alone to Bear — Set Woman Free, She Longs to Do Her Share."

(2) "Let Ohio Women Vote," a 20½" × 26¾" design depicting an allegorical woman figure with the sun and mountains behind her head. This particular image was quite popular during the Ohio campaign, and it appears on postcards, stamps, and stationery.

(3) "Watch Her Grow," a 12" × 19" black on tan poster, copyrighted 1913, that shows a woman growing in height in concert with the addition of suffrage states to the union.[14] This last piece was issued by the *Woman's Journal*, a publication that had been started by Lucy Stone in 1870, and was the source of several interesting but cheaply printed artistic broadsides. *The Suffragist*, the official journal of the Congressional Union and later the National Woman's Party, also was a source for inexpensive posters that resembled handbills.

(4) A colored poster that featured portraits of Anna Howard Shaw and Jane Addams with a scene from the "Votes for Women" photoplay was sold by NAWSA for fifteen cents each at the shop at its national headquarters in New York. The poster was designed to advertise the play, but NAWSA assured potential customers that it was "useful for general purposes."[15]

Rose O'Neill was purported to be among the "Lap-Board Ladies," a group of women who rode the New York City subway trains carrying pro-suffrage placards that refuted the propaganda of the anti-suffragists, whose messages appeared on the advertising space on those same trains.[16] The suffragists themselves advertised on subways as well as on trolley cars, and often created elongated posters or modified existing images for this purpose. In addition to O'Neill's own contribution of the March of Babies trolley poster, other examples of suffrage trolley signs depict a woman standing between two servicemen sons with the accompanying legend "We Give Our Men Our Time Our Lives If Need Be — Will You Give Us the Vote?," a man pointing directly at the observer while admonishing, "Men of New Jersey — Be Just! Vote 'Yes' on Woman Suffrage October 19th," and images of the faces of six women with the legend, "You ask us to walk with you, dance with you, marry you, why don't you ask us to vote with you? Vote YES on Woman Suffrage October 19th."[17] The "You ask us" question also appeared on a poster created by Ethel McClellan Plummer for the Empire State campaign committee. Her design, which featured a stylish couple standing together under an umbrella, stood eight feet in height and was hung in theater lobbies and on billboards throughout New York City during the 1915 state effort.[18]

The Lap-Board Ladies' subway campaign was not the only demonstration in which placards were employed. Mrs. I.F. Mackrille, for example, writing for the *Woman's Journal*, told of her organization's experiences with them, advising other suffragists how to use the medium most effectively: "We advertised 100 placards for one month at a cost of $200 exclusive of printing. Different texts were used, and on the advice of experts, the placards were not crowded with printed matter. The copy was as crisp as possible. 'Give your girl the same chance as your boy,' 'Women pay taxes, give those who pay some say,' were two of the texts used. Each placard also bore the sentence, 'Vote for Woman Suffrage — fourth place on the ballot.' Street car advertising is most valuable in the beginning of a campaign and unless the treasury permits the use of larger spaces than we engaged, I question the advisability of advertising in a small way at the end of a campaign."[19]

One of the more popular non-placard posters was commissioned by the Men's League for Women Suffrage. In the upper left hand corner of the piece, Theodore Roosevelt, with his finger extended, is seen declaring, "Let the People Rule!" Below and to the side are a series of vignettes, including a group of men bearing a banner that says "We're the People," an assemblage of animals including lions and giraffes, alluding to Roosevelt's Africa trip, with the motto, "We're the Animals," and a group of women with a banner that questions, "We're what?"[20] This design, by Clifford K. Berryman, who was famous for his Theodore Roosevelt "Teddy Bear" cartoons, was also used on a black-and-white postcard put out by the New York Suffrage Association and additionally graced the front page of one of its newsletters.

In general, the anti-suffragists avoided the reliance on display and memorabilia that characterized the campaign of their adversaries. Therefore, they did not produce much in the way of poster art, although they occasionally sponsored a poster contest. An exception to this relative lack of graphic propaganda is an 18" × 30" lithograph by Tom Fleming designed for the October 19, 1915, referendum in New Jersey. It pictured two women, one a loving mother with babe in arms, and the other a strident suffrage activist with Medusa-like hair. It asked the male voter, who after all would decide the question, "Which Do You Prefer — The Home or Street Corner for Woman — Vote No on Woman Suffrage October 19th."[21] The poster aimed to heighten the fear many men had about suffrage — that extending the franchise would transform women from the traditional romantic form that they had imaged them to be to that of the repulsive, militant harridan whose main desire, apparently, was to make the world ugly and discomforting to men. It was in response to this fear that many suffrage organizations, such as NAWSA, argued that giving the vote to women would place them in the position of being better wives or mothers, because they could help legislate matters that enhanced the quality of the home such as ensuring the purity of milk and providing for educational opportunities for their children.

World War I provided another opportunity for women to image suffrage as part of the traditional American landscape. The problem, of course, was that once the war was on everyone's minds, suffragists had to be careful lest their public activities to secure the franchise appear diversionary and, hence, unpatriotic. Accordingly, posters appeared portraying suffrage as a responsible adjunct to the war effort. In one drawn by C.D. Batchelor, a Pulitzer Prize–winning editorial cartoonist whose work often appeared in the *Woman's Journal* and its successor, *The Woman Citizen*, a soldier points out his mother to Uncle Sam and argues: " She has given me to Democracy; give Democracy to her." In another, whose image was also incorporated on a trolley placard, a woman stands between her soldier husband and soldier son over the inscription: "We give our work, our men, our lives — if need be — will you give us the vote?" The poster was designed

This illustration by C. D. Batchelor, Pulitzer Prize winning cartoonist, originally appeared on the cover of the Sept. 29, 1917, issue of *The Woman Citizen*.

originally by Evelyn Rumsey Cary, but typically appears in most versions without her signature.

In general, then, the pro-suffrage American art posters tended to portray women either as the ideal mother or as a Pre-Raphaelite or art nouveau goddess-like figure. One should be cautious, however, about inferring too much about suffrage tactics from art posters alone, for there are too few of them that survive in America. For a larger picture of the relationship of art to the suffrage movement, we have to turn to magazine and newspaper illustrations and to suffrage postcards. It would be helpful if there were period records as to why American suffrage groups chose to purchase the specific varieties for resale of English posters that they did, for that might give us a better reflection of movement strategies and intent.

In England, decorative artist posters were either printed or published by the Artists' Suffrage League, for which Lisa Tickner lists fifteen different examples, and the Suffrage Atelier, to which she attributes forty-five more, not all of which are extant. In addition, Mrs. Pankhurst's Women's Social and Political Union was responsible for at least nine more titles and the anti-suffrage forces for seven, although at least two of their designs may have appeared only in postcard format.[22] The Artists' Suffrage League was founded in 1907 by Mary Lowndes as a society of professional women artists who donated their talents to help the cause. They were loosely affiliated with the National Union of Women's Suffrage Societies, and were responsible for creating graphic suffrage banners, pamphlets, and postcards, as well as posters. Their counterpart, the Suffrage Atelier, was formed two years later, in 1909, by Laurence and Clemence Houseman, and while it had loose ties with the more militant Women's Freedom League, its products were theoretically available to any legitimate suffrage group. Its membership was open to amateurs as well as professionals, and it permitted artists to take a percentage of profits, if any, from the sale of their work.

Many of the British posters resembled large and elaborate editorial cartoons, and many were created either to allude or to respond to a specific political issue or campaign. Many were produced for parliamentary general or by-elections. Emily

Ford's "Factory Acts," for example, which was distributed by the Artist's Suffrage League in 1908, dealt specifically with new laws that allegedly protected the female factory worker, but which were drawn up without the workers' say. Mary Lowndes' 1912 "Justice at the Door" poster alluded to the exclusion of women from the reform bill debate. Alfred Pearse, who signed his designs as "A. Patriot," illustrated a poster for the WSPU for the January 1910 general election that served as an indictment against the Liberal government for force-feeding suffrage prisoners. The Atelier launched a series of posters dealing with the "No Vote — No Tax" campaign waged by a number of suffragists, and, furthermore, responded to such issues as "The Cat and Mouse Act" and the effects of sweat labor on women. Also appearing on posters were references to the Conciliation Bill, the Insurance Bill, and to current political leaders, including the prime minister.

According to Lisa Tickner, these posters were distributed in particular contexts for particular audiences. One might find them posted in shops, at railway stations, at meetings and exhibitions, and even "at home." Some newsagents were prepared to display "Votes for Women" posters free of charge if they were guaranteed that twelve customers would buy a copy every week of the WSPU paper. The Women's Freedom League promoted poster parades. Participation in these events was problematic, as it was extremely difficult to carry a sandwich board for any distance on which these posters had been mounted. Women replaced the wooden boards with lighter cardboard sheets, but walking was still difficult.[23] One such parade of note did occur in June of 1912 when a procession of about thirty suffragists walked past the door of the House of Commons bearing boards with such notices as "Women Tortured in English Prisons" and "Citizens, Stop It!"[24] In 1913, Mrs. McGowan and Mrs. R.C. Bentnick organized a poster brigade as a nonmilitant response to some of the tactics of the WSPU. In advertising the event, they asked, seemingly frustrated, "If [nonmilitant suffragists] do not do this, then we want to know what they are prepared to do to get the Vote."[25]

The Pethick Lawrences were especially fond of poster parades, and organized several to promote special issues of *Votes for Women*, including the Christmas issue for 1913, after they had taken back control of the periodical following their expulsion from the WSPU. They also reported on a "new kind of poster parade" held in February 1914 just after the king had opened Parliament. A number of various suffrage organizations took part in the procession, including members from their own Votes for Women Fellowship, who carried red, white, and purple boards that demanded "Votes this Session"; the Actresses Franchise League, who followed with "Now is the Hour" and "Delays are Dangerous"; and the Cymric League, whose slogans were in Welsh.[26]

The National Union of Women Suffrage Societies (NUWSS), the Artists' Suffrage League, and the Suffrage Atelier all promoted competitions with monetary prizes to encourage submission of creative designs. Dora Meeson Coates won the first NUWSS competition in 1907 with her design "Political Help," which portrayed "Mrs. John Bull" refusing to feed her children, who all had such allegorical names as Trade Unions, Primrose League, and the Liberal Federation, out of a bowl labeled "Political Help" until she had first served herself. The Artists' Suffrage League took over these competitions from the NUWSS in 1909, and jointly awarded the first prize of four pounds to W.F. Winter for his "Votes for Workers" and to Duncan Grant for his "Handicapped." Grant, who was later to become known for his participation in the Bloomsbury Group, which included the novelist Virginia Woolf, drew an image of a woman floundering about in a stormy sea with only a pair of oars to row her to safety while a man in a sailboat designated "Votes" nonchalantly passed her by.[27]

In 1911, the League sold seven of their posters in bulk to NAWSA, which then advertised them in the *Woman's Journal* for twenty-five cents each and pictured all. The seven included the aforementioned "Votes for Workers," "Handicapped," and "Political Help," along with Emily Ford's "Factory Acts," Mary Sargent Florence's "What's Sauce for the Gander Is Sauce for the Goose," Emily J. Harding Andrews' "Coming In with the Tide/Mrs. Paddington," and John Harvey Drew's "Won't You Let Me Help You, John?"[28] What is interesting about this assortment is that many of the posters refer specifically to English political issues. Yet, apparently, NAWSA felt that that the colorful graphics of these posters would nevertheless appeal to American women. This must have been the case, because in their national catalog, published a year or two later, NAWSA increased the number of English posters that it was selling to twelve.[29]

Despite the appeal of posters and despite the number of varieties that were produced, costs were always a problem and lack of outside support did cut down on actual production, particularly for the League. In a letter to the NUWSS journal *The Common Cause* in 1910, Mary Lowndes outlined the situation. Color posters were expensive to produce (some early posters were hand-colored for this very reason) and to be able to sell them at cost at four pence each, the League had to order at least a thousand copies from the printer. Because many titles sold off slowly, the League in order not to lose money was reluctant to order new designs until the old ones had sold out. The WSPU sold topical posters for the 1910 elections for only twopence each, but apparently these editions were subsidized from organization funds. Because of funding problems, the League virtually halted any production of posters after their first four years in existence. The financial situation was better with respect to the Atelier. The organization was able to produce more varieties because many of their posters were done in smaller sizes, on cheaper paper, and in black-and-white block printing. When they went to commercial printers to publish larger and more colorful posters, their expenses were as much or more than those of the League. Their "Anti-Suffrage Ostrich" poster, for example, produced in 1912, cost five pence. To further offset production costs, the Atelier sponsored fundraising fairs. They also possessed a hand press and printed many of their own designs.[30]

So effective were English posters that the government in 1914 began to enforce old acts to restrict where they could be placed. A graphic poster showing a woman breaking her chains and protecting her child from the specter of infant death that was published by the International Suffrage Alliance was banned from all public hoardings of London in late July 1914. Around the same time a contract between the National Union of Women's Suffrage Societies with the London General Omnibus Company was circumvented by intervention of the commissioner of police. The suffrage group wished to display on buses a poster that appealed to the public to support "law-abiding suffragists" by becoming members of the Society. The commissioner, however, citing the Metropolitan Carriage Act of 1869, maintained that the display of any advertisement on public carriages was subject to the approval of his office, and, for safety reasons, it had long been his practice to forbid "advertisements of a political character," including the suffrage design. In addition to intense outcries from suffragists over the ruling, the *Manchester Guardian* bitterly protested what it felt to be arbitrary censorship. [31]

Although suffrage posters on both sides of the Atlantic were an integral part of the campaign, their survival rate was low. They were printed to be posted and displayed, not collected, and most were eventually ripped down and destroyed. Still, many were illustrated with both passion and skill, and, as a body, they represent a significant statement from the artistic community about their responses to the suffrage movement and the various issues that accompanied it.

Ribbons

The use of the printed political ribbon in America extends as far back as the first quarter of the 19th century, when crudely drawn items appear celebrating in one fashion or another such figures as Thomas Jefferson, James Madison, and James Monroe. The first extensive campaign use of ribbons, however, occurred during the 1840 election, when William Henry Harrison ran against Martin Van Buren. Over 150 different varieties of lapel material exist for Harrison, although far fewer numbers are known for his rival. Early ribbons were not always campaign related; some were commemorative, some mourning, and some related to movements and causes, rather than to candidates. Beginning around 1850, for example, items were produced for temperance issues as well as for the "Know-

Nothings," sometimes known as the Native American Party or the American Republican Party. Most ribbons were made of silk until 1864 when cotton and linen gradually become the fabric of choice. Silk ribbons were used largely as bookmarks, although pinholes in some surviving examples indicate that they were also worn, probably to marches and rallies. Following the various Lincoln campaigns, however, ribbons moved from the book to the lapel. Once there, they became the campaign item of choice until the end of the century when celluloid buttons began to replace them. [1]

It is not known when the first printed suffrage ribbons were manufactured, although certainly homemade varieties surface relatively early in the history of the movement, and, apparently, were quite popular. During the failed campaign in Kansas in 1867, which attracted Susan B. Anthony, Elizabeth Cady Stanton, and Lucy Stone, among others, supporters wore homemade yellow ribbons, the color taken from the sunflower, Kansas' state flower. The idea of the yellow ribbon as a suffrage symbol soon spread quickly. By 1876, Marie Le Baron could write a song called "The Yellow Ribbon," which reminded female activists "We wear a yellow ribbon upon our woman's breast." [2] By the time of the second Kansas campaign in 1887, the pro-suffrage journal *Justicia* could proclaim that yellow had been "adopted as the distinguishing badge of the woman suffrage army." [3] In 1894, Mary Livermore introduced the yellow ribbon and its attendant suffrage symbolism to supporters in her home state of Massachusetts. [4] In 1920, Laura Johns, to whom credit is given as the originator of the yellow Kansas ribbon, sent a letter of regret to the delegates at the NAWSA victory convention that she could not attend, noting "Isn't it tragical that I cannot be present to see the finish and be decorated with the yellow ribbon badge of which I was the author?" [5]

The third formal campaign in Kansas in 1894 also resulted in the production of a graphic ribbon, one of the few printed examples of nineteenth-century varieties that have survived. Measuring 2⅛" × 6¼" and produced in the now established colors of black-on-yellow, it featured the image of a dove underneath the legend "Equal Suffrage — We Wage a Peaceful War."

Below the dove are the words "Kansas Amendment—1894." It was distributed by the journal *The Farmer's Wife*, which was published in Topeka, and the ribbon sold for a dollar per dozen and six dollars per hundred. The journal, which had but a scant three-year run from 1891 to 1894, was edited by Emma D. Pack and published by her husband, Ira. The paper promoted populist issues, derived in part from the platform of the People's Party with which Ira Pack was associated, and supported women's rights, an elevation of women's economic status, and prohibition. The dove ribbon, however, was possibly the only suffrage artifact that the paper ever distributed.[6]

An early and formalized use of ribbons as convention badges occurred at the 1888 meeting of the International Council of Women that was assembled by the National Woman Suffrage Association and met March 25 to April 1 at Albaugh's Opera House in Washington, D.C. There were sixteen differently colored badges issued to delegates, various committee members, and the press. As officers for the committee of arrangements, Elizabeth Cady Stanton and Susan B. Anthony wore a black-and-gold ribbon, the badge committee itself wore pink, and general delegates wore white.[7] It is not known whether or not these were printed ribbons, although they probably were, but they could have been simply cut out of cloth. A period photo of international delegates to the convention, most of whom are wearing a nondescript ribbon, leaves little in the way of clues.[8]

It is extremely difficult to find examples of printed suffrage ribbons, however, prior to the 1890s, perhaps indicating that most of these early ribbons and badges were crafted as one-of-a-kind pieces by individual suffragists and were not manufactured commercially.

No convention ribbons for the National Woman Suffrage Association have apparently survived if any were ever made, but when the group merged with the American Woman Suffrage Association in 1890, examples appeared within the next few years. The first National American Woman Suffrage Association (NAWSA) ribbon recorded by the APIC project was from the 27th annual convention, held in Atlanta in early 1895.[9] Although the project does not record

examples from every convention that followed, it is quite likely that they were produced. Many convention programs identify ribbons as part of the credentials packet and instruct delegates where to pick them up.[10] One of the more interesting delegate items, not a ribbon but a celluloid disk suspended from a hanger, was issued for the 1905 convention in Portland, and it pictured the famous Native American woman Sacajawea.[11] She was honored by NAWSA that year for her heroic contributions to the Lewis and Clark expedition. Anna Howard Shaw noted, "Next to 'Suffrage Night,' the most interesting feature of the exposition to us was the unveiling of the statue of Saccawagea [*sic*]."[12] But there were other ribbons and badges issued for this convention. Lucy Stone's daughter, Elizabeth Blackwell, was impressed by the "yellow ribboned delegates" roaming through the streets of the city.[13] One of the delegates to the 1911 NAWSA convention in Louisville expressed a similar reaction in a note to the *Woman's Journal*:

"We all have yellow badges [and other accouterments] on our dresses and coats ... and as we go about in dozens or scores or hundreds the onlookers receive the fitting psychological impression and we find them thinking of us as victors and conquerors."[14] The official yellow convention badge for that year that the correspondent was alluding to was actually a nondescript 2" × 7" silk ribbon containing the words "Suffrage Convention—Louisville, KY.—1911."

Not all of NAWSA's

One of few National American Woman Suffrage Association convention ribbons on which the organization failed to identify itself.

formal meetings were necessarily national conventions open to delegates. In 1897, the national leaders met at a conference at the First Baptist Church of Minneapolis on November 15 and 16 that was held in conjunction with the state convention of the local Political Equality Club. The event was noted with a 2" × 6" black-on-yellow ribbon that celebrated the participation of both organizations. Susan B. Anthony was present at the gathering and autographed several of these ribbons.[15] The Political Equality Club of Minnesota was originally organized as the Woman Suffrage Club of Minneapolis in 1868, and was renamed as the Equality Club in 1897. It was disbanded following the passage of the national suffrage amendment in 1920. The club hosted many Minneapolis Woman Suffrage Association annual conventions as well as the NAWSA annual convention held in 1901.

Many conventions produced multiple ribbons, one for

the delegates and another versions for officials and helpers, including ushers and pages. Some ribbons, though not most, came attached to a metal hanger. Technically, the term "ribbon" is used only for items that consist of nothing but a strip of cloth. A "ribbon badge" is a ribbon that has an added attachment, such as a celluloid disk or a metal nameplate.[16]

One of the earliest known ribbons printed for meeting of a local suffrage group was that for the 1894 convention of the New York Woman Suffrage Association, held in Ithaca.[17] At the bottom of the ribbon, following identification of the organization, the convention, the city, and the year, appeared the words "Souvenir of the 600,000 Petition." The allusion was to a petition drive earlier in the year when the state of New York planned to hold a constitutional convention. One of the issues to be considered was whether or not women should be granted the right to vote. Governor Roswell Flower was in favor of the franchise extension and also wanted women to serve as delegates to the convention. He introduced a bill to the legislature that would have given him the power to appoint women delegates, but his proposal was declared unconstitutional and women, consequently, were not granted a formal voice on behalf of their own cause.

The suffrage forces, however, still seeing grounds for optimism, started a major petition drive to push for the franchise extension amendment. The campaign was run out of Susan B. Anthony's home in Rochester. Anthony, now seventy-four, spoke in all sixty counties in New York on behalf of the proposition. An independent magazine, *The Illustrated American,* ran a contest in conjunction with the drive in which it awarded a hundred-dollar prize to the best essay on the question, "Shall Women Be Granted Full Suffrage?"[18] Suffragists had hoped to obtain a million signatures on the petition, but they were able to gar-

Left: Susan B. Anthony, who was in attendance at this conference, signed several of the backs of the ribbons, including this example; *right:* One of the most commonly preserved of all suffrage ribbons from the 19th century.

ner only 600,000, and those with the help of labor organizations, other suffrage groups, and the Grange. The amendment was eventually defeated, 98–58.[19] The ribbon that was issued for the November 12–14 suffrage convention that followed the defeat not only served as an identification badge, but also recognized the efforts of those who had worked so tirelessly to obtain names for the petition.

The New York Woman Suffrage League (NYWSL) also helped, along with the New York Woman Suffrage Association, to secure names for the state drive. At the doors of Chickering Hall in New York, where the annual convention of the NYWSL was held on February 26 and 27, 1894, there were tables set aside for the signing of the petition, each topped with little bows of yellow ribbon suffrage badges. These items were sold for five cents each by persons whom *The New York Times* characterized as "charming young women." No one who had signed the petition was allowed to leave the hall without putting on the ribbon.[20] Because no surviving examples have been located, is not known whether these ribbons were manufactured items or handmade.

There were NYWSA ribbons from the 1897 convention in Geneva, the 1898 convention in Hudson, and the 1899 gathering in Dunkirk. Other surviving ribbons from NYWSA conventions include the 32nd annual meeting in Glens Falls in 1900 through the 39th in Geneva in 1907, along with an isolated piece from the 46th in Rochester in 1914, although doubtlessly others were issued for the intervening years.[21] Some of these ribbons come with a photo button or hanging celluloid honoring such leaders as Elizabeth Cady Stanton, Emma Willard, Susan B. Anthony, Anna Howard Shaw, and Carrie Chapman Catt. NYWSA was one of the few suffrage groups to so honor leaders by picturing them on any type of memorabilia, although some of these buttons were issued in memoriam. In England, however, the practice of honoring current workers and leaders, whether on buttons or postcards, was rather common.

In 1894 also, an organization devoted to homeopathy, the COUFTDO, provided a ribbon for their gathering in Bath, New York, on August 16 that portrayed a couple kissing along

with the legend "Female Suffrage No Show Here." Other ribbons issued by lodges and professional organizations contained a similar attempt at humor and satire not necessarily mean-spirited in intent. The fact that suffrage is the object of humor indicates to what degree the issue had penetrated popular culture of the period.

Many other state organizations issued ribbons for their local conventions, although, because of the ephemeral nature of these pieces, it is not clear whether they did so each year with any consistency. The Pennsylvania Woman Suffrage Association used ribbons for at least seven of their meetings. Other groups issuing badges include associations in New Jersey, Nevada, Michigan, Ohio, California, and Iowa. Activists in Utah, one of the first suffrage states, wore a black-on-red ribbon that proudly proclaimed, "Utah Has Womans' [sic] Suffrage." [22] California women, who had hoped to win the franchise in 1896, produced a silky yellow ribbon with frayed ends for their convention in November of that year.[23]

The Missouri State Woman Suffrage Association, which was affiliated with NAWSA, held its annual meeting in April 1919, for which it produced a ribbon. A year earlier, the St. Louis League of the Association had invited the NAWSA to hold its 1919 national convention in St. Louis. The national group accepted, and the meeting took place in March 23–29, an event that Carrie Chapman Catt was later to describe as "the best convention ever held anywhere."[24] Both the state and the national groups used the same manufacturer for their ribbon designs, and the two pieces are virtually identical except that the local version contains the wording "Missouri Suffrage Convention," whereas NAWSA's indicates "National Suffrage Convention." The national ribbon also was attached to an embossed, die-cut metal bar that featured the image of Saint Louis, the 13th-century monarch who is the only canonized king of France and the icon of the Missouri convention city.

The majority of extant suffrage ribbons are convention items, although sufficient varieties were made for other occasions. Those that simply proclaim "Votes for Women" in black lettering on a yellow background probably were intended for marches and parades, not conventions, although they could have been worn at both types of events. An interesting black-on-yellow ribbon from an unidentified source states simply "Municipal Suffrage for Women," indicating a campaign where women, if they could not vote in a presidential election, were nevertheless attempting to gain local suffrage access.[25] There were at least five or six mock Belva Lockwood ribbons made for the satirical "Mother Hubbard" marches held throughout the country (see **Belva Lockwood and the Equal Rights Party**). Additionally, ribbons were produced for a suffrage ball that was held in Lynn, Massachusetts, on October 13, 1915, an unidentified suffrage "bazar" for an unknown place and year, a National Suffrage School that took place in Baton Rouge, Louisiana, February 22–24 in an unidentified year, and several precinct worker or poll watcher ribbons for referenda that were held in California and New Jersey in 1911 and 1915 respectively.[26] NAWSA issued for the holidays a thin ten-yard ribbon bolt that sold for twenty-five cents and repeated over and over again, "Merry Christmas — Votes for Women."[27] Because this bolt was made for decorating and wrapping, it is most often found today cut up into pieces.

An undated and unadorned black-on-yellow ribbon exists for the Men's League for Women Suffrage that was probably a marching ribbon, perhaps for the New York event of 1910, the first big suffrage parade, where the eighty-seven men who took part with the rest of marchers up Fifth Avenue were jeered by the crowds that lined the sidewalks. The idea for the League may have come from Max Eastman in 1909, when he was a young professor at Columbia University, and its name may have been modeled after the English association that had been formed by Herbert Jacobs in 1907. In 1910 James Lees Laidlaw, a prominent New York banker whose wife was also heavily involved in the suffrage movement, assumed the presidency. From 1910 to 1917, the League was extremely active in the New York suffrage movement, holding district rallies, public dinners, theatrical performances, balls, and various other campaign events. Men's leagues were formed in other states, including New Jersey, whose chapter issued a button on a ribbon for an unidentified event or rally. In October 1912, *The Woman Voter* issued a special league number with accompanying sketches and pictures.[28]

The California Equal Suffrage Association, whose members attempted to show creativity in their production of even standard memorabilia such as campaign stationery, wrestled with the purpose and function of the convention ribbon. Was it merely intended to be an identification piece that allowed the wearer entrance to convention events or should it be used to promote the cause? In 1909 the Association opted for promotion over identification at their meeting in Stockton. The badges for that year bore the words "Votes for Women" in large type instead of "Delegate" so that all could read and know that the suffragists were in town. In very small type at the bottom of the ribbon were the initials of the Association and the place and date of the convention.[29]

There are a limited number of known suffrage ribbons from England, despite the superior merchandising of memorabilia by

Left: The local Missouri ribbon and the 1919 National American Woman Suffrage Association St. Louis convention ribbon were very similar in design; *right*: there were several men's suffrage societies with similar names — this example is probably from New York.

British activists and their focus on "wearing the colors." The WSPU did offer a few "Votes for Women" woven ribbon badges for sale at one English penny, the same price they charged for most of their buttons or badges.[30] There are several possible reasons for their relative absence. The English held far fewer suffrage conventions than did their American sisters, and thus did not have as compelling a need for identification or delegate badges. Moreover, while many English suffrage associations were very concerned about display at public meetings and marches, the exhortation to "wear the colors" may have focused more on what type of dress the activist wore as opposed to whatever ribbons she might have attached to it. In America, those organizations that were more militant or more assertive in their tactics, such as Alice Paul's NWP, actually produced far fewer ribbons than their more conservative counterparts, perhaps adopting other forms of visual rhetoric to achieve notice. While certainly American marchers, militant or not, could and did wear parade ribbons on occasion, it was the sash and not the ribbon that drew attention of onlookers.

Rolling Pin

A novelty manufactured by the Bleazby Brothers of Detroit that could have been mocked by the anti-suffragists if it had become popular enough was "A Tiny Rolling Pin" that they promoted in the March 30, 1912, issue of the *Woman's Journal*. In their advertisement, they noted, "We've had the Big Stick, now let's have the Big Rolling Pin; roll out the opposition; roll in Votes for Women." Each pin was priced at ten cents and consisted of a small wooden piece to which a cheap piece of paper with printed suffrage phrases had been glued.[1]

Rubber Stamps

In an effort to promote the cause, suffragists frequently stamped their postcards and envelopes with a "Votes for Women" rubber stamp, particularly when suffrage Cinderella stamps were not available. There are a number of varieties of rubber stamps,

but one of the first was issued by NAWSA in 1911 and sold for fifteen cents.[1]

Sashes

One of the more ubiquitous symbols of the suffrage movement, particularly during the period of mass parades and demonstrations from about 1910 to 1915, was the suffrage sash. Draped around the shoulders, extending down to the waist, and often worn in conjunction with a parade "uniform" with hat or other standard mode of dress, the sash was a strong visual statement to the onlooker of the intensity of the movement. Most sashes contained no slogan other than the standard "Votes for Women," their colors along with the numbers of women who wore them in a demonstration providing the main messages. NAWSA's official color of yellow did not stand out by itself, but the multitude of sashes on women who marched in one of their parades presented a sea of color whose meaning was unmistakable. The Woman's Suffrage Party of New York was one of the few organizations to print its name on the sashes that it issued, but these sashes, with their yellow background, also relied heavily on color to draw attention during parades and demonstrations.

Sashes were worn in marches throughout the country, but they were especially in evidence in many of the vast parades held in New York City. Theodore Roosevelt was invited to head the Men's League for Equal Suffrage contingent

Most suffrage sashes, unlike this example from the Woman Suffrage Party, did not identify the issuing organization.

that marched in a "Votes for Women" parade there on May 4, 1912. Also taking part was Mrs. Belmont's Political Equality Association (PEA). Mrs. Belmont, who always made a point of not personally displaying the dark blue official color of her association, wore simply a white gown with a hat trimmed in black. Marchers from the PEA, however, all wore "Votes for Women" sashes, along with twenty marshals from the same organization.[1] When Harriot Stanton Blatch's Women's Political Union held a dress rehearsal for the parade in April, all women taking part wore the tricolor sash of the union.[2] Sashes were also on prominent display in a march that took place along Fifth Avenue in October 1912 that involved approximately 20,000 demonstrators and 400,000 onlookers. Anna Howard Shaw, departing from the traditional yellow of NAWSA, wore a "great blue sash." One of the other marchers was Inez Milholland, who, when asked by an onlooker if she was not cold in her flimsy outfit, answered without knowing that exposure and exhaustion on behalf of the cause would, in part, be responsible for her death, "I will never get cold in a cause such as this."[3]

On the cover of the official program for the spectacular suffrage "Banner-Parade" held on October 23, 1915, Frances Maule Bjorkman and Mrs. Henry Brueres of the WPU are pictured in their purple, green, and white "Votes for Women" sashes registering potential paraders. The program itself contains much information about the proscribed rules for dress for marchers from the different suffrage organizations taking part, including a general warning to all participants, "especially the youthful ones — against wearing their hats [many of which were "official"] rakishly upon the side of their heads."[4] When Rosalie Jones and Ida Craft led a pilgrimage to Albany, all of the marchers wore suffrage sashes or stoles upon which the words "Votes for Women" were imprinted, and passed out both literature and buttons along the way.[5]

But sashes were worn for other reasons and on other occasions than parades. In fact, in NAWSA's supplemental catalog of literature and supplies, they are referred to not as "parade sashes" but instead as "usher's sashes" and sold at three dollars and fifty cents per dozen.[6] Even in its main literature and supplies catalog, where

NAWSA calls them sashes, their main purpose was listed as "For ushers."[7] When Emmeline Pankhurst was about to return to England in January 1912, she made an appeal for funds before a rally of Harriot Stanton Blatch's Women's Political Union. Ushers, dressed in purple, green, and white sashes, passed baskets up and down the aisles, collecting approximately $5,000 in the process.[8] The sashes probably were those of the WPU, but it is possible that Pankhurst brought the draping over from England as the WPU and the WSPU shared the same colors, although the lettering on the English version was more stylized. Alice Paul's Congressional Union (CU) had a special sash made up in purple, white, and gold, not with the organization's name or even a suffrage slogan imprinted on it but with the simple word "usher" to indicate its purpose. The colors of the sash were so ostensibly emblematic of the organization that no other specific identification was necessary.[9] In fact, the traditional CU sash, which was later used when the CU morphed into the National Woman's Party, contained no words at all, just the group's colors. These sashes can be seen on occasion in period photos of women picketing the White House.

In general, sashes could be worn at any time activists wished to identify themselves visually with the movement, whether or not they were acting collectively or as individuals. Women at suffrage stands at bazaars often dressed in sashes, as did speakers on platforms. When Emmeline Pankhurst came to New York in October 1909 and appeared before a meeting of Harriot Stanton Blatch's League of Self-Supporting Women at Carnegie Hall, she was embraced by Kate Keegan, wearing a sash in purple, green, and white. Keegan had been a prisoner with Pankhurst at her first incarceration at Holloway.[10] Two suffrage speakers on a portable platform in Harlem in 1913, addressing a small crowd on the subject of the franchise and education, had to abandon their speeches when someone in the crowd threw, first a paper bag filled with water and then another bag, this one filled with small shards of glass.[11] The hostility which the pair generated may have been occasioned as much by their visible sashes as by their audible words. At a meeting of Italian suffragists, attended in part by women editors of Italian newspapers wishing to find writers familiar with both the suffrage movement and the Italian language, participants all wore yellow sashes after attending a torchlight parade.[12] Presumably the purpose of the sashes was to draw attention to suffrage from the Italian community as well as to serve as a bonding instrument among the attendees to the meeting.

Bonding and solidarity became an issue for suffragists, who had rented a booth at the Woman's Industrial Exhibition in the New Grand Central Palace in New York in March 1912. The women had taken their booth at the last minute, much to the chagrin of some of the exhibition's organizers, who returned their rental check and forbade them from distributing suffragist literature at the event. The women proceeded to obtain a court injunction to open their booth once again. Many of the suffragists then began to walk around the hall in suffrage sashes emblazoned with the words "Votes for Women," and were joined in their demonstration by women from other exhibits. The anti-suffragists in the hall, including Mrs. Arthur Dodge, a notorious opposition activist who was also vice president of the exhibition, attempted to get the women to take off their sashes, but they merely refashioned them about their necks, making certain that the suffrage message was visible.[13] Suffragists were refused a booth the following year, but they returned as demonstrators, wearing purple, green, and white sashes, and walked about the hall for two hours. There were no incidents, although one male onlooker did ask the women why they had worn sashes instead of buttons.[14]

Because sashes relied more on size and color than lettering to convey their message, it is rare to find an example with a slogan other than "Votes for Women." Variations do exist, but their differences tend to be nondescript and relegated to such matters as the size of the sash itself or the width of the yellow or purple bands attached to it. While suffragists often kept their sashes as personal souvenirs, they do not appear to have been collected by them in the same fashion that buttons, stamps, postcards, and ribbons were. Most sashes were constructed to be draped around the shoulders of the wearer. Hence they were issued in a "loop" design, with whatever words were imprinted on them visible on both the front and back of the demonstrator. Some of the cheaper varieties were one-sided only, and were pinned to the front of the dress or blouse rather than draped around the wearer. Over the years, some antique dealers, in an effort to double sales, have cut looped varieties into two pieces, so the historian or collector should be aware.

In England, sashes were also a significant part of a suffrage "uniform," perhaps even more so than in the United States. The WSPU's plea to its members and sympathizers to "wear the colors" often involved the donning of a purple, green, and white sash with the words "Votes for Women" imprinted on it. The WSPU sash was, for the most part, a standard issue, differing primarily from the American WPU version in its larger and more ornate lettering. Women can be seen wearing them in numerous photographs and postcards from the period as part of the "suffragette look," which often included a light-colored dress and hat. Sashes could be purchased from the Woman's Press as early as 1908, where they were advertised as a form of regalia called "bandoliers" at two shillings and six pence each. When the Pethick Lawrences split with Emmeline Pankhurst in 1912 and took the journal *Votes for Women* with them, the WSPU began publishing a new periodical, *The Suffragette*, which did not include the extensive advertising for the variety of novelties that their previous publication had, but still promoted various forms of marching regalia, the sash becoming so synonymous with WSPU activities.

The WSPU was not the only English suffrage group to rely on sashes to communicate their message. When the National Union of Women Suffrage Societies began their famous Land's End to London march in July 1913, pilgrims wore the recommended uniform, which included a red, green, and white shoulder sash along with matching haversacks. Various types of sashes can also be seen at times on the shoulders of members of the Women's Freedom League.

Scarves

More than 10,000 scarves in purple, green, and white, the colors of the Women's Social and Political Union, were sold in London during the great demonstration at Hyde Park in 1908, where women were urged to show their colors. Dry goods stores were also cleaned out of ribbons in these shades, which women fashioned into belts and men into cravats. Both sexes also used these ribbons to make badges and rosettes.[1]

Sheet Music, Songsters and Records

The theme of women's rights, both pro- and anti-, both serious and comic, has had an extensive history in the tradition of American popular music, making its first appearance in printed form at least fifty years prior to the first woman's rights convention in Seneca Falls in 1848. Suffrage lyrics can be found in newspapers, single-page broadsheets, sheet music, and songsters. Their study provides another serious glimpse into the development of the power relationship between men and women in America.

The earliest recorded lyrics dealing with the theme of women's rights appeared in *The Philadelphia Minerva* on October 17, 1795, a newspaper whose title suggests an appeal to female readership. The song itself, published without music, was called "Rights of Woman" by "a Lady." It urged women not to be awed "by man your tyrant lord," to "endure no more the pain of slavery," to declare your "equal rights," and to find in "Wolstoncraft [sic], a friend," an allusion to the British writer Mary Wollstonecraft, whose *A Vindication of the Rights of Woman*, published a scant three years earlier, in 1792, argued that women are not inferior to men, but only appear to be so primarily because of a lack of education.[1]

Women's rights, particularly in terms of the marital relationship, was a popular theme in American music, even before Seneca Falls. The issue made its appearance in early nineteenth-century music as a type somewhat akin to the later Victorian parlor song. As a rule, most Victorian parlor songs were highly sentimental, romanticizing and glorifying femininity and woman's "traditional" role as homemaker. Many parlor songs were written for reputable singers who introduced them in music halls, and were published later in sheet music form and sold to the general public, primarily women, to play at home on the fortepiano, an instrument that was gaining popularity.[2]

But those songs that dealt with women's rights had a defiant edge to them and involved a rejection of the socially approved and compliantly domesticated image of woman that appeared in most later parlor music. For example, a song written by C.E. Horn and published in Baltimore in 1813 urged women to "slip over" the word "obey" during a marriage ceremony that "was so wish'd for and dreaded." An 1830 song titled "No, No, I Never Will Marry," by an anonymous composer, declared that the singer would "rather lead monkies [sic] forever, than be led by that ape called man." Alexander Lee's "I'll Be No Submissive Wife," first published in 1835 with a sentimental cover picturing a woman in a garden, was also emphatic in its lyrics. The narrator asserts that she will "not be a slave for life," will not say as other women have that she will "love, honor, and obey," and that she will not give in to a "humdrum husband" who demands that she stay at home. This particular song proved to be so popular that it went through at least four more distinct editions with different covers within the next ten years.

Other songs expressed the theme that women actually rule over men, despite their characterization as the "weaker sex." These songs had such titles as "Woman Rules You Still (As Sung by Mad. Anna Thillon)"(1840), and "The Lords of Creation Men We Call" (1840). Since men wrote several of these songs, it is not always easy to judge whether their intent was serious or satirical. Also, the original music hall performers who popularized these pieces could twist the words to give them either a comedic or a reflective emphasis.[3] But, no matter what their intent, these songs are strong evidence of the fact that the topic of women's rights was embedded in popular American cultural thought prior to Seneca Falls.

What appears to have been more popular with women in the mid-nineteenth century than message lyrics were those songs that dealt with the new fashion of the bloomer. Crew lists at least 25 different examples of sheet music on the subject that were published between 1851 and

1853, many with sentimentalized covers picturing women in "bloomers" and often carrying parasols. The songs were often dedicated to Amelia Bloomer herself.[4] The majority of these compositions were simply dances with such titles as "The Bloomer Schottische," "The Bloomer Polka," "The Bloomer Quadrilles," "The New Costume Polka," "The Bloomer Waltz," and "The Bloomer Quick Step."

Amelia Jenks Bloomer, born in Homer, New York, in 1818, was a social activist who was interested in both temperance and suffrage, and attended the first Woman's Rights Convention in 1848. She married Dexter Bloomer around 1848 and wrote on social issues for his newspaper, *The Seneca Falls County Courier*. She started her own paper in 1849 called *The Lily*, which was dedicated to the cause of temperance. But with encouragement from Elizabeth Cady Stanton, she also tackled women's issues. She was particularly interested in dress reform, believing that the typical costume for women, involving confining and health-debilitating corsets and several petticoats, was in need of change. She favored a new style involving short dresses or skirts over bulging trousers that gathered at the ankle, much in the manner of fashion in the Middle East and central Asia. Bloomer did not originate the style, which nevertheless became named after her. Fanny Wright of the New Harmony Socialist Commune wore a version of it in the 1820s. It was introduced to Bloomer by the temperance activist Elizabeth Smith Miller and also worn in public by the actress Fanny Kemble. For many, the new form of dress was a woman's rights issue, not only because of Bloomer's suffrage sympathies, but also because it addressed the topic of women's freedom in terms of her right to be comfortable in what she wore. Newspapers of the period, perhaps in part fearful of the emerging issue of women's rights, often ridiculed the style, but an inherent sympathy among many women for what Bloomer was attempting to do was, obviously, a reason for the proliferation of the subject in period sheet music, albeit for only a short period of time. Bloomers made a reappearance in the 1890s with the advent of the bicycle, but there was not an appreciable corresponding resurgence of the style as a topic in sheet music and song.

Following the Seneca Falls Convention, the subject of women's rights in sheet music took on a political edge where previously it had been confined to the social sphere. Two songs published in the early 1850s specifically alluded in their titles to that convention and to the other suffrage meetings that followed, "The Woman's Rights Convention Waltz," arranged by Julia Baker and published by William Hall in New York, and "Woman's Rights, a Right Good Ballad Rightly Illustrating Woman's Rights Music and Poetry Rightly Written for the Womans Rights Conventions by Kate Horn (Not One of the Womans Rights Conventions)." The latter piece, obviously an oppositional response to female empowerment though written by a woman, argued that it was a woman's right to act as a wife to a legislator but not to mount the stand and act as a commentator, and it was her right to rule the house and brave "petty troubles" but not her right to rule the "head" and treat him as her "petty slave." Other songs found in sheet music format, while not directly mentioning women's rights conventions, dealt with the issues that evolved directly out of those gatherings, whether it was the question of women's rights generally or the topic of voting rights specifically. Titles include "Woman's Rights," published in 1853 by Fanny Fern and sung by Wood's Minstrels, "Woman Is Going to Vote," with words by Luke Collins and music by J.P. Webster, published in 1868, and "Clear the Way for Woman Voting," also published in 1868, with words and music by John W. Hutchinson and performed by the Hutchinson Family Singers.

In discussing the suffrage songs that evolved after 1848, Francie Wolff divides them into two types: rally songs and songs of persuasion, a helpful categorization as long as one realizes that these lines of demarcation were not necessarily absolute. According to Wolff's division, rally songs were those songs that attempted to inspire or rouse women to action. They were usually sung to the tune of familiar songs, so that when lyrics were passed around at suffrage gatherings, all could join in because everyone knew the melody. The two most common types of tunes that were thus modified were religious hymns and patriotic anthems. The use of hymns can partly be explained by the religious backgrounds

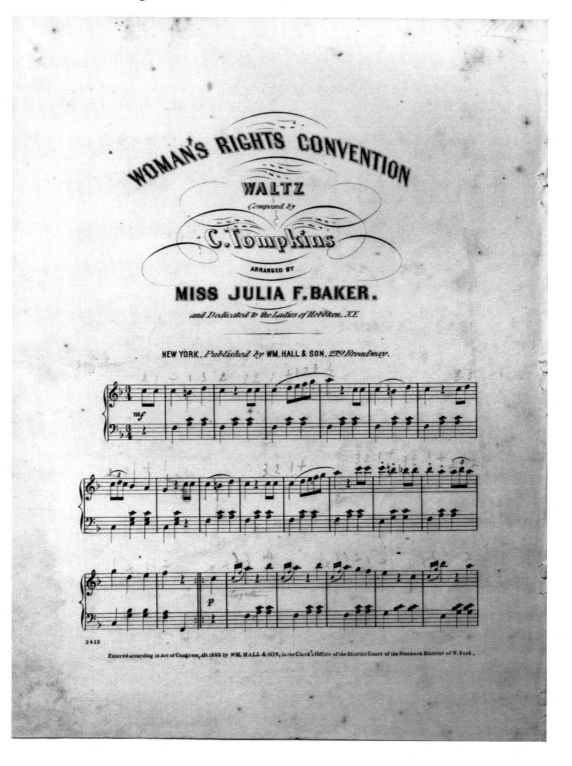

Quite probably the first allusion to Seneca Falls in American sheet music.

of many of the early suffragists. Lucretia Mott was a devout Quaker, Olympia Brown was an ordained minister in the Universalist Church, and Anna Howard Shaw was an ordained Methodist minister.[5] But there were rally songs written by and for traveling minstrel groups such as the Hutchinson family, who often attended suffrage events and attempted to inspire those present with their compositions. These songs usually but not always contained their own original melodies.

The other category of pro-suffrage songs which Wolff describes are songs of persuasion and were argumentative rather than rallying in content; they explained why women wanted the vote, presented the virtues of motherhood and the injustice of taxation without representation, and proposed notions of what the world would be like if women had the vote.[6] While rally songs were generally printed on single sheets of paper, now sometimes termed "broadsides," or in suffrage songsters, it was these songs of persuasion that were more likely to find their way into sheet music format and subsequently into the parlor. The woman who played songs of persuasion on the pianoforte or on the piano, perhaps while singing them, was instructor to her audience. She was not so much rallying those around her, although that could very well have been a by-product of the performance, she was enlightening friends and family to the justice of the cause in the nonthreatening environment of the home.

Whether through rally songs or songs of persuasion, music was now intertwining itself with the suffrage movement. And the publications that began to illustrate the theme were but a small reflection of many songs and orchestrations that were raised at suffrage rallies, meetings, and other events. An important group in developing a suffrage musical tradition was the Hutchinson family, precursors to the protest singers of the 1960s. The ensemble consisted at various points of all thirteen children of Jesse Hutchinson, a New Hampshire farmer. The Hutchinsons sang about the rural life they knew, but also focused on songs involving abolition, war, temperance, and woman suffrage. Not all thirteen sang at the same time; some served only as temporary fill-ins for absent members. The group finally split into two ensembles in 1859,

called the Tribe of Asa and the Tribe of John, each led by sons of Jesse Hutchinson. Both groups were also advertised on occasion as the Hutchinson Family Singers. Not only were the Hutchinsons composers and performers of suffrage songs, they often attended suffrage rallies, and both John and Asa were friends with Elizabeth Cady Stanton.

In several of the early books of the six-volume *History of Woman Suffrage,* Elizabeth Cady Stanton reflects on a number of occasions relating to her interactions with the family and how they worked to help the cause. In 1855, for example, John Hutchinson, writing to accept an invitation to appear at the convention in Saratoga that year, noted, "We are all interested in Woman's Rights and in liberty for all humanity.... We will consult together, and if we can make up a quartette we will try to be with you to sing once more our songs of freedom for another struggling class."[7] The Hutchinsons also took a very active role in the Kansas campaign of 1867. John Hutchinson co-wrote with P.P. Fowler "The Kansas Suffrage Song," a rally piece to the tune of "Old Dan Tucker," which was "sung at the meetings and concerts during the grand campaign" in that state and "at the polls in Leavenworth, by the Tribe of John, on the day of the election."[8] On May 14, 1868, the Hutchinson family opened the annual meeting of the American Equal Rights Association with their song "We Come to Greet You."[9] In her return to Kansas in 1881, where the Hutchinsons were taking part in the campaign, Stanton noted that what suffrage speakers "could not do with reason and appeal, the Hutchinsons, by stirring the hearts of people with their sweet ballads, readily accomplished."[10] In addition to the Kansas piece, John Hutchinson also wrote and composed other songs for the cause, including "Clear the Way for Woman Voting" (1868), "The Fatherhood of God and Brotherhood of Man" (1868), "Vote It Right Along" (1869), "One Hundred Years Hence" (1876), and the tune for "The Good Time Coming" (1889).

While additional pieces of original sheet music on the suffrage theme, some pro-, some anti- continued to be produced throughout the remainder of the 19th century, it was the rally songs printed on single song sheets or gathered together in songsters that still proved to be the most popular. Among the various titles can be found "Fill the Ranks with Voters"—to the tune of "Glory Hallelujah" (1888), "Woman and the Ballot"—to the tune of "Mollie and the Baby" (1888), "Give the Ballot to Mothers"—to the tune of "Marching Through Georgia" (1888), and "The Equal-Rights Banner"—to the tune of "The Star Spangled Banner" (1889).

While many rally songs were printed up for a specific meeting or rally, their popularity among suffragists became so pervasive that various suffrage organizations and journals collected them and published them for regional or even national distribution. The South Dakota Suffrage Association, for example, issued a twenty-page songster in 1888 that could be picked up at its headquarters in Huron for ten cents.[11] For fifteen cents, the American Woman Suffrage Association in 1889 sold through the *Woman's Journal* a woman suffrage leaflet that contained the words to thirteen rally songs, including Rebecca Hazard's "Give the Ballot to the Mothers" and Rev. C.C. Harrah's "The Equal Rights Banner." In 1897, just seven years after the American Woman Suffrage Association had merged with its counterpart rival, the National Woman Suffrage Association, the *Woman's Journal* sold another version of the leaflet. This follow-up contained but eight songs. Both versions began with the words to "The Battle Hymn of the Republic," by Julia Ward Howe. The inclusion of this song was no accident. Howe was a noted New England suffrage leader, who helped found the American Woman Suffrage Association in 1869. The patriotic song "America" can also be found on other rally sheets, indicating that not all songs sung at suffrage gatherings necessarily focused on the franchise, and that many of them contained a strong patriotic element. Utah suffragists, although they were busy planning for a display at the Columbian Exposition in Chicago in 1893, still managed to collect and publish a songbook in 1892.[12]

When NAWSA published its *Manual for Political Equality Clubs* in 1896, it outlined the structure of six possible meetings for suffragists and included prayers and words for rally songs. These lyrics included Marie Le Baron's "The Yellow Ribbon" (to the tune of "The Wearing of the Green"), Sophia Hale's "The Breaking Day" ("Webb"), the Rev. C.C. Harrah's "The Equal Rights Banner" ("The Star Spangled Banner"), Harriet H. Robinson's "Columbia's Daughters" ("Hold the Fort"), Rebecca N. Hazard's "Give the Ballot to the Mothers" ("Marching through Georgia"), and the anonymous "Press On" ("Maryland, My Maryland"), "The New America" ("America"), and "Woman's Crusade" ("John Brown").[13] The focus on song in this manual was a strong indication of the degree of importance that it had for the national organization to rally their supporters.

In England, the Women's Social and Political Union published seven militant songs in 1907 as part of a "Votes for Women" pamphlet." In 1908, they issued another song sheet leading with "The Women's Marseillaise." In the same year, Alicia Adelaide advertised in the WSPU paper four songs that she had written and published, including ""Fight On," "Clipped Wings," and "Marching On." Laura Morgan-Browne, who had campaigned for the cause since the end of the nineteenth century, wrote "The Purple, White, and Green," to be sung to the tune of "The Wearing of the Green."[14]

Rally sheets and songsters remained popular up until 1920, when women finally received the constitutional right to vote. Perhaps the one with the widest distribution was the "Equal Suffrage Song Sheaf," a 1912 collection of twenty-five songs compiled by Eugenie M. Raye-Smith that was dedicated to the Rev. Anna Howard Shaw. California women printed up a tricolor sheet entitled "Suffrage Campaign Song for California" for their successful 1911 effort in that state. Charlotte Perkins Gilman, the author of the widely circulated feminist short story "The Yellow Wallpaper," wrote "Another Star," also for the California campaign, using the tune of a popular 1860s song "Buy a Broom." The original piece derived from a Bavarian drinking song about brushing away the insects that annoy you. The argument of Gilman's composition was that women would clean up politics the same way that they cleansed the house of obnoxious creatures and objects. Even the program for the "Victory Convention" of the New Jersey Woman Suffrage Association contained nine songs to enable delegates to celebrate with music their successful battle.[15]

One of the most popular of all collections of rally songs, going through several editions.

But as the twentieth century approached, more and more the theme of suffrage was advancing into the parlor, accompanied by a variety of newly composed songs designed specifically to be published in sheet music format. Many of these titles had an official or semi-official suffragist status, but a number were also popular pieces, sold at local music shops and not at a suffrage headquarters. The lyrics of these commercial music shop pieces, both pro- and anti-, indicated the degree to which suffrage was now present in the national consciousness. Both types were also greatly enhanced by new printing technologies that allowed for the cheap use of color on their covers to attract potential buyers.

Nettie Bacon Christian wrote one of the more intriguing semi-official songs in 1895 and dedicated it to Helen M. Gougar, who was president of the Indiana Suffrage Association. The title of the song, "American Citizens Who Cannot Vote — The Indian, the Chinaman, the Idiot and the Woman," reflected a racist theme common to the iconography of many a pro-suffrage illustration. The anger that some suffragists had

towards minority groups who could vote while they could not was often extended as well to African Americans, to immigrants in general and to Italians in particular. Other sheet music titles with at least some degree of official tie-in include: Lila C. Bliven's "Give Us the Ballot — Dedicated to the Political Equality Club of Emmetsburg, Iowa" (1897), the 1914 song "Fall in Line — Suffrage March," sold by the New York State Woman's Suffrage Association, "Hurrah! Votes for Women," written by Lillian Hart Durand in 1914 and "Dedicated to the Suffrage Movement in New Jersey," another 1914 piece entitled "Suffrage Marching Song," that was "Officially Approved and Sold for the Benefit of the Equal Suffrage Cause" by the Massachusetts Woman Suffrage Association, and "Woman Suffrage Song — 'Victory,'" distributed by the Woman Suffrage Party of Luzerne County, whose headquarters was located in Wilkes-Barre, Pennsylvania. The Women's Political Union published "The Women's Political Union March," which they sold at their headquarters in New York City for twenty-five cents, and

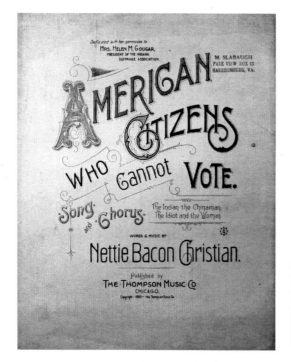
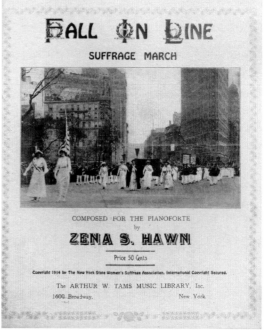

Left: Although pro-suffrage, the song, unfortunately, reflects some of the over-all cultural racism of the period; *right*: this march was reflective of the popularity of banner parades in New York prior to the 1915 referendum.

which featured the Clarion image, so common to their campaign memorabilia.

Even the anti-suffrage forces had at least one "official" representation in sheet music in the song written by Phil Hanna entitled "The Anti-Suffrage Rose," published by the Women's Anti-Suffrage Association, located in Boston. Red, along with black and white, was one of the colors of the opposition, and the antis often represented it through the symbol of a rose. An earlier satirical song, "Belva, Dear, Belva, Dear!," written, composed, and published by M.H. Rosefield in 1888, was part of a large scale burlesque effort to discredit the presidential campaign of Belva Lockwood. It is probably the only known piece of presidential sheet music, pro- or anti-, devoted exclusively to a woman candidate prior to the passage of the Federal Suffrage Amendment in 1920, although there are scattered references to Victoria Woodhull in some.

The sheet music for "November," written by Ella H. Lowe and Edward Johnson and published in Suffern, New York, in 1915, recounts a little-known event in suffrage history. Suffragists in the fall of that year honored NAWSA's president, Anna Howard Shaw, by presenting her with a Saxon automobile, painted in the suffrage color of yellow. The words of the music do not allude directly to Shaw's gift, but do refer to a tour in a comparable yellow Saxon to win the vote in November. Perhaps as a result of this donation, the Saxon automobile became loosely associated with the suffrage movement. On April 6 of the following year, Alice Snitjer [or Snitzjer] Burke and Nell Richardson were sent out by the National Woman Suffrage Association on a tour of twenty-five states to promote the cause of suffrage. They did so in a Golden Flier Saxon, similar to that appearing on the sheet music cover. Burke and Richardson were also featured in a magazine ad for the Saxon,[16] which may have been the first time in advertising history that women were used to endorse an automobile to attract women buyers. The tour was not an easy one. They suffered privations crossing through the desert and the Badlands. They were on the

Left: The cover of this music sheet contains both the official color (red) and the official flower (the rose) of the anti-suffrage forces; *right*: the Saxon Auto Company, whose car is shown here, established a strong relationship with the suffrage movement.

Mexican border during raids, and their car had to be pulled out of the water during floods.[17]

Perhaps the most spectacular use of a suffrage song at any rally or demonstration in America was the performance of Ethel Smyth's "The March of Women" at a massive demonstration in Washington on May 9, 1914, organized by the Congressional Union for Woman Suffrage. Delegates from every congressional district in the country marched up the Capitol steps to present suffrage resolutions to members of Congress. A chorus of 1,000 voices, all trained by Mrs. Appoline M. Blair, sang Smyth's march, which, unlike most marches, contained words.[18] All of the members of the chorus wore white gowns with green stoles and ivy on their heads. Smyth was a member of the English WSPU, and her song was originally published in sheet music format by the union's literature department, the Woman's Press, and a "vocal card with words" was also available.[19] It was played for the first time on January 21, 1911, at the Suffolk Street

By the second decade of the 20th century, suffrage had entered into the mainstream American cultural fabric as illustrated by this song from the *Ziegfeld Follies*.

Galleries to welcome those who had been imprisoned following Black Friday in November 1910.[20] The cover illustration, designed by Margaret Morris, contained an extremely colorful depiction of women marching with the standard-bearer carrying a "Votes for Women" flag in the WSPU colors of purple, green, and white. Later, when Smyth was imprisoned in Holloway for her suffrage activities, it was reported that she heard her song being sung by other suffragist prisoners in the courtyard. She then moved her cot to her window, stood on it, and conducted her song through her bars with a toothbrush.[21] There were several simple black-and-white versions of Smyth's song published in America, but none with an illustrated cover in color as the WSPU's version was.

In both England and America, many suffrage groups and individuals working within those groups frequently advertised their suffrage compositions in both regional and national publications. Editors of those periodicals gave notice to new song sheets with the same zeal that they promoted postcards, perhaps with some consideration of future advertising revenue. Alice Stone Blackwell, for example, announced in late June 1909 in the *Woman's Journal* that Crane and Company of Topeka, Kansas, had just published a "Suffrage Song Book." The firm took out an ad in the publication the next week. Also variously promoted and/or advertised in the *Woman's Journal* were "The Suffrage Marching Song" from the Massachusetts Woman Suffrage Association, "The First Rose of Suffrage," from the company of Richards and Richards of Illinois, which was an agent for suffrage literature, "Fall in Line," from the New York State Woman Suffrage Association, and Pauline Russell Browne's collection of "Woman's Suffrage Songs," sold by the Woman's Franchise League of Indiana. NAWSA sold "The Woman's Battle Song" by Elizabeth Bullock, "Equality" by Helena Bingham, "Votes for Women" by Maria Louise Carlton, and the identically titled "Votes for Women" by Nellie H. Evans, each for twenty-five cents.[22] Alicia Adelaide Needham's collection of four suffrage songs, "Marching On," "Daughters of England," "Fighting On," and "Clipped Wings," received notice in an October 1908 issue of *Votes for Women*, and was extensively advertised the following November. Also promoted was "Give Her a Vote, Papa" from the publisher Stanley Webb. The Wimbledon branch of the WSPU advertised its song leaflet, which included "A Free Field" and "Freedom of Speech."[23]

Popular sheet music with suffrage themes, those pieces sold commercially in stores and not through suffrage outlets such as periodicals and movement shops, reflected a variety of period genres, including ragtime ("That Ragtime Suffragette" from the *Ziegfeld Follies of 1913*), show tunes ("The Militant Suffrage Song" from Charles Dillingham's' *Old Town of 1909* and "Votes for Women" from *They Loved a Lassie*, produced in the same year) along with marches and two-steps ("Twentieth Century Woman Two Step March" of 1906 and the English "Suffragettes One or Two Step" of 1913). Often they delineated a topsy-turvy world in which women, now hypothetically having obtained the vote, were forcing men to do their jobs. In "No Suffragettes for Mine," a beleaguered husband is doing the wash; in "Mind the Baby, I Must Vote Today," an unconcerned woman is seen leaving the house to exercise her rights to the franchise while her incompetent husband deals with a howling child; "Everybody Works but Ma— She's an Advocate of Woman's Rights" and "Since My Margarette Become-a-da Suffragette," in which a submissive Italian immigrant is down on his knees pleading for mercy from his dominatrix girlfriend. Anti-black satire is present in "The Darktown Suffragette Parade."

Not all popular songs were satiric or derisive. Perhaps the biggest seller among such sheet music as determined by surviving copies was the popular edition of "She's Good Enough to Be Your Baby's Mother and She's Good Enough to Vote with You," with lyrics by Alfred Bryan and music by Herman Paley, published with two different covers by Jerome H. Remick in 1916. Both covers portrayed a smiling young wife and a small infant or baby. Even though the ultimate purpose of this piece appears to have been commercial, it reinforced several of the arguments that suffragists, particularly those from the mainstream, were making: those who would most benefit by the vote were not the harridans and the desexed creatures of anti-suffragist propaganda, but rather the women that men most re-

The composers of this song combined a bias against immigrants with ridicule toward the suffrage movement.

spected, their wives and mothers; the vote would not overturn the traditional marriage relationship and make women bosses, but rather it would enable mothers to do a better job watching over the home; and, finally, if men entrusted their children to their wives, surely a highly responsible task, then were these same women not able to handle the less onerous task of voting? The same themes were echoed in Richard O'Connor's "In 1920 I Will Vote for You," whose cover depicts a patriotic motif through images of the American eagle and the Liberty Bell, thereby legitimizing suffrage as a movement that was in keeping with traditional American democratic principles. The number of popular songs in the decade between 1910 and 1920 that dealt directly with or alluded to the theme of suffrage and its inevitable effects, good or bad, on the social structure, is a strong indication of how much the issue was integrated into the core of American culture.

America and England were not the only countries where suffrage sheet music made an appearance. In France, several songs are known, including "Marche des Suffragettes," with words and music by Isoline Azzara Grinberg, and "Le Droit des Femmes," with words by Montehus and music by G. Grier, who published the piece. The satirical "J'n'ai jamais pu comprendr' ca!" by L. Henry Lecomte and Abel Quielle, took a bemused look at the emerging feminist movement, including voting rights agitation. In the Netherlands, sheet music for "Hollandsche Keis-rechtjuffers" by S. DeHaas and J.C. Van Kerkvoorde depicted on its cover an illustration of four suffragists marching with a banner proclaiming "Vrouwenkiesrecht," the Dutch equivalent of "Votes for Women."

There are period Edison cylinders and phonograph records with suffrage themes, but most of these are talking comedy pieces and not musical selections. The music recordings that were made include A. Liberatti's "Suffragettes March," Charles A. Prince's "The Suffragette Militante," and George Reneau's "Woman's Suffrage." The titles of the comedy records show a genre that offered a fairly conventional response to the issue of women's rights and include "Schultz on Woman's Suffrage," "Old Country Fiddler on Woman Suffrage," "Mr. Dooley's Address to the Suffragists," "The Suffragette Street Scene" and "Uncle Henry Sees the Suffragette Parade."[24] In general, they featured a country bumpkin, an elderly disconnected man, or an immigrant attempting to make sense out of a modern phenomenon.

Shirts and Socks

The *Woman's Journal* reported that so many men in England wanted to show that they were believers in equal suffrage that an unnamed manufacturer put out for them a special "suffragette shirt," with stripes of purple, white, and green, the colors of the WSPU, along with socks in the same design. According to the journal, there was some demand for these articles,[1] although none appear to have survived today.

Soap

Various forms of suffrage or "Votes for Women" soap, generally made of glycerin, were sold in both England and the United States. The English firm of J. and A. Miller, Soap Works, advertised "The Suffragette Toilet Soap," noting that it was "made and used by Suffragettes," that sold in a box of three "tablets" for one shilling and two pence.[1] The WSPU sold a box of four bars with "Votes for Women" molded into each and the cover containing a stamp of Sylvia Pankhurst's design of a woman sowing the seeds of woman's suffrage.[2] The author has in his own collection an oval bar of similar design that he purchased from an English source. By 1914 a commercial manufacturer in America had made a "special soap" that was dedicated to suffrage and from which at least one suffrage organization was given a percentage of the sales.[3] In 1915, the Women's Political Union, based in New York, issued small cakes of soap bearing in purple and green letters the following words, "Votes for Women!/Equal Suffrage/Means Clean Politics/Use This Soap and Do Justice/for Women."[4] No inventory lists of sales are known, and thus it is impossible today to determine how popular various brands of suffrage soap were. Many of these soaps were used as intended, and those that were not are subject to age cracking, two factors responsible for their low survival rate today.

Spoons

In her study *Selling Suffrage,* Margaret Finnegan notes the relationship between the evolution of the suffrage movement and the growing consumer culture of America in the late nineteenth and early twentieth centuries. Part of this new culture involved an increasing emphasis on commodities: things that could be manufactured and bought that were not necessarily essential to sustain life.[1] While one might debate the significance of the reactions of suffragists, both conservative and radical, to the growing influence of mercantilism in American culture, it is clear that manufactured memorabilia that could be sold in suffrage shops and bazaars played an increasingly important role in promoting the idea of the franchise. What we might today term suffrage ephemera from the nineteenth century — sheet music, broadsides, and ribbons — was issued originally for a purpose, to rally supporters at a meeting, to provide information as to when the next lecture would be, or to serve as a means of identification. Any collector appeal was generally secondary. However, as suffragists themselves saw the potential in commodities to raise money for the cause, an increasing quantity of suffrage memorabilia emerged in the marketplace, objects that had little or no primary functionality other than to be appreciated and collected, at the same time raising money for the cause.

One of the earliest of the pure suffrage collectibles to appear was the souvenir suffrage silver spoon. The first modern collector's spoon of any sort, suffrage related or not, is generally acknowledged to be the one patented in 1881 by Myron H. Kinsley for the completion of the Niagara Falls suspension bridge. What made this spoon a collectible was the fact that there was no pretense whatsoever that the purchaser would ever actually use Kinsley's spoon as an eating utensil.[2] Ten years later, Millie Burtis Logan of Rochester, New York, designed the first suffrage variety, a silver grapefruit spoon, that featured a bust of Susan B. Anthony at the tip of the handle, her name, and the words, "Political Equality."[3] The back was engraved "1892," stamped "sterling," and trademarked with an "S" in a scroll, indicating that it was made by Frank W. Smith, a silver manufacturer from Gardner, Massachusetts. Despite the date, the spoon was available for sale a year earlier, in 1891, as the original jeweler's circular that accompanied it indicates.[4] At least three additional spoons are known in this design, a 4½" demitasse, a scalloped, slotted variety of the same size, and a 5¾" dinner spoon, all sterling but not all containing the manufacturer's mark. Logan's mother was Anthony's cousin,[5] so, in all probability, the spoons were sold as some form of suffrage fundraiser.

Probably the earliest minted collector's spoon for the suffrage movement, featuring a bust of Susan B. Anthony.

The only known collector's spoon issued by National American Woman Suffrage Association.

Other suffrage spoons include an official NAWSA demitasse that was made by the Watson Company. Inscribed in the bowl is the legend "National Woman Suffrage Convention 1912." On the top of the handle is the word "Philadelphia," the site of the convention, followed by various images associated with the city, including the city seal, a portrait of William Penn, Independence Hall, an eagle, and the Liberty Bell. There are additional scenes on the rear. This piece is probably the only collector's spoon produced by NAWSA. The firm of George Homer of Boston made a 5½" sterling spoon, numbered 724, on which the words "Votes for Women" were embossed on a handle that featured openwork daffodils at the top. It is not known whether this was an official issue.

Another spoon merely contains the word "Equality" in the bowl. Patented in 1912, it is nevertheless engraved "1915" on the stem. While "Equality" is a common enough demand made by advocates for a variety of causes, the fact that this is of the suffrage period and that the term has associations with Anthony probably identifies it with the movement. The year 1915 suggests that it was minted for use in the eastern states campaign of that year, when Pennsylvania, New York, Massachusetts, and New Jersey all held referenda on the suffrage issue, all going down to defeat. One of the rarest of the suffrage spoons was made in 1904 in the Netherlands for the International Woman Suffrage Alliance. The spoon contains the legends "Votes for Women" and "Jus Suffragii ['Right to Vote']," the latter adapted by the IWSA as their official motto. It was made by Cornelis Rietveld, an active silversmith from 1865 to 1912 in the town of Schoonhoeven.

The *Woman's Journal*, always eager to increase its circulation, gave away free pieces of flatware to readers who were able to obtain a prescribed amount of new subscriptions. Theoretically, if a reader applied herself diligently, she could obtain a full service. However, these pieces of flatware, spoons, knives, and forks, did not have any engraving or other indication on them that suggested they were tied to the movement in any way, and probably were utilitarian rather than souvenir in conception.

Stamps, Cinderellas, Stickers and Labels

The use of non-philatelic stamps (sometimes referred to as Cinderellas[1]), stickers, and labels to advertise and advance the cause of suffrage was heavily influenced by two sources, the political or propaganda stamp, which had its origins in America in the mid–19th century, and the poster or advertising stamp, which had a brief but momentous run during the years 1912 to 1915. But as important as the stamp format was to advertise the movement, suffragists printed a variety of other forms of small, colorful paper items to serve such purposes as luggage labels, bookplates, window stickers and the like. Anna Howard Shaw, for example, had made a personalized bookplate that pictured a small cherub carrying a "Votes for Women" pennant.

Political stamps, resembling postage stamps in size and appearance and designed to promote a presidential aspirant, can be traced as far back to at least 1856 with the candidacy of John C. Frémont, just nine years after the appearance of the first acknowledged U.S. postage stamp in 1847. Several portrait souvenir stamps are known for Frémont's presidential run containing such slogans as "Free Land, FREE LABOR, FRE-MONT," and "Fremont and Our Jessie [Fremont's wife]"[2] The next presidential campaign, in 1860, included items for Abraham Lincoln, his main opponent, Stephen A. Douglas, and third-party candidate John C. Breckinridge. The use of these early Cinderellas on behalf of presidential candidacies coincided with the appearance of numerous varieties of campaign envelopes, which also featured portraits and slogans of various national and state nominees lithographed on the upper left of the cover.

But while stamps and labels are known for

most national politicians throughout the latter half of the nineteenth century, political Cinderellas were not produced in abundance until the McKinley and Bryan campaigns of 1896 and 1900, just prior to the appearance of the first woman suffrage stamp in the first decade of the twentieth century. They continue to be a source of political advertising right up to the present, despite current U.S. postal restrictions, with certain candidates such as Franklin D. Roosevelt, Wendell Willkie, and Richard Nixon eliciting especially numerous varieties from their supporters.

The development of the political campaign stamp in the nineteenth century most probably influenced the creation of the political cause stamp in the twentieth. In addition to woman suffrage, one of the earliest if not the earliest cause to produce Cinderellas, there were also stamps for civil rights organizations and movements, with examples from the NAACP dating from the late 1920s until present times, labor movements, including the IWW and the AFL-CIO, the NRA, the Ku Klux Klan, Social Security, Prohibition, antiwar, and others. The first American Christmas seal was created by Emily Bissell in 1907. Bissell was a Red Cross volunteer who wished to raise money for a small Delaware sanitarium, and sold copies of her design at a penny each. Easter Seals did not make their appearance until much later in 1934.

The second major influence on the development of the woman suffrage Cinderella was the advertising poster stamp, a larger and more graphic type of label than its political predecessor. According to Robert C. Bradbury, this new format of the Cinderella evolved in the second decade of the twentieth century, when advertisers changed the form of earlier Cinderellas, creating perforated and nonperforated labels that resembled miniature posters rather than postage stamps to promote their products.[3] These stamps became highly collectible, and their evocative colors, their imaginative designs, their commercial intent, and their general aesthetic appeal made them more suitable items for placement in an album or scrapbook than for embellishment on the front of an envelope addressed to a friend. While many thousands of varieties of the poster stamps were published, the popularity of this second format lasted but three years, from 1912 to 1915, after which advertisers generally turned to other forms of media to promote their products, although post–1915 advertising poster stamps are known. But the effect of the poster format on the political and cause stamp was profound. While some stamps continued to be printed to resemble officially issued government types, many produced by cause groups such as woman suffrage associations adopted the appearance of the poster stamp in size, design, and color because the new medium conveyed the suffrage message in a far more graphic and striking fashion than did the older variety.

Kate M. Gordon, as part of her corresponding secretary's report, introduced the earliest known woman suffrage stamp to the delegates at the 1903 national convention of the National American Woman Suffrage Association. She characterized the design on the item as that of "a college girl in cap and gown holding a tablet inscribed: 'In Wyoming, Colorado, Utah and Idaho women vote on the same terms as men' to offset the prevailing ignorance of this fact."[4] The stamp, in government postal format, was printed in blue on a white background and measured 1" × 1½". Although these stamps were affixed to various parts of envelopes and letter sheets, they were supposed to "be placed on the lower left hand corner of letters sent by those who believe in political equality."[5]

There are other scattered references in varying specificity to stamps and labels to promote the cause of equal franchise throughout the national convention reports in *The History of Woman Suffrage*. In her secretary's address, delivered to the convention in 1904, Elizabeth J. Hauser, for example, told of the progress in the printing and distribution of literature and memorabilia after NAWSA had moved its national headquarters from Warren, Ohio, to New York City. Printed products included 2,000 each of Lucy Stone and Elizabeth Cady Stanton birthday souvenirs, Christmas blotters and "10,000 suffrage stamps."[6] These stamps went through several more printings for a total cost of $45, and, at the time of Hauser's report, had brought in $59.25.[7]

In 1909, Mrs. Harold Dudley Greely and

Mrs. Rheta Childe Doer, President and vice president respectively of the Cooperative Equal Suffrage League, journeyed to the White House to present President Taft, Senator Robert LaFollette of Wisconsin, and Associate Justice of the Supreme Court David Brewer with the first three copies of a new stamp that they had designed for national distribution. The stamp, in blue, contained at its center an image of the scales of justice in equilibrium. The top of the design featured the standard "Votes for Women" slogan, while the bottom proclaimed, "Taxation without Representation Is Tyranny." Around the border were the names of the four states that had conferred equal suffrage for women at that time, Idaho, Utah, Wyoming, and Colorado. The women wanted to give Taft a copy, but he insisted on paying the penny that they would be charging the public. They also wanted him to attach it to his next letter to Theodore Roosevelt, who was then on his famous trip to Africa. Taft demurred,

A copy of this stamp was given to President Taft, causing him an awkward moment.

promising that he would send it to Mrs. Taft instead.[8] This stamp was slightly redesigned the following year to celebrate the fact that Washington had become the fifth state to approve full suffrage to women. The copyright to the stamp was owned by the Cooperative Equal Suffrage League, which was paid a commission by every suffrage club or organization that sold the stamp.[9]

By 1911, suffrage stamps had become so popular among women that NAWSA saw fit to issue several types of these new labels to accommodate diverse usages. The corresponding secretary, Mary Ware Bennett, proudly giving an account of the rapid increase in both the size and role of her department and in the exchange of suffrage propaganda with the International Shop in London, told convention delegates, "We issued 45,000 of the little convention seals and the supply has hardly held out." Charlotte Shetter of New Jersey designed the seal for the 1911 Louisville convention, which was taken from the emblem of the International Suffrage Alliance, portraying an allegorical figure of a woman superimposed with the words "Votes for Women." Shetter was the former president of the Women's National Single Tax League, and her design first appeared on the print page of the May 27, 1911, issue of the *Woman's Journal*.[10] In addition to Shetter's design, NAWSA was also able, through the largesse of Helen Hoy Greeley of New York, to print 13,000 traditional suffrage stamps free of charge for use on letters,[11] probably for the official correspondence of the organization. Another delegate to this same convention, writing excitedly to the *Woman's Journal*, noted, "We all have votes-for-women tags on our baggage."[12]

That NAWSA envisioned multiple uses for stamps and labels and, accordingly, printed various types is further illustrated by their ad for suffrage products that appeared in the *Woman's Journal* for August 10, 1912. Labels and seals that the organization had for sale were divided into two categories, "Campaign Letter Seals" and "Votes for Women" stickers. The "new seal" was "especially designed to call attention to the campaign states" and was probably on the order of the new poster stamp format, selling for a penny each. The stickers were described as "A gummed

label for pasting on fences, posts, baggage, etc." and were cheaper at five cents a dozen.[13] A year earlier, NAWSA had issued a "Votes for Women" butterfly sticker that it advertised in the journal. The purpose of this sticker appears to have been decorative, as a notice in the journal proclaimed, "They stick tight wherever they light. Try them and see," and they were promoted as "good as favors at Fairs, Luncheons, and Teas."[14]

NAWSA was not the only suffrage group to issue stickers. The Michigan Equal Suffrage Association also advertised "Special Michigan stickers" at four cents a dozen out of its offices in Grand Rapids, Michigan,[15] and doubtless other organizations issued comparable products as well.

It is certainly possible that NAWSA printed campaign stamps in the older postage stamp format after 1912, but the new poster stamp became the standard issue to promote national conventions. In 1913, for example, the cover of the program for the convention that was held in Washington, D.C., contained a 1¾" × 2¼" stamp label

The National American Woman Suffrage Association issued this stamp for its conventions of 1913 and 1915, changing only the dates in the design.

that pictured the Capitol Dome and included the words "National Suffrage Convention" and "1913."[16] When the convention was held in Washington again in 1915, the same stamp reappeared, this time with the date changed and not affixed to the program as its predecessor had been. The 1914 poster stamp for the convention held in Nashville, Tennessee, pictured an American flag, an iconic image that did not often appear on other suffrage memorabilia.

The larger poster stamp format was especially in evidence during the eastern states campaign of 1915, where four northeastern states held referenda on the issue, New Jersey on October 19, and New York, Massachusetts, and Pennsylvania on November 2. A generic stamp for the latter three states pictured the 1913 flag bearer, Cora Anderson Carpenter, standing in front of the Capitol, with the accompanying exhortation, "Vote for the Woman Suffrage Amendment — November 2nd 1915."[17] Other stamps for the

Although she is not identified here, this stamp pictures Cora Anderson Carpenter standing in front of the Capitol Building.

campaign illustrated a map of the suffrage and non-suffrage states, a town crier shouting out "Vote *Yes* for Woman Suffrage," and a woman with child casting her ballot. The town crier stamp was issued by the New Jersey Woman Suffrage Association, and was sold nationally at twenty-five cents a hundred for the benefit of the New Jersey campaign fund.[18]

The stamp with the illustrated map was designed by Caroline Katzenstein, executive secretary of the Equal Franchise Society of Philadelphia, and it came in two versions, one of which referenced Pennsylvania for the upcoming 1915 referendum in that state, and the other without that reference for national distribution. A local reporter in Reading noted, "all suffragists are enthusiastically in favor of the new sticker" and that "suffrage headquarters are busy sending them to every part of the union."[19] Even assuming that the reporter's enthusiastic words were derived in part from a suffrage press release, it does appear that suffrage stamps were very popular throughout the country.

The Women's Political Union, founded by Harriot Stanton Blatch in 1910, issued at least two small varieties of stamps in their official colors of purple, green, and white just prior to the group's merge with Alice Paul's Congressional Union in 1915. The affiliated Women's Political Union of New Jersey, organized by Mina C. Van Winkle, distributed a poster-style stamp of Blind Justice holding the ballot, probably around 1915, the time of the four-state campaign. The more conservative New Jersey Woman Suffrage Association printed a stamp two years earlier that pointed out, "Votes for Women — New Jersey Women Voted 1776–1807 — Why Not Now?"[20] The largest of the known American poster stamps, a product of the Massachusetts Woman Suffrage Association, pictured a group of women holding up a banner that proclaimed, "Women Are People." Even the Socialist Party produced a stamp that announced, "Half a Million Women Socialist Votes in 1916."

Christmas, a holiday that was celebrated through other suffrage products such as postcards, special holiday issues of suffrage publications, Christmas stockings, ribbons, and small posters, found its way onto the movement stamp. There were several Cinderellas featuring the de-

A poster stamp containing the official design of the Women's Political Union of New Jersey.

sign of Santa bringing "Votes for Women" in his sack that were modeled after similar postcards. They were the invention of the Just Government League of Baltimore, which planned to install decorated booths in stores, where suffrage volunteers would urge women buying Christmas presents to paste a suffrage stamp on each.[21] Most likely, they were used also as a suffrage version of the Christmas seal, which had been introduced to the nation less than a decade earlier. When California became a suffrage state in 1911, local activists printed a stamp in "bright Christmas red" that was an adaptation of the design showing Liberty welcoming the new star.[22] Another Christmas stamp urged "Peace on Earth — Goodwill to Men and Votes for Women." This last stamp drew ridicule in a verse published by the New York State Association Opposed to Woman Suffrage, in which the author, Margaret Doane Gardiner, complained that when suffragists "rave and ramp of 'Man the Tyrant,' some their sex-antagonism veil. 'Good-

will to Men' is only on the stamp."[23] In any event, no other holiday apart from Christmas was so honored with any type of suffrage label or seal.

The suffrage stamp was an international phenomenon. Emmeline Pankhurst's WSPU sold several varieties of stickers and one large window seal based on a design by Pankhurst's artistic daughter, Sylvia. A sheet of 32 transfer labels with recurring anti-suffrage designs was issued in England sometime between 1908 and 1914. These labels were perforated and issued in sheets like regular postage stamps.[24] A set of eight dual-language poster stamps was issued for the International Woman Suffrage Congress held in Budapest in 1913, and highly graphic items were also produced in Germany, Austria, Sweden, Denmark, and the Netherlands. An early French example, portraying an allegorical figure of a woman with a tablet inscribed "Droits de la Femme," was based upon the design of an actual 1902 postage stamp that celebrated the "Rights of Man."[25]

Any of the above stamps could be pasted on envelopes for mailing, but what appears to have been also a popular item for this purpose was neither the political stamp nor its poster counterpart, but a small rounded seal that simply stated "Votes for Women." These small seals were not nearly as colorful and as graphic as other types of suffrage Cinderellas, but they did identify the sender of the letter as a supporter of the female franchise and they were inexpensive. Stamps, stickers, and seals of whatever type, because of their high visibility and graphic appeal on letters, postcards, pieces of luggage, and books, while certainly not a major form of propaganda, nevertheless were not insignificant in their attempt to get the suffrage message across. That they had much appeal to women of suffrage sympathies is perhaps reflected in the number of examples that survive today in both collectors' albums from the period and on surviving postal envelopes.[26]

Stationery — Envelopes and Letterheads

The first postal envelopes with a woman suffrage imprint were probably produced in the early 1870s, and they gained increasing use throughout the remainder of the century through to 1920 when the suffrage amendment was finally passed. Because these early envelopes are generally undated, however, and because accounts of their issuance are difficult to come by, one often has to look to the postmarks of surviving copies for hints as to when various varieties were first printed. Occasionally, an envelope was issued in conjunction with an event, which helps in dating. To acknowledge the nation's centennial in 1876, for example, the National Woman Suffrage Association (NWSA) had printed a provocative piece in several designs that listed the officers of the organization, along with four "Centennial Questions." These included "Why should women, more than men, be governed without their consent?" and "Why should women, more than men, be taxed without representation?"[1] The questions mirrored concerns in a "Declaration of Rights for Women"[2] that was passed out by Susan B. Anthony and four other suffragists at a Fourth of July centennial celebration held at Independence Hall in Philadelphia.[3]

Various NWSA envelopes that followed throughout the nineteenth century listed officers of the organization along with suffrage-related slogans.[4] Edward M. Davis, President of the Citizen's Suffrage Association, located in Philadelphia, issued his own envelope in the 1880s that could be purchased at fifty cents a hundred and included not only a substantial argument for suffrage but also an allusion to a tract that he had published on the issue. Davis was the son-in-law of Lucretia Mott, and was characterized in *The History of Woman Suffrage* as "one of the most untiring workers in the cause."[5]

Other early envelopes were printed by the American Woman Suffrage Association, before its merger with NWSA in 1890, the Massachusetts Woman Suffrage Association, the New York Woman Suffrage Association, and the International Council of Women that was assembled by NWSA. Leaders such as Susan B. Anthony, Anna Howard Shaw, and Harriet Taylor Upton often imprinted their own name alongside a generic organizational design to use for their personal correspondence. Such was the case when around 1896, NAWSA developed its new logo, the year "1848," the date of the Seneca Falls Convention, placed in the middle of the Kansas state sunflower, an early symbol of the movement. This logo appeared not only on stationery that could be personalized but also on a political action manual, the 1898 convention program, and on a stickpin. Based on surviving letters, generic announcements, and mailed leaflets, the majority of envelopes issued in the nineteenth century were used primarily for business purposes, be they personal or organizational. Later, they were also used for mass mailings of announcements and campaign material.

Many a twentieth-century envelope contained little more than the imprint of the organization that issued it and its address, along with the name of either the president or the secretary. A few were more elaborate. The Cambridge Political Equality Club printed a variety with the traditional map of the suffrage and non-suffrage states, the Empire State campaign of 1915 issued an envelope with its rising sun motif, and the Ohio Woman Suffrage Association employed the

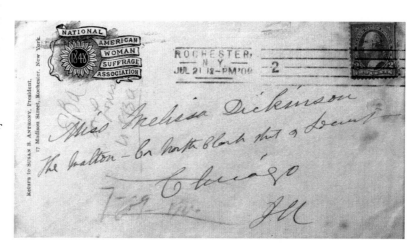

Susan B. Anthony's imprint on the newly designed official envelope of the National American Woman Suffrage Association.

same rising liberty design on its cover that had appeared around the same time on a poster, a postcard, and a button. Envelopes, like letterheads, were not strictly campaign souvenirs in the same fashion as buttons, ribbons, and Cinderellas were. However, the numbers that have survived separated from their inside contents suggest that at least some suffragists kept them as memorabilia.

The California Equal Suffrage Association (CESA) took such great pride in some of the envelopes it had printed that it sent notice of new varieties to the *Woman's Journal*, which both promoted their sale and encouraged other organizations to follow California's lead. The journal described the first envelope of the CESA as "the most popular Literature ever sent out in the State." The envelope pictured a poster in the upper left corner, with the phrasing "Women Vote in Four States, Why Not in California?" The first edition of 5,000 quickly sold out to local organizations at a price of a third of a cent in lots of two hundred or more.[6] A second design, printed in yellow, as was the first, expanded the text to include the words "Women Vote in 29 States for Local or School Offices. Women Vote for President in Wyoming, Colorado, Utah, and Idaho, Why Not in California." The CSEA offered to alter the address line on the envelope to that of any other club in the state that wished to purchase the design for its own use.[7] The California suffragist and collector of suffrage memorabilia Alice Park even designed yellow "Votes for Women" letter paper for the same campaign that was "convenient for use with the new California envelopes."[8]

Letterheads, however, typically came without slogans, but occasionally they could include a design, such as NAWSA's 1895 illustration of a rounded image containing an arrow bursting through the clouds. This was replaced the following year with the 1848 Kansas sunflower motif that was also featured on stickpins. What most letterheads did offer, however, was a complete or nearly complete listing of officers, which, in the case of some organizations, could be somewhat extensive, along with the Association's address. The layout of multiple names was generally done with extreme care, resulting in conspicuously attractive designs even though there were no illustrations per se that were present on the piece. On occasion, some portions of the sheet could be highlighted in color as seen in examples from the Massachusetts Woman Suffrage Victory Parade Committee and the New York State Woman Suffrage Party. In 1915, the New York State Association Opposed to Woman Suffrage, under the presidency of Alice Hill Chittenden, printed a letterhead in pink, which, on occasion, served as the official color of the anti- forces instead of red. When George Francis Train ran for president of the United States in 1872, his campaign letterhead listed his platform, which included "Woman Suffrage," probably the

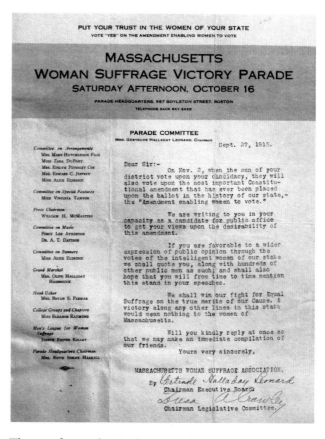

The use of any color, in this case yellow, in suffrage letterheads is rare.

first time the issue had appeared in print in this format.

Some letterheads were printed or mimeographed with messages designed to elicit donations from supporters, announce upcoming events, or rally support for impending legislation. Thus, in addition to the list of officers' names and local association addresses, they provide other hard-to-find information for the suffrage historian.

At least one suffrage organization, the Massachusetts Woman Suffrage Association (MWSA), saw the potential propaganda value to listing officers on their letterheads. One of the "most active and efficient" officers in the group used the letter paper in her general correspondence as well as in official business in order to advertise the fact that eminent persons believe in equal suffrage. A man to whom she had recently sent a letter, not about suffrage at all, was "amazed by our list of vice-presidents," for he had assumed that "only short-haired women and long-haired men" thought that women deserved the vote. As a result of that letter, four members of his family joined the Winthrop Equal Suffrage League, and the MWSA began selling its letterheads to the general public at ten cents for twenty sheets through the *Woman's Journal*.[9]

Suffrage stationery was, at times, promoted as a Christmas present. For the 1912 holiday season, NAWSA offered two "Votes for Women" designs at fifty cents and a dollar a box.[10] The *Woman's Journal* suggested that men who were wondering what to give their wives for Christmas should give them a box of stationery like that fashioned by Charlotte C. Rhodus of Chicago. Her envelopes and letter sheets contained a picture of her four-year-old boy along with the inscription "Why Can't Mother Vote?"[11]

Emmeline Pankhurst's Women's Social and Political Union sold a complete line of stationery, including notepaper, envelopes, and a writing pad, all decorated with Sylvia Pankhurst's medallion in the colors of the union.[12]

In America, commercial suffrage stationery was available also, although most such products appear to have had some sort of connection with official suffrage groups. The Cargill Company of Grand Rapids, Michigan, for example, primarily noted for its set of thirty suffrage aphorism post-cards that had been endorsed and approved by NAWSA, also issued "Suffragist Stationery" in two grades, regular and deluxe. The regular issue was printed with the emblem of "The Blot on the Escutcheon" design in four colors that had graced its postcard set, and consisted of one quire of both letter sheet and envelope that sold for a dollar a box subject to postal rates. The deluxe set consisted of the same design, but steel die embossed, for two dollars and fifty cents a box. As with the cards, the stationery was also marketed as a potential fundraiser.[13]

Statues and Statuettes

There were several women sculptors who created pieces celebrating or commemorating the suffrage movement, including Gertrude Boyle, whose *Woman Freed*, depicting a naked woman spreading her wings, appeared at the end of the campaign, and Adelaide Johnson, who produced representations of Susan B. Anthony, Lucretia Mott, and Elizabeth Cady Stanton to celebrate ratification of the Nineteenth Amendment. These three works are now housed in the Smithsonian. The only sculptor whose efforts appear to have been merchandised for popular sale by the American suffrage movement is Canadian-born Ella Buchanan. Her work *The Suffragist Arousing Her Sisters*, originally sculpted in 1911, was reproduced and sold as 12" × 16" photogravures, postcards, and cast statuettes at various local headquarters throughout the country. It was also emblazoned on large felt pennants issued by the Woman Suffrage Party. It featured the central figure of the suffragist blowing her clarion, surrounded by "Degradation" (identified on one postcard as "Prostitution"), fallen with her right hand upon the foot of "Vanity," who is unmoved and simpering. Also included in the scene are "Conventionality," listless, with her face averted and her eyes closed, and "Wage Earner," kneeling and appealing to the suffragist for help.

In England, Edith Downing created statuettes of Christabel Pankhurst and Annie Kenney, which she sold at her studio at Chelsea for five pounds, five shillings, and two pounds, two shillings, respectively.[1]

Stove and Pie Safe

Not truly a "novelty," a "Woman's Rights Cooking Stove," manufactured by Burdett, Potter, and Smith of Troy, New York, was mentioned with approval for its name in an 1870s issue of Susan B. Anthony and Elizabeth Cady Stanton's paper *The Revolution*.[1] The author has heard of but not seen a "Woman's Rights" pie safe from about the same period. Although obviously not ubiquitous, these products indicate a slow but emerging realization on the part of advertisers that there was an evolving woman's market and that advertising for even common household objects needed to be framed in such a way as to respond to their needs and interests.

Suffrage Drink

At the Savoy Hotel in London, there was a "so-called American bar for the delectation of residents only" that served a drink called "the Suffragette." It consisted of a small amount of lemon juice, a bit of orange peel, a peppermint leaf, a small piece of cucumber, some sugar, and a large amount of ginger ale. The English publication *Votes for Women* characterized its taste "as stimulating and insinuating as the energetic and persuasive ladies out of compliment to whom the beverage has been named."[1] No menu or other period ephemera from the Savoy that either lists or describes this drink is readily available.

Suffrage Shops

Partially to aid in the distribution of the large volume of leaflets, tracts, brochures, and memorabilia that the movement was generating, many suffrage organizations, both in America and in England, opened up suffrage shops to the public.[1] These shops could housed within general headquarters, as were both the NAWSA and Michigan Equal Suffrage Association versions, or they could be located in separate storefronts, such as the one set up by the WPU in 1913. These storefronts, whose windows were decorated with pennants, posters, and other colorful suffrage products, served as advertisements in themselves to passersby for the suffrage cause, whether people purchased any of the merchandise or not. In addition, some suffrage organizations and clubs sent out traveling wagons from which literature, papers, and memorabilia could be sold.

The main NAWSA shop, operating out of the national office at 505 Fifth Avenue in New York City, issued several catalogs that listed for sale booklets, pamphlets, and flyers but also promoted "Votes for Women Regalia," bannerettes, the common "Votes for Women" button with a gold background, various pins, glove purses, calendars, notepaper, "Votes for Women teacups" with gold lettering-on-white enamel, and several varieties of suffrage-related postcards.[2] While these catalogs generally contained a listing of items that had been specifically made for NAWSA, they sometimes included material issued by other organizations. One catalog, for example, offered a dozen different English posters, priced at $1.25, along with a dozen postcards at three cents each.[3] In addition, the shop advertised in the *Woman's Journal*, selling, along with much of the above, such items as sheet music, campaign letter seals, "Votes for Women" stickers and blotters, and ushers' sashes.[4] It catered to both drop-in and mail order customers, with discounts given to those individuals and organizations that ordered quantities of a hundred or more of an item. Recognizing the propaganda potential in simply having the shop itself, NAWSA urged supporters to "Come to National Headquarters" for "help and suggestions in campaigns, for literature, for campaigning regalia and supplies."[5]

NAWSA opened up a second shop in Atlantic City, New Jersey, in 1916, the same year they held their national convention there. The novelties they had for sale included "Votes for Women post-cards, pencils, stationery, drinking cups, yellow crepe paper caps, streamers and banners, favors, place cards, playing cards, horns, pins, paper napkins, doilies, Kewpies [sic] dolls, balloons, and fans."[6] In an ad printed on the back page of the convention program for their 23rd annual convention, the New Jersey Woman Suffrage Association advertised for delegates and friends to visit their headquarters at 33 Halsey Street in Newark for "Fancy Articles for Christmas Presents ON SALE." It is unclear as to whether or not these articles included specifically suffrage memorabilia as opposed to general merchandise, but they probably did.[7]

Harriot Stanton Blatch's Women's Political Union, which perhaps relied more heavily on visual rhetoric than did NAWSA, also operated a shop. It underwent several transformations before the union was incorporated into the National Woman's Party. The Women's Political Union was first known as the Equality League of Self-Supporting Women and was founded by Blatch in 1907 to bring working women into the movement. In July 1910, the group erected a suffrage newsstand in front of their headquarters at 43 East Twenty-Second Street in New York City, where they sold suffrage ribbons, buttons, and postcards, and suffrage tracts.[8] When the League evolved into the WPU later that year, the reformed organization opened up a more ambitious suffrage shop at their new headquarters at 46 East Twenty-Ninth Street. Teasing the public that they were planning to sell suffrage cigarettes at the shop's inaugural in December, the WPU passed out chocolate cigarettes instead, presumably much to the delight of Lucy Gaston Page of the Anti-Cigarette League, who had come from Chicago to attend the event. Most of the items that they had for sale were in the purple, green, and white colors of the WPU, including silk hosiery, small bags, handkerchiefs, and "Little Mary," the suffrage doll.[9]

When the WPU issued the first issue of their journal in January 1913, they included a small ad for their headquarters and shop, proclaiming that "We always have on hand a supply of good suffrage literature, and the latest books, buttons, badges, and novelties, carrying out the union's colors — purple, green, and white."[10] However, in late 1913, the WPU began to experiment with a separate "suffrage shop" in a downtown storefront away from headquarters, which featured a daily program of speeches along with other events. The shop apparently attracted large numbers of working women and men who were eager to learn more about the movement. In the spring of 1914, Blatch's organization purchased a horse-drawn wagon formerly used as a lunch van and turned it into a roving shop. The side of the wagon could be folded down, and speakers were able to come forth and address whatever crowd had gathered. The shop also sold, in ad-

dition to literature, such campaign paraphernalia as the colorful WPU Clarion buttons, pencils, and cigarettes. Whether these cigarettes were once again made of chocolate is not known. Later in the year, the store moved to a more permanent location on Fifth Avenue, and was managed by such prominent socialites as Vera Whitehouse, whose husband was an investment banker, Louisine Havemeyer, a wealthy art collector, and Helen Rogers Reid, wife of the *New York Herald's* publisher.[11] One of the highlights for the store in 1915 was "Grandmother's Day" on April 24, an event that Blatch had to miss because her granddaughter, Harriot Stanton Blatch de Forest, had chicken pox.[12] A "Roving Shop" was also still in operation in 1915, however, that sold, among other things, a purple, green, and white button with the "Votes for Women" slogan on it for a penny each.[13]

Alva Belmont's Political Equality Association (PEA) headquarters was located on 15 East Forty-First Street in New York. The PEA operated a different kind of retail establishment for its supporters. The group's offices contained a "Department of Hygiene" that sold "Victory Toilet Preparations," including various skin creams, violet water, a dandruff remedy, camphor ice, liquid shampoo, castile soap, tooth powder, and tooth paste[14] but, more importantly, served as a beauty salon for suffragist sympathizers. Mrs. Belmont saw the development of women to be associated not only with the right to vote but also with their appearance, and she brought in experts to help women in the use of cosmetics.[15] She later gave her consent for an advertisement in which she endorsed Pond's face cream. The Department of Hygiene was located above the suffrage shop that was connected to the Association's lunchroom. The shop did sell "Votes for Women" ceramic creamers for twenty-five cents each,[16] and, while there is no record of it, activist clerks also may have sold other pieces from Belmont's famous Newport ironstone set. The lunchroom was originally operated by Mary Donnelly when the Association's headquarters was located on Thirty-Fourth Street. When it was moved to Forty-First Street, however, Donnelly, who had been known as "the suffrage Queen," found to her dismay that potential lunchroom customers were directed immediately to Belmont's beauty parlor upstairs instead, so she resigned.[17]

Belmont's headquarters also became a subject of local notoriety during Emmeline Pankhurst's visit there in October 1913. Anthony Comstock, head of the New York Society for the Suppression of Vice, had obtained a warrant for the arrest of anyone selling the WSPU publication *The Suffragette,* which Belmont's association was doing. Comstock was concerned primarily about a series of articles that Christabel Pankhurst had written for the paper about "white slavery," remarking that he did not propose to have "the sewage of Europe" spread about New York. The crisis may have been averted by the fact that the Association had sold all of its remaining copies prior to the serving of the warrant and thus no evidence was on hand to support the charges.[18] However, in November, Comstock's forces were back again, threatening to arrest two of Belmont's workers for selling Christabel Pankhurst's book *Plain Facts About a Great Evil,* which contained the offending articles. Comstock relented when Mrs. Belmont took full responsibility for the sale of the book, which she withdrew from the headquarters' shelves. Comstock, who had no problem arresting "self-supporting" women who were making fifteen to twenty dollars a week in salary, was reluctant to take into custody a person of Mrs. Belmont's social stature and held off making a final decision on the matter until he had returned from a "purity congress" in Minneapolis.[19] No further action appears to have taken place.

Mrs. Belmont's Political Equality Association produced several buttons, a suffrage celluloid mirror, and various pamphlets that were probably on sale at one time or another at her headquarters on Forty-First Street or when her organization occupied offices above NAWSA's on Fifth Avenue.[20] However, it is not clear how large the sales volume for these products was, or indeed if there were many sales at all apart from those of *The Suffragette* during its brief moment in the spotlight. Mary Gray Peck may reflect Carrie Chapman Catt's own antipathy to Mrs. Belmont in her biography of the NAWSA leader when she observes, "[Mrs. Belmont's] offices at headquarters were palatial. She could be seen only by appointment, and her organization could not be seen at all."[21]

One other suffrage shop that opened in New York City in 1914 was that operated by Mrs. Norman deR. Whitehouse at 663 Fifth Avenue. Working with her on the venture were such women as Mrs. Ogden Reid, the publisher; Mrs. Theodore Roosevelt, Jr.; Mrs. Gifford Pinchot, wife of the governor of Pennsylvania; and Mrs. Charles S. Whitman, wife of the governor of New York. The shop sold literature, ribbons, badges, and pencils.[22] When the Woman Suffrage Party planned to open a suffrage store in Boston, they appealed through the *Woman's Journal* for a donation from a suffragist of an unoccupied shop in Ward 10 or 11.[23]

A suffrage shop that also operated out of headquarters and was patterned much after NAWSA's was that of the Michigan Equal Suffrage Association, which sold "literature published by the National American Woman Suffrage Association," as well as their own materials. One of their catalogs lists such items as two varieties of "Votes for Women" buttons, four versions of "Votes for Women" bannerettes, several postcards, including "special Michigan postcards," stickers, paper napkins, and lantern slides.[24]

There were at least two suffrage shops operating in California during the two main franchise campaigns in that state, both located in storefronts detached from any official headquarters. The earlier, and certainly one of the first such shops in America, was opened in Los Angeles on Broadway with the help of a hundred-dollar donation from an anonymous woman. The managers of the shop did everything possible to make it attractive with "flags, engravings, and furnishings." Various suffrage newspapers were kept on file, and literature was available for distribution. Among the items for sale were stationery, photographs, and medallions.[25] During the successful 1911 campaign in the state, the College League of California opened up a storefront on Market Street in San Francisco, where "the passer-by was lured within and won by the fine display of pennants and literature to vote for the amendment. It attracted the attention of hundreds who had never heard of the subject, as impossible as this latter idea appeared to us."[26]

Mary B. Anthony[27] opened up a shop in 1916 in Providence, Rhode Island that sold campaign materials and supplies. According to Elizabeth Upham Yates, it "became and active center of propaganda."[28] After the suffrage amendment was finally passed, the shop was used to teach a civics class. The New Jersey Woman's Suffrage Association apparently had some sort of retail outlet at its headquarters at 33 Halsey Street in Newark where they sold literature, pennants, and buttons.[29]

Even the opposition experimented with a small sales area in one of their offices. In late October 1915, just prior to the November 2 suffrage referendum in New York State, the headquarters of the New York State Association Opposed to Woman Suffrage at 37 West Thirty-Ninth Street remained open every night until ten for a week to accommodate customers. They sold "anti-suffrage buttons, pennants, and literature."[30]

It is clear from available records that suffragists conceived of their shops to be more than strictly commercial establishments; they also used them as meeting places for lectures and other events, as gathering places that beckoned people to drop by and discuss suffrage-related matters, and as advertising devices that attempted to appeal to the public through brightly arrayed windows. Despite a sometimes impressive inventory of campaign regalia and memorabilia, including the occasional novelty item, the main product for sale in these shops was literature in one form or another. Literature made the reader aware of the premises on which the argument for suffrage was based and provided responses to deal with opposition claims. The campaign regalia that these shops offered was essential for parades and demonstrations, for such material not only drew the attention of onlookers but also suggested the depth and power of the suffragists. Other memorabilia allowed the purchaser to "ingest" the cause, to achieve a physical connection of one sort or another to the movement by owning a souvenir of it. But the focus of the stores was on literature. A period photo of the Connecticut Woman Suffrage Association's headquarters in Hartford indicates the typical multifunctions of such establishments. On the left side of the room are file cabinets, desks, and women working on the campaign. On the right is a table with literature, a woman behind a cash register, and a display case with books and various types

of memorabilia, including books and a tea set that may or may not have been suffrage inspired.[31]

It was the English suffragists, far more than their American sisters, however, who experimented with the commercial possibilities of sales of memorabilia at such stores, not only to raise funds but also to develop public awareness by spreading the iconic images and colors of the movement into as many households as possible. The growth of the sales of English suffrage memorabilia was enhanced by two main factors: the introduction to the public by the WSPU in 1908 of their official colors of purple, green, and white, and the growth of the Woman's Press, the publishing arm of the WSPU, when it was placed under the direction of Frederick Pethick Lawrence in 1907.

The WSPU colors were in prominent display at their first major demonstration at Hyde Park on June 21, 1908, when 700 banners with various slogans were printed in purple, green, and white.[32] Suffrage supporters were asked to "wear the colors," and a number of merchants responded by making, advertising, and selling products in the WSPU color scheme. Annette Jacobs and Caprina Fahey, dressmakers, created procession hats and corsets for the June 17, 1911, demonstration[33]; Annie Steen, a producer of ornaments for women, sold a line of Christmas jewelry "in Gold and Silver Set With Stones in the Colours"[34]; William Owen offered women Kremlaine material, the "finest ALL WOOL unshrinkable Blouse Material ... in many beautiful designs, using solely the Suffragette Colours"[35]; one could buy "Home-Made Cakes iced in the colours of the WSPU" from the Home Restaurant in London and bathe with "Suffragette Toilet Soap" from J. and A. Miller[36]; and Scott Brothers, Hurst Nurseries, urged suffragists to buy their floral displays of color for an upcoming demonstration in 1911. The brothers previously had designed floral arrangements in the colours of the NWSPU, the Actresses Franchise League, the Younger Suffragists, and the Men's Political Union.[37]

The WSPU, through its publishing arm, the Woman's Press, issued much suffrage memorabilia in the colors at its various shops throughout London and the rest of England, but these shops carried only a limited stock of clothing items. Perhaps the leadership preferred, as Diane Atkinson suggests, that merchants initiate and manufacture fashions and accessories themselves, hesitating to engage much at all in joint ventures.[38] Whatever the case, it is clear from the number of ads that appear in *Votes for Women* and other journals of the period that many merchants who directed their advertising to suffrage supporters sold their suffrage-related wares at their own shops and not at the WSPU's, an indication, perhaps, of how widespread the movement had become. Merchants continued to sell suffrage-related goods throughout the campaign despite the fact that some shop windows advertising these goods were vandalized by suffrage opponents, as were the official suffrage shops themselves.

In the early days of the WSPU, the literature department was structured within the context of the WSPU itself, and, in general, restricted itself to the sale of newspapers, pamphlets, and postcards. The total sales of such material in 1906 brought in but sixty pounds. In 1907, a more ambitious literature department, called the Woman's Press, was created on a "distinct basis," theoretically but not actually separate from the WSPU, with Frederick Pethick Lawrence serving as its first secretary. As Lawrence was to point out later, however, the name "Women's Press" was a misnomer, "as we never did any printing ourselves."[39] Wholesale and retail sales were initiated in a special room at the WSPU headquarters at Clements Inn, and income increased dramatically in a single year to £600. After the Hyde Park demonstration of 1908 with its introduction of the official colors, income again increased to the point where in 1910, sales were averaging a £1,000 month.

On May 5, the Woman's Press moved to its new shop at 156 Charing Cross Road, decorated in front by a large street clock made by Synchronome Company that spelled out "Votes for Women" on its face. By then, a number of local suffrage shops had already appeared all over the country, and their merchandise, consisting of literature and "the colors," was supplied in part by the Woman's Press.[40] The opening of the Charing Cross shop by Evelyn Sharp and Fanny Brough was so successful that, during its first week of operation, the pair sold sixty pounds of "Votes for Women" tea alone to one customer in addition to impressive sales of other items.[41] Besides tea, the shop carried postcards, a special album to put them in, tea sets, canvas bags in which to sell *Votes for Women,* dolls with suffrage posters on their shoulders, pendants, and badges. Several of the items for sale, including postcard albums and china tea sets, were designed by Sylvia Pankhurst, who was trained at what is now the Royal College of Art, South Kensington. During the Christmas season, there were a number of special yuletide items offered that were intended mainly for suffragists but some for their children as well, including Cabinet Mincemeat, Christmas crackers "containing instead of the usual paper caps and toys, articles of prison dress, miniature handcuffs, etc.," "militant jam with stones," or the "stoneless variety (stones extracted for other purposes)," various dolls, Christmas cards, boxes of "Votes for Women" greetings, and the games "Panko" and "Pank-a-Squith."[42]

Shops with connections to the Woman's Press and the WSPU proved to be extremely popular, not only in terms of the sale of suffrage materials, but also as a gathering place for women to meet and to develop plans for upcoming events. Diane Atkinson lists nineteen such WSPU shops in operation between 1907 and 1914 in the greater London area.[43] Their very success, and their very colorful window displays, unfortunately, made them a tempting target for anti-suffrage vandals, who often sought revenge after WSPU members themselves destroyed or marred public property. Students from the nearby university attacked the Bristol shop on Queen's Road, managed by Mary Blathwayt, in October 1913. The Shop-on-Blackett Street had its windows broken on three separate occasions, and it was fully ransacked following the suffragist arson attack at Newcastle. And in 1912, medical students smashed the windows of the Woman's Press headquarters itself in Charing Cross Road. Much of this destruction is depicted in period photographs that have been widely reproduced on postcards and in newspapers, the English public having a fascination both with suffrage vandalism and its retaliatory response.

In 1912, several events occurred that significantly affected the Woman's Press and the sale of suffrage memorabilia. Frederick Pethick Lawrence, in a rift with the Pankhursts, "departed" from the WSPU to found another suffrage organization, the Votes for Women Fellowship. About the same time, the WSPU moved to new headquarters at Lincoln's Inn, abandoning its Charing Cross base. It continued to offer literature in the entrance hall of the new building, but little else, although many regional shops continued to function as retail outlets for suffrage goods. Lawrence, who retained the rights to the former WSPU official publication, *Votes for Women*, continued to advertise some novelties such as badges in the paper, but on a more limited basis than he had before. With the start of the war in 1914, the WSPU perhaps considered that the act of producing suffrage novelties was inappropriate for the times, and the organization no longer traded even in a limited way in such commodities as tea, chocolates, cigarettes, writing paper and the like, focusing more on political and educational activities, and concentrating on their sale of propaganda and the WSPU colors.[44] While memorabilia such as postcards and parade regalia were still manufactured by various other English suffrage groups, most of their novelty items were also produced prior to the war.

Other organizations beside the WSPU operated suffrage retail outlets. The Women's Freedom League founded a limited network of shops in Battersea, Croyden, Glasgow, and Edinburgh, opening up additional establishments in 1913 in Harringay and Crystal Palace and Anerley.[45] The Bristol and West of England branch of the National Society for Women's Suffrage added such a shop to its premises in 1909. The Cambridge Women's Suffrage Association rented its first permanent committee room in Benet Street in early 1911, where they provided literature and information. The Suffrage Atelier sold postcards, posters, and processional and platform banners at its offices on Robert Street in the Strand, along with taking mail orders. In 1910, Sime Seruya opened up her International Suffrage Shop at 31 Bedford Street, third floor, in a room lent to her by Edith Craig.[46] Seruya, born in Lisbon, Portugal, was an actress by profession and co-founder with Winifred Mayo in 1908 of the Actresses' Franchise League. She announced plans for the formation of her suffrage shop in an ad-

vertisement that appeared in an October 1909 issue of *Votes for Women*, indicating her intention also to open a restaurant on the premises.[47] Her enterprise moved on March 27, 1911, to a new, more spacious location at 15 Adam Street in the Strand, opposite the Adelphi Theater, where one could buy "feminist literature of all kinds" and rent a "large room for meetings" and "two good little offices."[48] The shop lasted until August 1913, when it held a "Great Closing Sale" of its remaining stock, including photographs, stationery, ribbons, and fixtures. A "Miss Timms," who was in charge of book sales, set up a temporary replacement at the Adam Street address in an attempt to continue the literature sales.[49] Despite the closing notice, the "temporary shop" still kept the name of the original establishment, and, attempting to retain its lecture and meeting room activities, it moved to new quarters on Duke Street in the Strand. It was still afflicted with financial problems, however, partly generated by the war, and it sent out an urgent appeal for £150 in donations to stay open.[50] Although on financially precarious footing, it managed to survive throughout the war, the only suffrage shop to do so.[51]

It is quite probable that some suffrage shops both in America and in England were not intended to be permanent fixtures, but may have been set up hastily to accommodate demonstrators at scheduled rallies and conventions. The permanent shops themselves could vary in size, some of them no larger than a small room, others occupying several floors of a building. It does appear, though, that whenever possible, a shop was integrated with other activities of the sponsoring organization, thereby connecting merchandise with political activity. The shop could also serve as a recruiting device, drawing in potential activists for those establishments that had show windows with an attractive window display of suffrage products, such as postcards, badges, sashes, and tea sets.

Susan B. Anthony *Bas-Relief* Plaster of Paris Wall Plaque

In June 1891, Mary S. Anthony copyrighted a 7¼" round white plaster of Paris bas-relief bust

Mary Anthony's copyrighted bas-relief plaque of her sister. No other suffrage piece by Anthony is known at present.

of her sister to be sold as a fundraiser for the Political Equality Club of Rochester. While earlier items were produced that, in addition to their functionality, can be considered suffrage memorabilia, this was one of the first pieces made that appears to have been made exclusively for a collector's market. The plaque, which Ida Husted Harper terms a "medallion,"[1] had a wire loop embedded at the top for hanging. Husted Harper borrowed the design for the cover of her famous biography of Anthony. An example of this piece is currently on display at the Susan B. Anthony House in Rochester, New York.

Tin Bird

One prize of the suffrage campaign was a nearly foot-long die-cut tin bird put out by the Massachusetts Woman Suffrage Association and bearing the names of Gertrude H. Leonard and Teresa Crowley. Printed in blue, black, and dark yellow colors, it urged, "Votes for Women Nov. 2." It was part of a large publicity effort on behalf of the 1915 campaign in the state that also included "Votes for Women" kites, propaganda films, and a pilgrimage to Worcester. Approximately 100,000 of these birds were placed in "conspicuous places throughout the State."[1] There was a hole in the middle of the bird, allowing it to be nailed up as a decoration on barns, fences, dead trees, and garages. Massachusetts's suffragists were able to obtain permission to place these birds on telephone poles outside of city limits. All of this took place on July 17, 1915, which local activists termed "Suffrage Blue Bird Day."[2]

Tin Thread Holder

One of the most intriguing of all of the buttons that was issued by Massachusetts activists was a 1½" yellow, green, black and white celluloid that proclaimed itself to be "A Souvenir of Sarah's Suffrage Victory Campaign Fund" and urged its wearers to "Help Cut the Fetters." In another form, this celluloid was used as the cover for a tin thread holder, which was sold by suffragists to raise money for the campaign. An advertisement that appeared in a 1915 issue of the *Woman's Journal* illustrates the incentives that were attached to its sale: "$500 is Awaiting Whom? This amount is now ready for the 17 prizewinners in Sarah's $25,000 Suffrage Victory Campaign. Are *You* one of them? In order to make a correct list of winners, so that prizes may be distributed AT ONCE, it is essential that each participant in this recent Campaign SEND IN A PERSONAL RECORD OF THE SALES OF THREAD HOLDERS MADE DURING THE CAMPAIGN—with her Local League President's O.K. and statement that the proceeds from these sales have been duly collected and turned in—one half to State League Headquarters in Boston and on half to the Local League Headquarters. It will be to your advantage to send this information AT ONCE to the Thread Holder Company (Official Headquarters for Sarah's Suffrage Victory Campaign) 246 Summer Street, Boston, Mass."[1]

The button and the thread holder celebrate Sarah G. Bagley, founder of the Lowell (Massachusetts) Female Labor Reform Movement. Born in 1806 in Candia, New Hampshire, she came to Lowell in 1837 to work as a weaver at the Hamilton Manufacturing Company. In 1840, she contributed a piece entitled "The Pleasures of Factory Work" to the *Lowell Offering*, the sentiments of which were incompatible with the ideas of the editor, Harriet Farley, who did not think it fitting that the female employees criticize the male owners of the factories. Bagley, however, quickly became disenchanted with the poor working conditions and low wages that women were subject to, and in December 1844, she founded and became first president of the Lowell Female Labor Reform Association. One of the first acts of this group was to initiate a petition to limit the working day to a maximum of ten hours. She continued to work for reform, but in 1846, she became the first woman telegraph operator, accepting a job as superintendent of the newly opened Lowell telegraph office. Her previous notoriety made this new position a source of humor in the newspapers, with one wag quoted in the *Boston Journal* wondering whether a woman in her position "could keep a secret." She eventually went back to the mills for about five months in 1848, but when her father came down with typhus, she left Lowell and slipped from public record and public view.[2]

Toys, Games and Dolls

There was an interesting representation of various suffrage toys, games, and dolls produced not only by official sources but also by commercial manufacturers, particularly for the Christmas trade. Many of these dolls and toys, however, saw limited issue, and many were homemade and sold at bazaars and at suffrage shops. The first suffrage group to show significant interest in these novelties was the Women's Social and Political Union in England, which was responsible for the creation and sale of board and card games, dolls, puzzles, and other such items from 1907 to 1914, when both the departure of the Pethick Lawrences in 1912 and the ominous presence of World War I resulted in the limiting and then cessation of their production. Elizabeth Crawford notes that these board and card games brought suffrage into domestic circles where "more rabid propaganda might not have been welcomed."[1] Commercial manufacturers, observing the cultural impact that suffrage had on the public, also created a variety of items. However, the overwhelming majority of their products had a comic or satirical flavor to them and were designed for those who had anti- rather than pro-suffrage sentiments.

Advertisements and commentary in suffrage publications suggest that the intended audience for many games and toys was not children but the suffragists themselves. A 1909 article in *Votes for Women*, for example, listing Christmas merchandise the union had for sale, noted that "no better way could be found of popularizing the purple, white, and green," and that their Christmas crackers contained "instead of the usual paper caps and toys articles of prison dress, miniature handcuffs, etc."[2] An advertisement for the game "Pank-a-Squith" in the same issue indicates that it was intended to help the purchaser "play,

give away, and talk about ... the Cause."[3] Another ad lists a "doll with a poster on her shoulders" and a shilling jar of "Cabinet Mincemeat."[4] Alice Paul's Congressional Union, however, did sell a "Suffrage Jigsaw Puzzle" that was specifically marketed for children to interest them in suffrage. It cost thirty cents and was on sale at headquarters or could be ordered through the mail from Mrs. John Jay White in Washington, D.C.[5]

"Pank-a-Squith" was a multicolored board game, first available in 1908 in England, that concerned the attempts of a "suffragette" to get from her home to the House of Commons. To arrive there, she had to cross fifty squares, each with its own vignette involving prejudices, injustice, and opposition. The game came with six metal suffragette figures and dice. Another board game along similar lines but of much cheaper manufacture, also available in 1908, was entitled "Suffragettes In and Out of Prison Game and Puzzle." Copyrighted by Whitworth Hird Ltd. of Norwich and London, the game consisted of a large maze, and players had to find their way out of Holloway prison by casting a die and moving counters. That this game was of private manufacture is indicated by the advertisement for the *Morning Leader* that was printed on its packaging.[6] The educational theme of "Pank-a-Squith" was mirrored also in a variety of suffrage card games that were issued in both England and the United States [see **Playing Cards and Card Games**].

One early item that was made by F.H. Ayers of Aldersgate Street in London in 1908 also had an educational intent. Called the "Suffragette Puzzle to Get Bill through Parliament," it was a rounded, wooden dexterity game. Its title alludes to the failure of suffragists to get the Women's Suffrage Bill passed that was introduced in 1907 in Parliament but ran out of time to become law. Game players were instructed to take "the Bill," which was represented by a metal pin, and push it through an opening in the standing doorway to the House by means of a tin die-cut "Suffragette" attached to a thin metal rod. Once through, the bill had to be manipulated upright into the Speaker's table. Concealed under the door and table, however, were two magnets that made the task virtually impossible. It sold for one shilling each and was briefly advertised in

Votes for Women in time for the 1909 Christmas season.[7]

Apart from games, it would seem quite natural for groups and commercial firms to include dolls in their inventory of suffrage toys available for the public to purchase. And a number of dolls were sold as fundraisers at suffrage shops and bazaars in both England and America, although it is not always clear from period descriptions if all of these dolls were suffrage related. At the National Suffrage Bazaar that climaxed Carrie Chapman Catt's first year as NAWSA's president, for example, Mrs. William McKinley and Mrs. Theodore Roosevelt sent in dolls of undefined description for "the doll booth,"[8] which may not have had an explicit suffrage connection. In Auburn, New York, there was a store associated with the local headquarters whose window contained suffrage products in yellow, including banners and dolls.[9]

Many dolls, even those that were distributed by "official sources," were at least partially handmade and of limited edition. When the Women's Political Union opened up their shop at 46 East Twenty-Ninth Street in New York in December of 1910, they featured "Little Mary, the Suffrage Doll," who was "beautifully gowned in handmade garments."[10] Liska Stillman Churchill of Denver was under contract from the Woman Suffrage Party of New York to produce a number of dolls by a method that she had "invented." Churchill took donated kid gloves, used or otherwise, and fashioned two of the fingers to make legs, two others for arms, the wrist buttoned or sewn up, and the back forming the head. She decorated the resultant dolls in the costumes of a "Chinaman," an Indian, and a bride, and they were sold for fifty cents, 75 cents and $1.25 respectively. She also made Jane Addams, Carrie Chapman Catt, and Dr. Anna Howard Shaw dolls. There was no attempt to personate individually the suffragists who were so celebrated, but the forenamed dolls were made from the gloves of these suffragists, and the WSP charged a premium for them.[11] An attractive, well-dressed suffrage doll was sent to Winston Churchill when he served as Home Secretary in 1910 and 1911. Churchill was engaged in prison reform, and the doll, which carried a letter addressed to him, was designed to ask for equal treatment for

suffrage prisoners, particularly those who had been assigned to Holloway.[12]

One of the more interesting dolls was that made by Mabel Drake Nekarda and advertised in the *Woman's Journal.* She promoted the doll as one that "entertains and enlightens little girls," advertising special rates for fairs and bazaars. In an accompanying article, Nekarda related how the idea for the doll came about. She was at a suffrage parade with her four-year old daughter, Helena, who was fascinated by the yellow sashes women wore that proclaimed "Votes For Women." She asked her mother if she could ever vote one day. When her mother replied that she could as long as she did not forget her desire when she played with her dollies. Helena responded that her dolly could help her to remember the struggle if she could dress her up just like the marchers. Nekarda agreed, and Helena's vision became the inspiration for the doll, whose body was shaped in the form of a ballot box and trimmed with a yellow pennant.[13]

For Christmas 1909, Mrs. Alva Belmont gave away 2,000 dolls to poor children, each one dressed with a "Votes for Women" sash. It is not known whether these dolls were specially made for the occasion or if the sashes had been added to an everyday commercial product.[14] A Rose O'Neill Soap Kewpie doll is also known with a red, white, and green sash with the same slogan.[15] McLoughlin Brothers, which, starting in the nineteenth century produced a number of highly colorful children's books and games, issued a sheet of six paper doll costumes, one of which was that of a suffragist, complete with a petition and a "Votes for Women" hat.

In what was obviously intended as satire, one unidentified commercial manufacturer produced a mildly grotesque bisque suffragette that carried two cymbals in her hands. When her stomach was pressed, the hands came together causing the cymbals to strike. The doll was partially handmade. Its head, with a plaster straw hat, is of uniform manufacture, but its dress varies from copy to copy, indicating that it was individually sewn from cloth at hand.[16] The same bisque head was used for a Jack-in-the-box figure that featured a "Votes for Women" sash wrapped around her shoulder. There were several varieties of Jack-in-the-box suffrage toys sold commercially in both England and the United States, the implication being that the suffragette was a scary figure indeed. Another satirical item was a boxed bisque doll called "The Jumping Suffragette—How the Suffragette Lost Her Head." Painted in the WSPU colors of purple, white, and green, the doll appears innocent enough, but its head is removable, presumably as a form of ridicule. One of the few other manufactured dolls known to exist was made by the Excelsior Corporation as part of its automatic toy series. Satirizing both African Americans as well as the suffragists, the figure portrays a black woman, perhaps an attempt to recall Sojourner Truth, as a stump speaker for woman's rights. When wound up by a key, the doll pounded up and down on a rectangular or circular podium.

Suffragists not only manufactured and made dolls, they also, on occasion, sponsored exhibits of dolls to draw attention to the cause. One such exhibit in Sioux Falls, South Dakota, attracted derisive comments from men opposed to equal franchise. One asked, "Are people who play with dolls capable of reforming politics?" The local paper defended the exhibit, noting that men were capable of creating a more ominous display of "Whiskey bottles, beer casks, court records of bride transactions and crooked election monkey-shines, photographs of demagogues and crooks who have been elected to office, or come dangerously close to it, and volumes of lies and blackguardism."[17]

Other suffrage toys, some of which may have been intended originally for children, were gobbled up by adults as mementos of the campaign. As part of a rally in 1915 on Wall Street in New York, for example, "dignified" brokers enthusiastically grabbed for suffrage souvenirs passed out by the Woman Suffrage Party of Manhattan. Among these objects were "little whirligig rattles" which had "Votes for Women" stamped on them.[18] Several varieties of these spinners survive. They featured tin die-cuts of either a fish in a bowl or a bird in a cage that moved up and down a spiral rod. The Woman Suffrage Party produced another example that contained a yellow linen pennant at the top of the piece upon which the organization's name was printed.

Because of the war, production of pro-suf-frage toys, games, and dolls appears to have virtually ceased in America in 1917, just as it had in England in 1914. However, despite the efforts of many suffragists to contribute to the war effort, at least one anti-suffragist, writing in *The New York Times*, attempted to link the movement back to the novelties that it had distributed during happier times. The editorialist condemned suffragists for distracting the public mind from the conflict at hand and squandering "thought, emotion, time, and money on negligible or minor objects." He called upon Congress to resist the "vociferations and bulldozing of women who have lost all sense of proportion and patriotic values" and are dandling "the suffrage doll before a country called to wounds, suffering, and death." He concluded with a call: "Let us be done with toys."[19] But it is clear that the suffragists themselves, while engaged in suffrage activities and the passage of the federal amendment, had already ceased to produce toys and similar campaign souvenirs. The editorialist was, in all probability, not so much concerned with material objects as he was with what he paternalistically felt to be the triviality of ideas that were advanced by the suffrage cause.

Still, prewar toys, dolls, and games did serve a purpose other than providing souvenirs of a historical movement. They domesticated the suffrage issue by framing it with children's amusements and brought it into the context of traditional home-life.

Train Transfers

Special tickets were made for "Suffrage Transfer" day, held in Boston on July 24, 1915, and were handed out at various "Transfer Stations" throughout the city. The transfers were printed to resemble those issued by the Boston Elevated, but they contained "suffrage propaganda," together with the following transfer privilege: "Constitutional Amendment Suffrage Transfer. The bearer having expressed himself in the presence of one of the suffrage conductors as being opposed to the amendment giving the women of Massachusetts the right to vote, is hereby given a transfer to the line on which a large majority of the voters will ride on Nov. 2, 1915. Not transferable. Time-Right now. Transfer good only in the right direction. From Anti-Suffrage to Equal Suffrage. Good only if punched with the heart punch."[1]

Umbrellas and Parasols

One of the most striking and visible elements of many parades and demonstrations was that of a contingent of women bearing parasols or umbrellas. Some brief examples include a May Day parade in Los Gatos, California, in 1909 when a group of six girls formed the rear of the marchers and floats and carried white parasols that included the words, "Votes for Women," a parade featuring the green, white and violet umbrellas of the Women's Political Union of New Jersey to advertise an appearance in Newark of Mrs. Pankhurst on December 4, 1911, a suffrage umbrella parade in Flatbush, Brooklyn, in 1913 conducted by the Women's Political Union, and a rally in Delaware, where "Votes for Women" umbrellas were in evidence not only in a rally tent, but also in one section of the Chamber of Commerce "boost fair" parade, whose marchers carried "Do-It-for-Wilmington" umbrellas.[1] A color postcard from the 1915 New York State Fair exists showing two women in front of the Women's Political Union booth, both holding suffrage umbrellas, one with the words "Tea Every Afternoon," the other with the WPU initials. St. Louis suffragists had ordered a number of parasols for a "Golden Lane" celebration. When they were finished, they sold the surplus through the *Woman's Journal.*[2]

It is possible that many of these demonstration umbrellas were handmade by local activists. To accommodate the heavy demand for such parade accouterments, however, NAWSA began merchandising umbrellas in the summer of 1913 and selling them for one dollar each and ten dollars a dozen. They promoted them as good for advertising the cause at street meetings, summer resorts, and county fairs. The design consisted of yellow and white in alternate sections, with "Votes for Women" on the white sections.[3] Several of these umbrellas exist with the names of states hand-lettered on the yellow segments. The states and territories listed, such as Idaho, Oregon, and Alaska, suggest that the umbrellas were part of a demonstration to celebrate those states

and territories where women were allowed to vote for president.

The Women's Social and Political Union organized a regular series of "parasol parades" during the summer months in England to promote sales of its newspaper, *The Suffragette.* During the rainy season, volunteers carried umbrellas instead. The parasols carried the name of the paper in black letters set against a white background. Such "parades" were similar to the poster parades that the WSPU and other English suffrage organizations often held.[4] At a parade in Birmingham in 1911, several women carried similar umbrellas marked with the words "Votes for Women."[5]

Valentines and Penny Dreadfuls

While its antecedents can be traced back to the love letters of the Middle Ages, the modern valentine card probably evolved in the late 18th and early 19th centuries from period decorated love notes. Lovers at that time began to embellish their letters with pinpricking and cutwork, resulting in an effect similar to fine lace. The more artistic adorned their love notes and the envelopes that contained them with calligraphy. Merchants, eager to develop new markets, assisted by producing decorative add-ons to attach to these letters and by experimenting with the early forms of the valentine card, replete with printed verses, ballads, and engravings. Guides were published, such as *Kemish's Sixpenny Annual and Universal Valentine Writer* (1797) and Thomas Hughes' *Hymen's Rhapsodies* (1800), for those who were insecure about expressing their sentiments or who felt that they lacked knowledge concerning the rituals of the love relationship. Although courtly love traditions dating back to the Middle Ages[1] generally portrayed the male as the pursuer, books such as J.L. Marks' *The Lady Valentine Writer* (circa 1850) instructed women also about valentine etiquette. Early valentines were hand delivered, but after the development of cheap postal services in both England and America in the 1850s, many valentines were sent through the mails instead. There are examples of commercially produced valentines in England from the period of 1820–1850 from such publishers as Meek, Windsor, Mullord Brothers, and Kershaw. Esther Howland (1828–1904) is credited with introducing the mass production of valentines in America in the late 1840s. Her father had a stationer's shop in Worcester, Massachusetts, where she experimented with various types of design and manufacture.[2]

At the same time commercial valentines were being produced there developed an antiphonal form, variously called the "vinegar valentine" or the "penny dreadful."[3] Printed on cheap paper (sometimes cardboard) these comic valentines portrayed in a cruel way ugly women, vulgar men, and people with unpleasant personalities. In general the message was that no one would want to be a valentine to someone as grotesque as the type of person portrayed in the image. It is not clear whether such messages were simply collected as amusing drawings or whether they were actually sent through the mails either as a joke or as a deliberate insult. Nevertheless, there were a number of "vinegars" produced on both sides of the Atlantic from about 1840 to the first quarter of the 20th century. They represent an anti-romantic vision, for one could hardly imagine the true lover engaging in such behavior. The vinegar valentine did not necessarily need to mention Valentine's Day or even love at all; its implicit message was that the character portrayed had distanced himself or herself from the possibility of any type of love relationship.

Thus, by the time of Seneca Falls in 1848, elaborate valentines, whether hand-fashioned or commercially produced, were a popular part of American and English culture. And perhaps it is not surprising that the first references to the woman's rights movement appears in the penny dreadful and not the traditional valentine, and that even in the twentieth century the movement was often imaged in cards celebrating February 14 with attendant insults and ridicule. The suffrage cause was regarded by many as a destabilization of the traditional romantic relationship between men and women, between the lover and the object of his veneration. According to the construct that developed as far back as the courtly love tradition of the 12th century and was still in effect for many, woman, through her beauty, purity, and grace, ennobled man, who

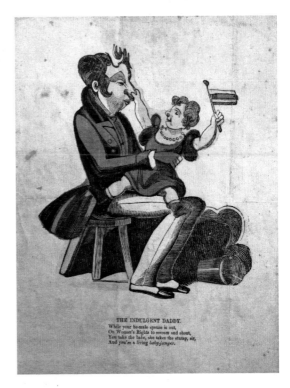

THE INDULGENT DADDY.
While your he-male spouse is out,
On Woman's Rights to scream and shout,
You take the babe, she takes the stump, sir,
And you're a living baby-jumper.

The image here plays upon the fear of men that any extension of women's rights would involve a reversal of gender roles.

looked to her as a source for inspiration and betterment. She had attained her position, however, by disassociating herself from the mundane world. To the extent that she involved herself in it (by voting, for example), she lost her noble qualities. She was not a valentine, but an anti-valentine, a scold, a harridan, even a she-devil that was to be avoided, and not sent love messages to.

Some examples of early penny dreadfuls, which were often hand-colored, include the image of a beleaguered father taking care of an infant who is pinching his nose. The accompanying verse, addressed to "The Indulgent Daddy," declares, "While your he-male spouse is out / On Woman's Rights to scream and shout / You take the babe, she takes the stump sir, / And you're a living baby-jumper." Another shows a woman with a buggy whip riding a man while boasting, "Pshaw! All womankind now want their rights, / The female world have suffered far enough. / I for one am ready for to strike, / To make a man a slave is what I like." A small, lithographed American card from about 1860 that is labeled "Woman's Rights" again continues the reversal of roles theme. On it, a wife points to her husband, who is taking care of the children, while admonishing him, "Quiet the Baby my dear and send Billy to school, and when I get the stable swept, I'll tell you about the races."

At their most vicious, penny dreadfuls would depict the suffragist as a mean-featured woman whose ugly looks and ugly ways inherently precluded her from ever attracting a man. At their most indulgent, however, hope was given that the young, attractive, but deluded suffragist, who had not as yet developed the grotesque features or personality of the professional activist, might yet see the light and respond to her traditional feminine instincts. In a penny dreadful from the 20th century, for example, such a woman, who is labeled "The Suffragette," is pushing her hand down on a modern Cupid, who has dropped his arrows. The verse

SUFFRAGETTE

You blow because you now can vote
With men at each election,
But should a strong wind come along
'Twould blow off your complexion.

Even when women could vote, some men charged that they did not have the *gravitas* to take their responsibilities seriously.

warns her, "You may think it fun, poor Cupid to snub, / With the hand of a Suffragette, / But he's cunning and smart, aye, there's the rub / Revenge is the trap he will set." Other 20th-century examples suggest that female trivialities will overwhelm the desire to vote. One woman is ridiculed: "You blow because you now can vote / With men at each election, / But should a strong wind come along / 'Twould blow off your complexion." Another is criticized: "You boast of women's suffrage / And what you'll do next fall. / If your 'Whist' meets on election day, / You'll ne'er show up at all."

While there are other examples of the vinegar valentine surviving in its cheap, large paper format into the 20th century, the theme of the suffragist as the anti-valentine, the one whose movement activities automatically excluded her in terms of appearance, character, and personality from being a love object, entered into mainstream forms, the Valentine's Day commercial holiday card and the Valentine's Day postcard. While elaborate cards decorated with lace and fine lithography were still manufactured for the lover who wished to acknowledge his love in a significant way, cheaper, mass-produced cards were available, along with the postcard, for people to send en masse to their friends, relatives, and even distant acquaintances as well as to those with whom they may have been involved romantically. The fact that these cheaper forms of cards often lacked the personal quality of the more expensive valentine allowed them as a genre to move away from individualized sentiment and to deal more with general social or cultural comment, such as the suffrage question.

The majority of suffrage valentines produced in America were negative towards the movement, but not necessarily in a vicious way. Lovers, after all, were still attempting to attract the objects of their desire and not to insult them. So, those men opposed to the movement did set down their lines of demarcation — they did not want a suffragette for a valentine — but the cards they sent out to convey that message generally portrayed scenes of innocence, often involving children, not harridans. One postcard, for example, that was addressed "To a Suffragette Valentine" portrays a small but sweet-looking girl reading a book who is told, "Your vote from me you will not get, I don't want a preaching suffragette." Another that pictures cute vegetable people (there was a fad beginning in the 1880s to portray various fruits and vegetables as people) comes with the accompanying message, "Valentine Greetings. The suffragettes can rule, they say / And splendid they may be, / But the girl who can rule the kitchen, / Oh, that's the girl for me."

In general, though, the theme of suffrage appears primarily on cards that women gave to men rather than on cards sent by men to women, at least in the later days of the movement. Moreover, there was a decent sampling of commercially produced valentines and valentine postcards designed for women to send to men assuring them that they had not been tainted by the movement and thus were eligible for their love. One card, drawn and copyrighted by Frances Brundage, proclaims, "I am not a little suffragette, / To the polls I never go, / But a vote To-day I'd like to cast / And elect you as my beau." Another that pictures the image of a woman superimposed over a heart lets the recipient know "I couldn't be a suffragette, I'm not a modern woman yet." A third portrays a young girl admonishing her shy beau, "You can speak out young man — I'm not a suffragette." Some valentines let the recipient know that, while the sender had strong suffrage sentiments, love transcended all and that love and suffrage were ultimately antithetical. One card declares "I am a little suffragette, / I have the thing down fine, / But I will gladly give it up / to be your Valentine." Another serves as a statement of reflection, asking St. Valentine to speed up the day that she can obtain the vote "Ere I lose this heart of mine" to a beau.

Many woman-to-man valentine cards that touched on the subject of suffrage, however, tied the individual's willingness to love a man directly to his position on female voting rights. The message was usually conveyed through pictures of the interactions of children. Children were non-threatening, they counteracted the image of the suffrage harridan that anti-suffragists loved to promulgate, and they reflected a life in the mainstream, not an alien movement on its edge. One card, drawn by the artist Charles R. Twelvetrees, famous for his "Twelvetrees

The negative message on this valentine is a strong indication that the sender was not mailing it to his beloved.

This valentine, which expresses the idea that love surpasses any desire for the vote, must have reflected a concern among at least some women that suffrage was an impediment for a relationship.

Kids," is representative of most. A determined little girl with her arms folded warns a sad-looking little boy, "I may look like a demure little miss, but this I'll say, 'No vote, no kiss.'" Another card shows a large heart upon which the words "My hero" are engraved. A young girl gives the heart to a young boy carrying a "Votes for Women" sign. This card reassures the recipient that the male is still the controlling force in the relationship, and that the traditional image of the male protector is still in force, but that heroism now involves the courage to extend the vote. Several valentines show young girl speakers on a podium declaring "No Votes, No Hearts."

All of the suffrage valentines discussed so far were produced by commercial publishers. Thus, while the range of sentiments they conveyed were what these manufacturers assumed would sell, they may or may not be reflective of how suffrage activists viewed the love relationship, particularly love in its popularly conceived forms. The only known suffrage valentine card, and a postcard at that, that was probably distributed by an official suffrage source, pleads, "To My Valentine — Have a Heart! Vote for Woman Suffrage in November." The center of the card contains a rhyme: "The rose is red / The violet's blue / We want the vote / As well as you!" Although the card does not list its source, its "official" status is suggested not only by its reference to the coming November referendum, but also by its black-on-yellow colors. The same verse encased in the same heart design appears on a suffrage fan that bears the imprint of the National Woman Suffrage Publishing Company for the November 6, 1917, referendum in New York.

But suffrage groups did not necessarily ignore the holiday. In 1912, members of the Just Government League of Maryland sent to their legislature a valentine that bore a large red heart labeled "Votes for Women," and a little Cupid with bow and arrow aimed at it. The inside message read, "Cupid with his silver dart / Has secured this longed-for heart, / So I send it you

Left: This card, picturing a young girl with a ballot under the legend "To My Valentine," has a simple message. I am your sweetheart, but I come with a strong desire for suffrage that you need to respect; *right:* Based upon its address and cancellation, this card was probably issued for the 1917 referendum in New York. It reiterates the theme that love involves respect and that respect involves the vote.

with mine; / Will you have it, Valentine?"[4] In 1915, the New Hampshire State Suffrage Headquarters was responsible for sending out a packet of literature to their local legislators that included 400 suffrage Valentines and tickets for the suffrage film "Your Girl and Mine."[5] For February 14, 1916, Alice Paul's Congressional Union (CU) organized an event where they bombarded President Wilson along with Congress with "Dripping Hearts and Rhymes."[6] The union claimed over 1,000 valentines were received by senators and representatives from their various districts as a result of their actions.[7] Reflective of the earlier history of the valentine, many contained hand-drawn illustrations and rhymes that were composed specifically for the recipient. Some were polite — the card sent to Wilson certainly was — but several contained digs at those politicians whom the CU had judged to be hostile to the movement. Consciously or by coincidence, the earlier tradition of the vinegar valentine was called upon to point out the person whose behavior and attitude isolated him from the mainstream, but this time they offered the possibility of redemption and inclusion. To Charles Pope Caldwell of New York went the message "Though hostile to us by report / We will besiege the Caldwell fort / With our aggressive staff. / There's every hope for victory / Because you see, already we / Have won the better half." Despite his opposition, Caldwell's wife was a suffragist. Edward William Pou, who was described by *The Boston Herald* as an "arch-enemy" of the suffrage movement,[8] received an elegantly drawn card showing a man delivering a bouquet of flowers to his beloved with the message warning "The rose is red / The violet's blue / But VOTES are / Better, Mr. Pou." Robert Lee Henry, chair of the House Rules Committee, was given an acrostic with his name urging him to hurry to bring to the floor a resolution supporting suffrage. President Wilson, whose public behavior reflected an infuriatingly ambivalent position about suffrage to activists, received a well-drawn card showing a group of women passing out hearts instead of rose petals. On it, he was questioned, "Will you be our Valentine if We will be your Valentine?"[9]

If the American suffrage valentine, vacillating back and forth between pro- and anti- sentiments, was in the main gentle in its treatment of the subject, the English tradition was not. British anti-suffrage valentine cards could be so hostile in their treatment of the subject, so graphic in depicting the ugliness of the suffrage sympathizer, that one assumes that they were seldom if ever sent to one's beloved and were intended as social statements and not as messages of love. This was especially true with the genre of the postcard. One card, for example, portraying a woman with an elongated tongue, points out, "If't was not for / That tongue of thine / You should be my Valentine. / Cut off a Yard / or Two and Yet / You'll still have more than a suffragette." Another shows a vocal suffragette with a fierce toothache, to the delight of the versifier, who finds her pain the only thing that can make her "hold her jaw." A third, which obviously was not designed in any fashion to promote romance, pictures a jailer inside Holloway Prison, and is addressed "To a Suffragette." The accompanying verse carries home the message: "Oh my Valentine, my dear, How I wish that you were here." Other cards remind women, "While you remain a suffragette, a Valentine you'll never get," and that activists can find a suffragette imp in their tea instead of a beau outside. Apart from postcards, there were few English valentine cards, one of the few exceptions being that of a suffragette in a harem skirt with glued-on popping eyes that was issued by the prolific printing house of Raphael Tuck.

To view the history of the suffrage Valentine, at least in America, is to see a slow journey of the integration of the ideas of the movement into mainstream life. What was obviously a strong feeling on the part of the anti-suffragists that the franchise and the traditional male-female relationship could not coexist, particularly in the area of romantic love, was beginning to break down. Existing valentine cards right up to the time of the passage of a national suffrage amendment in 1920 can still reflect some of this feeling, but the earlier hostility was beginning to mitigate, as reflected in the evolution of valentine suffrage imagery.

Victoria Woodhull

During the course of her life, Victoria Woodhull was a stockbroker, a feminist, a clairvoyant, an advocate for labor, a part-time prostitute, a lecturer, a writer, and a newspaper publisher. She ran for president of the United States in 1872, the first woman ever to do so, and had additional, albeit abortive, "campaigns" in 1880 and 1892. Her first run was unconstitutional for reasons other than her gender. Born on September 23, 1838 in Homer in Licking County, Ohio, she would have been only 34 had she won the election, a year below the legal requirement. Her 1872 run caused a significant rift within the suffrage movement itself, resulting in an intense dispute between Elizabeth Cady Stanton and Susan B. Anthony that may have hurt the progress of the cause. Her notoriety became even further established when on November 2, 1872, the weekly newspaper that she published with her sister, Tennie C. Claflin, exposed the affair between Elizabeth Tilton and Henry Ward Beecher, probably the most prominent theologian of his day. Woodhull was immediately arrested for sending obscene materials through the mail, and spent Election Day in jail, unable to vote for herself, even if she had been allowed access to a ballot box.

Woodhull was the fifth of seven children born to Reuben Buckman ("Buck") Claflin and Roxanna Claflin. Her father's reputation was rather shady. He was a gambler, sold snake oil made of alcohol and opium, brought frivolous lawsuits, and backed get-rich schemes. Her mother was a clairvoyant, probably influencing her daughter's interest in spiritualism, a topic that often appeared in her newspapers. In 1868, the two sisters, Victoria and Tennie C., headed to New York; there they became acquainted with Cornelius Vanderbilt. With his influence and help, the sisters became stockbrokers; Tennie C. was rumored to have had an affair with their benefactor.

Always known for her feminist ideology, Woodhull caused a sensation on April 2, 1870, when, in a letter published in the *New York Herald*, she announced her intention to run for president in the next election, the first woman ever to take such a step. In May 14 of that same year, with their Wall Street profits, she and Tennie C. published the first issue of *Woodhull and Claflin's Weekly*, which had an intermittent run for the next six years and was to provide a forum for her

candidacy as well as for her views on a variety of topics, including suffrage, spiritualism and economics.

After having impressed delegates to the National Woman Suffrage Association (NWSA) Convention in Washington in 1871 with her appearance before the House of Representatives Judiciary Committee on the topic of voting rights for women, Woodhull became a fixture among suffragists and a heroine to many. Just prior to the 1872 NWSA national gathering in New York City, she announced that this was to be a joint convention of the suffrage organization and her newly formed People's Party. Susan B. Anthony was furious, and had no intention of allowing Woodhull to take over the convention for her political advancement. However, Elizabeth Cady Stanton, who at that time admired Woodhull, took the opposite point of view, and resigned her presidency over the issue. Despite Anthony's attempt to keep the meeting in order and suppress any talk about endorsing a woman candidate for president, Woodhull did manage to speak, and invited all delegates to attend the People's Party Convention the next day at Apollo Hall. It was there that the name of the party was changed to the Equal Rights Party (previously in the *Weekly*, Woodhull had referred to it as the "Cosmo-Political Party"), and Woodhull was nominated as its first presidential candidate. She selected Frederick Douglass to be her running mate without asking for his permission. Douglass never acknowledged the nomination, but neither did he ask for his name to be withdrawn.

The campaign had a rocky start and even rockier finish. Suffragists had assumed, based on hints from Woodhull herself, that she was a wealthy woman who could promote her own candidacy and provide funds for getting her name on the ballot. This was not the case. To raise money for the campaign, her then husband, Colonel James Harvey Blood, proposed issuing non-interest-bearing bonds that would become redeemable when the Equal Rights Party came into power. Delegates quickly purchased bonds worth $1,600. But money became not only a campaign issue but also a personal problem. Woodhull lost the support of her investment friends by taking an anti–Wall Street stance in her campaign. She could not afford her house, and, because of her notoriety, no one would rent to her. In addition, she was facing lawsuits because of nonpayment of bills. Horace Greeley's *Tribune* decided not to mention her candidacy, and other papers followed suit. On June 22, she had to suspend publication of her newspaper temporarily because it was losing money. She ran afoul of federal obscenity laws, and she and her sister spent Election Day in jail. There are no recorded votes for her, and no extant ballots, if any were ever published. A campaign that had much promise in conception turned out to be a disaster for the suffrage movement.

Woodhull divorced Colonel Blood in 1876 and moved to England the following year. There she attempted to gain respectability and repudiated many of her earlier positions, including her stance on free love. In 1879, in an apparent attempt to impress British society, she announced that she would run again for the presidency. Her

campaign, however, involved little more than having a supplement published in London to the *American Traveler* that contained her portrait over the caption "Victoria Woodhull. Candidate for the Presidency of the United States."

She became acquainted with a wealthy banker, John Biddulph Martin, and married him in 1883 over objections from his family. With his financial backing she made a modest third run for the presidency in 1892. In terms of memorabilia, the campaign is represented primarily by a single item: an announcement of her intentions that appeared on the first page of a leather-bound pamphlet called "A Page of History," which delegates to the NAWSA Convention in Chicago that year found placed in their seats. The pamphlet also contained extravagant praise about her from Elizabeth Cady Stanton, Susan B. Anthony, and Isabella Beecher Hooker. However, all the quotations were at least twenty-five

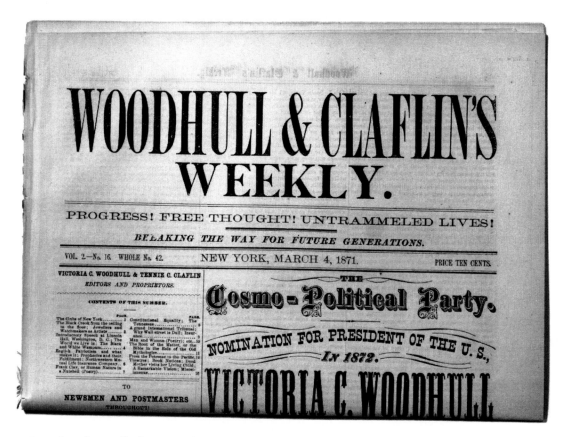

Even though Woodhull apparently never printed any official ballot for her candidacy, this newspaper version ran for four months in her paper in 1871.

years old. Woodhull told reporters that her nomination for president had been sponsored by NAWSA, but Lucy Stone called her own press conference to announce that no such support had ever been given.

In England, with the help of husband and daughter, Woodhull launched the *Humanitarian,* a somewhat conservative paper that was modeled after *Woodhull and Claflin's Weekly* and dealt with topics of sociology, women's rights, and politics. The magazine was published from 1892 to 1901, but, with the death of her husband in 1897, Woodhull gradually lost interest in publishing, shut down the journal, and retired to the countryside, where she died on either June 9 or 10, 1927.[1]

There are a number of pieces of extant ephemera relating to both Victoria Woodhull and her sister Tennie C. Claflin. However, given the lack of funding, very little of it relates to Woodhull's presidential campaigns, particularly

items that are non-satirical. There is the previously mentioned "campaign biography" by Theodore Tilton (**see Campaign Biographies**). Theodore Hake records a small picture in a brass frame with the legend "Victoria C. Woodhull President for 1872," but there is no information about who produced it and under what circumstances.[2] Issues from all six years of publication of *Woodhull and Claflin's Weekly* are still extant. Those published between January 28 and May 20, 1871, feature advertisements on the front page of "The Cosmo-Political Party Nomination for President of the U.S. in 1872. Victoria C. Woodhull—Subject to Ratification by the National Convention." It was a tradition in American newspapers going back to the 1830s to include a ballot-type advertisement of candidates that they supported for local and national office. At times, these ballots were cut out for the purpose of actual voting, and were deposited in ballot boxes on Election Day along with "official" bal-

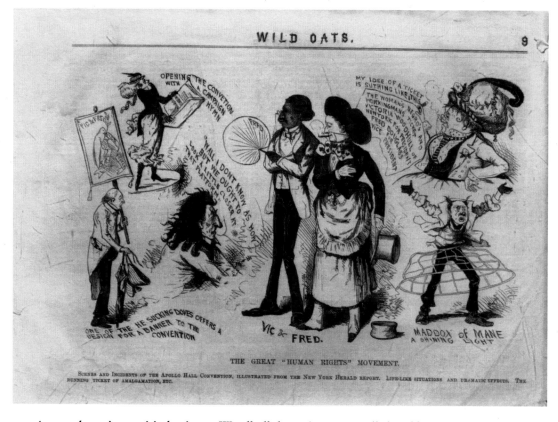

Among the various satirical swipes at Woodhull shown in a paper called *Wild Oats* is a racist message concerning her proposed running mate, Frederick Douglass.

lots from party or government sources. The June 6, 1872, edition of the satirical paper *Wild Oats* ran a full-page series of vignettes on the Apollo Hall convention, including a cigar-smoking Woodhull ("Vic") standing next to Douglass ("Fred"), labeling it the "Running Ticket of Amalgamation." One of the scenes shows delegates rushing to buy the bonds that were used to finance the campaign; another shows them running away when called upon to donate $200 each.[3] No copies of these bonds are known today, but they may exist. Another satirical paper, *The Great Carnival—National Republican*, also took note of Woodhull's run with a front-page cartoon of the carnival arriving with Woodhull in an open coach holding a "For President Mrs. Woodhull" sign.[4]

There are several *cartes de visite* that picture both Victoria and Tennie C. (**see Cartes de Visite and Cabinet Photos**). Most of these cards, apart from a few such as the one printed by Howell on Broadway in New York, do not list the studio at which they were taken. Two identify the sisters as "Stock Broker," which may mean that they were printed prior to the campaign of 1872 when Woodhull lost her Wall Street support. One bust portrait of Tennie C. shows her wearing men's clothing. Several cabinet photos of both Woodhull and Claflin exist, as well as one produced by Bradley and Rulofson of San Francisco of Woodhull's daughter, Zulu Maude. The two trade cards known that picture the sisters were drawn from photographic images appearing on *cartes de visite*, and do not contain an advertiser's imprint. Perhaps the sisters were too controversial for any manu-

Most *carte* images of Woodhull and Claflin allude to their occupations as stock brokers and not to their suffrage sympathies.

facturer to be willing to identify his product with their notoriety. One other photographic piece is a stereo card view of Woodhull issued as part of a "Popular Celebrities" series by an unknown firm. An image by Van Der Weyde that was captioned "Victoria Claflin Woodhull Now Mrs. John Biddulph Martin" was sold in London sometime after her marriage there in 1883.

Issues of the *Humanitarian,* which had a nine-year run in England, are rare. Perhaps even rarer still, however, is a publication produced in London in 1881 called *Woodhall and Claflin's Journal.* Although labeled Vol. XII, No. 3, this may have been the only issue of the paper. It was little more than a justification of Woodhull's life to the British, and it contained a denial of many of her positions of the past. It included a copy of Woodhull's divorce notice from Colonel Blood, attempting to squelch rumors, perhaps, that the two were still married, a denial that she

had ever advocated free love, attributing the charge to the calumny of Stephen Pearl Andrews, an endorsement from Elizabeth Cady Stanton, a notice that she had changed the spelling of her last name to "Woodhall" to reflect her English ancestry,[5] and a selected portion of the transcript from the Beecher trial, ostensibly vindicating her.[6]

Harper's Weekly ran several engravings of Woodhull in the early 1870s, which are often reprinted today. The most famous is that by Thomas Nast, who drew her as "Mrs. Satan" on a mountaintop, holding a piece of paper upon which is inscribed "Be Saved by Free Love." Above her on the trail is a woman in rags, carrying as burdens an alcoholic husband and several children, who rejects her by shouting, "Get thee behind me, (Mrs.) Satan."[7] Far more flattering is an 1871 illustration showing Woodhull before a ballot box asserting her right to vote, something that she would have done for

Woodhull only printed one issue of this journal, which was designed to enhance her standing with the English by denying the truth about the scandals that infected her past.

herself in 1872 if she had not been incarcerated.[8] *Harper's* also ran an illustration without comment of Woodhull and Claflin in 1871, identifying them both as stockbrokers.[9]

In 1872 appeared two advertising items that, while not mentioning Woodhull by name, were probably inspired by her candidacy in that year. The first was an advertising booklet called "Morning, Noon, and Night" that was designed to promote various medical nostrums. An illustration to one of its vignettes pictures a woman candidate for president named Lucy Kissem addressing a crowd of "strong-minded sisters on the platform" and "apron-string men" standing below her. Obviously hostile to advocates for woman's rights, the copywriter, in what is perhaps a veiled allusion to Woodhull's stance on free love, notes that few of "the male wretches" that Kissem is denouncing would object to woman's "rule," if "all the ladies who claim political equality" were "as good-looking" as Kissem.[10] There is also a cigar box from the period for a product called "Woman's Rights." The label portrays a woman running for president as a candidate for the "Woman's Rights" Party. Dressed in bloomers, she is exchanging cigars with men electioneering for "the Regular Democrat Ticket." One of her own supporters, a male, is also dressed in bloomers, suggesting, as does the medical booklet, that men who support equal rights would do so only because they were "effeminate." While there is no overt allusion to free love, the woman's inclination to be outrageous by shattering social restrictions strongly suggests Woodhull.[11]

It is unfortunate that there are so few official artifacts produced surrounding Woodhull's three attempts to become president. What outside memorabilia does survive, however, suggests strongly that Woodhull fascinated people of the era more as a personality than as a political candidate.

Women's Oversea Hospitals and Suffrage War Efforts

There were at least three different 7/8" celluloid buttons issued that promoted the Women's Oversea Hospitals and the Women's Apparel Unit of the Women's Oversea Hospitals. All three pins are suffrage related and are a reflection of NAWSA's desire to help with the war effort, unlike Alice Paul's National Woman's Party, which was determined to keep its focus on suffrage. The Apparel Unit was also responsible for a graphic poster showing a starving mother and child, pleading "Don't Let Them Die — You Can Save Them — Send Contributions to the Women's Apparel Association — Women's Apparel Unit of Women's Oversea Hospitals. USA."[1]

The Women's Oversea Hospitals had their inception when a group of women physicians and surgeons, most of whom were connected in some capacity to the New York Infirmary for Women and Children, wanted to serve their country during wartime by providing their services to sick and wounded soldiers. Because the Medical Reserve Corps of the United States Army refused to admit women and because even the Red Cross did not accept women surgeons, they offered themselves as war volunteers through the French High Commission to the French government, and, as an all-women unit, were eagerly accepted. The French had their own prejudices against women surgeons, but their need for their services was far greater than that of the Americans. The National American

The first of several buttons issued for the Women's Oversea Hospitals and its various units.

Woman Suffrage Association, at its annual convention in December of 1917, agreed to support this hospital unit and undertook to raise $125,000 for its maintenance for one year. Mrs. Charles L. Tiffany of New York submitted the plan to the assembled delegates at the request of Carrie Chapman Catt. [2]

The first group sailed for France on February 17, 1918, expecting to set up a hospital in a war-devastated area. Before they could establish their hospital, however, the villages to which they had been assigned were taken over by the Germans. About half the group, headed by Dr. Caroline Finley, who had preceded the group to France, also now found themselves called to military service. The remaining volunteers were finally settled in Chateau Ognan, near Senlis, on the road to Compiègne, an area that was frequently bombed by German planes on their way to Paris. Immediately upon their arrival, the women were overwhelmed with the number of wounded who streamed in, and, despite being understaffed, they treated 650 men in a period of thirty-six hours. Later, when the Germans were driven back from the area, the status of Chateau Ognan was changed from that of an evacuation area to that of a base hospital, and Unit No. 1 still maintained a presence there when the armistice came.

Shortly after the first group of women had set up operation at Chateau Ognan, the French government asked the remainder to go to the Department of Landes in the south of France. Dr. Alice Gregory, with a group of fifteen women, including a carpenter, a plumber, a chemist, and a chauffeur, reached an area called Labouheyre early in April 1918, and worked to set up a hospital of twenty-five beds, which opened on July 4 as Unit 2. In the neighborhood were several engineering camps of the United States Army, and the doors and hospitality of the hospital were always open to them. The Women's Apparel Association affiliate of the Oversea Hospitals took over operation of the Labouheyre unit in August 1918. This affiliate was formed under the direction of a national organization of businesswomen engaged in the garment trades. They assumed not only the costs of running the hospital but of its entire maintenance from the beginning.

In May 1918, Mrs. Raymond Brown, a vice president of NAWSA, was sent to France to inspect the work of the Women's Oversea Hospitals (WOH). When she returned to New York in July, she came with a request from the Service de Santè that the hospitals set up a unit of 300 beds for the treatment of soldiers who had been gassed. A field operation (Unit 3) was organized, and equipment such as hot shower baths and a large disinfecting apparatus was designed and manufactured and placed on the docks in New York in September ready for shipment. Owing to freight congestion, however, it did not arrive in France until November, after the war's end.

After the armistice, the WOH remained in France to care for refugees and repatriates. In addition, they dealt with wounded soldiers of various nationalities along with cases of typhus. The work of the WOH came to an end on September 1, 1919. It had the support not only of suffragists, but also of other organizations such as the Civitas Club of Brooklyn, the Sorosis of New York, the Colony Club, Bonwit Teller, and the Stage Women's War Relief. With the exception of the Scottish Women's Hospitals, the WOH provided the first women surgeons known in the French military. Overseas directors of its various units, which consisted of 74 women from across the U.S., included Dr. Caroline S. Finley, Dr. Alice Gregory, Dr. Marie K. Formad, and Dr. Marie Louise Lefort. The WOH was funded by a final total of $178,000 that had been raised by NAWSA's state affiliates. Dr. Finley returned to America as both a lieutenant in the French army and a member of the Order of the British Empire. Three American women surgeons and one nurse were awarded the Croix de Guerre by a grateful French nation.[3]

At least six small paper stickpins exist bearing the name of the Scottish Women's Hospitals. At the outbreak of the war, Elsie Inglis, who helped to found the Scottish Women's Suffrage Federation, proposed that women's medical units be allowed to help at the front. Assisted by the National Union of Women's Suffrage Societies, one of the more conservative of the English groups, she created the Scottish Women's Hospitals Committee, which sent a woman's medical unit to France. Later, in 1915, she led a group of women to the Balkan front. Despite temporarily being held prisoner during an Austrian offensive, Inglis and her staff eventually sent fourteen medical units to various locations in France, Serbia, Corsica, Salonika, Romania, Russia and Malta. In December 1914, Katherine Mary Harley, active in the NUWSS and sister of a leading suffragist, Charlotte Despard, joined the first unit of the Scottish Women's Hospitals. She worked in France and Serbia before she was killed by a shell at Monastir.

Suffragists from other countries also helped with the war effort. Canadian activists, whose intent was to provide women for business and industry to replace those men who had been called up for duty, issued a ⅝" black-on-orange pin that contained the name "Suffragists War Auxiliary." Through their efforts, over 30,000 women were given positions in munitions factories, more than 5,000 in civil service, and thousands more in banks, offices, factories, and on farms.

The United States government was likewise concerned with the loss of men to the workforce. Accordingly, the secretary of war, through the Council of National Defense, set up the Woman's Committee to coordinate the work of women throughout the country to offset the effect of the loss of male workers, both to the national economy and to the war effort. Dr. Anna Howard Shaw, honorary president of NAWSA, was selected to chair this committee that consisted of a number of prominent women leaders, including: Mrs. Philip North Moore, of St. Louis, Missouri, president of the National Council of Women of the United States; Mrs. Josiah Evans Cowles, of Los Angeles, California, president of the General Federation of Women's Clubs; Maude Wetmore, of Newport, Rhode Island, chairman of National League for Women's Service; Carrie Chapman Catt, of New York, New York, president of the National American Woman Suffrage Association; and Ida M. Tarbell, of New York, New York, a publicist and writer.[4] Not all was harmonious on this committee. Wetmore and Tarbell were anti-suffragists, and Shaw felt frustrated by both the general lack of authority of the committee and poor treatment by male bureaucrats. Still, Shaw's tireless efforts in Washington led to her receiving

the Distinguished Service Medal in March 1919 for her efforts. Several buttons were issued for the Woman's Committee, including a celluloid button for a Nebraska affiliate. They were worded either "Woman's Committee — Council of National Defense" or simply "Woman's Council of Defense," and printed with a vignette in the patriotic colors of red, white, and blue.

One of America's main concerns was with the food supply, and the Woman's Committee was responsible for coordinating the efforts of various groups of women throughout the country to bring in the harvest in 1918. They were officially designated collectively as "the Woman's Land Army" and unofficially referred to as "farmerettes." More than 20,000 city and rural women during the period from 1917 to 1919 worked on farms, driving tractors, plowing fields, planting, and harvesting. As was the case with

Report from the National American Woman Suffrage Association underscoring its link to the Women's Oversea Hospitals units and to the war effort itself.

Rosie the Riveter during World War II, the "farmerette" became a wartime icon.[5] A 1¼" multicolored celluloid pin picturing a harvested wheat field surrounded by images of fruits and vegetables was issued to honor their efforts.

The Woman's Committee and the Woman's Land Army were not official suffrage organizations. Nevertheless, many suffragists, feeling the need to participate in the war effort, extended to them their enthusiastic support. And while it is difficult to access, suffragists' participation in the war effort and their patriotic service on the home front may have created the climate that finally made possible the passage of a Federal Suffrage Amendment.

Notes

Advertising Trade Cards

1. Dave Cheadle and W.H. "Bill" Lee, *Soapine Did It* (Englewood, Colorado: TCCA, 2000) 3.

2. Kit Barry, *The Advertising Trade Card* (Munson, Massachusetts: Blatchley's, 1981) 5.

3. The standard scholarly work on the history and development of the trade card, an account of the various printers and publishers of cards, a discussion of the various types of printing used in the process, and the trade card's parallel history with the advertising poster can be found in Robert Jay, *The Trade Card in Nineteenth-Century America* (Columbia: University of Missouri Press, 1987).

4. Jay, 39. Some additional thoughts about distribution, albeit from a less scholarly perspective, can be found in John Kaduck, *Advertising Trade Cards* (Des Moines: Wallace-Homestead, n.d.) 7.

5. Barry, 6.

6. Interestingly enough, however, there is a brief mention of a product called the "Woman's Rights Cooking Stove" by the Burdett, Potter, Smith and Company of Troy, New York, as early as 1870 in Susan B. Anthony's *The Revolution* 12 May 1870: 300. Cooking stoves were often advertised on cards, but no card has turned up as yet promoting the "Woman's Rights" version.

7. See the speculations of Kevin Mac Donnell, "Cards by Charlotte Perkins Gilman," *The Journal of the Trade Card Collectors Association* Fall 2001: 3. Other useful sources dealing with Gilman's involvement with trade cards include Denise D. Knight, "An 'Amusing Source of Income': Charlotte Perkins Gilman and the Soapine Connection," *The Journal of the Trade Card Collectors Association* Summer 2001: 8–12, and the aforecited *Soapine Did It*. Cheadle and Lee's study does not mention Gilman by name, but it does include full color reproductions of most Soapine and Kendall Soap designs that both Knight and Mac Donnell attribute to her.

Baked Goods and Other Foodstuffs

1. Advertisement, *Votes for Women* 1 Oct. 1909: 8.

2. Advertisement, *Votes for Women* 20 Nov. 1909: 137.

3. Advertisement, *Votes for Women* 3 Dec. 1909: 152.

4. "Trinkets and Songs of the Suffragists," *New York Times Sunday Magazine* 28 June 1914: smb.

5. "Unreported Utterances," advertisement, *Votes for Women* 26 Feb. 1909: 389.

6. "A New Cracker for the Cause," *Woman's Journal* 8 Nov. 1913: 359. In its extensive history from 1870 to 1931, the *Journal*, founded by Lucy Stone and Henry Browne Blackwell, was variously titled *Woman's Journal*, *The Woman's Journal*, *Woman's Journal and Suffrage News*, and *Woman Citizen*. To simplify matters, it shall be cited as *Woman's Journal* or *Woman Citizen* throughout this study.

Balloons

1. Harriet Taylor Upton, "Suffrage Changes the Ohio Map — Ten Thousand Balloons for Ohio," *Woman's Journal* 22 June 1912: 198.

2. "Kansas to Have Balloon Day," *Woman's Journal* 15 June 1912: 1.

3. "Votes for Women Toy Balloons," advertisement, *Woman's Journal* 8 June 1912: 182.

4. "Suffrage Campaign Is at High Pressure," *New York Times* 30 Oct. 1915: 4.

5. "Boston to Have Victory Parade," *Woman's Journal* 28 Aug. 1915: 276.

6. "New York Party Has Big Fete," *Woman's Journal* 4 April 1914: 107.

7. "Yellow Balloons and Trouble," *Woman's Journal* 7 Nov. 1908: 177.

Ballots and Ballot Boxes

1. Eleanor Flexner, *Century of Struggle: The Woman's Rights Movement in the United States,* rev. ed. (Cambridge: Belknap Press of Harvard University Press, 1975) 146.

2. There is a well-known full-page engraving in the 13 Nov. 1880 edition of *Harper's Weekly*: 724 of colonial New Jersey women casting ballots while several white men and an African American look on.

3. Another well-known engraving, this one from the front page of *Frank Leslie's Illustrated Newspaper*

from 24 Nov. 1888, illustrates a scene from the polls at Cheyenne, where women are casting their ballot through a window.

4. eBay item 160503635227 listed 7 Nov. 2010 and currently in author's collection.

5. *Plain Instructions for the Assessment and Registration of Women Voters* (Boston, 1888), author's collection. It was not always easy for women to run for office even in those elections in which they were allowed to participate. When Bertha E.H. Berbert was nominated to be the second school commissioner of the county of Westchester in New York in 1899, she had to satisfy the objections of Joseph B. Shea by pledging not to marry her opponent. Shea was concerned that some years ago he had nominated a woman for school commissioner who had fallen in love with her Democratic rival and subsequently lost the election. Berbert's "pledge" was irrelevant as her elderly opponent was already married. She went on to win the election and held office for 6 years until the Republican machine refused to nominate her again in 1905. Clippings from *New York Times* 15 Oct. 1899 and 5 Oct. 1905.

6. "Women Voting at the Municipal Election in Boston on December 11," *Harper's Weekly* 15 Dec. 1888: 959, 965; and "The Municipal Election in Boston — December 11th — The Old Style Canvasser and the New," *Frank Leslie's Illustrated Newspaper* 22 Dec. 1888: 320.

7. All of the above items are in the author's own collection.

8. Elizabeth Cady Stanton, Susan B. Anthony, and Matilda Joslyn Gage, eds., *History of Women Suffrage, Vol. II, 1861–1876* (New York, 1882) 180–81.

9. *Speech by Tennie C. Claflin, Candidate for Congress for the 8th Congressional District, at the German Mass Meeting, Held at Irving Hall, New York, Friday Evening, August 11, 1871* (New York, 1871).

Banks

1. "Suffragists Watch This Space," advertisement, *Woman's Journal* 22 Feb. 1913: 63.

2. An example of the bank alluded to here can be found in the extensive holdings of Gil Gleason of California.

Belva Lockwood and the Equal Rights Party

1. For a far more complete discussion of Lockwood's two presidential runs, see the following from which most of the above discussion was taken: Jill Norgren, *Belva Lockwood: The Woman Who Would Be President* (New York: New York University Press, 2007) 124–42, 155–68.

2. "An Amusing Burlesque Reception to Belva Lockwood," *New York Times* 4 Nov. 1884: 1.

3. "Fun in Essex Street," *New York Times* 30 Jan. 1885: 2.

4. "Belva Lockwood Parade," *Mystic Press* 28 Oct. 1884, and "Belva Lockwood Brigade," *Stonington Mirror* 1 Nov. 1884, clippings.

5. For a fuller description, see W.L. Purcell, *Them Was the Good Old Days, in Davenport Scott County, Iowa* (Davenport: Purcell, 1922).

6. "A Mother Hubbard Parade," *New York Times* 3 Nov. 1888: 1.

7. Jack Wilson, "Belva Lockwood for President," spec. issue of *The APIC Keynoter* Summer, Fall, Winter (2008): 10, 12.

8. "The True Story," *New York Times* 12 Jan. 1885: 4.

9. Norgren, 94–5.

10. "Another Scandal," *New York Times* 12 Oct. 1884: 8. A scant 25 years after this controversy, the Elswick Cycle Company of England began to manufacture a special suffrage bike in the purple, green, and white colors of Emmeline Pankhurst's Women's Social and Political Union.

11. The campaign card, a copy of the *Equal Rights* newspaper, the ballot, and the Duke tobacco card are in the author's collection. The palm card is pictured in Jack Wilson's article on Belva Lockwood in *The APIC Keynoter* suffrage issue. See page 10.

12. Wilson, 10–12.

13. This ribbon currently forms part of the collection of Gil Gleason.

14. Norgren, 166; Edmund B. Sullivan and Roger A. Fischer, *American Political Ribbons and Ribbon Badges, 1825–1981* (Lincoln, Massachusetts: Quarterman, 1985) 225.

15. See "Grover Cleveland: 1894 Sugar Trust Mechanical Stickpin," *Heritage Political and Americana, May 21, 2011, Dallas, Item 38146*, 69. This brass shell badge shows a woman arrayed in the Mother Hubbard style of dress with "Sugar Trust — Don't Expose Me" inscribed on her skirt. When the skirt is lifted, a cowering Grover Cleveland figure appears, in much the same pose as that of Benjamin Butler on the Lockwood item. The similarity of the two items suggests that there may have been a "genre" of this novelty during the period.

16. [Sheet Music] M.H. Rosenfeld, "Belva, Dear, Belva Dear!" Located in the Belva Lockwood Collection 1830–1917 of the New York State Library SC21041. Jill Norgren also cites a printing of this song in the [New York] *Morning Journal*, July 29, 1888, in her study on Lockwood, 274.

17. One of the earliest Salt River cards on which a suffragist's name appears was an extremely racist piece issued by the opponents of John C. Fremont, the first true Republican candidate for president in 1856. Lucretia Mott is labeled, along with William Lloyd Garrison, as leaders of "the Black Republicans" on a steam scow named *Disunion*. Others under attack on the card were "Wooley Heads," "N_____ Thieves," "Underground R.R. Directors," Fremont's wife, Jessie, and Frederick Douglass. In author's collection.

18. "A Belva Lockwood Club," *Frank Leslie's Illustrated* 1 Nov. 1884: 169, 171.

19. Front cover, *Judge* 18 Oct. 1884.

20. Front cover, *Puck* 17 Sept. 1884.

21. *The Presidency — Sketches and Portraits of All the Candidates* 1888: 7.

22. In many states and localities, women could vote for and run for such offices as school committee prior to their achieving the presidential franchise. In some areas, technicalities of the law expressly forbade women from voting for various offices, but theoretically did not prohibit them from running for those same positions. When Elizabeth Cady Stanton ran for Congress in New York in 1866, she was permitted on the ballot, although she could not vote for herself.

23. *Brooklyn Daily Eagle Almanac 1890* (Brooklyn, 1890) 218.

24. Frances E. Willard and Mary Livermore, eds., *A Woman of the Century: Fourteen Hundred Seventy Biographical Sketches Accompanied by Portraits of Leading American Women in All Walks of Life* (Buffalo, New York, and Chicago, 1893). Hamilton Willcox challenged both figures, asserting in an interview with *New York Times*: "Mrs. Beckwith is the woman who made herself utterly ridiculous by pretending to be a candidate for Mayor of Brooklyn, when she had no party behind her and no nomination. As far as I know, she did not get one vote." Willcox's statement, however, contains many errors that undoubtedly resulted from his pique at having had his authority to be president of the New York Peace Society recently challenged by Beckwith. "Hamilton Willcox Makes a Sharp Answer in the Peace Society Quarrel," *New York Times* 25 July 1893: 8.

25. "Emma Beckwith Dies," *The Brooklyn Daily Eagle* 2 Dec. 1919: 2.

26. Receipt of payment from Mrs. A.D. Morgan to T. Charters, 4 Nov. 1889 in author's collection.

27. "A Chance for Brooklyn," *New York Times* 29 Oct. 1889: 5.

28. "Women Talk of French History," *New York Times* 13 Dec. 1893: 8.

29. "A Woman for Mayor," *Aurora Daily Express* 5 Nov. 1889: 2. The taunt may have derived from a popular music hall song of the era, "Whoa Emma," composed by John Read in 1877. The song concerns the adventures of man whose new girlfriend is subject to insulting chants when he takes her for a walk. "Whoa Emma" seems to have then become a derisive "catch phrase" soon after the appearance of the song. John Read, "Whoa Emma" (New York, 1877).

30. "Contested Election," a one-page printed petition dated 17 Jan. 1893 in author's collection.

Bicycles

1. "Votes for Women Bicycles," *Votes for Women* 25 June 1909: 847.

Blotters

1. Harriet Taylor Upton and Elizabeth J. Hauser, eds., *Proceedings of the 36th Annual Convention of the National American Woman Suffrage Association* (Warren, Ohio: William Ritezel, 1904) 16.

2. *Proceedings of the 37th Annual Convention of the National American Woman Suffrage Association* (Warren, Ohio: The Tribune Co., 1905) 24.

3. "Another Suffrage Blotter," *Woman's Journal* 14 Feb. 1911: 45. The list of those who could vote included "white men, black men, red men, drunken men, lame men, sick men, rag men, bad men, dead men." Those who could not vote were listed as "idiots, convicts, and women." This blotter was issued about the same time as another suffrage blotter with similar sentiments appeared independently of it in New York.

4. "Cargo of Yellow Blotters," *Woman's Journal* 18 March 1911: 83.

5. Advertisement, *Votes for Women* 4 March 1910: 104.

6. "Mississippi Valley Suffrage Conference," supplement to *Woman's Journal* 10 May 1912: 3.

Buttons and Badges — American

1. Edmund B. Sullivan, *Collecting Political Americana* (New York: Crown, 1980) 33.

2. Ted Hake, *Encyclopedia of Political Buttons, United States, 1896–1972* (New York: Dafran House, 1974) 5.

3. Edmund B. Sullivan, *American Political Badges and Medalets 1789–1892* (Lawrence, Massachusetts: Quarterman, 1981) vii.

4. Hake, 5.

5. A sampling of these pins, photographed in full color, can be found in Hake, *The Button Book*.

6. Agnes Gay was one of the founding members of the American Political Items Collectors (APIC), and is a member of their hall of fame.

7. Ella O. Guilford, "Wanted — Suffrage and Amendment Buttons for a Collection," advertisement, *Woman's Journal*, 1 April 1916: 111.

8. Much of Alice Park's collection of suffrage memorabilia is now part of the suffrage holdings at the Huntington Library in California. See Ellen DuBois and Karen Kearns, *Votes for Women: A 75th Anniversary Album* (San Marino: Huntington Library, 1995) 41.

9. Alice Park, "Wear the Badge," *Woman's Journal* 27 Sept. 1913: 306. A photograph of her badge collection in its entirety appears in Sara M. Algeo, *The Story of a Sub-Pioneer* (Providence, R.I.: Snow and Farnham, 1925) 275.

10. "Wear Your Badges," *Woman's Journal* 11 May 1912: 151.

11. Helen Loop, "Wear a Button," *Woman's Journal* 15 April 1916: 125.

12. Nora Emerson Drew, "Advertising Suffrage — The American Substitute for Militancy," *McCalls Magazine* June 1913: 11.

13. "Victory Won for Buttons," *Woman's Journal* 8 Feb. 1913: 41.

14. *Women's Political Union of New Jersey Campaign*

Year Handbook (Newark: Women's Political Union of New Jersey, 1914) 28–9.

15. "All Records Broken in Illinois — 'Votes for Women' Buttons," *Woman's Journal* 24 April 1909: 68.

16. "Suffrage Cheers for Mrs. Pankhurst," *New York Times* 21 Oct. 1909: 1.

17. "Rich Variety of Foreign Regalia," *Woman's Journal* 11 Jan. 1913: 16.

18. In March of 2011, a shell badge from South Dakota was auctioned off on e-Bay (Item 110660469528) that might have been issued earlier than the NAWSA pin. Featuring an embossed set of the scales of justice, used by the South Dakota Equal Suffrage Association as its symbol, along with the initials "ESA," it was accompanied by a period note indicating that "this pin was given to Mrs. A.R. Bouney by Susan B. Anthony before equal suffrage." The ESA had its first convention in 1890 when Anthony was in South Dakota to help with the state campaign that year. Records indicate that a Mrs. Bouney was a resident of the state at that time. If the note was correct and if Anthony obtained the pin during her efforts in the campaign (it may have been given to her at a later date), the South Dakota piece would then have preceded the NAWSA item by about six years in date of issue. I would like to thank Chase Livingston for providing me with this information.

19. *Harriet May Mills and Isabel Howland, Manual for Political Equality Clubs* (Philadelphia, 1896) inside cover.

20. Margaret W. Brown, "Medals Awarded Mrs. Carrie Chapman Catt, Leader in the Woman Suffrage Movement," *The Numismatist* Feb. 1952: 115.

21. *Manual for Political Equality*, inside cover.

22. Author's own collection.

23. *"Proceedings of the Thirtieth Annual Convention of the National American Woman Suffrage Association, Held in Washington, D.C.,"* Feb. 13–19, 1898.

24. "Peddle Tea for Suffrage," *New York Times* 12 May 1912: clipping.

25. Ida Harper Husted, ed., *History of Woman Suffrage, Vol. V, 1900–1920* (New York: National American Woman Suffrage Association, 1922) 557.

26. Harper, *History,* Vol. V, 471.

27. "Gleanings," *Woman's Journal* 15 Feb. 1913: 50.

28. Information gathered from names of various suffrage organizations and manufacturers listed on the back papers to these buttons, all from the author's collection.

29. "'Hikers' Reach Capitol," *New York Times* 8 Jan. 1914: 2.

30. *NAWSA Headquarters Newsletter* 25 Nov. 1916: 9.

31. "'Voter' Buttons at Exposition — Western Women Show Panama-Pacific Fair that Thousands Like and Use the Ballot," *Woman's Journal* 8 May 1915: 149.

32. Advertisement, *Votes for Women* 25 Nov. 1909: 138.

33. "New Suffrage Buttons," advertisement, *Woman's Journal* 11 March 1911: 79.

34. "Votes for Women Buttons," advertisement, *Woman's Journal* 29 July 1911: 240.

35. "TEN STAR BUTTON READY NOW," advertisement, *Woman's Journal* 16 Nov. 1912: 363.

36. *Catalog of Woman Suffrage Literature and Supplies* (New York: National American Woman Suffrage Association, n.d.) 16. While there is no date of issue attached to this catalog, it was advertised for the first time in the March 16, 1912, issue of *Woman's Journal*: 87. Since the six stars pin was not issued until after California had become a suffrage state in 1911, the catalog probably appeared about the same time as did the advertisement.

37. *Supplementary List and Catalog of Supplies* (New York: National American Woman Suffrage Association, n.d. but circa 1912–16) 6.

38. *NAWSA Headquarters Newsletter* 25 Nov. 1916: 9.

39. "Votes for Women Badge," *Woman's Journal* 31 Oct. 1908: 176.

40. Selina Solomons, *How We Won the Vote in California* (San Francisco: New Woman, circa 1912) 41.

41. "A Novel Celebration," *Woman's Journal* 25 Feb. 191: 59. NAWSA sold at least two different Susan B. Anthony buttons at its New York headquarters in 1912, along with a portrait pin for Anna Howard Shaw that was issued in 1911. *Catalog of Supplies,* 16. The Shaw pin was probably the same piece that was alluded to in the *New York Times* the following year: "Tours for Women in Radiant Garb," *New York Times* 26 Aug. 1913: 9.

42. eBay item 310210597677, April 6, 2010.

43. Katherine H. Adams and Michael L. Keene, *Alice Paul and the American Suffrage Campaign* (Urbana: University of Illinois Press, 2008) 92.

44. "Begin Police Grill," *Inaugural Edition of the Washington Post* 4 March 1913: 7.

45. "5,000 Women March, Beset by Crowds," *New York Times* 4 March 1913: 5.

46. "Suffrage Button Pool," *New York Times* 29 May 1915: 20.

47. Adams and Keene, xvi–xviii.

48. A fuller and "official" account of the hunger strikes and "the Night of Terror" can be found in Doris Stevens, *Jailed for Freedom: American Women Win the Vote* (New York: Boni and Liveright, 1920).

49. Adams and Keene, 240.

50. *The Clarion* Dec. 1999: 7.

51. Mary Gray Peck, *Carrie Chapman Catt* (New York: H.W. Wilson, 1944) 168–69.

52. All buttons referred to in this paragraph are from the author's own collection.

53. "Women Begin A New Fight for Suffrage," *New York Times* 1 Dec. 1915: 13.

54. "Case Against Suffrage," *New York Times Magazine* 9 Sept. 1917: 55.

55. "Notice," *Votes for Women* 5 Dec. 1913: 139.

56. "Suffrage First Campaign," *Votes for Women* 21 Nov. 1913: 113.

57. Author's collection.

58. "Suffrage Pledge to Car Men," *New York Times* 25 Aug. 1915: 11.

59. "What Mrs. Belmont Has Done for Women, and What She Has Spent on Her in the Suffrage Cause, All Set Forth By Herself, to Last Cent," *New York Times* 9 March 1910: 1. In the same report, Belmont also listed expenditures of $150 for dolls for the Sittig Christmas tree and $18 for dolls for the actor's fair. The rental of "National, State, and own offices" for two years was $8,200, and the cost of furnishings for those same offices was $8,000.

60. Ida Husted Harper, ed., *History of Woman Suffrage, Vol. VI, 1900–1920* (New York: National American Woman Suffrage Association, 1922) 441.

61. "News from the States — Connecticut," *Woman's Journal* 30 Sept. 1916: 317.

62. "Another Suffrage Pet," *Woman's Journal* 1 July 1916: 216.

63. Harper, *History,* Vol. V, 405.

64. Harper, *History,* Vol. VI, 286–87.

65. Harper, *History,* Vol. VI, 553–55.

66. *Fifty Years Old and Proud of It* (Philadelphia: League of Women Voters of Pennsylvania, 1970) 6.

67. The suffrage referendum passed in Kansas, Oregon, and Arizona, but failed in Michigan and Wisconsin as well as in Ohio.

68. It may have been this pin that Harriet Taylor Upton was writing about to the *Woman's Journal*, which the periodical referred to as "a neat yellow button bearing the words, 'Ohio the Sixth.' According to Taylor Upton: 'Our button seems to have stirred up the Massachusetts Antis to a white heat. They do not seem to know that the Constitutional Convention, which is in the future, and the Ohio Legislature, which is in the present, are not the same thing. There is no suffrage bill before the Ohio Legislature, but they continue to send the legislators quantities of literature.'" "Ohio the Sixth," *Woman's Journal* 18 Feb. 1911: 51.

69. "Antis Break Law," *Woman's Journal* 17 Aug. 1912: 262.

70. "Suffrage Supplies," advertisement, *Woman's Journal* 24 May 1913: 167.

71. Mae Silver and Sue Cazaly, *The Sixth Star: Images and Memorabilia of California Women's Political History 1868–1915* (San Francisco: Ord Street Press, 2000) 68.

72. Solomons, 41. Solomon's book was distributed by NAWSA as a handbook for other state organizations, and it was advertised in their *Supplemental Catalog* that was probably distributed between 1912 and 1916. The cover design by Elmer S. Wise, a fifteen-year old schoolboy, was taken from a poster that he presented to the Votes for Women Club (p. 40). It depicted an allegorical figure in blue holding a gold star.

73. "State Correspondence — California," *Woman's Journal* 29 April 1911: 134.

74. Solomons, 47.

75. Solomons, 41.

76. Solomons, 40.

77. Harper, *History*, Vol. V, 717. There is no listing of this intricately designed 2 3/4" ¥ 4 1/2" multicolored butterfly pin in the APIC Suffrage Project, but one is owned by a California collector Gil Gleason.

78. Silver and Cazaly, 69.

79. Harper, *History,* Vol. V, 264.

80. "State Correspondence — Washington — Badges," *Woman's Journal* 19 June 1909: 99.

81. Mildred Tanner Andrews, *Washington Women as Path Breakers* (Dubuque: Kendall/Hunt, 1989) 4.

82. Harper, *History,* Vol. VI, 342–7. The new Missouri association was generally conservative in its approach to activities on behalf of suffrage. At one of their early organizing events, they invited the English woman, Ethel Arnold, then touring the country to speak to them, featuring her as a "suffragist but not a 'militant.'" When Emmeline Pankhurst, whose English WSPU was associated with the more radical elements of the movement, came to speak in Odeon, she was excused on the basis that her "charming personality set at rest all fears as to the ill effect of suffrage, even of the 'militant' variety."

83. "Red Rose as Antis' Badge," *New York Times* 4 May 1914: 13.

84. "Antis Mine Jersey Against Suffrage," *New York Times* 13 Oct. 1915: 5.

Buttons and Badges — English

85. Mary L. Parr, "The Importance of Wearing the Badge," *Votes for Women*, 19 March 1909: 450.

86. "A Purple, White, and Green Web," *Votes for Women* 9 July 1909: 913.

87. "West of England," *Votes for Women* 23 July 1909: 984.

88. "Wearing the Badge," *Votes for Women* 27 Aug. 1909: 1116.

89. "The Holiday Campaign," *Votes for Women* 3 Sept. 1909: 1136.

90. "Our Post Box," *Votes for Women* 11 Nov. 1910: 90.

91. Elizabeth Crawford, *The Women's Suffrage Movement: A Reference Guide 1866–1928* (London: UCL Press, 1999) 304.

92. Crawford, 304.

93. Advertisement, *Votes for Women* 11 Dec. 1909: 216.

94. Advertisement, *Votes for Women* 8 July 1910: 676.

95. The WFL was probably responsible for several flag pin varieties. On a postcard of Marguerite Sidley that was photographed by Foulsham and Banfield and where she is identified as a member of the WFL, she is seen wearing a tri-color "Votes for Women" flag badge on her bosom that differs in design from the more common gold-on-white variety.

96. Based on age and manufacturing type of items in author's collection. At least several of these items probably were made around the time of the League's inception in 1883.

97. Crawford, 567.

98. Emmeline Pankhurst, *My Own Story* (New York: Hearst's International Library, 1914) 15.

99. No exact count of these badges has ever been made. On its website, the Primrose League pictures a substantial number of "jewels" and badges, issued to reflect various offices of the League, various levels of membership, and various types of service, including political involvement. See <http://primroseleague.lead hoster.com/index2.html>.

100. See, for example, <http://www.chagbmcollec tions.blogspot.com/2011/10/primrose-league-for-em pire-and-liberty.html>.

101. The British Museum website, citing several sources, indicates the popularity of these badges among women. In her books on village life in the 1880s and 90s, one author, Flora Thompson, noted that "the pretty little enameled primrose badge, worn as a brooch or lapel ornament, was so much in evidence at church on Sunday." Another writer in The Lady's Realm argued that "the sight of the Primrose League badge has in some cases done as much to win recruits as the ablest of addresses and most eloquent of appeals." <http://www.britishmuseum.org/explore/ highlights/highlight_objects/cm/p/primrose_league_ badge.aspx>

102. This pendant came in two different versions, one selling for 2 s., the other for 3 s., 6 d. "Xmas Gifts at the WSPU Shops," *Votes for Women* 10 Dec. 1909:170.

103. All three of these images are displayed in their purple, green, and white colors in Liz McQuiston, *Suffragettes to She-Devils: Women's Liberation and Beyond* (London: Phaidon Press, 1997): 35.

104. Pankhurst, 45–46.

105. "Literature for the Election," *Votes for Women* 24 Dec. 1909: 203.

106. This pin is pictured in McQuiston, 34.

107. Advertisement, *Votes for Women* 26 Aug. 1910: 778.

108. Crawford, 305.

109. Advertisement, *Votes for Women* 26 Aug. 1910: 778.

110. "The Albert Hall Meeting — Its Significance to Our Members," *Votes for Women* 16 April: 533.

111. "A Lie Nailed to the Counter — Biting Charge Against Miss Garnett Dismissed," *Votes for Women* 6 Aug. 1909: 1037.

112. "On the Cover," *The Clarion*, Summer (2006): 2.

113. Special issue of the *Keynoter*: 35.

114. "The Procession of June 13," *Woman's Journal* 30 June 1908: 98.

115. Crawford, 304.

116. An image of one of these pins, albeit identified as a WSPU badge, appears in McQuiston, 42.

117. Crawford, 308.

118. "'Votes for Women' Badge," *Woman's Journal* 31 Oct. 1908: 176.

119. Crawford, 308.

120. According to Elizabeth Crawford, Sargant was not happy with her design, but it was produced anyway. She also designed and donated a banner to the League. Crawford, 308.

121. Elizabeth Freeman, "Letter from an American," *Woman's Journal* 7 Jan. 1911: 4.

122. eBay auction item #220569659226, March 11–13, 2010.

123. "The Badges," *Votes for Women* 18 July 1913: 620. In announcing the availability of the badges, the Pethick Lawrences indicated that, after having filled initial requests, "hardly more than one hundred are left over." However, the order from the manufacturer may not have been much more than that. Elizabeth Crawford notes that "there does not seem to have been an overwhelming rush to join the VFWF," and their lack of success and the formation of the United Suffragists in 1914 probably is the main reason why the Pethick Lawrences gave to that society *Votes for Women* in July for use as its official paper. Crawford, 698.

124. "Special Announcements," *Votes for Women* 12 Dec. 1913: 159; "New Fellowship Badge," 20 Feb. 1914: 314; and advertisement, 27 Feb. 1914: 327.

125. What was missing was an image of the daffodil, representing Wales.

126. "Ridicule for British 'Anti's,'" *Woman's Journal* 12 Dec. 1908: 197.

127. Mrs. George Lowell, "A Suffrage Festival," *Woman's Journal* 22 Aug. 1908: 133.

Calendars

1. "Announcement," *Publisher's Weekly* 17 Aug. 1895: 219.

2. This presentation copy currently is located in the collection of Rose Gschwendtner.

3. Clipping, Miller NAWSA Suffrage Scrapbooks, 1897–1911, Library of Congress, Scrapbook 8, 106.

4. "College Suffrage Calendar," *Woman's Journal* 6 Nov. 1909: 117.

5. *Equal Suffrage League of Virginia Suffrage Calendar, 1912,* Equal Suffrage League of Virginia Papers, ca. 1909–1935, Box 7, Folder 421.

6. "1916 Suffrage Calendars," advertisement, *Woman's Journal* 27 Nov. 1915: 381.

7. *Social Referendum League of Maine Calendar, 1917,* located in the Maine Historical Society, Collection 1876, Box 3, Folder 5.

8. *Supplementary Catalog of Supplies,* 7.

9. "New Literature," advertisement, *Woman's Journal* 1 Nov. 1913: 351.

10. Alice Stone Blackwell, "Suffrage Calendar Card," *Woman's Journal* 28 Nov. 1914: 316; "Pocket Calendars," advertisement, *Woman's Journal* 27 Nov. 1915: 381.

11. "Suggestions for Christmas Gifts," *NAWSA Headquarters Newsletter* 25 Nov. 1916: 9.

12. "The Most Suitable New Year Gift," advertisement, *Woman's Journal* 7 Jan. 1914: 7.

13. "Mrs. Belmont Quit Suffragists? No!" *New York Times* 12 Feb. 1911: 10.

14. Clipping, Mudd Library Collection, Yale University, New Haven, Connecticut.

15. Crawford, 60.

16. "Notice," *The Nation* 56. 1440 (1892): 84, and "Women Suffrage," *Timaru Herald,* Rorahi LVII, Putanga 1689, 18 Huitanguru 1895: 4.

17. "Notice," *The Common Cause* 25 Nov. 1909: 437.

18. "Notice," *The Common Cause* 15 Dec. 1910: 596.

19. Advertisement, *Votes for Women* 19 Nov. 1909: 123.

20. "The Woman's Press Christmas Bazaar," advertisement, *Votes for Women* 11 Nov. 1910: 82.

21. "Calendars for the New Year," advertisement, *Votes for Women* 5 Jan. 1912: 232.

22. "Notes," *Woman's Journal* 10 Oct. 1908: 164.

23. "Editorial Notes," *Woman's Journal* 2 Oct. 1909: 157.

24. *The Woman's Rights Almanac for 1858. Containing Facts, Statistics, Arguments, Records of Progress, and Proofs of the Need of It* (Worcester, Massachusetts, 1858). Although this work was published anonymously, Harriet Jane Hanson Robinson attributes it to Lucy Stone and the Rev. Thomas Wentworth Higginson: *Massachusetts in the Woman Suffrage Movement* (Boston, 1881) 259. Harriet Jane Hanson was a worker in the Lowell Massachusetts mills in the 1830s and 40s. She married William Stevens Robinson, the editor of the *Lowell Courier,* in 1848. Following the Civil War, both became active in the Woman's Rights Movement.

Campaign Biographies

1. William Miles, *The Image Makers: A Bibliography of American Presidential Campaign Biographies* (Metuchen, N.J: Scarecrow Press, 1979) ix.

2. Sullivan, *Americana,* 59.

3. William Burlie Brown, *The People's Choice: The Presidential Image in the Campaign Biography* (Baton Rouge: Louisiana State University Press, 1960) xiii.

4. James B. Hart, "They All Were Born in Log Cabins," *American Heritage,* Aug. 1956: 103.

5. Sullivan, *Americana,* 59.

6. Theodore Tilton, *Victoria C. Woodhull, A Biography* (New York, 1871).

7. Barbara Goldsmith, *Other Powers: The Age of Suffrage, Spiritualism, and the Scandalous Victoria Woodhull* (New York: Alfred A. Knopf, 1998) 288.

8. Tilton, 4, 32.

9. These quotations are taken from Goldsmith, 289.

10. "Captain Miller," *Hero of Tippecanoe or the Life of William Henry Harrison* (New York, 1840) 118.

Cartes de Visite *and* Cabinet Photographs

1. There are a number of various histories of *cartes* and cabinets, including Lou W. and Lois McCulloch, *Card Photographs: A Guide to Their History and Value* (Atglen, Pennsylvania: Schiffer, 1997); W.C. Darrah, *Cartes de Visite in Nineteenth Century Photographs* (Gettysburg: W.C. Darrah, 1981); and William Welling, *Photography in America: The Formative Years—1839–1900* (New York: Thomas Y. Crowell, 1978).

2. At times, there are clues on the card itself that make its intent obvious. A *c.d.v.* that has been heavily retouched or identifies its subject in a formal way such as "Mrs. Woodhull, Stockbroker" is, most probably, a commercial product. Personal *c.d.v.*'s that were intended for family and friends can sometimes be identified as such through "record keeping" notations on the card in pencil or ink. The author, for example, has a *c.d.v.* of Belva Lockwood from her days as headmistress at Union School in Lockport, New York. The penciled note on the back indicates that the portrait is of "Mrs. Belva A. McNall [the last name of her deceased husband, Uriah] 1860–61 at Lockport, N.Y. afterwards Belva Lockwood D.C. candidate for presidency given to me while a student in Lockport." It appears to have been a practice prior to the advent of the school or college yearbook for students and faculty to exchange *c.d.v.'s,* which were then saved in a photo album. The author has seen such albums from a variety of institutions including Lafayette College and Yale. Such may have been the case here. *C.d.v.'s* were introduced for popular use in the country circa 1859, so it appears that Lockwood took early advantage of the new form of photography.

3. The broadside is pictured in Robert P.J. Cooney, *Winning the Votes: The Triumph of the American Woman Suffrage Movement* (Santa Cruz: American Graphic Press, 2005) 11.

4. Mary Gabriel, *Notorious Victoria* (Chapel Hill, North Carolina: Algonquin Books of Chapel Hill, 1998) 182.

5. See, for example, *The Revolution,* 21 Jan. 1869: 35 (front page).

6. Advertisement, *Manual for Political Equality Clubs, Philadelphia: National American Woman Suffrage Association,* Harriet May Mills and Isabel Howland, Compilers, 1896, inside page of front cover. At the same time NAWSA distributed photographs of its leaders, it also sold autographs of "great Reformers, Statesmen, Members of Congress, and other celebrities." While the manual does not indicate such, it is possible that some of the cabinet photographs of suffragists were autographed. This is one of the few instances in which NAWSA actively promoted images of its leaders for sale to the public.

7. "Portraits of Mr. Blackwell," *Woman's Journal* 9 Oct. 1909: 162.

8. "Last Photograph of Julia Ward Howe," adver-

tisement, *Woman's Journal* 14 Jan. 1911: 16; and "Pictures of Miss Anthony," *Woman's Journal* 11 March 1911: 79.

9. "A True Republic and Other Songs, " advertisement, *Woman's Journal* 28 Sept. 1912: 310.

10. Advertisement, *Votes for Women* 3 Feb. 1911: 300.

11. "Photographs," advertisement, *Votes for Women* 22 March 1912: 394.

Ceramic Figures

1. Crawford, 109.

2. Ralph Kovel and Terry Kovel, *Kovels' New Dictionary of Marks: Pottery and Porcelain 1850 to the Present* (New York: Crown, 1986) 112.

China and Dinnerware

1. *Supplementary List*, 7.

2. "Trinkets and Songs of the Suffragists," *New York Times Sunday Magazine* 28 June 1914: smb.

3. For the period in question, Maddock pieces were stamped with the initials "GV" along with a number. The initials stood for George V, and the number indicated the year of his reign, which began in 1910, when the item was manufactured. Thus a bread plate from the set that is stamped "GV" with a "III" below it means that the piece was made in 1913. Not all extant pieces from this set have a number, but to be stamped with the king's initials means that they could not have been manufactured prior to 1910.

4. Ida Husted Harper, "What Do the Newport Suffrage Meetings Mean?" *The Independent* 9 Sept. 1909: 579; Julie Powell and Robin Powell, "Woman Suffrage Brummagem Items," *The Clarion* March 2000: 14–15; Janet W. Buell, "Alva Belmont: From Socialite to Feminist," *The Historian*, 229–31; and items from the author's own collection. The information regarding dispersal of the service and the destruction of inventory records by a fire is contained in an e-mail that was sent to me by Paul F. Miller, Curator of the Newport County Preservation Society.

5. Advertisement, *Votes for Women* 9 Oct. 1909: 31.

6. "WSPU China," advertisement, *Votes for Women* 3 Feb. 1911: 300.

7. "Scottish Exhibition," *Votes for Women*, 13 May 1910: 538.

8. Crawford, 108.

Chocolates

1. *Printer's Ink: A Journal for Advertisers 1888– 1938* 184. 4 (1938): 278.

2. An example of this box is now in the collection of Chris Hearn.

3. "Buy Your Chocolates," advertisement, *Votes for Women* 4 Nov. 1910: 79.

4. "Our Christmas Bazaar Now Open," advertisement, *Votes for Women* 18 Nov. 1910: 116.

Christmas Cards

1. "Plan for Christmas," *Woman's Journal* 18 Nov. 1911: 365.

2. "Suffrage Christmas Presents," *Woman's Journal* 7 Dec. 1912: 391.

3. "Suffrage Holiday Cards," advertisement, *Woman's Journal* 1 Nov. 1913: 351.

4. "Our Christmas Card," supplement to *Votes for Women* 12 Dec. 1907: xxxix.

5. "Christmas Publications," *Votes for Women* 1 Oct. 1908: 2.

6. "Buy Your Christmas Presents and Support the Cause by Dealing at the Kensington 'Votes for Women' Shop," *Votes for Women* 3 Dec. 1909: 150.

7. "Special — WSPU Christmas Cards," advertisement, *Votes for Women* 18 Nov. 1910: 116.

8. "Special Announcements," *Votes for Women* 12 Dec. 1913, 159.

9. "Christmas Cards," *Votes for Women* 21 Nov. 1913: 119.

Cigarettes and Tobacco

1. Advertisement, *Votes for Women* 26 Aug. 1910: 778.

2. "Under the Clock," *Votes for Women* 1 July 1910: 651.

3. Advertisement, *Votes for Women* 26 May 1911: 571.

4. "Suffragettes Find a Christmas Counter," *The Evening Standard (Ogden City, Utah)* 6 Dec. 1910: 7.

5. "Silk Hosiery in Their Flag; Women's Suffrage Shop Also Has a Stock of Cigarettes-Chocolate," *New York Times* 16 Dec. 1910: 3.

6. "Cigarettes Start a Suffragist Row: 'Votes for Women' Smokers Sold at the Victoria Gives Heavy Blow to Cause," *New York Times* 17 Sept. 1912: 6.

7. "Ready for Suffrage Week," *New York Times* 7 Sept. 1912: 6.

8. "Cigarettes," 12 Sept. 1912: 6

9. "'Lysistrata' in Open Air," *New York Times* 15 Sept. 1912: 15.

10. Harper, *History*, Vol. VI, 471.

11. "Tells How She Outwits Antis," *Woman's Journal* 30 Oct. 1915: 345.

12. An example of this particular variety of sheet music can be found in the collection of Danny O. Crew. See Danny O. Crew, *Suffragist Sheet Music* (Jefferson, N.C.: McFarland, 2002) 374.

13. From the collection of Chase Livingston.

14. For the complete story of Eddie Bernays and the campaign to turn women into smokers, see E. Michael E. Jones, *Libido Dominandi: Sexual Liberation and Political Control* (South Bend: St. Augustine's Press, 2005).

Clarion Figure

1. For the discussion of the English origin of the Clarion design along with that of Watt's poster, I am

indebted to Lisa Tickner's account in *The Spectacle of Women: Imagery of the Suffrage Campaign 1907–14* (Chicago: University of Chicago Press, 1988) 211–13. Many of the facts in this section about the NUWSS, the controversies involved in the use of the Clarion image, and references to *The Common Cause* first appear in her fine study.

2. Crawford, 136.

3. As quoted in Tickner, 211.

4. "25231 Super Rare Suffrage Pinback," Heritage Grand Format Auction #659, February 26–27, 2007, Dallas, Texas, 54.

Clocks and Watches

1. "A 'Votes for Women' Clock," *Votes for Women* 6 May 1910: 514.

2. "Under the Clock," *Votes for Women*, 13 May 1910: 533.

3. "Bits and Pieces," spec. issue of *The APIC Keynoter* Summer, Fall, Winter (2008): 132.

Coffee and Tea

1. "Suffrage Coffee," advertisement, *Woman's Journal* 29 April 1916: 143.

2. Solomons, 44.

3. "Suffrage Tea in a Special Box," advertisement, *Woman's Journal* 18 May 1912: 158.

4. "Votes for Women Tea," advertisement, *Votes for Women* 29 April 1910: 496.

Colors

1. Crew, 66. There was another suffrage song with a similar title of undetermined date written by Fannie Holden Fowler to the tune of "Marching Through Georgia." The opening lines are "Put on the yellow ribbons, friends, the color of the sun,/It is the signal of the dawn, our glittering gonfalon,/Wear it for our glorious cause till Equal Rights are won!" "The Color Yellow," *The Clarion* Aug. 1997: 5.

2. Mills and Howland, 33.

3. Anna Howard Shaw with Elizabeth Jordan, *The Story of a Pioneer* (New York: Harper & Brothers, 1915) 242.

4. "Show Your Colors," *Justicia* 1.4 (December 1887): 4–5.

5. Rev. Anna Howard Shaw, Alice Stone Blackwell, and Lucy Elmina Anthony, *The Yellow Ribbon Speaker* (Boston, 1891).

6. Mary Livermore, "Show Your Colors," *Woman's Journal* 5 May 1894: 137.

7. Rachel Foster Avery, "From National American Suffrage Headquarters," *Woman's Journal* 6 June 1896: 180.

8. Kenneth Florey, "The First Suffrage Button," spec. issue of *The APIC Keynoter* Summer, Fall, Winter (2008): 37.

9. Harper, *History,* Vol. 54.

10. Harper, *History,* Vol. VI, 481–82.

11. Solomons, 5.

12. Harper, *History,* Vol. VI, 168.

13. Harper, *History,* Vol. VI, 332.

14. "Welcome Dr. Shaw with Tea and Dance," *New York Times*, 18 April 1915: 14.

15. Harper, *History,* Vol. VI, 349.

16. Harper, *History,* Vol. VI, 452.

17. Harper, *History,* Vol. VI, 462.

18. Harriot Stanton Blatch and Alma Lutz, *Challenging Years: The Memoirs of Harriot Stanton Blatch* (New York: G.P. Putnam's Sons, 1940) 131–2.

19. "Blue Ribbon Suggested for Women Who Oppose Vote," *New York Times* 8 Nov. 1912: 12.

20. Ads for the jewelry of Mappin and Webb and Annie Steen ran through a number of issues of *Votes for Women*, the official organ of the WSPU. See, for example, *Votes for Women* 1 Oct. 1909: 16 and 7 Jan. 1910: 210.

21. Catalog, Historical and Popular Culture Americana, February 26–27, Dallas: Heritage Auction Galleries, 2007, 54.

22. "Tours for Women in Radiant Garb," *New York Times* 26 Aug. 1913: 9.

23. *Women's Political Union of New Jersey Campaign Year Book 1914* (Newark: Women's Political Union of New Jersey, 1914) 35.

24. Adams and Keene, 144.

25. Alice Stone Blackwell, "Malicious Misrepresentation," *Woman's Journal* 10 May 1913: 148.

26. Quotation from the journal *Votes for Women* issue of 14 May 1908, cited by David Fairhall, *Common Ground* (London: I.B. Tauris, 2006) 31.

27. Why gold was substituted for the green of the WSPU is not known. Edith Mayo speculates that whatever the reason "it may have helped win acceptance for this least traditional of groups." Edith Mayo, "Votes for Women," *The APIC Keynoter* Fall 1982: 9.

28. See, for example, various images of NWP memorabilia with yellow rather than gold as one of the three colors in the spec. issue of *The APIC Keynoter* Summer, Fall, Winter (2008).

29. "Official Bulletin," Washington, July 3, 1917.

30. "Vast Suffrage Host Is on Parade To-Day," *New York Times* 4 May 1912: 22.

31. "Suffrage Paraders Beckon Roosevelt," *New York Times* 2 May 1912: 11.

32. "4,000 Women March for Suffrage Cause," *New York Times* 2 Nov. 1913: 13.

33. Alice Edith Abel, "Red and White Do Not Have a Bad Connotation," *New York Times* 7 Nov. 1913: 12.

34. "Brave Suffragists Save 'Anti' from Sea," *New York Times* 18 July 1915: 15.

35. Alice Stone Blackwell, "A Fitting Badge," *Woman's Journal* 2 May 1914: 140.

36. Helen Fraser, *The Common Cause* 25 Nov. 1909: 433.

37. A.M. Allen, "The Red, White, and Green," *The Common Cause* 26 May 1910: 99.

38. *Program, Votes for Women Suffragettes Demonstration in Hyde Park, Sunday, June 21st, 1908*, 3–4.

39. Christabel Pankhurst, "The Political Importance of the Colours," *Votes for Women* 7 May 1909: 514.

40. Diane Atkinson, *Suffragettes in the Purple White & Green* (London: The Museum of London, 1992) 17.

41. "Color and Ginger," *Woman's Journal* 20 Aug. 1910: 138.

42. When various differences led to the expulsion of Sylvia Pankhurst and her East London Federation of the WSPU from the parent organization in 1914, she renamed her group the East London Federation of Suffragettes and added red to the organization's official colors. In a press release, members of the reconstituted organization emphasized that the addition of the new color did not indicate in any way that they were allied to the Socialists. "Red Added to the Colors," *Votes for Women* 13 Feb. 1914: 306.

43. In a brief note for 17 Oct. 1908 ("Varied Suffrage Colors," 167), the *Woman's Journal* noted that the League "has just adopted yellow, which has been the chosen color of suffragists in America." Extant buttons from the League are in yellow, not gold, but perhaps, like NAWSA, the League did alternate on occasion yellow and gold.

44. Crawford, 137; and "Order of March," *Votes for Women* 16 June 1911: 613 and 10 July 1914: 638.

45. *Votes for Women* 30 May 1913: 503.

46. Tickner, 265.

47. "The 'Votes for Women' Fellowship," *Votes for Women* 15 Nov. 1912: 98.

48. Alice Stone Blackwell, "Anti-Suffrage Colors," *Woman's Journal* 16 Nov. 1912: 364.

Cookbooks

1. As Edith Mayo notes, "Especially after the turn of the century, suffrage rhetoric based upon motherhood and the 'special' qualities of women became almost pro forma.... The essence of the argument was that women were 'specially suited'—they wanted the vote to fulfill women's traditional role and not to transform it...." As Mayo cautions, however, this was not the approach of the "National Woman's Party militants." Edith Mayo, "Votes for Women," *The Keynoter* 82. 3: 10.

2. Clinton Political Equality Club, *Choice Recipes Compiled for the Busy Housewife 1916* (Clinton, N.Y.: The Courier Press, 1916) title page.

3. Equality Club, 72.

4. Hattie A. Burr, ed., *The Woman Suffrage Cook Book* (Boston, 1896) title page.

5. Susan B. Anthony and Ida Husted Harper, *The History of Woman Suffrage, Vol. IV* (Indianapolis: The Hollenbeck Press, 1902) 704.

6. Burr, vii.

7. Linda Deziah Jennings, comp., *The Washington Women's Cookbook* (Seattle: Wash.: Trade Register Print) 1909.

8. L.O. Kleber, *The Suffrage Cookbook* (Pittsburgh: The Equal Franchise Federation of Western Pennsylvania, 1915).

9. *Choice Recipes.*

10. *For Better Baking ... Votes for Women, 1913.* A copy of this booklet, bearing the imprint of the kings County W.S.A. of New York, of which R.C. Talbot-Perkins was president, reached the desk of one of the editors of the *Woman's Journal*, and was favorably commented on in the September 13, 1913, issue of that publication on page 295.

11. Harper, *History,* Vol. VI, 676.

12. Harper, *History,* Vol. VI, 677.

13. "Washington — Treasurer's Report," *Woman's Journal* 31 July 1909: 123.

14. Alice Stone Blackwell, "Cook Book," *Woman's Journal* 24 July 1909: 117.

15. "Suffrage Women to Open a Grocery," *New York Times* 19 Feb. 1913: 8.

16. Kleber, 8.

17. "Cookbook Will Silence Enemy," *Woman's Journal* 9 Oct. 1915: 325; "The Best Cooks are Suffragists," advertisement, *Woman's Journal* 30 Oct. 1915: 349.

18. Ella M.S. Marble, ed., *Wimodaughsis Cook-Book* (Washington, D.C., 1892).

19. Gloria Moldow, *Women Doctors in Gilded Age Washington: Race, Gender, and Professionalization* (Champaign, Illinois: University of Illinois Press, 1987) 140–2.

20. Teresa Zackodnik, *Press, Platform, Pulpit: Black Feminist Ethics in the Era of Reform,* Knoxville (Tennessee: University of Tennessee Press, 2011) 233.

21. Elizabeth Driver, *A Bibliography of Canadian Cookbooks 1825–1949* (Toronto: University of Toronto Press, 2008) 278.

Cosmetics

1. *Votes for Women* (New York: Political Equality Association, n.d.) 9.

2. "Mrs. Belmont Plans Beauty Repair Shop — Her Suffrage Headquarters Will Provide a Cosmetic Course for Her Followers," *New York Times* 19 Oct. 1911: 1.

Counterstamps

1. A number of suffrage counter stamp pieces have appeared recently in Internet auctions, all on coins of the period, although there is really little way for the average person to tell when, exactly, the piece was counterstamped. The online descriptions for some of these coins do label them, however, as counterfeits. Because of the number of "faked" pieces available, it is difficult to know how widespread the practice of counter stamping was during the suffrage period.

Dust Mops

1. "Chemical Dust Mops and Marless Holders," *Woman's Journal* 28 Sept. 1912: 310.

Eggs

1. "Suffrage Women to Open a Grocery — From Which All Goods, Even the Eggs, Will be Stamped 'Votes for Women,'" *New York Times* 19 Feb. 1913: 8.

2. "Col. Ida Craft Gets a Prize for Cookies," *New York Times* 27 March 1914: clipping.

Endorsements in Magazines

1. The names of both Elizabeth Cady Stanton and Belva Lockwood appear as endorsers of the soap in a sixteen-page "Fairy Art Book" that was published by the company as a promotional piece in 1899. The booklet included "11 art selections" in full color to encourage women to keep the piece as a collectible, while presumably considering the soap for future purchase. It also included endorsements from other famous women, but it is interesting to see how suffragists were beginning to enter the mainstream of American culture at the very end of the century, at least from the perspective of women.

2. Belva Lockwood's name appears alongside those of nine other women endorsing Fairy Soap in a separate advertisement. Lockwood is identified as "the most prominent woman attorney." Most of the other women cited achieve acknowledgment through their marriage to distinguished men, primarily politicians. The list includes "Mrs. Charles Fairbanks, wife of Sen. Fairbanks, Indiana," "Mrs. Marion Butler, Wife of Sen. Butler, North Carolina," "Mrs. B.R. Tillman, Wife of Sen. Tillman, South Carolina," and "Mrs. W.A. Harris, Wife of Sen. Harris, Kansas."

3. "Curtain the Exterior for Harmony," advertisement for the Quaker Lace Company, clipping from unidentified magazine, with unidentified date. In author's collection.

4. For a more complete account of Lockwood's endorsement of Nervura and her own attempt at creating a company to distribute nerve tonic, see Norgren, 151–2.

5. Copies of all of these ads are in the author's private collection. Most, including those featuring Elizabeth Cady Stanton, appeared multiple times in a variety of magazines of the era.

6. Advertisements, *Votes for Women* 13 Feb. 1914: 306 and 9 Jan. 1914: 222.

Face Cloth

1. "Notes and News," *Woman's Journal* 24 June 1911: 200.

Fans

1. Lou W. McCulloch, *Paper Americana* (San Diego: A.S. Barnes, 1980) 157.

2. "Votes for Women Fans," *Woman's Journal* 9 Aug. 1913: 255; "Suffrage Fans — Comfort for the Hot Weather," *Woman's Journal* 26 Jan. 1913: 239.

3. An example of this fan can be found in the collections of both Chase Livingston and Rose Gschwendtner.

4. "Women Make Plea for Wall St. Votes," *New York Times* 16 Sept. 1915:11.

Flyswatter

1. "Special Novelties for County Fairs," *Woman's Journal* 8 July 1916: 223.

Garden Seeds and Sticks

1. Advertisement, *The Suffragist* 20 May 1916: 12.

2. Spec. issue of *The APIC Keynoter* Summer, Fall, Winter (2008): 108.

3. "Plan a State Garden," *Woman's Journal* 6 March 1915: 78; "Suffrage Garden Grows Popular," *Woman's Journal* 27 March 1915: 102; "The Seed For Your Suffrage Garden," *Woman's Journal* 27 March 1915: 101.

4. *Garden Primer. How to Plant and Care for a Vegetable Garden* (New York: Isaac Goldman Company, Printers for Mayor Mitchel's Food Supply Committee. Distributed by the Albany Branch of the N.Y. State Woman Suffrage Party, 1917).

5. Clipping of advertisement from a July issue of *Woman Voter* provided to me by Robert Cooney.

6. "Suffragette Colours — Sweet Pea Seeds," *Votes for Women* 18 Feb. 1909: 368.

Handkerchiefs

1. "Suffrage Campaign Emblems," *Woman's Journal* 22 July 1916: 239.

2. "Handkerchiefs for Xmas Presents," *Votes for Women* 17 Dec. 1909: 184.

3. "The Purple, Green & White," *Votes for Women* 15 Dec. 1911: 173.

Jewelry

1. "Suffragist Jewelry," advertisement, *Woman's Journal* 15 Oct. 1910: 171. This particular advertisement, along with the similar Cargill piece that ran along side it, were probably the first two full-page ads for a suffrage product in the *Journal* after it had been transformed into newspaper format.

2. Agnes E. Ryan, "Suffrage and Styles — Special Woman Suffrage Day at the National Style Show," *Woman's Journal* 4 Feb. 1911: 33.

3. "The Popular Name," *Votes for Women* 1 Sept. 1911: 773.

4. "Jewelry for Suffrage," *New York Times* 26 July 1914: 11.

5. Harper, *History,* Vol. V, 616–17.

6. Peck and Catt, 323–24.

7. Shaw and Jordon, 237.

8. Shaw and Jordon, 301.

9. Harper, *History,* V, 447.

10. Elizabeth S. Goring, "Suffragette Jewellery in Britain," *Omnium Gatherum: A Collection of Papers— The Decorative Arts Society 1850–Present, Journal 26,* 2002: 85.

11. Crawford, 308.

12. Goring, 98.

13. Goring, 87.

14. Crawford, 309.

15. Advertisement, *Votes for Women* 17 Dec. 1909: 183. This same advertisement appeared in a number of issues of the journal.

16. *Votes for Women* 1 Oct. 1909: 16.

17. Crawford, 309.

18. "New Year Presents," advertisement, *Votes for Women,* 3 Jan. 1913: 211.

19. Advertisement, *The Suffragette* 13 Jan. 1913: 179.

20. Advertisement in *The Trial of the Suffragette Leaders* (London: The Woman's Press, 1908) 49.

21. "Xmas Gifts at the WSPU Shops," 170.

22. A picture of the Murphy enamel, both front and back, can be found in Irene Cockroft and Susan Croft, *Art, Theater and Women's Suffrage* (Twickenham, England: Aurora Metro Press, 2010) 93.

23. Goring, 94.

24. One correspondent to the WSPU official journal, *Votes for Women* 21 June 1909: 279, did suggest that "the Union colours should be termed Green, White, and Violet, i.e., 'Give Women Votes,'" but the lack of a responsive follow-up in the paper indicates that the suggestion was not taken up even as supplementary to the official symbolism. Alice Stone Blackwell, though, seemed to have been unaware of Mrs. Pethick Lawrence's official gloss of the colors of the WSPU and assumed that they stood instead for "Give Women Votes" (Alice Stone Blackwell, "Malicious Misrepresentation," *Woman's Journal* 10 May 1913). The mistaken attribution occurred earlier in 1909 in an anonymous column in the *Woman's Journal* entitled "More Suffrage Postcards" that may have been written by Blackwell. In describing a set of three suffrage postcards that had just been published by "Mr. D.C. Coates, the columnist noted their colors and commented 'Green, white and violet are the colors of the Women's Social and Political Union. They are said to stand for 'Give Women Votes'" (*Woman's Journal* 31 July 1909: 124). The Women's Political Union of New Jersey did adopt "violet" rather than "purple" as one of its three official colors, because the "initials of their names are also the initials of the words "Give Women Votes." However, in the organization's campaign handbook for 1914, Mrs. Minnie J. Reynolds, the WPUNJ's secretary and state organizer, contributed a poem in which she commented on the symbolic meanings of "the Purple, White and Green [not Violet]," and their importance to the suffrage cause (*Women's Political Union of New Jersey Campaign Yearbook* [Newark, WPUNJ, 1914] 4, 35). Despite the occasional substitution or confusion of violet rather than purple as an official color, no one from the period ever seems to have advocated or even suggested that the resultant gloss of 'Give Women Votes'" either was or should be used as a "secret code." Colors were used to command public attention, not hide from it.

Magazine Covers and Illustrations

1. All magazines and illustrations referenced are in the collection of the author.

2. Dickens' character of Dolly Varden was a vain, flirtatious girl known for wearing a colorful costume with a distinctive calico pattern. In America, the name appears to have taken on a political meaning involving that of irresponsible and inconsistent reform. On the front page, for example, of the 6 June 1872 edition of *Wild Oats,* a satirical newspaper, there is an illustration on the front page of the "Cincinnati Dolly Varden Platform" in shambles. This platform consisted of support for such issues as "Female Suffrage [*sic*]," "Free Trade," "Free Rum," "Amnesty," "KKK," and "Temperance." The figure of Dickens' original Dolly Varden was popular enough in America that the publisher Lee and Walker of Philadelphia could publish in the same year a "Dolly Varden Quadrille" that featured a chromolithographed cover in dazzling color of well-dressed woman, including, presumably, the title character. The sheet music illustration, however, was devoid of political symbolism.

3. For a complete discussion of magazines of the period, see Frank Luther Mott, *A History of American Magazines, Volume III, 1865–1885* (Cambridge: Harvard University Press, 1938) and *A History of American Magazines, Volume IV, 1885–1905* (Cambridge: Harvard University Press, 1957).

4. Richard Samuel West, *Satire on Stone: The Political Cartoons of Joseph Kepler* (Urbana: University of Illinois Press, 1988) 52.

5. See his comments, for example, throughout his best-selling memoir, Edward Bok, *The Americanization of Edward Bok* (New York: Charles Scribner's Sons, 1920).

6. "'Votes for Women'—As Seen by Edward Bok," *New York Times* 18 April 1909: unpaginated clipping.

7. Richard Barry, *What Women Have Actually Done Where They Vote* (New York: New York State Association Opposed to Woman Suffrage, n.d.).

8. *The Truth Versus Richard Barry* (New York: National American Woman Suffrage Association, n.d.).

9. Elisabeth Israels Perry, "Introduction: Image, Rhetoric, and the Historical Memory of Women," *Cartooning for Suffrage* by Alice Sheppard (Albuquerque: University of New Mexico Press, 1994) 6.

Millinery and Accessories

1. Advertisement, *The Suffragist* 13 May 1916: 9.

2. "Our Hat in the Ring," *The Suffragist* 20 May 1916: 5.

3. Advertisement, *The Suffragist* 3 June 1916: 2.

4. "Suffrage Paraders Beckon Roosevelt," *New York Times* 2 May 1912:11.

5. *Supplementary List*, 7; "Suffragists Should Have a Glove Purse with Votes for Women Button," advertisement, *Woman's Journal*, 4 May 1912: 142.

6. "Always Wear the Colors," *Votes for Women* 10 Sept. 1908: 448.

7. Advertisements, *Woman's Suffrage Edition — The Detroit Times* 3 June 1912: 21–2, 24.

8. Advertisements, *Chicago Examiner — Women Voters' Edition — Published and Edited by the Illinois Equal Suffrage Association* 11 Aug. 1913: 15–16, 19, 22, 25.

9. "Fashion Preferences of Famous American Women," *Supplement to The Illustrated Milliner (Hats from Paris & New York)* October 1915: 3.

10. "Notable American Women," *Supplement to The Illustrated Milliner* September 1915: unpaginated fold-out.

11. Various ads for The Woman's Press of the WSPU in *Votes for Women* indicate that Pankhurst's organization sold such clothing accessories at its shops as purse bags in leather, ribbons, belts with either black buckles or Haunted House buckles, ties, and motor scarves.

12. Advertisements, *Votes for Women* 26 May 1911: 562–63, 572.

13. Advertisements, *Votes for Women* 2 June 1911: 578.

14. Advertisement, *Votes for Women* 17 June 1910: 621.

15. "Concerning Dress," *Votes for Women* 1 Oct. 1908: 5, "Suffragettes and the Dress Problem," *Votes for Women* 22 Oct. 1908: 54, "Dress in the Colours," *Votes for Women* 5 March 1909: 413; and "Dress in the Colours," *Votes for Women* 26 March 1909: 483.

16. Krista Lysack, *Come Buy, Come Buy: Shopping and the Culture of Consumption in Victorian Women's Writing* (Miami: Ohio University Press, 2008) 145–50.

17. "Hats for Women," advertisement, *Votes for Women* 28 Jan. 1909: 303.

18. "Votes for Women," advertisement, *Votes for Women* 21 May 1909: 705.

19. "Union Men Assist Suffrage Workers," *New York Times* 6 June 1916: 15.

Miniature Bissell Carpet Sweepers

1. Anthony and Harper, *History of Woman Suffrage* Vol. IV, 942.

2. This fan is in the collection of Ronnie Lapinsky.

Paper Bags

1. Martha Wentworth Suffren, "30,000 Paper Bags," *Woman's Journal* 30 July 1910: 121.

Paper Napkins

1. "National Headquarters Newsletter," *Woman's Journal* 1 July 1911: 204.

2. "Those Missing Paper Napkins," *Woman's Journal* 29 July 1911: 237.

3. *Woman's Journal* 27 March 1909: 52.

4. "The Popular Souvenir," *Votes for Women*, 2 July 1909: 876.

Pencils

1. "Suffrage Novelties," *New York Suffrage Newsletter* Jan. 1912: 2.

2. "Suffrage Pencils," advertisement, *Woman's Journal* 13 Aug. 1913: 247. This particular advertisement ran for several issues after its initial appearance. The advertisement for penholders came in the October 11 edition of the periodical.

3. "Quaker City Has Big Pencil Day," *Woman's Journal* 28 Feb. 1914: 72.

4. "Wives of Soldiers Seek Financial Aid," *New York Times* 1 July 1916: 3.

5. "Ready for Suffrage Week," *New York Times* 7 Sept. 1912: 6.

6. R.A. Lawrence, "Selling Suffrage Pencils," *New York Times* 19 Oct. 1913: 14.

7. "Our Offer to Members of the NWSPU and Their Friends," advertisement, *Votes for Women* 18 Feb. 1909: 367.

8. "Will You Help the Cause?" advertisement, *Votes for Women* 5 June 1914: 552.

Pennants

1. See Herbert Ridgeway Collins, *Threads of History: Americana Recorded on Cloth 1775 to the Present* (Washington, D.C.: Smithsonian Institution Press, 1979). For his study, Collins, who was a curator of political history at the Smithsonian, had access to their collection. Also Theodore L. Hake, *Political Buttons Book III*, Sullivan, *Americana*, 168, and Heritage Auction, 2009, 105.

2. This advertisement appeared in multiple issues of *The Suffragist*, including 13 Dec. 1913: 48.

3. Solomons, 72.

4. *Supplementary List*, 6.

5. Solomons, 41.

6. Heritage Historical and Vintage Popular Culture Americana, November 12–13, 2007 (Dallas: Heritage Auction Galleries, 2007) 142.

7. "Suffrage Paraders Beckon Roosevelt," *New York Times* 2 May 1912: 11.

8. Harper, *History*, Vol. VI, 678.

9. Harper, *History*, Vol. V, 420–21.

10. Harper, *History*, Vol. VI, 403.

Pennsylvania Liberty Bell Campaign

1. Harper, *History*, Vol. VI, 553–55.

2. "Liberty Bell for Women," *New York Times* 28 March 1915: 8.

3. "The Woman's Liberty Bell — Silent Until November 2," flier, Pennsylvania Woman Suffrage Association, Harrisburg, Pennsylvania, n.d.

4. "Suffrage Liberty Bell; Women from Pennsylvania Entertained Here on Way to Troy," *New York Times* 31 March 1915: 6.

5. "Liberty Bell," *Times*, 28 March 1915.

6. "The New Liberty Bell for Pennsylvania Women," admission ticket, 1915.

7. "New Liberty Bell Cast; Suffragists Participate in Ceremonies at Troy Factory," *New York Times* 1 April 1915: 7.

8. Harper, *History*, Vol. VI, 556.

9. "Suffrage Liberty Bell," *Times*, 31 March 1915.

10. Harper, *History*, Vol. V, 160.

11. All of the above items are in the author's own collection, except for the flier, which can be found at the Liberty Bell Museum, located in Rocky Hill, Connecticut.

Pillow Tops

1. "Pillow Top and Back," advertisement, *Woman's Journal* 25 May 1912: 166.

Playing Cards and Card Games

1. When NAWSA first advertised these decks of cards on page 175 of the 31 May 1913 edition of the *Woman's Journal,* it announced that there would be "four different backs" available, not one, and that these would be in the colors of yellow, black, and white and also purple, green, and white. Each deck would sell for 25 cents. Plans may have changed prior to publication, as only one design is known and that in both purple, black (not green), and white and yellow, black, and white. In a later printing, blue appears to have replaced the original purple. One can understand why NAWSA may have dropped green as a color in the proposed purple, green, and white deck as it may not have wished to become too closely associated with the colors of either the more militant WPU in America or the WSPU in England.

2. Harper, *History*, Vol. V, 13. NAWSA seems to have been quite serious and inclusive about its anti-gambling policies. When Mrs. Alva Belmont, the prominent socialite and suffrage leader, offered to raffle off "one of her prize porkers to the suffrage cause" at a 1911 Suffrage Fair, she was refused. The organizers of the fair "did not allow any raffling," and *Woman's Journal* commented, "this, we believe, has been an invariable rule at all Suffrage Fairs." The rebuffed Mrs. Belmont decided then to sell chances on the pig at her own fair in Hempstead, New York, in April of that year, where the *Journal's* editors conceded that she was "free to hold any number of raffles on her own responsibility." "Suffrage Pigs," *Woman's Journal* 8 April 1911: 1.

3. "Tours for Women in Radiant Garb," *New York Times* 28 March 1915: 8.

4. *Woman's Journal* 3 July 1913: 214.

5. *Times Sunday Magazine*, 28 June 1914: smb.

6. *Votes for Women* 3 Dec. 1909: 157.

7. Crawford, 235.

8. Crawford, 235.

9. Atkinson, 43.

10. "New Suffrage Game Out," *New York Times* 23 April 1910: 10. See also "A Suffrage Game," *Woman's Journal* 14 May 1910: 78. The game was offered as a free premium by the *Journal* for anyone bringing in a new subscriber.

11. "'Constitution' A Campaign Game," *Woman's Journal* 9 Sept. 1916: 294.

Postcards — American

1. McCulloch, 75.

2. McCulloch, 75.

3. An excellent introduction to the "Real Photo" card, along with accompanying illustrations, is Robert Bogdan and Todd Weseloh, *Real Photo Postcard Guide: The People's Photography* (Syracuse: Syracuse University Press, 2006).

4. "Get Out Your Cameras," *Woman's Journal* 25 Sept. 1909: 153.

5. Unless otherwise noted, all references to postcards are from the author's own collection.

6. "She Was Bound to Vote," *New York Times* 7 Jan. 1887: 1.

7. Many of these "postcards" had blank reverses and could be used, therefore, as simple handouts rather than as mailers, although many of them are addressed.

8. Solomons, 55.

9. "Few Seats for Men on Suffrage Day," *New York Times* 23 Feb. 1911: 3.

10. "Mrs. Dodge Charges a Poison-Pen Plot," *New York Times* 30 Oct. 1916: 9.

11. *Supplementary List,* 6.

12. "The Enemies It Has Made," *Woman's Journal* 18 July 1908: 114.

13. The set came in an envelope bearing the imprint of the press along with the statement "Herein are half dozen thoughts of earnest folk concerning Women Suffrage." Some of these "thoughts" include "In the progress of civilization, woman suffrage is sure to come," "Taxation without representation is Tyranny," "Governments derive their just powers from the consent of the governed," and "A nation cannot remain half slave and half free."

14. Solomons, 40, 74.

15. Harper, *History*, Vol. V, 372, 482, 532. It is unfortunate that while the *History* at times gives the total figure for the year of the number of items that its publishing company produced, it does not list separately the sales of postcards.

16. The Anna Howard Shaw card was part of a set of three portrait cards issued by a "Miss A.E. Hufstader, of Fredonia, New York" in 1911. The other two subjects were Susan B. Anthony and Frances E.

Willard. Willard, who was famous for her temperance activities, was also a staunch suffragist, just as many suffragists were staunch believers in temperance. Hufstader unveiled the set in a brief announcement in *The Woman's Journal* for July 15 of that year.

17. Ellen Carol DuBois, *Harriot Stanton Blatch and the Winning of Woman Suffrage* (New Haven: Yale University Press, 1997) 258.

18. Some of these "aphorisms," each stated separately on an individual card, are as follows: "Equal Suffrage is neither more nor less than simple justice"; "The Declaration of Independence was the direct result of taxation without representation. Either exempt WOMAN from taxation or grant her the right of Equal Suffrage. What is Sauce for the GANDER is sauce for the goose"; "Beware of MAGAZINES and NEWSPAPERS which are opposed to WOMAN SUFFRAGE. THERE'S A REASON"; and "Any Man who denies WOMAN is his equal mentally, simply casts a slur on his MOTHER." The entire set of 30 is numbered 101–130. Card 111, with the message "Advocating special sex legislation is a detriment to the cause of Woman Suffrage—EQUAL SUFFRAGE knows no sex," appears with far less frequency than the other 29. Because some women may have felt that certain protection by law was needed for women the slogan may have been somewhat controversial and withdrawn soon after its publication.

19. "United Equal Suffrage States of America," advertisement, *Woman's Journal* 15 Oct. 1910: 172.

20. "Equal Suffrage Week," advertisement, *Woman's Journal* 22 Oct. 1910: 177–78.

21. "Agents—The Cargill Company," advertisement, *Woman's Journal* 14 Oct. 1911: 326.

22. Katherine Milhous, "A Moving Picture," *Woman's Journal* 11 March 1916: front cover.

23. "Blind Justice—Can This Be Justice?" *Woman's Journal* 19 June 1909: front cover; and "New Suffrage Postcard," *Woman's Journal* 18 Sept. 1909: 152.

24. "The Appeal of Womanhood," *Suffragist* 27 June 1914: front cover.

25. Carrie Harrison, prep., "The First Munition of War," *Suffragist* 6 Feb. 1915: front cover.

26. The child in the picture was Mary Ware Dennett's youngest, and the card was available from the Massachusetts Woman's Suffrage Association at two for five cents. After an announcement about the card appeared in the January 8 issue of the *Woman's Journal*, it was featured on the front cover of the periodical the next week. It was common practice for suffragists to photograph their children holding up suffrage propaganda and then transferring the image to a postcard. "Another Suffrage Card," *Woman's Journal* 8 Jan. 1910: 5.

27. Entitled "*This* is allowed to vote," the card portrays an Italian Immigrant, a Jew, a Black, and a Chinese Man, but notes that a woman is denied a parliamentary vote. It was issued in support of a "Resolution for Women's Suffrage" that was introduced on February 17, 1910.

28. "Four Voters," *Life* 16 Oct. 1913: cover. The illustration, titled "Four Voters," shows a respectable but un-franchised woman, dressed in white, indicating her purity, surrounded by four men who could vote: a member of the Black Hand (precursor to the Mafia) carrying a knife, a drunken laborer, an effeminate man, and an African American male, dressed as a dandy and strutting his importance.

29. "New Suffrage Postcards," *Woman's Journal* 11 July 1908: 112.

30. "If You Are a Suffragist," *Woman's Journal* 17 July 1915: 228.

31. *Official Program—Votes for Women Pageant and Parade—Hartford, Conn. May 2, 1914* (Hartford: Connecticut Woman Suffrage Association, 1914) 5.

32. "Mrs. Thomas Hepburn Joins Militants—with Mrs. Toscan Bennett She Leaves the State Association," *Meriden Morning Record*, 13 Sept. 1917: 6. Emily Pierson, the state organizer for the CWSA, had also abandoned the group the previous month for the Woman's Party. Under Hepburn's leadership, the CWSA had adopted for its official colors the purple, green, and white of the militant English group, the WSPU, but the colors themselves were not enough apparently to persuade many members of the CWSA to become more aggressive in their pursuit of the franchise. Several other Connecticut newspapers also recorded Hepburn and Bennett's departure that same day, including *The Hartford Courant* and *The Day*.

33. eBay item 310217870819, May 8, 2010.

34. Many of Kehrhahn's photographic postcards were preserved as campaign memorabilia by WSPU members and eventually found their way into the Celia and U.I. Harris collection of suffrage ephemera. This collection is now owned by the Elizabeth Cady Stanton Fund, whose president is Coline Jenkins, great great granddaughter of Stanton. Currently the fund makes these cards accessible to the general public and to scholars through traveling exhibits as part of its educational efforts.

35. For a more complete listing of publishers of English suffrage photo postcards, along with the names of photographers whose work often appeared on these cards, see Crawford, 546–49, 562–64.

36. Harper, *History*, Vol. VI, 451–52. One interesting badge associated with the march was not made by Jones or her supporters but by a group of electrical workers called "The Sons of Jove" that met weekly at the Hotel Emerson in Baltimore. On February 25, when Jones and her army were scheduled to arrive in that city, the "Baltimore Jovians" had printed up a ribbon and celluloid badge welcoming "the Suffragette Pilgrims." The souvenir may or may not have had a satirical intent. See an image of this badge in spec. issue of *The APIC Keynoter* Summer, Fall, Winter (2008): 95. There are several buttons with the legend "We Are Hikers Not Pikers" that also may be related to Jones' expedition.

37. Gertrude M. Price, "A Day with Gen. Jones

and Her Army," *The Bay City Times* 26 Feb. 1913: un-paginated clipping, collection of author.

38. Adams and Keene, 76–92.

39. Such was the case with two cards from the Wall series that were pictured in the June 27 and July 4, 1914, issues of the *Woman's Journal.*

40. One such card asserts that the speech was that of Lady Morris at Berkeley Hall in London on Nov. 4, 1908. Another claims that the same words came instead from a suffrage meeting in Omaha, Nebraska. Obviously, both attributions are spurious.

41. A collection of seventy-nine different cards on the pants and Harem Skirt theme was assembled by Frank Corbeil and sold in a Heritage Gallery Auction on November 18, 2009.

Postcards — English

42. Crawford, 562.

43. Crawford, 562.

44. Advertisement, *Votes for Women* 18 Feb. 1910: 329.

45. Crawford, 562.

46. These cards are in the collection of Rose Gschwendtner.

47. Scenes of domesticity were not restricted to the WFL. Even Sylvia Pankhurst, daughter of the militant Emmeline Pankhurst, is pictured pacifying a baby on a card published by the Press Photo Company sometime after May 27, 1913, when she had formed the East London Federation of Suffragettes.

48. Advertisement, *The Trial of the Suffragette Leaders,* 49.

49. Diane Atkinson, *Mrs. Broom's Suffragette Photographs* (London: Dirk Nishen, n.d.) 2.

50. *Program, Political Peepshows (Political Cartoons in Model)* (London: The National Women's Political and Social Union, 1909).

51. Tickner, 16–17. The winner of the first poster prize was Dora Meeson Coates for "Political Help," and the poster was later published by the NUWSS.

52. "Artists' Suffrage League," *Votes for Women* 9 Oct. 1909: 30.

53. There is no complete list known. The author has 24 ASL cards in his private collection and knows of no others. However, more varieties in all probability do exist.

54. "English Cartoon Buttons," advertisement, *Woman's Journal* 13 May 1911: 152.

55. Ian McDonald, *Vindication! A Postcard History of the Women's Movement* (London: Deidre McDonald, 1989) 44.

56. Front page illustration, *Woman's Journal* 13 March 1909.

57. Tickner, 21.

58. Tickner, 22.

59. "The Two Asquiths," *Votes for Women* 19 Nov. 1909: cover; 10 Dec. 1909: 69; and 24 Dec. 1909: 203.

60. "More Suffrage Postal Cards," *Woman's Journal* 6 Feb. 1909: 24.

61. "A Kitten for Mrs. Catt," *Woman's Journal* 16 Jan. 1909: 10.

62. McDonald, 61.

Posters — Art and Propaganda

1. Many of these early broadsides are pictured throughout Robert P.J. Cooney, *Winning the Vote.*

2. Anthony and Harper, Vol. IV, 28. Actually, there is at least one speech of Anthony's that was preserved, and that was a lengthy one delivered in a number of districts of the counties of Monroe and Ontario prior to her trial in June 1873 for voting. It is transcribed as part of the thick pamphlet in an edition of 3,000 copies that Anthony printed up in 1874 and distributed to both supporters and law libraries. *"Address of Susan B. Anthony," An Account of the Proceedings of the Trial of Susan B. Anthony on the Charge of Illegal Voting at the Presidential Election in Nov. 1872* (Rochester, N.Y., 1874) 151–78.

3. "International Suffrage Fair," *Woman's Journal* 28 Sept. 1912: 308.

4. Sheppard, 29.

5. Vernon D. Jordon, *Around the Korner, Women's Suffrage and Rose O'Neill* (Des Moines: privately printed, 2009) 5.

6. Jordon, 10.

7. Solomons, 40.

8. "Art Notes," *New York Times* 4 March 1915: 8.

9. "Suffrage Posters Bear Messages to Voters," *New York Times Sunday Magazine* 3 Oct. 1915: 58–9.

10. "Suffrage Poster Contest," *New York Times* 15 Oct. 1915: 6.

11. "Suffrage Art Prizes," *Woman's Journal* 8 April 1911: 104.

12. "The Purple, Green, and White in America," *Votes for Women* 20 Jan. 1911: 256.

13. An illustration of this poster, a copy of which is in the holdings of the Sophia Smith Collection of the Woman's History Archive of Smith College, Northampton, Massachusetts, appears in Paula Hays Harper, "Votes for Women? *A Graphic Episode in the Battle of the Sexes," Art and Architecture in the Service of Politics,* eds. Henry Millon and Linda Nochlin (Cambridge: MIT Press, 1978) 152.

14. Illustrations of these first two posters appear in Heritage Auction, 2007, 60–61, and the third in the June 12–13 auction from the same house, 68.

15. "New Literature and Supplies," *Woman's Journal* 28 Sept. 1912: 311.

16. Susan K. Scott, "Rose Cecil O'Neill: America's First Female Cartoonist Fought for Women's Suffrage," *The Ozark's Mountaineer* March/April 2010: 7.

17. An image of this poster can be found in Heritage Auction, 2007, 61. For the second and third, see Heritage Auction, May 13–14, 167.

18. An image of this poster can be found in Cooney, 289.

19. Mrs. I.F. Mackrille, "Street Car Advertising," *Woman's Journal* 8 June 1912: 183.

20. "New Suffrage Poster," *Woman's Journal* 1 April 1911: 99.

21. An illustration of this poster, a copy of which is in the holdings of the Rare Book Room of the New York Public Library, appears in Paula Hays Harper's article in *Art and Architecture*, 152.

22. Tickner, 250–53.

23. Tickner, 47.

24. "Poster Parade," *Votes for Women* 28 June 1912: 639.

25. "Volunteers Wanted for Poster Brigade," advertisement, *Votes for Women* 18 April 1913: 412.

26. "A New Kind of Poster Parade," *Votes for Women* 13 Feb. 1914: 304.

27. Tickner, 16–17.

28. Advertisement, *Woman's Journal* 14 Jan. 1911: 14.

29. *Catalog of Supplies,* 17.

30. Tickner, 20–21, 42–46.

31. "Two Banned Posters," *Votes for Women* 3 Aug. 1914: 686.

Ribbons

1. For histories of the rise and development of the political campaign ribbon, see Sullivan*, American Political Ribbons*, and Sullivan, *Collecting Political Americana*, 113–24.

2. Crew, 132.

3. *Justicia,* 1.

4. Mary Livermore, "Show Your Colors," *Woman's Journal* 5 May 1894: 137.

5. Johns quoted by Peck, 321–22.

6. Thomas R. Burkholder, "The *Farmer's Wife,* 1891–1894 — Raising a Prairie Consciousness," *A Voice of Their Own: The Woman Suffrage Press, 1840–1910,* ed. Martha M. Solomon (Tuscaloosa: University of Alabama Press, 1991) 155.

7. *Program for The International Congress of Women Assembled by the National Woman Suffrage Association, March 25th to April 1st, 1888* (Washington, D.C., 1888) 2, 3, 15.

8. Cooney, 62–3.

9. "Ribbons and Badges," spec. issue of *The APIC Keynoter* Summer, Fall, Winter (2008): 120.

10. See, for example, the programs for the 1913 and 1917 conventions, held in Washington, D.C., and Atlantic City, respectively.

11. This badge is pictured in Silver and Cazaly, 52.

12. Shaw, 289.

13. Harper, *History,* Vol. V, 119.

14. Harper, *History,* Vol. V, 311.

15. Autographed examples of this ribbon are in the collections of Gil Gleason and the author.

16. Sullivan, *Americana,* 124.

17. The Association was formed in 1869, and this was their 26th annual convention. See Harper, *History,* Vol. VI, 440.

18. Undated clipping from *The Illustrated American.*

19. Anthony and Harper, Vol. IV, 847–52.

20. "Pleas for Political Equality," *New York Times* 28 Feb. 1894: 4.

21. Examples of NYWSA ribbons are pictured on the Library of Congress website and the spec. issue of *The APIC Keynoter* Summer, Fall, Winter (2008). This issue, put together from contributions of woman suffrage collectors and historians, pictures the largest grouping of movement ribbons every published. There are no additional NYWSA ribbons listed in Sullivan and Fischer's study *American Political Ribbons and Ribbon Badges 1825–1981.*

22. Spec. issue of *The APIC Keynoter* Summer, Fall, Winter (2008): 112–20.

23. This delegate ribbon is pictured in Silver, 47.

24. Harper, *History,* Vol. VI, 351.

25. Spec. issue *Keynoter,* 132.

26. Spec. issue *Keynoter,* 112–20.

27. Advertisement, *NAWSA Headquarters Newsletter* 25 Nov. 1916: 9.

28. Harper, *History,* Vol. VI, 486.

29. "State Correspondence — California," *Woman's Journal* 20 Nov. 1909: 190.

30. Advertisement, *Trial.* 49.

Rolling Pin

1. "A Tiny Rolling Pin!" advertisement, *Woman's Journal* 30 March 1912: 102.

Rubber Stamps

1. "National Headquarters Letter," *Woman's Journal* 1 July 1911: 204.

Sashes

1. "Suffrage Paraders Beckon Roosevelt," *New York Times*, 2 May 1912: unpaginated clipping.

2. "Dress Rehearsal of Suffrage Parade," *New York Times* 21 April 1912: unpaginated clipping.

3. "400,000 Cheer Suffrage March," *New York Times* 10 November 1912: unpaginated clipping.

4. *Banner-Suffrage Parade,* 5.

5. "Suffragists Plan Albany Pilgrimage," *New York Times* 10 Dec. 1912: unpaginated clipping.

6. *Supplemental List of Supplies,* 5.

7. *Catalog of Supplies,* 17.

8. "Pankhurst Speech Opens Pocketbooks," *New York Times* 6 January 1912: unpaginated clipping.

9. An example of this sash, probably worn by Frances Williams to a Congressional Union Convention in Washington, was auctioned off by Heritage Galleries in 2010. 22 May. *Catalog, Heritage Political and Americana, May 22, 1910* (Dallas: Heritage Auction Galleries, 2010) 56.

10. "Suffrage Cheers for Mrs. Pankhurst," *New York Times* 21 Oct. 1909: unpaginated clipping.

11. "Shower Women with Glass," *New York Times* 1 August 1913: unpaginated clipping.

12. "Italian Suffrage Meeting," *New York Times* 16 Nov. 1912: unpaginated clipping.

13. "Suffragist Battle at Industry Show," *New York Times* 16 March 1912: unpaginated clipping.

14. "Suffragists Invade Show," *New York Times* 2 March 1913: unpaginated clipping.

Scarves

1. "Notes and News," *Woman's Journal* 11 July 1908: 112.

Sheet Music, Songsters and Records

1. Crew, 8–9. All future references to published suffrage lyrics and songs, unless otherwise noted, are either from this volume or from the author's own collection.

2. Lori Deter, "The Image of Women in Nineteenth Century Parlor Songs," thesis, Tulane University, 1981.

3. In reacting to some of these earliest protest songs, one must be especially cautious. The 1863 song by William Brough "Let Us All Speak Our Minds If We Die for It" is described by Francie Wolff, despite its male authorship, as being "one of the earliest feminist songs and it is also one of the most militant" (Francie Wolff, *Give the Ballot to the Mothers: Songs of the Suffragists—A History in Song* (Springfield, Missouri: Denlinger's, 1998) 45. The program notes to the Folkways Records compendium of suffrage songs term this "the most outspoken feminist musical statement that we have been able to find" (*Songs of the Suffragettes*, Folkways, 1958). However, Mrs. T. German Reed, who performed it in the role of Mrs. Naggit, obviously presented it as satire in English music halls as denoted by her character's name. It is entirely probable, then, that many, if not most, of the American music hall renditions of this same song were intended to expose militant feminism to ridicule and not to advance the cause of women's rights.

4. Crew, 19–36.

5. Wolff, 5–6.

6. Wolff, 44.

7. Elizabeth Cady Stanton, Susan B. Anthony, and Matilda Joslyn Gage, *History of Woman Suffrage, Vol. I, 1848–1861* (New York, 1881) 627.

8. Elizabeth Cady Stanton, Susan B. Anthony, and Matilda Joslyn Gage, *History of Woman Suffrage, Vol. II, 1861–1876* (New York, 1882) 934.

9. Stanton, Anthony, Gage, Vol. II, 309.

10. Stanton, Anthony, Gage, Vol II, 232.

11. Crew, 108.

12. Anthony and Harper, Vol. IV, 942.

13. Mills and Howland, *Manual*.

14. Crawford, 644–45.

15. *Program Victory Convention New Jersey Woman Suffrage Association 1869–1920 Robert Treat Hotel, Newark, New Jersey.*

16. *Heritage Auction*, 2009, 122.

17. Harper, *History*, Vol. V, 481–82.

18. "Washington Demonstration," *The Suffragist*, 25 April 1914: 5.

19. Advertisement, *Votes for Women* 31 March 1911: 436. The Woman's Press sold the card for 1 d., a pianoforte arrangement with words for 3 d., and an edition with a pictorial cover in color for 1/6.

20. Crawford, 645.

21. "Great May 9th Demonstration," *The Suffragist* 2 May 1914: 5–6. See also "The Women's March in Prison," *Votes for Women* 15 March 1912: 378.

22. Alice Stone Blackwell, "Suffrage Song Book," *Woman's Journal* 26 June 1909: 104. Also from the *Woman's Journal* 6 July 1912: 215; 18 April 1914: 127; and 2 May 1914: 143.

23. *Votes for Women* 8 Oct. 1908: 23; 15 Nov. 1908: 103; 7 Jan. 1909: 253; and 18 Feb. 1909: 387.

24. Author's collection.

Shirts and Socks

1. "Notes and News," *Woman's Journal* 27 Aug. 1910: 142.

Soap

1. Advertisement, *Votes for Women* 1 Oct. 1909: 8.

2. Atkinson, 51.

3. "Trinkets and Songs," smb.

4. "Bits and Pieces," *The Clarion*, Dec. 2001: 5.

Spoons

1. Margaret Finnegan, *Selling Suffrage* (New York: Columbia University Press, 1999).

2. For an account of the historical evolution of the collector's spoon, see Donna H. Felger and Dorothy T. Rainwater, *American Spoons: Souvenir and Historical* (Atglen, Pennsylvania: Schiffer, 1997).

3. Stanton, Anthony and Gage, Vol. II, 917.

4. Located in *Guide to the Lindseth Collection of American Woman Suffrage* [ca. 1820–1920], Collection Number 8002 — Division of Rare and Manuscript Collections, Cornell University Library, Box 14 Series VI.

5. Anthony and Harper, Vol. IV, 298.

Stamps, Cinderellas, Stickers and Labels

1. James Mackay has defined the term "cinderella" as "virtually anything resembling a postage stamp, but not issued for postal purposes by a government postal administration..." James Mackay, *Philatelic Terms Illustrated*, 4th ed. (London: Stanley Gibbons, 2003) 27.

2. For a comprehensive catalog of both political and cause stamps, see Mark Warda, *Political Campaign Stamps* (Iola, WI: Krause, 1998).

3. Bradbury, *Advertising Poster Stamps.*

4. Harper, *History,* Vol. V, 60.

5. Clipping from the Miller NAWSA Suffrage Scrapbooks, 1897–1911, from the collection of Elizabeth Smith Miller and Anne Fitzhugh Miller located in the Library of Congress, JK1881 .N357 sec. XVI, no. 3–9 NAWSA Collection.

6. Harper, *History,* Vol. V, 93.

7. Upton and Hauser, 16.

8. "Four Idols of American Suffragettes," *Ogden Standard* 29 April 1909: 4.

9. Helen K. Hoy, "The 'Votes for Women' Stamp," *Harper's Weekly Advertiser:* undated clipping but probably 1909, in the collection of author.

10. "The Convention Seal," *Woman's Journal* 3 June 1911: 172.

11. Harper, *History,* Vol. V, 313–14.

12. Harper, *History,* Vol. V, 11.

13. "Ammunition for the Campaign," *Woman's Journal* 10 August 1912: 3. There is no design of this description that is listed either in Warda or appears in other APIC collector sources. It is possible that NAWSA may have been anticipating a future design.

14. Advertisements, *Woman's Journal,* 18 Nov. 1911: 367 and 25 Nov. 1911: 375.

15. *Price List Special Michigan Literature* (Grand Rapids: Michigan Equal Suffrage Association, n.d.) 2.

16. *Program, Forty-Fifth Annual Convention* (Washington: National American Woman Suffrage Association, 1913) cover.

17. Cooney, 293.

18. "Town Crier Poster Stamps," advertisement, *Woman's Journal* 9 Oct. 1915: 325.

19. "New Suffrage Stamps Designed," *Reading Eagle* 2 April 1915: 18.

20. "Notes and News," *Woman's Journal* 8 March 1913: 78.

21. "Santa Claus to Aid Suffrage," *Woman's Journal* 9 Dec. 1911: 389. The stamps sold for a penny each.

22. "The New Sticker or Seal," *Woman's Journal* 2 Dec. 1911: 383.

23. *Voice of the People: A Lament Together With a Prophecy* (New York: The New York State Association Opposed to Woman Suffrage, n.d.) 5.

24. McQuiston, 58.

25. eBay item 300411019086, 1 April 1910.

26. Often the postmark on the envelope on which a cinderella is affixed can give us a rough idea as to when the stamp was issued. A stamp that was published to honor Susan B. Anthony appears on an envelope, cancelled sometime in 1907, which was sent out from NAWSA headquarters when it was still located in Warren, Ohio. Anthony died in March of 1906, so this is probably a memorial piece printed right after her death or in the following year.

Stationery — Envelopes and Letterheads

1. The description of all envelopes and letterheads in this category are taken from the author's collection.

2. *Declaration of Rights of the Women of the United States By the National Woman Suffrage Association, July 4th, 1876.* Author's collection.

3. Flexner, 175.

4. One such slogan that appeared on several varieties of NAWSA cards was "'Governments derive their power from the consent of the governed.' The ballot is consent. Why should woman be governed without her consent?"

5. Elizabeth Cady Stanton, Susan B. Anthony, and Matilda Joslyn Gage, *History of Women Suffrage, Vol. III, 1876–1885* (Rochester, N.Y., 1887) 45.

6. "California," *Woman's Journal* 25 Sept. 1909: 155.

7. "Equal Suffrage Envelopes," *Woman's Journal* 9 Oct. 1909: 164.

8. "Suffrage Letter Paper," *Woman's Journal* 23 Oct. 1909: 171.

9. "Use Suffrage Letter Paper," *Woman's Journal* 28 March 1908: 51.

10. "Christmas Presents," advertisement, *Woman's Journal* 7 Dec. 1912: 391.

11. "A Hint for Christmas," *Woman's Journal* 18 Dec. 1909: 206.

12. "WSPU Stationery," *Votes for Women* 24 March 1911: 406.

13. "United Equal Suffrage States," *Journal,* 172.

Statues and Statuettes

1. "Statuettes of Miss Christabel Pankhurst & Miss Annie Kenney," advertisement, *Votes for Women* 28 May 1909: 739.

Stove and Pie Safe

1. *The Revolution* 12 May 1870: 300.

Suffrage Drink

1. "Drinking 'The Suffragette,'" *Votes for Women* 20 Aug. 1909: 1094.

Suffrage Shops

1. At NAWSA's 1913 national convention, it was decided that literature had become so large a feature of the organization that a separate publishing company had to be created to deal with the demand. In 1917, Esther G. Ogden, president of that publishing company, noted that they had published over 10,000,000 pieces of literature for the New York campaign alone. At the Victory Convention of 1920, Mrs. Ogden reported that the company had printed over 50,000,000 pieces of literature in total during her tenure. Harper, *History,* Vol.V, 532, 614.

2. *Catalog of Supplies* and *Supplemental List of Supplies*, both issued by NAWSA. The original catalog, based on advertisements for similar material contained therein that appeared in *Woman's Journal* throughout the year of 1912, appears to have been published in that year. The supplement probably was published not long after.

3. Cited in Tickner, 324.

4. "Ammunition for the Campaigns," *Woman's Journal* 10 Aug. 1912: 255.

5. *Supplemental List,* 8.

6. "Suffrage Shop for Atlantic City," *Headquarters Newsletter 2,* 15 Aug. 1916: 4.

7. *Twenty-Third Annual Convention of the New Jersey Woman Suffrage Association ... November 13–14, 1913,* 4.

8. "To Help the Suffragists," *New York Times* 14 July 1910: 6.

9. "Silk Hosiery in Their Flag," *New York Times* 16 Dec. 1910: 3.

10. Advertisement, *The Women's Political World,* Vol. I, No. 1 6 Jan. 1913: 8.

11. DuBois, 154. The use of old horse drawn lunch wagons to promote suffrage was a relatively common device to advertise the cause. A number of period postcards from the period portray such suffrage wagons. An undated card sent from Hartford, Connecticut in the author's collection depicts, for example, four women standing in front of a wagon upon which are written advertisements for *The Women's Journal.* Since several of the women are wearing bags in which to carry the paper, it is clear that this wagon had a mercantilistic side to it as well.

12. "Grandmother's Day at Suffrage Shop," *New York Times* 25 April 1915: 10.

13. "Suffrage Button Pool," *New York Times* 29 May 1915: 20.

14. *Votes for Women* (New York: Political Equality Association, n.d.) 9.

15. "Mrs. Belmont Plans Beauty Repair Shop — Her Suffrage Headquarters Will Provide a Cosmetic Course for Her Followers," *New York Times* 19 Oct. 1911: 1.

16. "Trinkets," *Times*: smb.

17. "Lunchroom Queen Quits Mrs. Belmont," *New York Times* 30 January 1912: 20.

18. "Prosecute Sellers of 'Suffragette,'" *New York Times* 24 Oct. 1913: 6.

19. "Comstock After Belmont Workers," *New York Times* 11 Nov. 1913: 10.

20. Accompanied by Inez Milhollend, Alva Belmont sold "Belmont suffrage buttons" as well as literature outside the Twenty-Seventh Assembly District Headquarters of the Woman Suffrage Party at the Hotel Normandie in October of 1910. "Suffragist Boom Starts," *New York Times* 22 Oct. 1910: 9.

21. Peck, 170.

22. "Notice," *Woman's Journal* 31 Oct. 1914: 288.

23. "Wanted a Suffrage Store," *Woman's Journal* 30 Nov. 1912: 379.

24. *Price List— Special Michigan Literature,* 2.

25. Anthony and Harper, Vol. IV, 501–2.

26. Solomons, 55.

27. Not Susan B. Anthony's sister, Mary Stafford Anthony.

28. Harper, *History,* Vol. VI, 570.

29. "New Jersey Woman's Suffrage Headquarters," advertisement, *Woman's Journal* 28 Sept. 1912: 310.

30. "Suffrage Campaign to End with a Rush," *New York Times* 26 Oct. 1915: 5.

31. Photo from the Hartford Collection at the Hartford, Connecticut, public library.

32. *Hyde Park Programme,* 3.

33. Advertisement, *Votes for Women* 26 May 1911: 572.

34. Advertisement, *Votes for Women* 1 Oct. 1909: 16.

35. Advertisement, *Votes for Women* 31 Dec. 1909: 216.

36. Advertisements, *Votes for Women* 1 Oct. 1909: 8.

37. Advertisement, *Votes for Women* 26 May 1911: 564.

38. Atkinson, 24.

39. Frederick Pethick-Lawrence, *Fate Has Been Kind* (London: Hutchinson, 1942) 73.

40. "A Votes for Women Clock," *Votes for Women* 6 May 1910: 514.

41. "Under the Clock," *Votes for Women* 13 May 1910: 533.

42. "Xmas Gifts at the W.S.P.U Shops," *Votes for Women* 10 Dec. 1909: 170.

43. Atkinson, 49.

44. Atkinson, 48.

45. John Mercer, "Shopping for Suffrage: The Campaign Shops of the Women's Social and Political Union," *Women's History Review* 18.2 (2009): 297.

46. Crawford, 634–35.

47. "Suffrage Trading Scheme," *Votes for Women* 29 Oct. 1909: 72.

48. "International Suffrage Shop," advertisement, *Votes for Women* 24 March 1911: 404.

49. "The International Suffrage Shop's Farewell," advertisement, *Votes for Women* 6 Aug. 1913: 654.

50. "The International Suffrage Shop," *Votes for Women* 19 Feb. 1915: 175.

51. See Crawford, 635.

Susan B. Anthony Bas-Relief Plaster of Paris Wall Plaque

1. Ida Husted Harper, *Life and Work of Susan B. Anthony,* Vol. II, (Indianapolis, 1899): 917.

Tin Bird

1. Alice Stone Blackwell and Teresa A. Crowley, "Massachusetts," Ida Husted Harper, ed., *The History of Woman Suffrage, Vol. VI* (New York: National American Woman Suffrage Association, 1922) 285.

The History mistakenly attributes this to 1919, but this appears to have been a misprint. The discussion surrounding the introduction of the Tin Bird is about the 1915 campaign, the day for balloting being November 2, the date on the bird.

2. "Blue Birds Help in Bay State," *Woman's Journal* 22 May 1915: 159; "Bluebird Day in Bay State," *Woman's Journal* 17 July1915: 228.

Tin Thread Holder

1. Advertisement, *Woman's Journal* 15 May 1915.
2. I am indebted to Sarah Baldwin for much of this information from her article "Sarah's Suffrage Victory," *The Clarion* Sept. 2003: 6–7.

Toys, Games and Dolls

1. Crawford, 235.
2. "Christmas Gifts in the Colours," *Votes for Women* 27 Nov. 1909: 137.
3. *Votes for Women* 27 Nov. 1909: 141.
4. "Xmas Gifts at the WSPU Shops," *Votes for Women* 10 Dec. 1909: 170.
5. "A New Suffrage Game," *The Suffragist* 13 Dec. 1913: 40.
6. The game board is illustrated in Atkinson, 38.
7. "The Ladies' Puzzle," advertisement, *Votes for Women* 17 Dec. 1908: 207.
8. Peck, 115–16.
9. "The Local Headquarters; From Auburn," *The Woman Voter* May 1914: 20–21.
10. "Silk Hosiery in Their Flag," *New York Times* 16 Dec. 1910: 3.
11. "Old Glove Dolls New Suffrage Aid," *New York Times* 7 March 1915: 13.
12. "Suffrage Toys," spec. issue of *The APIC Keynoter* Summer, Fall, Winter (2008): 124.
13. Mabel Drake Nekarda, "The Suffrage Doll," *Woman's Journal* 9 Sept. 1911: 286. Accompanying ad appears on the same page.
14. "Concerning Women," *Woman's Journal* 1 Jan. 1910: 1.
15. "Rose O'Neill and the Suffragette Kewpies," spec. issue of *The APIC Keynoter* Summer, Fall, Winter (2008): 83.
16. "Suffrage Toys," spec. issue of *The APIC Keynoter* Summer, Fall, Winter (2008): 124. Other varieties are known.
17. "Doll Pageant Attracts Antis," *Woman's Journal* 9 Sept. 1916: 294.
18. "Women Make Plea for Wall Street Votes," *New York Times* 16 Sept. 1915: 11.
19. "Necessity and a Feminine Luxury," *New York Times* 24 Dec. 1917: 8.

Train Transfers

1. "Boston Transfers to Suffrage," *Woman's Journal* 24 July 1915: 236.

Umbrellas and Parasols

1. "Fourth of July Floats," *Woman's Journal* 19 June 1909: 97; *Woman's Journal* 5 July 1913: 214; *Women's Political Union of New Jersey Campaign Handbook* (Newark: Women's Political Union of New Jersey, 1914) 7; and "Delaware Women Stir State Fair," *Woman's Journal* 20 Sept. 1913: 302.
2. "Yellow Parasols Are on the Market," *Woman's Journal* 1 July 1916: 215.
3. "Votes for Women Umbrellas," advertisement, *Woman's Journal* 5 July 1913: 215.
4. A photograph of such a parasol parade appears in Diane Atkinson, *The Suffragettes in Pictures* (London: The Museum of London through Sutton, 1996) 14.
5. "A Votes for Women Parade in Birmingham," *Votes for Women* 4 Aug. 1911: 725.

Valentines and Penny Dreadfuls

1. Two excellent books on the Courtly Love tradition are C.S. Lewis's *The Allegory of Love: A Study in Medieval Tradition* and Maurice Jacques Valency's *In Praise of Love: An Introduction to the Love-Poetry of the Renaissance*.
2. Much of this discussion about the history of both Valentines and Penny Dreadfuls is taken from McCulloch, *Paper Americana*.
3. Some people restrict the term "penny dreadful" to early examples of potboiler fiction, not the valentine, which, hastily written and printed on cheap paper, cost but a penny.
4. *Woman's Journal* 10 Feb. 1912: 43.
5. Harper, *History,* Vol. VI, 405.
6. "Send St. Valentine to Plead for Votes," *New York Times* 14 Feb. 1916: 13.
7. "Valentines Pour in upon Congress," *The Suffragist* 19 Feb. 1916: 7.
8. "Suffragist Valentines for Congress," *Boston Herald* 14 Feb. 1916: 1.
9. "Suffragists Use Valentines in the Campaign for the Ballot," *The Worcester Post* 14 Feb. 1916: 1.

Victoria Woodhull

1. There are a number of excellent contemporary biographies of Woodhull, including Lois Beachy Underhill, *The Woman Who Ran for President* (Bridgehampton, N.Y.: Bridge Works, 1995) and Barbara Goldsmith, *Other Powers* (New York: Alfred Knopf, 1998). Much of the above information was taken from these two works.
2. Hake, *Buttons* III, 237, 252.
3. *Wild Oats — An Illustrated Journal of Fun, Satire, Burlesque, Hits at Persons and Events of the Day* 6 June 1872: 9.
4. *The Great Carnival, National Republican* 21 Feb. 1871: front page. No volume or number listed. This appears to be a one-time supplement or special issue of the *Weekly National Republican*.

5. Her daughter Zulu also changed the spelling of her name to Zula, perhaps to sound less African.

6. *Woodhall and Claflin's Journal* 29 Jan. 1881.

7. Illustration, *Harper's Weekly* 17 Feb. 1872: 140.

8. "Mrs. Woodhull Asserting Her Right to Vote," *Harper's Weekly* 25 Nov. 1871: 1109.

9. Illustrations, *Harper's Weekly* 5 March 1870: 157.

10. *Morning, Noon, and Night: A Medical Miscellaneous Annual—A Free Gift for All* (1872) 48.

11. An image of this box can be seen online at <http://cigarhistory.info/Cigar-lable_themes/Election_boxes.html> as part of Tony Hyman's collection in the National Cigar History Museum collection.

Women's Oversea Hospitals and Suffrage War Efforts

1. "Binding up the Wounds, Suffragists in World War I," spec. issue of *The APIC Keynoter* Summer, Fall, Winter (2008): p. 57.

2. Harper, *History,* Vol. V, 732.

3. *Women's Oversea Hospitals USA of the National American Women Suffrage Association* (New York: National Woman Suffrage Association Publishing Company, 1919).

4. Emily Newell Blair, *The Woman's Committee. United States Council of National Defense: An Interpretive Report, April 21, 1917–February 21, 1919* (Washington, D.C.: GPO, 1920).

5. For a full discussion of "the farmerette" and The Woman's Land Army, see Elaine F. Weiss, *Fruits of Victory: The Woman's Land Army of America in the Great War* (Washington, D.C.: Potomac, 2008).

Works Cited

Newspapers and Magazines

Appleton's Journal, Aurora Daily Express, Bay City [Michigan] *Times, Boston Herald, The Brooklyn Daily Eagle, Browning's Magazine, The Clarion, Chicago Daily Examiner, Collier's, The Common Cause, The Detroit Times, Everybody's Magazine, Frank Leslie's Illustrated, The Great Carnival — National Republican, Harper's Weekly, Judge, Life, Meriden* [Connecticut] *Morning Record, The Nation, NAWSA Headquarters Newsletter, New York Suffrage Newsletter, New York Times, Ogden* [Utah] *Standard, Puck, Reading* [Pennsylvania] *Eagle, The Revolution, The Saturday Evening Post, The Suffragette, The Suffragist, Timaru Herald, The Vote, Votes for Women, Washington Post, Wild Oats, Woman's Journal, Women's Political World, Women's Rights, Woodhall and Claflin's Journal, Woodhull and Claflin's Weekly, The Worcester* [Massachusetts] *Post, Work and Win, Young's Magazine*

Books, Pamphlets, Leaflets and Other Articles

Adams, Katherine H., and Michael L. Keene. *Alice Paul and the American Suffrage Movement.* Urbana: University of Chicago Press, 2008. Print.

Algeo, Sara M. *The Story of a Sub-Pioneer.* Providence, R.I.: Snow and Farnham, 1925. Print.

Andrews, Mildred Tanner. *Washington Women as Path Breakers.* Dubuque: Kendall/Hunt, 1989. Print.

Atkinson, Diane. *Mrs. Broom's Suffragette Photographs.* London: Nishen Photography, 1988. Print.

_____. *The Suffragettes in Pictures.* London: Sutton, 1996. Print.

_____. *Suffragettes in the Purple, White and Green — London 1906–14.* London: Museum of London, 1992. Print.

Barry, Kit. *The Advertising Trade Card.* Monson, Massachusetts: Blatchley's, 1981. Print.

Barry, Richard. *What Women Have Actually Done Where They Vote.* New York: New York State Association Opposed to Woman Suffrage, n.d. Print.

Blair, Emily Newell. *The Woman's Committee United States Council of National Defense: An Interpretive Report, April 21, 1917–February 21, 1919.* Washington, D.C.: GPO, 1920. Print.

Blatch, Harriot Stanton, and Alma Lutz. *Challenging Years: The Memoirs of Harriot Stanton Blatch.* New York: G.P. Putnam's Sons, 1940. Print.

Bogdan, Robert, and Todd Weseloh. *Real Photo Postcard Guide: The People's Photography.* Syracuse: Syracuse University Press, 2006. Print.

Bok, Edward. *The Americanization of Edward Bok.* New York: Charles Scribner's Sons, 1920. Print.

Bradbury, Robert C. *United States Advertising Poster Stamps.* Worcester, Massachusetts: R.C. Bradbury, 2008. Print.

Brooklyn Daily Eagle Almanac 1890. Brooklyn, 1890. Print.

Brown, Margaret W. "Medals Awarded to Mrs. Carrie Chapman Catt, Leader in the Woman Suffrage Movement." *The Numismatist* Feb. 1952: 115. Print.

Brown, William Burlie. *The People's Choice: the Presidential Image in the Campaign Biography.* Baton Rouge: Louisiana State University Press, 1960. Print.

Buell, Janet W. "Alva Belmont: From Socialite to Feminist." *The Historian* 52. 2 (1989): 229–31. Print.

Burkholder, Thomas R. "The *Farmer's Wife,* 1891–1894 — Raising a Prairie Consciousness." *A Voice of Their Own: The Woman Suffrage Press, 1840–1910.* Ed. Martha M. Solomon. Tuscaloosa: University of Alabama Press, 1991. 153–64. Print.

Burr, Hattie A., ed. *The Woman Suffrage Cook Book.* Boston, 1886. Print.

Captain Miller [pseud.]. *"Hero of Tippecanoe" or the Story of the Life of William Henry Harrison.* New York, 1840. Print

Catalog and Price List of Woman Suffrage Literature and Supplies. New York: National American Woman Suffrage Association, 1912. Print.

Cheadle, David, and W.H. "Bill" Lee. *Soapine Did It! An Illustrated History of Kendall's 19th Century Soap Advertising Campaign.* Englewood, Colorado: TCCA, 2000. Print.

Choice Recipes Compiled for the Busy Housewife. Clinton, N.Y.: The Political Equality Club of Clinton, 1916. Print.

Claflin, Tennie C. *Speech by Tennie C. Claflin, Candidate for Congress for the 8th District, at the German Mass Meeting Held at Irving Hall, New York, Friday Evening, August 11, 1871.* New York, 1871. Print.

Clinton Political Equality Club, eds. *Choice Recipes for the Busy Housewife 1916.* Clinton, N.Y.: The Courier Press, 1916. Print.

Cockroft, Irene, and Susan Croft. *Art, Theater and Women's Suffrage.* Twickenham, England: Aurora Metro Press, 2010. Print.

Collins, Herbert Ridgeway. *Threads of History: Americana*

Recorded on Cloth. Washington, D.C.: Smithsonian Institution Press, 1979. Print.

Cooney, Robert P.J. *Winning the Vote: The Triumph of the American Woman Suffrage Movement.* Santa Cruz: American Graphic Press, 2005. Print.

Crawford, Elizabeth. *The Women's Suffrage Movement: A Reference Guide 1866–1928.* London: UCL Press, 1999. Print.

Crew, Danny O. *Presidential Sheet Music: An Illustrated Catalog.* Jefferson, N.C.: McFarland, 2001. Print.

_____. *Suffragist Sheet Music: An Illustrated Catalog of Published Music Associated With the Women's Rights and Suffrage Movement in America, 1795–1921, With Complete Lyrics.* Jefferson, N.C.: McFarland, 2001. Print.

Darrah, W.C. *Cartes de Visite in Nineteenth Century Photographs.* Gettysburg: W.C. Darrah, 1981. Print.

Declaration of Rights of the Women of the United States — By the National Woman Suffrage Association, July 4th, 1876. n.p., 1876. Print.

Deter, Lori. "The Image of Women in Nineteenth Century Parlor Songs." Thesis. Tulane University, 1981. Print.

Dix, Dorothy. *Votes for Women.* New York: The Political Equality Association, n.d. Print.

Dowson, Aubrey, comp. *The Women's Suffrage Cookery Book.* London: Women's Printing Society, n.d. Print.

Drew, Nora Emerson. "Advertising Suffrage — The American Substitute for Militancy." *McCalls Magazine* June 1913: 11. Print.

Driver, Elizabeth. *A Bibliography of Canadian Cookbooks 1825–1949.* Toronto: University of Toronto Press, 2008. Print.

DuBois, Carol. *Harriot Stanton Blatch and the Winning of Woman Suffrage.* New Haven: Yale University Press, 1997. Print.

DuBois, Ellen, and Karen Kearns. *Votes for Women: A 75th Anniversary Album.* San Marino: Huntington Library, 1995. Print.

"Fashion Preferences of Famous American Women." *Supplement to The Illustrated Milliner (Hats from Paris & New York)* October 1915: 3. Print.

Felger, Donna H., and Dorothy T. Rainwater. *American Spoons: Souvenir and Historical.* Atglen, Pennsylvania: Schiffer, 1997. Print.

Finnegan, Margaret. *Selling Suffrage: Consumer Culture & Votes for Women.* New York: Columbia University Press, 1999. Print.

Flexner, Eleanor. *Century of Struggle: The Woman's Rights Movement in the United States,* rev. ed. Cambridge: The Belknap Press of Harvard University Press, 1975. Print.

Florey, Kenneth. "The First Suffrage Button." Spec. issue of *The Keynoter* Summer, Fall, Winter (2008): 37. Print.

For Better Baking ... Votes for Women. n.p., 1913. Print.

Gabriel, Mary. *Notorious Victoria: The Life of Victoria Woodhull, Uncensored.* Chapel Hill, North Carolina: Algonquin Books of Chapel Hill, 1998. Print.

Garden Primer. How to Plant and Care for a Vegetable Garden. New York: Printers for Mayor Michel's Food Supply Committee, distributed by the Albany Branch of the N.Y. State Woman Suffrage Party, 1917. Print.

Goldsmith, Barbara. *Other Powers: The Age of Suffrage, Spiritualism, and the Scandalous Victoria Woodhull.* New York: Alfred A. Knopf, 1998. Print.

Goring, Elizabeth S. "Suffragette Jewelry in Britain." *Omnium Gatherum: A Collection of Papers — The Decorative Arts Society 1850–Present Journal* 26 (2002): 84–99. Print.

The Great Carnival, National Republican 21 Feb. 1871: 1. Print.

Hake, Theodore. *The Button Book.* New York: Dafran House, 1972. Print.

_____. *Political Buttons Book III, 1789–1916.* York, Pennsylvania: Hake's Americana, 1978. Print.

Harper, Ida Husted. *Life and Work of Susan B. Anthony.* 3 vols. Indianapolis and Kansas City, 1899. Print.

_____. "What Do the Newport Suffrage Meetings Mean?" *The Independent* 9 Sept. 1909: 579. Print.

Harper, Paula Hays. "Votes for Women? A Graphic Episode in the Battle of the Sexes," *Art and Architecture in the Service of Politics.* Eds. Henry Millon and Linda Nochlin. Cambridge: MIT Press, 1978. 150–61. Print.

Hart, James B. "They All Were Born in Log Cabins." *American Heritage* August 1956: 5. Print.

Hoy, Helen K. "The 'Votes for Women' Stamp." *Harper's Weekly Advertiser,* undated clipping but probably 1909, in the collection of author. Print.

Jay, Robert. *The Trade Card in Nineteenth-Century America.* Columbia: University of Missouri Press, 1987. Print.

Jennings, Linda Deziah. *Washington Women's Cookbook.* Seattle: The Washington Equal Suffrage Association, 1909. Print.

Jones, Michael E. *Libido Dominandi: Sexual Liberation and Political Control.* South Bend: St. Augustine's Press, 2005. Print.

Jordon, Vernon D. *Around the Korner: Women's Suffrage and Rose O'Neill.* Des Moines: Wings, 2009. Print.

Kings County Woman Suffrage Association. *For Better Baking — Votes for Women.* New York: Kings County W.S.A., 1913. Print.

Klamkin, Marian. *American Patriotic and Political China.* New York: Charles Scribner's Sons, 1973. Print.

Kleber, L.O., comp. *The Suffrage Cook Book.* Pittsburgh: The Equal Franchise Federation of Western Pennsylvania, 1915. Print.

Knight, Denise D. "An 'Amusing Source of Income': Charlotte Perkins Gilman and the Soapine Connection." *The Advertising Trade Card Quarterly* Summer 2001: 8–12. Print.

Kovel, Ralph, and Terry Kovel. *Kovel's New Dictionary of Marks: Pottery and Porcelain — 1850 to the Present.* New York: Crown, 1986. Print.

Lawrence, Vera Brodsky. *Music for Patriots, Politicians, and Presidents: Harmonies and Discords of the First Hundred Years.* New York: Macmillan, 1975. Print.

Mac Donnell, Kevin. "Trade Cards by Charlotte Perkins Gilman." *The Advertising Trade Card Quarterly* Fall 2001: 18–25, 28. Print.

Mackay, James. *Philatelic Terms Illustrated,* 4th ed. London: Stanley Gibbons, 2003. Print.

Marble, Ella M.S., ed. *Wimodaughsis Cook-Book, Washington, 1892.* Print.

Mayo, Edith. "Votes for Women." *The Keynoter* Fall 1982: 4–11. Print.

McCulloch, Lou W. *Paper Americana: A Collector's Guide.* San Diego: A.S. Barnes, 1980. Print.

_____, and Lois McCulloch. *Card Photographs: A Guide to Their History and Value.* Atglen, Pennsylvania: Schiffer, 1997. Print.

McDonald, Ian. *Vindication: A Post Card History of the Women's Movement.* London: Deirdre McDonald, 1989. Print.

McQuiston, Liz. *Suffragettes to She-Devils: Women's Liberation and Beyond.* London: Phaidon Press, 1997. Print.

Mercer, John. "Shopping for Suffrage: the Campaign Shops of the Women's Political and Social Union." *Women's History Review* 18.2 (2009): 293–309. Print.

Miles, William. *The Image Makers: A Bibliography of American Presidential Campaign Biographies.* Metuchen, N.J.: Scarecrow Press, 1979. Print.

Mills, Harriet May, and Isabel Holland. *Manual for Political Equality Clubs.* Philadelphia, 1896. Print.

Moldow, Gloria. *Women Doctors in Gilded Age Washington: Race, Gender, and Professionalization.* Champaign: University of Illinois Press, 1987. Print.

Morning, Noon, and Night: A Medical Miscellaneous Annual—A Free Gift for All. N.p., 1872: 48. Print.

Mott, Frank Luther. *A History of American Magazines, Vols. III-IV,* Cambridge: Harvard University Press, 1938. Print.

Norgren, Jill. *Belva Lockwood: The Woman Who Would Be President.* New York: New York University Press, 2007. Print.

Official Program—Votes for Women Pageant and Parade—Hartford, Connecticut May 2, 1914. Hartford: Connecticut Woman Suffrage Association, 1914. Print.

"On the Cover." *The Clarion* Summer 2006: 2. Print.

Pankhurst, Emmeline. *My Own Story.* New York: Hearst's International Library, 1914. Print.

Pankhurst, Richard. *Sylvia Pankhurst: Artist and Crusader.* London: Paddington Press, 1979. Print.

Peck, Mary Gray. *Carrie Chapman Catt: A Biography.* New York: H.W. Wilson, 1944. Print.

Pethick-Lawrence, F.W. *Fate Has Been Kind.* London: Hutchinson, 1942. Print.

Plain Instructions for the Assessment and Registration of Women Voters. Boston, 1888. Print.

Powell, Robin, and Julie Powell. "Woman Suffrage Brummagem Items." *The Clarion* March 2000: 14–15. Print.

The Presidency: Sketches and Portraits of All Candidates, 1888. n.p., 1888. Print.

Price List: Special Michigan Literature. Grand Rapids: Michigan Equal Suffrage Association, n.d. Print.

Printers Ink: A Journal For Advertisers 1888–1938 84.4 (1938). Print.

Proceedings of the 31st Annual Convention of the National American Woman Suffrage Association. Warren, Ohio, 1899. Print.

Proceedings of the 37th Annual Convention of the National American Woman Suffrage Association. Warren, Ohio: The Tribune Co., 1905. Print.

Program Council of Women Assembled by the National Woman Suffrage Association of the United States to Celebrate the Fortieth Anniversary of the First Woman's Rights Association. Washington, 1888. Print.

Program Forty-Fifth Annual Convention National American Woman Suffrage Association. New York: National American Woman Suffrage Association, 1913. Print.

Program Forty-Ninth Annual Convention National American Woman Suffrage Association. New York: National Woman Suffrage Publishing Co., 1917. Print.

Program Votes for Women Demonstration in Hyde Park, Sunday, June 21st, 1908. London: Women's Social and Political Union, 1908. Print.

Program the Prince's Skating Rink in Knightsbridge Exhibition Political Peepshows (Political Cartoons in Model]. London: National Women's Political and Social Union, 1909. Print.

Program Suffrage Banner Parade, New York: n.p., 1915. Print.

Program Victory Convention New Jersey Woman Suffrage Association 1869–1920 Robert Treat Hotel, Newark, New Jersey. Newark: New Jersey: Woman Suffrage Association, 1920. Print.

Purcell, W.L. *Them Was the Good Old Days in Davenport, Scott County, Iowa.* Davenport, Iowa: Purcell Printing Company, 1922. Print.

Robinson, Harriet Jane Hanson. *Massachusetts in the Woman Suffrage Movement.* Boston: Roberts Brothers, 1881. Print.

Sachs, Emanie. *The Terrible Siren: Victoria Woodhull 1838–1927.* New York: Harper & Brothers, 1928. Print.

Scott, Susan K. "Rose Cecil O'Neill: America's First Female Cartoonist Fought for Women's Suffrage." *The Ozark's Mountaineer* March-April 2010: 7. Print.

Shaw, Anna Howard, with Elizabeth Jordon. *The Story of a Pioneer.* New York: Harper and Brothers, 1915. Print.

_____, Alice Stone Blackwell, and Lucy Elmina Anthony. *The Yellow Ribbon Speaker.* Boston, 1891. Print.

Sheppard, Alice. *Cartooning for Suffrage.* Albuquerque: University of New Mexico Press, 1994. Print.

Silver, Mae, and Sue Cazaly. *The Sixth Star: Images and Memorabilia of California Women's Political History 1868–1915.* San Francisco: Ord Street Press, 2000. Print.

Solomons, Selina. *How We Won the Vote in California: The True Story of the Campaign of 1911.* San Francisco: The New Woman Publishing Co., 1911. Print.

Stevens, Doris. *Jailed for Freedom: American Women Win the Vote.* New York: Boni and Liveright, 1920. Print.

Stanton, Elizabeth Cady, Susan B. Anthony, and Matilda Joslyn Gage, eds. *History of Woman Suffrage Vol. I. 1848–1861— Vol. II. 1861–1876.* New York: Fowler and Wells, 1881–82; *Vol. III. 1876–1885.* Rochester, New York: Charles Mann, Printers, 1887; Susan B. Anthony and Ida Husted Harper, eds. *Vol. IV. 1883–1900.* Indianapolis: The Hollenbeck Press, 1902; Ida Husted Harper, ed. *Vol. V. VI. 1900–20.* New York: J.J. Little and Ives Company, Printers, 1922. Print.

Suffrage Liberty Bell— Silent Until November 2. Harrisburg, Pennsylvania: Pennsylvania Woman Suffrage Association, 1915. Print.

Sullivan, Edmund B. *American Political Badges and Medalets 1789–1892.* Lawrence, Massachusetts: Quarterman Publications, 1981. Print.

_____. *Collecting Political Americana.* New York: Crown, 1980. Print.

_____, and Roger A Fischer. *American Political Ribbons and Ribbon Badges 1825–1981.* Lincoln, Massachusetts: Quarterman Publications, 1985. Print.

Supplementary List of the Catalog and Price List of Woman Suffrage Literature and Supplies. New York: National American Woman Suffrage Association, n.d. (prob. 1915). Print.

Tickner, Lisa. *The Spectacle of Women — Imagery of the Suffrage Campaign 1907–14.* Chicago: University of Chicago P, 1988. Print.

Tilton, Theodore. *Victoria C. Woodhull: A Biography.* New York 1871. Print.

The Trial of the Suffragette Leaders. London: The Woman's Press, n.d. Print.

The Truth Versus Richard Barry. New York: National American Woman Suffrage Association, n.d. Print.

"25231 Super Rare Suffrage Pinback." Heritage Grand Format Auction #659, February 26–27, 2007, Dallas, Texas. 54. Print.

Underhill, Lois Beachy. *The Woman Who Ran For President: the Many Lives of Victoria Woodhull.* Bridgehampton, New York: Bridge Works Publishing Co., 1995. Print.

United States. *Official Bulletin — Vol. I, No. 46,* Washington: GPO, July 3, 1917. Print.

Upton, Harriet Taylor, and Elizabeth J. Hauser, eds. *Proceedings of the 36th Annual Convention of the National American Woman Suffrage Association.* Warren, Ohio: William Ritezel and Co., Printers, 1904. Print.

Voice of the People — A Lament With a Prophecy. New York: New York State Association Opposed to Woman Suffrage, n.d. Print.

Votes for Women. New York: Political Equality Association, n.d. Print.

Warda, Mark. *Political Campaign Stamps.* Iola, Wisconsin: Krause, 1998. Print.

Welling, William. *Photography in America: The Formative Years — 1839–1900.* New York: Thomas Y. Crowell, 1978. Print.

Weiss, Elaine F. *Fruits of Victory: The Woman's Land Army of America in the Great War.* Washington: Potomac Books, 2008. Print.

West, Richard Samuel. *Satire on Stone: The Political Cartoons of Joseph Kepler.* Urbana and Chicago: University of Illinois P, 1988. Print.

Willard, Frances E., and Mary Livermore, eds. *A Woman of the Century — Fourteen Hundred Seventy Biographical Sketches Accompanied by Portraits of Leading American Women in All Walks of Life.* Buffalo, 1893. Print.

Wilson, Jack. "Belva Lockwood for President." Spec. issue of *The Keynoter,* Summer/Fall/Winter (2008): 10–12. Print.

Wolff, Francie. *Give the Ballot to the Mothers: Songs of the Suffragists.* Springfield, Missouri: Denlinger's Publishers, 1998. Print.

The Woman's Rights Almanac for 1858 — Containing Facts, Statistics, Arguments, Records of Progress, and Proofs of the Need of it, Worcester, Massachusetts, 1858. Print. Attributed to Lucy Stone and the Rev. Thomas Wentworth Higginson.

Women's Oversea Hospitals USA of the National American Woman Suffrage Association. New York: National Woman Suffrage Publishing Co., 1919. Print.

Women's Political Union of New Jersey Campaign Year Book. Newark: Women's Political Union, 1914. Print.

Woodhall and Claflin's Journal. 12.3. (1881). Print. Despite the listed volume and number, this is probably the only issue of the journal.

Zackodnik, Teresa. *Press, Platform, Pulpit: Black Feminist Ethics in the Era of Reform.* Knoxville: University of Tennessee Press, 2011. Print.

Index

Numbers in *bold italics* indicate pages with photographs

324.6 FLO
Florey, Kenneth.
Women's suffrage memorabilia
: an illustrated historical

Index